$11.95

W9-AZQ-942

Computing Today

Della Cook

Computing Today
An Introduction to Business Data Processing

Joseph L. Sardinas, Jr.

Department of Accounting, School of Business Administration
University of Massachusetts, Amherst

Prentice-Hall, Inc.   Englewood Cliffs, New Jersey

**To my
mother and
father**

Library of Congress Cataloging in Publication Data

Sardinas, Joseph L
    Computing today.

    Includes bibliographies and index.
      1. Business—Data processing. I. Title.
HF5548.2.S236   658'.054   80-26694
ISBN 0-13-165092-0

Printed in the United States of America

10 9 8 7 6 5 4 3 2 1

Credits:
Art Director: Florence Dara Silverman
Production Editor: Eleanor Perz
Photo Researcher: Anita Duncan
Manufacturing Buyer: Ray Keating
Interior Designer: Andy Zutis
Cover Design: A Good Thing, Inc.
Cover Illustration: "Formes Lignes" by Yaacov Agam
  © 1974 Transworld Art Corp.
Line Art: Danmark & Michaels, Inc.
Unit Opener Photos: Bill Longcore

Prentice-Hall International, Inc., *London*
Prentice-Hall of Australia Pty. Limited, *Sydney*
Prentice-Hall of Canada, Ltd., *Toronto*
Prentice-Hall of India Private Limited, *New Delhi*
Prentice-Hall of Japan, Inc., *Tokyo*
Prentice-Hall of Southeast Asia Pte. Ltd., *Singapore*
Whitehall Books Limited, *Wellington, New Zealand*

Contents

Unit I

Introduction to
the Field of Data
Processing

v

Contents

Unit II

**Introduction
to Computer
Hardware**

11 FLOWCHARTS 295

12 PROGRAM PREPARATION 319

13 PROGRAMMING LANGUAGES 345

Unit IV
Data Processing Management

14 MANAGING THE DATA PROCESSING DEPARTMENT   367

15 COMPUTER SECURITY 389

16 TRENDS IN COMPUTER APPLICATIONS 413

Preface

About This Text

Today's students have grown up in the computer society; they constitute the first generation of which this can be said. They are science fiction fans who have seen the lines between fantasy and reality become blurred in their lifetime. Unawed by computers, many have already "played" with them in high school, and perhaps learned math and practiced spelling with them in elementary school. They already know that computers are complex and powerful. They also know that computers are *fun*.

That is the positive view projected in this introductory-level text on computers and their use in business data processing. It clearly describes how computers work from both the hardware and the software perspectives, along with the evolution of computers and business data processing.

In addition to being "fun," computer data processing has created some of the most challenging, exciting, and rewarding careers of our time. The understanding of this field, as presented in this text, will prepare students for continuing study in preparation for the jobs of the future. All essential concepts of computer use in data processing are presented here in a text that emphasizes today's technology for tomorrow's computer users and personnel.

Organization

This timely text is organized in four modules. Unit I, an *Introduction to the Field of Data Processing*, contains three chapters. Chapter 1, *Computers Today*, surveys the impact of electronic data processing on our society. In chapter 2, *The Past, Present, and Future of Data Processing*, the history of calculating devices is briefly summarized, and the remarkable technological advances that have brought us to the age of microprocessors are outlined. Chapter 3 presents an *Overview of Computers and Equipment*, introducing some key terms and concepts that will be discussed more fully in subsequent chapters.

Unit II, *Introduction to Computer Hardware*, is concerned with all the varieties of hardware. In chapter 4, *Input and Output Devices* are examined, with an emphasis both on traditional methods and on recent developments that have changed the procedures and appearance of input and output. Chapter 5 takes us into *The Central Processing Unit* to understand how computers operate, the special number systems and codes they use, and the new technology that provides vastly expanded primary storage in smaller mainframes. *Auxiliary Storage*, chapter 6, likewise emphasizes the technological advances that are blurring the distinctions between primary and auxiliary storage, while not ignoring older equipment still in service today. *Data Communications* are described in chapter 7, with a discussion of communications channels and networks from the inside-the-computer perspective, as well as from the computer-to-computer or computer-to-terminal perspective; this chapter also examines the most dramatic application of computer communications to date—distributed data processing.

Unit III, an *Introduction to Computer Software*, presents varied aspects of this topic in six chapters. In chapter 8, *Systems and Applications Software*, programming concepts are introduced; the focus is on the programs that actually run the machines and how they interact with the hardware and the application programs. Chapter 9, *Data Base Management*, discusses the newest techniques associated with data storage and retrieval, with a focus on the organization of a data base management system (DBMS). Chapter 10, *Systems Analysis*, discusses systems in business organizations, the "life cycle" of a system, and management information systems (MIS). Chapter 11, *Flowcharts*, explains their use at both the systems and programming levels; it also introduces decision tables as a supplement or alternative to flowcharting. *Program Preparation* is the subject of chapter 12, which takes a step-by-step approach to the logical processes—top-down programming, modularization—by which programs are developed; the importance of debugging and adequate documentation at every step in the process is emphasized. *Programming Languages* are described in chapter 13, with emphasis on the capabilities and specific applications for each of several widely used programming languages.

In Unit IV, *Data Processing Management*, the focus is on the real world— the world of work in a data processing department. Chapter 14, *Managing the Data Processing Department*, describes management responsibilities and department organization so that future employees will understand the perspective of management, and perhaps aspire to become managers themselves; job opportunities and career paths in data processing are outlined. In chapter 15, *Computer Security* is discussed from the perspective of the hazards to which computer installations are subjected and the precautions that may be taken to avoid them. Finally, chapter 16, *Trends in Computer Applications*, reviews the opportunities and trends of today that will define the business data processing world of the near future, and introduces thought-provoking issues, such as individual rights to privacy and priorities in technological development.

Features

Students often ask, "What does this course or textbook have to do with my future?" The pragmatic and practical perspective from which this book has been written provides answers to that question. In addition to the frequent descriptions of the working environment throughout the text, each chapter is introduced with a "real world" application relating to the material about to be covered. These applications are designed to ease the student into the subject matter of the chapter by showing it in a realistic context.

Other features to enhance student receptivity are also provided. At the beginning of every chapter, the topics to be discussed are outlined, and a little "comic relief" is provided by a cartoon that views, with tongue in cheek, the material that follows. A summary follows the text of every chapter, as do questions for student review.

One of the major problems faced by the newcomer to the field of data processing is the jargon, which seems to be both more extensive and more "imaginative" than that of most other fields. As a guide through the maze, this text introduces terms accompanied by an explanation or definition; the first appearance of a technical term is italicized for cross-reference to the Glossary at the end of the book. Also, at the end of every chapter, the terms the student should have learned are listed.

In the Appendix, three important computer programming languages are introduced through the imaginative use of an actual program. The amount of interest that would have accumulated on an investment of $24 from 1627 to 1981 is calculated in BASIC, COBOL, and Pascal. The small sum paid by Dutch settlers for the island of Manhattan thus provides the opportunity for explaining the syntax and vocabulary of the three languages most used today in business data processing. Students should be able to write simple programs on the basis of material contained in the Appendix and to read and understand a program written in any of these languages—and they will probably be eager for their first full-fledged programming course. Also in the Appendix is a useful list of the acronyms to which this discipline is devoted, and another of publications that might be of interest for further reading or reference.

Numerous diagrams in color have been designed expressly for this text, illustrating everything from the printing mechanisms of today's hard-copy output devices to the processes involved in structured programming. In addition, every chapter contains photographs variously showing the devices discussed, the data processing environment, or other relevant pictorial material.

Alternative Ways of Using This Text

The core of this text is formed by Units II and III, devoted, respectively, to hardware and software. The chapters in these two central modules can serve as the primary text for any introductory-level business data processing or computer course. The chapters in Units I and IV can be used in several ways, depending on the emphasis of a given course or the needs and interests of students and teacher. They can be assigned concurrently with the core curriculum chapters or as optional readings according to student interest. For example, in a strictly business-oriented learning environment, chapters 1 and 2 might be optional, while in a more general introduction to computers, chapter 14 might be optional. At the same time, however, Units I and II might provide the focus for a course in computers and society.

It is important that these six chapters not be overlooked. In these chapters, topics of grave concern today are discussed. Informed citizens cannot afford to be computer-illiterate; computer professionals cannot afford to ignore the valid concerns of the public. Computer data processing may take place inside a "black box," but it exists as part of a rapidly changing human environment and exists to serve the needs of human beings and their organizations.

Supplements

Both a Study Guide and an Instructor's Manual, which includes a Test Item File, are available as accompanying supplements to this text. The Study Guide reviews the highlights of each chapter, the technical terms introduced, and provides many self-test questions and problems.

The Instructor's Manual offers teaching suggestions and brief summaries of the contents of each chapter. It also contains the answers to the review questions at the end of every text chapter and to the discussion questions and problems in the Study Guide. The Test Item File contains over 750 true/false and multiple-choice questions in easy-to-administer parallel "A" and "B" test sets for each chapter. Many of the diagrams in the text are also included in the Instructor's Manual for use as transparency masters.

Acknowledgments

The publication of a textbook is a complex and time-consuming project. Many individuals provide special skills and knowledge, guidance, and encouragement. The list of acknowledgments, no matter how extensive, will always be insufficient.

First, I want to express my sincerest and warmest thanks to Marjorie Weiser, my editor, alter ego, indeed good friend. Marjorie's abundant creativity, limitless patience, constant good humor, and tireless efforts made this book possible. Without her there would be no book.

I am also deeply indebted to Susan Katz and Ronald Ledwith, who first interested me in this project. I would also like to give special thanks to the many other individuals at Prentice-Hall who contributed so importantly to the development and production of this book: Edward Glynn, market researcher; Ray Keating, book manufacturing buyer; Florence Silverman, art director; Eleanor Perz, production editor; Doug Thompson, college editor; Elinor Paige and Henrietta Nyman, editorial assistants; and Ernest Hursh, marketing manager. For professional assistance in the preparation of the manuscript, I am grateful to Thomas Adams, who also prepared the Glossary, Linda Midkiff, Evelyn Hu, whose technical knowledge and writing ability are reflected in the Appendix, Marvin Norworth, and Myra Dembrow. The Test Yourself questions were prepared by John M. Anderson, University of North Carolina at Wilmington; Richard C. Aukerman, Oklahoma State University; James Payne, Kellogg Community College, Michigan; Ralph A. Szweda, Monroe Community College, Rochester, New York; and Frank Severance, Lansing Community College, Michigan.

I wish also to thank the reviewers who read the manuscript during preparation and contributed numerous helpful suggestions relating to both content and format, especially Robert D. Chenoweth, County College of Morris, Dover, New Jersey, and Ralph A. Szweda, Monroe Community College, Rochester, New York; and also James Campise of Canyon Lake, Texas; James Harton, Computer and Technical College, University of Toledo, Ohio; Marvin Kushner, Borough of Manhattan Community College, New York; Jean Longhurst, William Rainey Harper College, Palatine, Illinois; Jack A. Fuller, School of Business, University of Northern Iowa, Cedar Falls; and Gerry Manning, School of Business, San Francisco State University.

In addition, many friends and colleagues contributed directly and indirectly to this book. Many thanks, first, to Richard Asebrook, Arthur Elkins, and Nancy Olzewski. Thanks are due also to the staff of the University of Massachusetts Whitmore Data Center, and especially Martha Little, and to the staff of the University of Massachusetts Computing Center, and especially Katy Cowles, for the many documents they made available. I extend very special thanks to Linda Overton who performed much of the library research for the book and to Anne Curran for additional library research. Finally, and perhaps most importantly, my thanks to Ronnie and Michael for their unfailing understanding and support.

Amherst, Massachusetts   J. L. S.

Unit 1
Introduction to the Field of Data Processing

Computers Today

© Computerworld

"It says 'Search Me'."

APPLICATION
Qube

On July 15, 1979, President Carter addressed the nation. Energy was the subject of his address, which may or may not have made history; only subsequent events will tell. But there can be no doubt that 7,600 viewers in Columbus, Ohio, set a historic precedent that night. With a two-way computerized television communication system called Qube, they gave the President, network commentators, and a national audience instant feedback by answering five questions. Their responses, punched into hand-held consoles, were relayed from Ohio to the NBC studios in New York, where they were tallied and broadcast within seconds.

Qube, Warner Communications' 30-channel cable television network, is based on four interrelated computer systems. One maintains the overall operation and collects both billing information and the two-way responses. It also checks the entire subscription roster every 6 seconds to determine which sets are in use and which response buttons were pressed last. Another poses the questions to viewers and compiles lists of their responses. A third does financial, technical, and marketing analyses, and the fourth is used mostly as a spare.

The Qube network contains 10 commercial television stations and 10 "premium" channels offering movies and cultural events. The remaining 10 "community" channels allow viewers to "talk back" by using five buttons on the channel selector. They have advised a rock star on the content of a concert, given opinions of food and other products, and even suggested the plot of a soap opera. Qube has 300 games in its memory bank, and can divide its audience into competing teams.

Four local colleges use Qube's two-way capability to teach courses for credit on TV. Students at home can answer questions posed by instructors in classrooms; reruns give students flexibility in arranging class schedules.

The system can do much more than simply serve as a connection between studio and living room. It can protect a home or office from break-ins or fires. When alerted by any of the variety of sensors installed in a home, alarms are sounded in the fire or police station, where a simultaneous printout provides the location, number of residents, location of the nearest fire hydrant, and other pertinent information. Another option is a medical alert system, which can alert appropriate agencies, such as an ambulance service, in an emergency.

Yet Qube is not without its critics. Civil libertarians worry about individuals' rights of privacy being violated, especially as more and more personal questions are asked and controversial issues are explored. Some fear the system's capability to accumulate data on the opinions of individuals, as expressed through their responses. Warner Cable has taken steps to protect the rights of viewers, by programming its computer to wipe out all records except those needed for billing purposes and for polling; in the latter instance, subscribers are warned several times during a program that their responses will be retained. Others are concerned about the effects of instant feedback on our democracy due to the increased temptations for politicians to play to the gallery. Some observers, on the other hand, are more optimistic, taking the view that any technology that expands expression will probably, in the long run, do more good than harm.

FROM THE time you are born until the time you die, computers will be tracking you and storing information about you, at times helping you and, perhaps, at other times making life difficult for you. No matter what field of employment you enter, you will be using computers as a tool to perform your duties, or computers will be used by others to assist you in your activities.

We as a society, indeed you as an individual, simply cannot escape the influence that computers have at present and will increasingly have in the future. Some people dislike computers; others love them and at times deal with or speak of them in humanlike terms. But no one in our society today can ignore them. To avoid a society in which all power lies with technocrats, every educated person must understand the capabilities of computers. A growing body of science fiction warns us of the consequences of letting only a select few decide what computers will do.

In this chapter, and in this course, you will learn to become comfortable with computers, by examining not only what they do but how they do it. You will become familiar with the different uses of computers, the variety of accessories that add special skills, and the terminology and concepts used by computer planners and operators.

The computerized world is a highly efficient one, processing the quantities of data and keeping the extensive records that are produced by and necessary to a postindustrialized society. But even the most sophisticated systems have their limitations. Programming errors, mechanical failures, and invasion of privacy are some potential hazards. Businesses are vulnerable to crippling losses if their computer systems or centralized records are lost, stolen, or tampered with. We will examine these and other issues related to the safe and secure use of computers in our world.

Although the primary focus of this book will be on the business uses of computers, we will also look into their applications in other areas. We will begin by surveying the influence these powerful machines have on our lives today.

Our Computerized World

Everyone is affected by computers every day—often several times a day and in widely diverse areas. For example, the person who makes a credit card purchase, renews a driver's license, takes a blood test, dials a long-distance telephone call directly, or opens a piece of promotional mail from a regional ballet company has had contact with the computers used in business, government, medicine, communications, and the arts. A typical day for many of us might well include all these, and more, interactions with a computer system.

Business

One hundred and thirteen million Americans have at least one bank-issued credit card. These small plastic rectangles have truly remarkable abilities. They give their owners automatic credit in stores, restaurants, and hotels, at home, across the country, and even abroad, and they make many banking services available as well. More and more of these credit cards have magnetic strips on the back, which can be read by automatic tellers, making it possible to withdraw or deposit money or purchase airline tickets or travelers' checks at terminals in scattered locations, whether or not the local branch bank is open.

Other banking applications of computers include automatic payroll deposits and preauthorized bill payments. For many of us the "cashless society" is not on the horizon—it's already here. Many banks are already using electronic funds transfer (EFT) systems, which will be examined more closely in a later chapter. These systems allow banks to clear checks with such speed that the process, which used to take a week or more, is now accomplished within a few days.

While computers offer these conveniences to consumers and bankers, they have many advantages for retailers too. Electronic cash registers can do much more than simply ring up sales. They can keep a wide range of records, including who sold what, when, and to whom. This information allows business proprietors to keep track of inventories by showing which items are being sold and how fast they are moving. Decisions to reorder or return merchandise to suppliers can then be made. At the same time these computers record which hours are busiest and which employees are the most efficient, allowing personnel and staffing assignments to be made accordingly. And they also identify preferred customers for promotional campaigns.

Computers are relied on by manufacturers for similar reasons. Computer-analyzed marketing reports can help to decide which products to emphasize now, which to develop for the future, and which to drop. Computers keep track of inventory, of raw materials on hand, and even of the production process itself.

But computers do much more than make commerce and control easier. Airlines, for example, rely on them for everything from filling seats to creating safe traffic patterns. The plethora of government regulations on varying types of fares with equally varying requirements would make ticket sales next to impossible without computers keeping track of them all. Ticket agents simply type your destination into a computer terminal; in a few seconds they are able to tell you the least expensive way to get where you are going (even if it is on another airline) and the flights on which seats are still available. Computers can even help you comparison shop for a rental car at your destination and reserve it for you.

Computers are also essential in air traffic control towers. Kennedy International Airport in New York is one of the busiest in the world, used by more than 80 airlines. Between 4:00 P.M. and 9:30 P.M. each day, a plane lands there every 90 seconds. A computer system in the control tower identifies each plane as it approaches and keeps tabs on its altitude and speed, permitting the air traffic controllers to give safe directions for landing.

Numerous other commercial enterprises, from theaters to magazine publishers, from gas and electric utilities to milk processors, bring better and more efficient services to consumers through the use of computers.

Government and Politics

Since the late 1960s, government officials and politicians have depended on computers increasingly every year. Voter registration lists, or selected portions of them, can be printed from computerized records, sharply cutting the time and costs of running an effective campaign, especially on the local level. For example, it is possible for political organizations and fund-raisers to obtain the names of registered party members who voted in the last primary and to concentrate their efforts on that group. And on election day computers tally the results and almost instantly are able to project the outcome on the basis of partial returns, district by district, even before all the votes are in.

At every level, government agencies use computers for general record keeping. The U.S. government had more than 6,000 computers in service in 1979—an increase of 1,000 since 1974. Also, in 1979 the White House installed a supersophisticated system that combined data processing with office automation and linked with computer systems in other government agencies and in private industry as well. The system is intended to coordinate the flood of information that streams through the Executive Office every day. Among the system's major features are correspondence and legislation tracking systems that will prevent items from getting lost or forgotten. Still in the planning and development stage is a domestic information system producing color-coded maps on screens, to

The Secretary of the Commonwealth of Pennsylvania, C. Dolores Tucker, entered the name of a candidate for State Senator into a computer in January 1976. This computer hookup, the first of its kind in the nation, kept track of more than 5,000 candidates who filed nomination petitions for more than 800 offices in the Pennsylvania primary election that year.

display demographic and other data. This system will be shared by 16 or more government agencies.

Computers used by the Census Bureau not only tabulate and organize data (see chapter 2) but also provide data in a variety of formats for use by other government agencies and by private industry. Computers used in law enforcement agencies keep crime statistics, check automobile licenses and registrations, and, among other things, can alert other departments about wanted individuals and stolen vehicles.

FBI files contain fingerprints of millions of veterans, police officers, civil servants, and bonded couriers, in addition, of course, to those of criminals. A specially designed computer system classifies each print by its characteristics and by the name and birthdate of each subject. It is able to select only the relatively few that are likely to match any sample sent for identification by any law enforcement agency. Only these few are sent for detailed analysis by a human expert, who thus does not have to spend days sifting through the millions of prints that the machine automatically eliminated. Local agencies can get prompt identification of print records sent by computer for comparison. At the same time they are given the criminal record, if there is one, of the individual so identified.

(UPI)

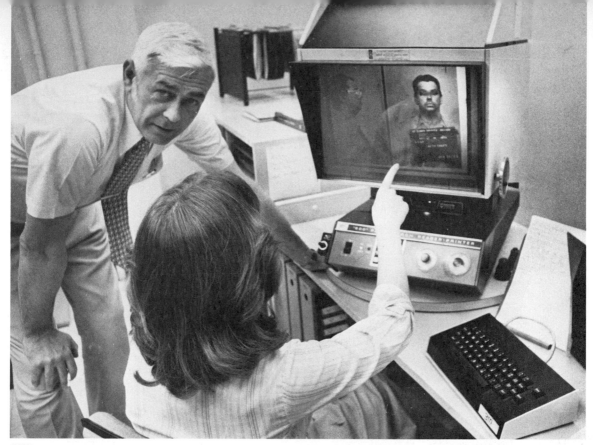

(UPI)

Government computers keep track of how much you have paid in withholding and property taxes, how much you owe, and how much has been credited to your social security account. These figures are used in the formulation of budgets, tabulating such factors as how much has been requested by each department or agency, how much was allocated and spent in the preceding year, and how much revenue can be expected from other tax dollars. Increasingly, mail is being sorted and routed as addresses are "read" by computers.

Some ways that municipal governments put computers to work include: analyzing population density by neighborhood, recording crime types and rates, and tracking traffic flow and operating traffic lights.

A minicomputer that calls up color photographs of suspects is used by detectives from the St. Louis County Police Department. Known as the Scientific Criminal Identification System, its memory contains information about more than 12,000 persons previously arrested in the county, as well as their images. When specifics of an event are entered on the keyboard, the system can present the viewer with pictures and data representing a number of likely suspects.

Medicine

Computer technology helps physicians and others in health fields to monitor patients' conditions and make diagnoses, conduct research, practice new techniques, and even plan special diet menus.

Computers aid in the treatment of critically ill patients in several

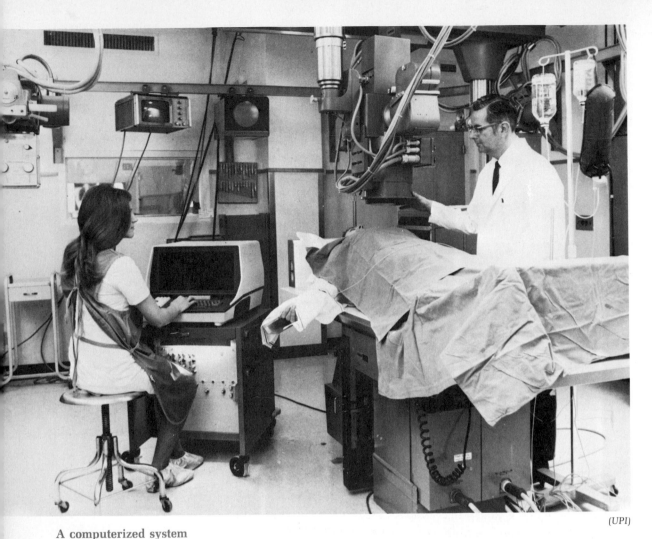

A computerized system from Honeywell's Test Instruments Division instantly displays and analyzes a patient's physiological data for a Denver cardiologist during a simulated catheterization procedure. Only a terminal and an operator, linked to a minicomputer, are added to the operating room.

ways. They can control fluid intake, regulating precisely the amounts of intravenous nourishment, blood, or other liquid infused. They can also detect stress and summon help if there are sudden changes in temperature, pulse rate, blood pressure, breathing, or fluid drainage.

Blood tests and other diagnostic procedures are often analyzed by computers, which are both faster and more accurate than human technicians, because they automatically check their own measuring devices. Computers are also able to keep track of more variables than humans possibly can; for example, computers can interpret blood sugar readings according to the patient's age, sex, and the amount of time that has elapsed since the last meal, all of which will affect how much sugar is in the blood at any particular time.

A student with cerebral palsy, Ann McClellan (left), operates a computer at the University of California at Irvine by breathing through a tube in Morse code. The Special Education Terminal System was constructed by then UCI student Charles Traynor (right) in 1975.

(UPI)

Computers can also relieve humans of the most time-consuming part of any physical examination by taking medical histories, thus freeing highly trained doctors and nurses from this essential but tedious chore and giving them more time for other aspects of patient care. The machines can be programmed to ask a series of basic questions and to ask for specific follow-up information when necessary. They can also be programmed to skip questions that are irrelevant in certain cases.

As medical and biochemical knowledge has grown at an ever-faster rate, and with more than 5,000 specialized scientific journals, it is impossible for any individual to keep abreast of all the latest developments. The computer system at the National Library of Medicine in Washington offers an index and research service so that physicians can quickly find the information they need. Other computer systems can print out a list of all known disorders that correspond to a given set of symptoms and a list of all known treatments, thus reducing the chance for errors of omission.

Computers may even be at work in the local pharmacy, checking the compatibility of the various drugs prescribed for a given customer. If the records show that several medical specialists have inadvertently prescribed medications that may either cancel out each other's effects or be dangerous to take in combination, the physicians can be notified and the treatment changed accordingly.

The Arts, Education, and Communications

Even the creative arts, the most human of endeavors, are influenced by computers. In fact, the new technology is becoming a

11

new medium, inspiring avant-garde artists who use digital computers to produce sounds and images that were not even imagined only a few years ago.

Film animation, titles, and credits, for movies and television, are today commonly produced by computer. Computer technology is used in the recording industry to modify sounds, to "revitalize" historic recordings, and to produce "larger-than-concert-hall" sounds.

Music is by nature a mathematical art and so particularly lends itself to computer applications. Composers like John Cage have used the random theory of mathematics to create new works with computer help. As early as 1962, "Music from Mathematics" was produced by Decca records to demonstrate how technology could imitate art by producing sounds similar to orchestra instruments and by creating new electronic effects.

Computers have, of course, also assisted the arts in more practical ways. Just as politicians rely on their voter lists, so administrators for theater companies, ballet troupes, and other artistic organizations rely on computer lists of potential patrons. Often these rosters come from magazine subscription lists and from past attendance records. Computers are also being used to catalog museum acquisitions; they were used by the Metropolitan Museum of Art in reconstructing the ancient Temple of Dendur, which was dismantled and shipped as 30,000 separate numbered stone pieces, from Egypt to New York.

Artistic criticism is also beginning to feel the effects of the computer age. For example, computer technology has been used to determine the linguistic structure of a written selection or to trace the influence of one writer on another. It is used to analyze the results of research in the physical, biological, and behavioral sciences, to analyze the fragments found in archaeological digs, or to compare the factors affecting the incidence of obesity. Computer applications in academia are only in their infancy. Modern researchers can analyze in 20 seconds data that once would have taken 11 *months* to process; they can also determine the significance of dozens of factors within a single study. A recent analysis demonstrated the impact of computer technology on psychological studies over the past 20 years. Between 1957 and 1978, the average number of people included in such studies had gone from 353 to 2,224.

More and more, high school students are considering the availability of computer facilities when they select a college. Already accustomed to computers in the classroom, they do not want to be deprived of these tools as they pursue their degrees. This trend is quite different from the one that prevailed over 10 years ago in the late 1960s, when most college students came in contact with computers only at registration. Today they use them to analyze their research and to learn all kinds of material. At the University of Illinois a system known as <u>PLATO (Programmed Logic for Automatic Teaching</u> <u>Operations)</u> uses the Socratic question-and-answer method to teach <u>150</u> subjects.

C.A.I. computer Aided Instruction

Elementary and high school teachers appreciate computerized instruction too. Unlike human teachers, machines have endless patience for rote drills, while at the same time stimulating several senses and being fun for young students to use. By freeing teachers from routine and repetitive tasks, computers enable them to give more personalized attention to individual students. The result: faster learning, longer retention, and higher achievement.

But of all the areas in which computers are used, the one with which most people are familiar is communications. Every time you pick up a telephone, you set a computer into action. We have all come to take for granted the direct dialing of long-distance calls, but new options now available include remote-call forwarding, which makes it possible for a call to a Boston number, for instance, to be answered from an affiliated office in Phoenix. In many offices telephones with tiny computers in them have made switchboards obsolete. These systems allow employees to receive calls directly and record the long-distance calls made at each extension, as well as route outgoing calls along the least expensive trunk lines, to mention only a few of their features.

Daily newspapers both report and make news in our computerized world. Computers set type, keep columns straight, and mechanically syllabicate words.

The applications of computers in communications and in the arts come together in the production of graphics, especially where color is concerned. Business executives, scientists, and others are finding that communication is more effective when color charts and graphs

(UPI)

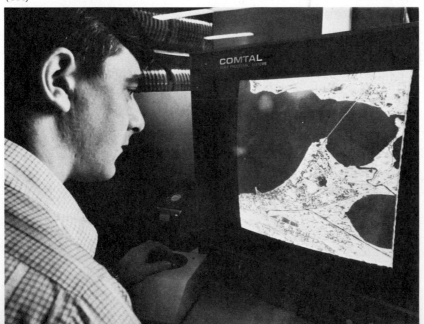

The city of New Orleans appears on a computer screen—Lake Pontchartrain is the larger black area—at the NASA computer center at Slidell, Louisiana. The color-coded picture was recorded by the Landsat satellite, which can identify almost anything on the surface of the earth by recording the amount of energy transmitted.

13

(UPI)

An engineer of the Firestone Tire and Rubber Company designs tire treads with the aid of a computerized graphic display system. This powerful electronic assistance eliminates time-consuming calculations and drawings.

are used to convey information. Color can be used to highlight important points or to tie concepts together.

Computer systems can store more than words in their memories; they can store such graphic representations as maps and diagrams. Municipalities are now indexing their tax rolls geographically, and utility companies are discovering the advantages of "automated" maps in planning, managing transformer loads, and pinpointing problems. Image processing helps the military see through camouflages, analyzes satellite pictures of the Earth so that scientists can determine areas suffering from plant diseases, and assists graphic artists in the preparation of art for advertising, television, and printing. Architects and construction engineers use these systems to simplify complex structural features through color coding. The application of computer color graphics is still new, and its potential is virtually unlimited.

Like fire, computer technology is basically a tool. If fire is used with control and care, it can heat our houses, cook our food, and energize industrial processes. But a fire that is carelessly set can bring disaster, and one that is deliberately set in order to collect insurance is a crime. Computers have similar potentials for abuse. Even in the few decades that they have been in widespread use, there have been instances of invasion of privacy and fraud. More innocently, human error or carelessness can lead to colossal snafus or petty annoyances. However, even without misapplication or abuse, computers would be a source of concern because of their revolutionary impact on the way we live.

Technological Unemployment

From the perspective of an individual, the greatest impact of computer technology is felt on the job. As computers are installed in the workplace, they change the ways in which work is done. And the people who formerly did the work may only know their traditional, although slower, skills; they may not be able to adapt to or learn to use the new devices. For example, the skills involved in hand-setting the type from which books, magazines, or newspapers are printed are very different from the skills needed to keyboard type in a word processing system. In the 1970s thousands of typesetters found themselves technologically unemployed, or encouraged to take early retirement, as print shops and newspapers all over the country switched to the new technology.

It is one thing to talk about "unemployment" in an abstract sense, by pointing out that as a result of computer installations some people will lose their jobs. It is a very different matter—and perhaps more accurate at that—to consider the individual workers who face emotional and financial strain as they are "displaced" by computers.

Overall unemployment rates have been higher during the past decade than at any time since the start of World War II. Much of that trend can be attributed to the entrance of more women into the labor force and to the predictable effect of the "baby boom" generation reaching working age. But computers are no small part of this trend, especially as it affects the unskilled and those trying to return to work after a long hiatus. It is often argued that computers have generally created more jobs than they have destroyed. Their increased use continues to eliminate many tedious, mundane, and repetitive jobs, but computers are also creating new careers, some of which will be examined later in this chapter.

15

An old composing room at *The New York Times*.

(*The New York Times Studio*)

When a work force is computerized, the threat of human obsolescence reverberates throughout the organizational hierarchy. While lower-level clerks and assembly-line workers may find their jobs have disappeared, middle managers may also find their responsibilities eroding. As computers replace workers, managers have smaller staffs to supervise. Departments may be merged, and expertise gained from human associates may be of little value in a roomful of machines. The structure of the organization itself changes as power shifts to the data processing staff, which has the necessary skills to

(*The New York Times Studio*)

A computerized composing room at *The New York Times*.

analyze computer functions and interpret computer-generated information. Even top administrators may feel threatened by their new dependency on the data processing staff, particularly if they themselves do not quite understand the technology.

Seminars and on-the-job training are helping to cushion the transition, for executives and clerical workers alike. Because many months may elapse between the time a computer system is designed and the time it is installed and operational, there is time to plan for a changeover. Natural attrition, as workers leave for other reasons, creates job openings to be filled by new staff members who are compatible with the computerized system. But wise personnel management will value experience and skills gained within the organization.

Craft workers, such as printers or skilled factory workers, do not fare as well as executives or clerical workers. Their skills are the ones that computers make truly obsolete, and society as a whole bears the cost of losing the value of their experience and retraining them for new jobs in the computer age.

Not even professionals and semiprofessionals are immune. Engineers, scientists, and technicians, for example, must constantly keep up with the latest technological innovations, or they risk being left behind as younger graduates with the most up-to-date knowledge and training enter the field.

One result of the transition to computers is a widespread suspicion of computers and resistance to their introduction, which can take forms ranging from lowered morale to actual sabotage. Uneasiness among employees is rooted in realistic fears about financial security, doubts about their ability to learn new skills, reluctance to be transferred away from long-time colleagues, and unwillingness to give up status or prestige that was conferred by their now-outmoded expertise. Some resistance to new computer systems is probably inevitable, but astute managers can reduce anxiety by keeping their employees fully informed and seeking their input during the planning stages.

It is important for all those concerned with the implementation of computer technology to take the human factor into account. The burden is on those who are conversant with computers to communicate their positive attitude to others and also to cushion the transition to a computerized society for those who have reason to resist change.

Invasion of Privacy

In our democracy, the individual's right to privacy may often be in conflict with the public's need to know. Governments use information in their files to plan and evaluate programs, enforce tax laws, issue security clearances, and so on. There is always the possibility that some of that information may be misused. Despite safeguards, no computer system yet developed is totally safe from either tampering or unauthorized use by someone many miles away, in another state, or perhaps even in another country.

Personal privacy. Like Hansel and Gretel who left a trail of breadcrumbs behind them, Americans have been scattering records for years. Credit bureaus and banks, licensing agencies and courts, educational institutions and the Internal Revenue Service maintain billions of files on millions of people. Birth and death certificates, school attendance records, marriage and driver's licenses—at these and other points of the life cycle the facts of our daily existence are entered into a data file somewhere.

Before computers were extensively used, individuals were protected by the very fragmentation of the information about them. Separate investigators who wanted to find out something had to travel to each place where documents were kept. They then had to deal with individual clerks who could be helpful but more often were not cooperative about granting access to their information.

Today, an investigator just has to sit down at a terminal and dial the appropriate computer on an ordinary telephone to obtain the information desired. Many records, now stored in centralized data banks, are readily accessible to users at widespread geographic locations.

But some of the data so efficiently stored and so readily accessed may be extraneous or even false. Errors of commission—false data —may result from careless verification procedures or from mistakes made in filling out the forms from which the data were taken. Errors of omission—incomplete data—are common, especially in police records, where officials may be diligent about recording arrests and lax about recording verdicts. Mistakes can also be compounded when information is exchanged between agencies, a common practice.

Some reformers advocate a single centralized national data center that would offer better protection of privacy than the current dispersed system. This data center would set tight controls on who would have access to information and for what purposes. The proposal, however, has been dropped in light of the simultaneously created possibility that the computers might be used for personal surveillance, especially as credit cards and electronic funds transfers vastly increase the trail of documentation we leave behind us.

International privacy. The flow of information through computerized channels across national borders has become a complex problem for all governments, including our own. Technical information is becoming an international commodity, but no body of international law has been developed as yet to govern its use. Some nations see the outflow of information as a threat to their security and sovereignty. Some U.S. business executives suspect that foreign nations that are reluctant to share data on economic resources and planning are trying to protect their own companies from American competition under the guise of protecting their privacy.

Nonetheless, many countries are trying to apply their own privacy laws to the flow of international data, making it difficult for businesses that have to cope with the conflicting regulations. Some national laws apply to private businesses as well as to government agencies and cover corporate as well as personal information. Laws also vary as to what kinds of information are considered privileged.

Possible solutions are now under consideration by two international agencies. The Organization for Economic Cooperation and Development, which includes the United States, Japan, Canada, Australia, and New Zealand in addition to European and other nations, advocates voluntary compliance with general guidelines. The Council of Europe is drafting a formal agreement that would be binding upon all the countries that sign it.

Fraud and Other Criminal Acts

Certain characteristics of computer systems make businesses and government agencies that use them vulnerable to fraud and other crimes on a monumental scale. In 1975 a $1 billion fraud drove the Equity Funding Corporation into bankruptcy. A New York savings bank lost $1.5 million to its embezzling chief teller; it took three years to discover his scheme.

Computers can help the unscrupulous to steal money and inventory, submit false claims for insurance payments, or copy sensitive information for blackmail or sale to competitors. Moreover, all of this can be accomplished without detection. The information and documents fed to computers are stored on magnetic tapes or disks, which can be quickly altered, substituted, or erased without anyone's knowledge. Centralized record keeping and the lack of physical documents also add to the risk of loss in case of fire (accidental or arson-caused). No amount of insurance can compensate for the loss of irreplaceable files.

Security precautions do exist, but they often lose out to demands for efficiency when choices have to be made during the design of a customized system. Many of the safeguards presently used can be bypassed by clever technical personnel.

19

According to some experts, one reason that criminal computer schemes can continue undetected for years is the belief that the systems are infallible and that computer-generated information is beyond question. Many computer frauds go unnoticed during routine audits and are only discovered either accidentally or when the thief makes a mistake.

In addition to the obvious abuses associated with embezzlement and deception, it is possible that computers have been used for attempted murder. In February 1980, a representation of an Aeroflot jetliner carrying the Soviet ambassador mysteriously disappeared from the computerized tracking system as it approached Kennedy Airport in New York. Some investigators feared it had been deliberately erased. That no midair collision resulted before the plane touched down has been credited largely to luck.

Human Error

Of course, people can misuse computers without having any insidious motives. They can simply make mistakes. Computers may take the blame, but human error is probably the greatest single problem in the data processing field.

A faulty program led to a $1 billion overpayment in Supplemental Security Income checks from the federal government. At a suburban newspaper, a fledgling technician was sent to perform routine maintenance on some computers, but he inadvertently skipped a few steps and the entire memory was wiped out. And numerous stories are told of credit card customers who received repeated bills for zero dollars and zero cents—and then were notified that their accounts had been turned over to a collection agency.

For all their elaborate hardware and sophisticated capabilities, computer systems are built on a human foundation, which includes occasional carelessness, incompetence, and misunderstanding. No system of checks and double-checks will ever remove the gremlins and glitches completely, and so—for better or for worse—computers will continue to reflect the touch of their human creators and programmers.

New Horizons in Our Computerized Society

The use of computers in business and government has, as we will see in the following chapter, a history that goes back only about 30 years. Computer applications in such fields as education, the arts, and medicine have been with us for only a little more than a dozen years. Some computer applications, such as artificial intelligence and robotics, are still in their infancy or just a gleam in their designers' eyes (see chapter 16). And one area of computer use, in existence barely five years, has already shown itself to be a booming mini-industry—an area made possible by mini- and microcomputers.

Personal Computing

In January 1977, almost 25,000 computers were in American homes, but more than two-thirds of them belonged to engineers, technicians, and computer professionals. Two years earlier these machines simply did not exist. But two years later, over 250,000 had been sold, almost all of them for family and small business use. Personal computing is rapidly becoming one of the fastest growing areas in our society, with new accessory products being unveiled almost every week.

Today, personal computers cost about as much as good stereo systems, putting them within reach of a substantial segment of the nation's consumers. These machines can play games with you, balance your checkbook, store your recipes or most-used telephone numbers, control your lights and appliances, and manage your family's energy and fuel consumption efficiently. Systems already developed will permit one home computer to be linked with another by telephone, thereby creating personal computer networks.

Until recently, one hindrance to the rapid spread of home computers was that they had to be programmed by their owners. For that reason their market was largely limited to specialists such as professionals or hobbyists. However, the products of software—programs for a variety of purposes on either cassettes or thin, flexible disks called "floppies"—are remedying that problem. Sold in retail computer stores—whose very existence is a measure of the growth in demand for personal computers and accessories—these programs are bringing home computers to an increasing audience, including the owners of small businesses, researchers in a variety of fields, and eventually the mass market. Programs range from strategy games, like checkers and bridge, to financial analyses that permit personal and business budget forecasting. They have spawned a new industry in which free-lance programmers have been compared to book authors, with software-producing firms likened to publishers.

Some computers designed for home use can be connected to television sets that are already part of virtually every American home. Video computer games have been available for several years, but the most sophisticated versions can be connected to an optional key-

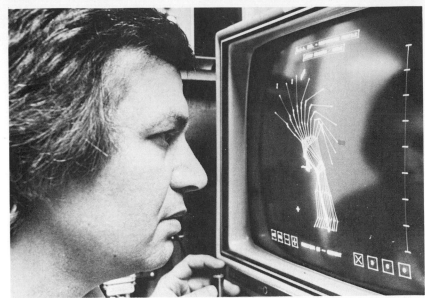

The movements of an
athlete training for the
Olympics are broken
down graphically by a
computer, and are used
to help athletes improve
their performance. Data
General donated this
computer to the U.S.
Olympic Committee in
1979.

(UPI)

board component that allows personal applications never before
possible in a television-based system. The initial collection of video
computer cassettes includes programs for 20 games (from backgammon to football), French lessons, astrological charting, custom-de-
signed exercise routines, and federal income tax computing.

Practicality aside, playing with computers has been growing more
popular each year. In addition to the smorgasbord of video games
available, there are assorted robots and electronic versions of classic
board games. One of the first games on the scene was computerized
chess, which challenged players who were either alone or without
good competition or who wanted to solve intricate chess problems.
More recently young children's games, available as single-purpose
computers that play spelling bee and quiz games or create simple
musical tunes, were marketed at relatively low cost.

The widespread acceptance of computers for amusement has significance beyond just providing a few enjoyable hours. It has probably led to wider acceptance of computers in other areas of life.

Career Opportunities

One of the most vital uses of computer technology is the generation of timely and relevant information needed for people to make
rational decisions. It is particularly evident in business, where computers directly affect general accounting, management, marketing,

and more. Every aspect of business today requires computer "literacy," whether for those who use the information it generates or those who design the systems and their components. Business is by far the field in which computers are used most frequently to perform the widest variety of tasks.

Thirty-five years ago, the ledgers or "books" that a company kept were literally that: books. In those days, 95 percent of the high-level financial professionals found it unnecessary to know anything about the computers of the day, and their subordinates may hardly have been aware that the machines existed at all. Today, a familiarity with data processing is a mandatory qualification for entry-level accounting jobs and highly desirable in most bookkeeping and clerical posts.

Accountants in the 1980s must be able to deal with electronic systems and the data produced by these systems in order to prepare the same financial statements, forecasts, budgets, marketing analyses, and other reports they have always been called upon to produce. As a result, current Certified Public Accountant (CPA) examinations ask questions pertaining to computerized audits, and nearly all accounting students are taking some computer courses.

Accountancy is an obvious example of a long-established profession that is being required to adapt to new techniques, but the same demands are creating opportunities for new types of employment in many other areas, as we have seen in this chapter. In the fields of medicine, the arts, education, retailing, manufacturing, architecture, as well as in other fields, the new technology is producing new procedures, enhancing productivity, spurring creativity—and creating new job opportunities.

Throughout its brief history the computer industry has grown so rapidly that the number of jobs available has continually expanded faster than the supply of personnel qualified to fill them. Engineers and analysts to design computer systems, programmers to direct their capacities, technicians to install and maintain them, and operators to run them are all in short supply. The U.S. Department of Labor has predicted that the number of computer scientists alone will grow to 230,000 by 1985, a 500 percent increase over the 42,000 individuals working in that capacity in 1978. Because there will continue to be a shortage of computer professionals for several years, this phenomenal increase is not expected to cause a glut. On the contrary, employment experts agree that computer technology will be among the best career opportunities in the coming decade.

The versatility of computer technology accounts for much of the optimism. As more diverse businesses apply computers to more varied aspects of their enterprises, the need for business programmers will grow, along with the need for systems designers. One of the most important new industry developments is distributed data processing, which allows branch offices to feed information to central data banks via direct computer links. Some banks and insurance companies are experimenting with the next logical step in that direction: They are placing computer terminals, which are tied to the office network, in the homes of employees. If this innovation proves feasible, it will reduce commuting, reduce energy consumption, and make jobs available to those who need or prefer to work from home. This possibility could also bring career opportunities to people who never had them before, such as the housebound handicapped.

For many individuals, computer careers can bring a great deal of occupational independence. As long as the current shortage persists, computer professionals will continue to be able, as they are at present, to change jobs frequently and seek new challenges, more responsibility, or more money. However, even after the boom passes, engineers, analysts, and programmers will still find tantalizing and practical opportunities to free-lance as consultants, either working on new systems or troubleshooting on old ones. The creative computer expert will always find new worlds to conquer.

Summary

Computers have already become ubiquitous. The most familiar applications are in business. Banks use them to administer credit card, checking, and savings accounts. Retailers and manufacturers use them at the point of sale and for inventory control and general record keeping. They also depend on computer-generated information in managerial decision making.

Similarly, agencies at all levels of government rely on computers for general administration and planning, for budgeting, and for numerous other purposes. Computers also assist local and national law enforcement agencies by providing instant access to vehicle registration files, police records, and fingerprint files.

In every science, from astronomy to zoology, computer applications can be found. In medicine, computers check bodily functions, perform tests and analyze the results, and help take medical histories and assist in diagnoses.

Computers can produce creative works of art and can also help students learn. They enable us to communicate easily with people all over the world through a network of telephone relays. Computer graphics are expanding their impact on printed media in government and business with the addition of such features as color coding and image-storing memories.

The proliferation of computer applications has raised some social and political concerns, especially in the areas of technological unemployment, invasion of privacy, and fraud. Records can be stolen, erased, changed, or duplicated without a trace of tampering. But the greatest source of difficulty is human error: computers can greatly magnify the impact of dumb mistakes by continually compounding them or by sharing them with other systems when information is electronically exchanged.

Computers have indirectly accelerated the pace of technical education, making it more essential than ever for professionals to keep abreast of the latest innovations in their fields in order to be competitive.

One of the newest benefits of computer technology is its personal use, as computers come into the home to help with household budgets, stimulate the intellect, and entertain with electronic toys and games.

All of these trends can be translated into career opportunities. Employers in many fields are looking for applicants who have some familiarity with computers. The demand for computer scientists, programmers, and technicians is expected to continue well into the future.

Sources of Additional Information

Dorf, Richard C. *Computers and Man*. San Francisco: Boyd and Fraser Publishing Co., 1974.

Klein, Jerome. "Computers and Medicine." *MD*, June 1975, pp. 84–96.

Krauss, Leonard I., and MacGahan, Aileen. *Computer Fraud and Countermeasures*. Englewood Cliffs, N.J.: Prentice-Hall, 1979.

Martin, James. *The Wired Society*. Englewood Cliffs, N.J.: Prentice-Hall, 1978.

"Pushbutton Power." *Time*, February 20, 1978, pp. 46–49.

Sanders, Donald H. *Computers in Society*. New York: McGraw-Hill, 1977.

Test Yourself

1. List three locations where data about you might be recorded.
2. Give one example of how computers store data in a form other than words.
3. What occupations are most likely to be affected by increased computerization? What occupations are most likely to be discontinued?
4. Why do employees often react adversely to a new computer installation? What might be done to improve employee acceptance? What can employees do on their own to prepare for the "computer age"?
5. Misuse of information can cause much damage not only by intentional criminal acts but also by human or machine error. What

are some major "blunders" that have been reported recently in the news media?

6. The use of minicomputers is rapidly expanding. How do you account for this? What are some of the applications for these machines?

7. Our own times are sometimes called the "age of computers." Why should a person considering a business career today have a basic knowledge of computers?

8. The computer industry offers excellent career opportunities. What are some types of jobs that are available within the industry?

2 The Past, Present, and Future of Data Processing

Reprinted from Infosystems, April 1979.
© Hitchcock Publishing Company.

APPLICATION
The First Computerized U.S. Census

The U.S. Constitution requires a national census every 10 years for the purpose of apportioning state representation in the House of Representatives. When the first U.S. census was taken in 1790, the census takers faced a relatively easy task. The U.S. population at that time was only about four million people, and the census questionnaire included only five items. Nonetheless, it took 18 months simply to collect the data. Also, hand tallying and paper and pencil were the only methods available for recording and tabulating data. When the tabulations were completed, the final printed report was 56 pages long.

The task of taking the census became much greater with each succeeding decade. Indeed, as the time approached for the 1890 census, the task had reached crisis proportions. The census of 1880 had counted a population of 50 million and used a questionnaire averaging 16 questions. The collection of data had taken no longer than in the first census a century before—18 months. But the methods of recording and tabulating data had hardly changed at all. The first of the printed reports (which eventually totaled 1,000 pages) was not published until 1887. And it was obvious that the 1890 census was going to face an even more serious problem: the population had grown substantially, and because of this increase, it looked as though the census would not be completed before the next census was due in 1900!

It is an old saying that necessity is the mother of invention, and so it was in the case of the 1890 census. A young statistician in the Census Bureau—Herman Hollerith—invented an electromechanical device that could tabulate data recorded on punched cards. At the census office, Hollerith (1860–1929) worked with Major John Shaw Billings, who was supervising the interpretation of vital statistics. It was Billings who mentioned to Hollerith that holes punched into cards might represent numerical data, and that a machine might be devised to "read" the holes in the cards. Hollerith set to work.

As a result of Hollerith's invention, the 1890 census took less than four years to complete—even though the population had grown to 63 million, the number of questionnaire items to 45, and the length of the reports to a total of 1,200 pages.

Hollerith's invention marked the beginning of what is now called data processing. But, as we shall see in this chapter, the history of devices for recording and tabulating data is thousands of years old. With Hollerith's machine the modern era of data processing can be said to have begun. But the development of data processing since Hollerith's time—and especially during the past 25 years—has been spectacular.

EVERYONE recognizes that computers are remarkable machines. Not the least remarkable thing about them is how rapidly they have developed in the past quarter century. Much of the effect that computers have had on our modern society is due to the "explosion" of computer availability and capacity.

In the early 1950s there were fewer than 1,000 computers in the United States (almost all of them owned by or operated for the federal government). Twenty-five years later, this number had increased to well over 200,000, or an average of one computer for every 1,000 people. Many of these computers were owned by or operated for private businesses, universities, local governments, and individuals.

Another mark of the development of computers is the overall increase in "computing power," or the total capacity of these machines. According to a common estimate, the computing power of computers has increased tenfold *every eight years* since the completion of the first all-electronic computer in 1946.

The Development of Computers: An Overview

Two major trends have marked the rapid evolution of computers: They have become ever *smaller* and ever *faster*. The same technological advances are responsible for both trends. The electronic circuitry that once would have filled a large room can now be fitted on a computer "chip" less than ¼ square inch in area. Moreover, the newest computers are performing calculations about *a million times faster* than computers available 25 years ago. The calculation speed of today's computers is measured in *nanoseconds* (billionths of a second).

To get a better idea of what this means, imagine a line 1 foot long (or, to be exact, 11.8 inches). This is the distance that light travels in a nanosecond. Compare that to the distance that light travels in a *second*: 186,000 miles, or the equivalent of nearly seven and one-half times around the world. When speeds of calculation become so great, the length of the wiring in the computer circuits themselves may become a major limiting factor. Thus, the miniaturization of computers has contributed significantly to their greater operating speeds.

Such speed of calculation is mind-boggling. Yet computer scientists expect to have even faster machines within the next 10 years! These computers will perform calculations in *picoseconds,* or trillionths of a second. Imagine a line measuring 1.2 inches. That would

29

represent the distance that light travels in 100 picoseconds! (Again, compare this to the distance that light travels in a single second.)

The miniaturization and increasing speed of computers are the results of advances in technology. Some of these advances have been so important that they have given rise to new "generations" of computers. The concept of a computer generation is not a precise one, but it does simplify the problem of distinguishing certain types of computers from others. The concept also makes it easier to outline a clear chronology of the development of computing machines.

Hollerith's electromechanical device is considered—along with the ancient abacus—one of the "earliest" machines. All machines of this type were "single-purpose" computing devices—that is, a change in purpose or function more or less meant having to build a new machine. During World War II, computer scientists began to develop "general-purpose" machines that could store their own instruction programs. Such machines could be given new instructions without having to be rebuilt or even rewired.

The so-called first-generation machines appeared in the 1950s. At that time, too, computers first became available commercially. Machines of this generation were characterized by the use of vacuum tubes in their circuitry. The vacuum tube (essentially an electronic switch) represented a tremendous advance in the history of computing machines. Unfortunately, vacuum tube machines also had serious limitations—they were big, hot, and expensive.

Then a tiny electronic device came along. This was the transistor, and it made second-generation computers smaller, cooler, and cheaper—and even more available.

Third-generation computers were characterized by simple integrated circuits (the earliest computer "chips"), which further reduced the space requirements for computers. With the development of large-scale integration (LSI), more circuitry could occupy the same chip space. LSI chips provided fourth-generation computers with greater computational power in an extremely small space. These machines represent the "state of the art"—that is, the stage of development reached by computers at the present time.

Considering the short time-span in which the first four generations have appeared, it is not surprising that computer scientists are already looking ahead to the fifth- and sixth-generation computers, which will characterize the 1980s and 1990s.

The explosive development of computer technology has been called the second industrial revolution. There certainly can be no doubt that computers—or rather their use in data processing—are having profound effects on our society (see chapter 1). But, aside from the many questions that this "revolution" has raised, there is the question of why it has occurred at all. Or, to put it another way, why do people need calculating machines? Indeed, have they ever truly needed them?

The Need for Computing Devices

Why do we need calculating machines? An obvious answer is: To take care of problems like the 1890 census. That census was an excellent example of the need for machines to process billions of pieces of information. More modern examples of our need for computing devices easily come to mind. In a world without computers, the operations of banks, many large industries, and the federal government would be much slower and more cumbersome than they are now. Credit cards probably would not exist. Landing a man on the moon would still be an impossible dream.

But these examples do not answer the more basic question of why people needed calculating machines in the first place, or indeed whether they ever needed them at all. The answer is rather surprising: The need for computing devices arises from a fundamental human need to count things.

Humans have been making computing devices since prehistoric times. People of the Stone Age marked bones, sticks, and stones to keep track of the repeating phases of the moon, the number of animals killed in a hunt, the number of rains in a season. The Sumerians, in the third millennium B.C., had three separate accounting systems, each with its own set of symbols, to record transactions involving grain, livestock, and landholdings. Without a counting system of some sort, such records could not have been kept. And counting requires numbers. The Egyptians could not have built the pyramids without a number system. In fact, without numbers many human enterprises would remain at the most rudimentary level, if they developed at all: trade, industry, science, and more. Government of any kind, and civilization as we know it, would be impossible.

The Development of Computing Devices: A Chronology

The Earliest Machines

The very earliest computing devices required some sort of physical effort from the user—tying knots in a rope, pushing beads on a wire, or turning a crank. Compared with the touch-sensitive keys of

31

Time Line of Computing History

3000	2500	2000	1500	1000	500	B.C.	A.D.	200	400	600	800	1000

● 3000–2000 B.C. Sumerians devised their own computing systems.

● 2700–2160 B.C. Pyramids built in Egypt.

● 1800–1400 B.C. Stonehenge built in England.

● 500 B.C. *Abax,* counting board, known in Greece.

● 600 A.D. Place-value

● 820 Indian

● 870 Zero

```
1200      1400      1600      1800      2000
```

otation of numerals originated in India.

umerals adopted by Arab mathematician al-Khwarizmi.

"0") invented as a concept and symbol in India.

● 1150 Abacus, or *suan pan* — movable "beads" on wires — used in China.

● 1202 Indian (arabic) numerals, zero, and place-value notation introduced in Europe by Leonardo of Pisa.

● 1550–1617 Napier invented logarithms, calculating system using "bones."

● 1642 Pascal invented adding machine.

● 1662 Slide rule invented.

● 1671 Von Leibniz invented "stepped reckoner."

● 1801 Jacquard used first punched cards –on a loom.

● 1822 Babbage developed "difference engine."

● 1823 Babbage invented "analytical engine."

● 1890 80-column punched card designed by Hollerith; used to tabulate U.S. census.

● 1896–1900 Hollerith invented sorting machine, card-punch machine, and semiautomatic tabulator.

● 1900 90-column punched card designed by Powers.

● 1924 Hollerith merged with two other companies to form IBM.

● 1925 First large-scale computer designed by Vannevar Bush and team.

● 1939–1944 Electromechanical computer MARK I developed.

● 1943–1946 First all-electronic digital computer, ENIAC, developed by Eckert and Mauchly.

● 1944 Von Neumann proposed the stored-program concept and use of binary numbers.

● 1944–1952 Von Neumann, Eckert, Mauchly, and others designed the EDVAC.

● 1948 Transistors invented.

● 1951 1st computer generation began: UNIVAC, first commercial computer.

● 1957 UNIVAC II and magnetic core memory developed.

● 1959 2d computer generation began: transistors were used in computer design.

● 1960 First commercial real-time data processing system, UNIVAC 490, was introduced.

● 1964 3d computer generation began: integrated circuits transformed computer technology.

● mid-1970s 4th computer generation began: mini- and microcomputers; LSI circuits on chips.

● 1978 Bubble memory first used commercially: very large scale integration began.

modern electronic computers, that seems like a lot of work and a slow way to get results. We may well question whether such "ancient" devices were worth the effort needed to operate them. But in judging the worth of any early machine, we must take into account other facts as well: the historical period in which it was developed, the purpose for which it was used, and the technological sophistication of the society in which it appeared. By these standards, all the earliest machines represented profound technological advances.

The abacus. Of all the computing devices ever invented, the abacus has been by far the most successful in terms of longevity and distribution. The term *abacus* is derived from the Greek word *abax* (or *abakos*), which means flat surface. It eventually was applied to a marked counting board on which pebbles, used as counters, were moved into various positions. (This led to our word *calculate*, from the Latin word *calculi*, meaning pebbles or stones.) The Greeks were known to have counting boards by the fifth century B.C., and perhaps even earlier. The abacus that is commonly known today consists of movable "beads" on wires. This type of abacus, or *suan pan*, appeared in China in the twelfth century A.D.

In this form the abacus is still widely used, especially in the Middle East and Asia, where it is as omnipresent as computerized cash registers and hand-held calculators are in the United States. There are two reasons for this popularity: The abacus is simple, and it is effective. In the hands of an experienced user, the abacus can compete with the best mechanical desk calculators. In late 1946 a contest was held in Tokyo between a U.S. Army finance clerk and a Japanese accounting official, using, respectively, a $700 electric desk calculator and a 25-cent abacus. Before a cheering audience of 3,000, the

Plaster cast of a Roman hand abacus; the original, of bronze, is in the Cabinet Médailles in Paris. Between the two rows of grooves are Roman symbols representing numbers from ¼ to 1,000,000. The counters, or *claviculi*, "little nails," are moved in the grooves to perform additive operations.

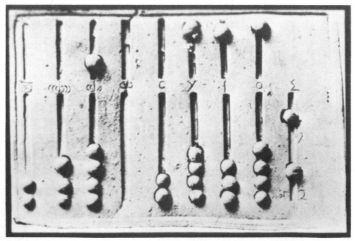

A Chinese abacus (*suan
pan*)

(Courtesy of IBM)

contestants solved problems in addition, subtraction, multiplication, and division involving 3- to 12-digit numbers. The electric calculator triumphed only in multiplication, while the abacus came out ahead in the other three categories, as well as in a final composite-process problem.

An abacus consists of parallel columns of beads strung on wires or rods, usually crossed by a wooden bar. Values are entered on the abacus by moving beads against the crossbar; each bead below the crossbar, when moved up, has a value of 1; each bead above the bar, when moved down, has a value of 5. The value of the beads in any one column is 10 times that of the beads in the next column to the right. In other words, the abacus is based on the decimal system and, in fact, has a "floating" decimal point, just as many of today's electronic calculators do. The unit value of a single bead is indicated by its *position* as one reads from right to left. The abacus is the first computing device known to use this type of positional notation in representing numbers. The concept of positional notation is discussed again in chapter 5, in the section on computing devices that use binary numbers.

Napier's "logs" and "bones." John Napier (1550–1617) was a Scottish mathematician who became famous for his invention of *logarithms.* The use of "logs" enabled him to reduce any multiplication problem to a problem of addition. (Napier's logs later became the basis for a well-known invention by another mathematician—the computing machine known as the slide rule, which was invented in

35

1662.) In 1617 Napier invented a computing device that consisted of a set of sticks with numbers printed on them. (The sticks were called "bones" because they were made of bone or ivory.) By ingenious methods, Napier could perform both multiplication and division with his "bones." Although the methods are too complex to be described here, Napier's "bones" represented a significant contribution to the development of computing devices.

Pascal's "arithmetic engine." The first successful mechanical calculator appeared in 1642, only 25 years after Napier had published his paper describing "bones." Its inventor was the French philosopher Blaise Pascal (1623–1662), who, like Napier, was also a mathematician. His "arithmetic engine" was a digital counting device that incorporated a number of features still found in modern mechanical calculators.

Approximately the size of a cigar box, Pascal's machine could add and subtract numbers containing up to eight digits. It had a hand-cranked mechanical gear system, in which a series of 10-toothed wheels or dials represented decimal numbers. The two wheels farthest to the right represented two decimal places; the next wheel to the left, "ones"; the fourth wheel, "tens"; the fifth wheel, "hundreds"; and so on. Each wheel was engraved with the digits 0 to 9, one digit for every tooth on the wheel.

Pascal's machine performed computations by counting integers. One of its important features was an automatic "carry." That is,

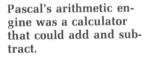

Pascal's arithmetic engine was a calculator that could add and subtract.

(*Courtesy of IBM*)

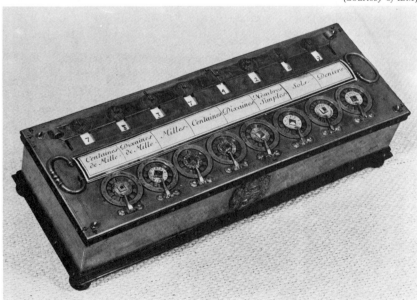

when one wheel was turned from 9 to 0, the next wheel to the left moved one digit. Addition was performed by "stepping" (hand turning) the appropriate wheels by the amount to be added. Subtraction required turning the wheels in reverse.

Pascal's arithmetic engine had one serious drawback: It could not be produced by the technology of the time. There was no industrial technology in the seventeenth century. Hand-turned parts could not supply the necessary accuracy. Precision machining, interchangeable parts, and mass production were more than 200 years in the future.

Leibniz's "stepped reckoner." The next major advance came half a century after Pascal's invention. It, too, was the work of a philosopher-mathematician—Gottfried Wilhelm von Leibniz (1646–1716) —one of the greatest scientific geniuses of his time. At the age of 26 he taught himself mathematics and then proceeded to invent calculus. He invented a calculator because he had never been taught the multiplication tables! He also proposed the use of a binary number system for mechanical calculators.

Leibniz's machine differed from Pascal's in several important respects. One of the most important differences was that Leibniz's device could multiply and divide directly, as well as extract square roots. Another was the use of stepped cylinders, each with nine teeth of varying lengths, instead of wheels. But Leibniz's "reckoner" was, like Pascal's engine, too advanced for the technology of its time. The working models constructed in 1694 and 1704 were never duplicated.

Jacquard's loom. Interestingly enough, the next important advance in the development of computing devices came from a field that had little association with science or mathematics—weaving. To produce a desired pattern when weaving cloth, selected warp threads must be lifted in a specific sequence, while a shuttle carries a weft thread between the lifted warps and those that are not lifted. The pattern is formed by lifting a different sequence of warp threads in each successive row. As early as 1725, French weavers were using continuous belts of perforated paper to select punched cards that, in turn, lifted the warp threads. In effect, the paper tape was a "stored" program for a specific weaving pattern.

Joseph-Marie Jacquard (1752–1834) was the first to successfully use punched cards both for storing information (on lifting the warp threads) and for controlling the machine (the program or sequence in which the threads were to be lifted). Jacquard's loom, exhibited in 1801, was a great commercial success. It was a milestone in the development of the textile industry, and was also one of the most im-

37

Babbage's difference engine

(Courtesy of IBM)

portant and far-reaching developments in the history of data processing.

Babbage's "engines." Charles Babbage (1792–1871) was an English inventor and mathematician with sufficient inherited wealth to indulge his many interests in science and technology. Although he was a genius, his name would be remembered by very few today if he had not invented two computing "engines."

In 1822 Babbage invented what he called the "difference engine." (The term "difference" refers to a mathematical technique.) One potential use for this calculator was the compilation of accurate navigational and artillery tables. The English government therefore underwrote the construction of a larger and even more accurate version. However, the difference engine fell victim to the same difficulties as the inventions of Pascal and Leibniz: The technology of the time could not produce it. Today we would classify the difference engine as a special-purpose digital computer because it had a fixed program.

In 1835, the year after Jacquard's death, Babbage conceived of the "analytical engine." This machine was designed to use two sets of Jacquard punched cards. One set carried the data, the other a sequence of operations (the program). Essentially the machine had two basic components: Its storage unit, or memory, would hold all possible numeric variables and the results of all previous calculations; its "mill" would process the data fed to it. "Feelers," or rods, plunged through the perforations in the cards, touching off the mechanism that would move numbers out of the storage unit and into the mill for processing. Among the many innovations incorporated in the analytical engine, at least two were revolutionary. The first enabled the machine to compare quantities and then *branch* (that is, "decide" which of two instructions or instruction sequences to follow). The second permitted the results of a calculation to change numbers and instructions already stored in the machine. With this ability, the computer could modify its own program.

Babbage described in detail what might have been the world's first working general-purpose (that is, programmable) computer. But his analytical engine was never built. Once again the technology of the time lagged behind the conception. It would not catch up until half a century after Babbage's death.

Hollerith's punched-card machine. The next major development was a step backward theoretically, but a considerable step forward technologically. Hollerith's machine could classify, sort, and add, but it would have been no match for the kind of machine envisioned by Babbage. Unlike Babbage, however, Hollerith had the advantage of electricity. In Hollerith's machine, as in Babbage's, the data to be processed were coded as holes in cards. Hollerith's punched cards, however, were passed between metal pins and trays containing mercury-filled cups. Whenever a metal pin encountered a hole in a card, it passed through the card and made contact with the mercury. As the pin touched the mercury, it closed an electric circuit and thus activated a counting mechanism. This arrangement made it possible to tabulate several different items at a time (several different holes in a card) on a single run of the cards through the machine. Electromechanical sensors had replaced Babbage's mechanical "feelers" in detecting perforations in cards.

A second and greater advantage of Hollerith's machine was also made possible by electricity. Babbage's analytical engine had been designed (of necessity) with a hand crank. In Hollerith's machine, electrical relays powered the tabulator. A "relay" is an electromechanical switching device. It consists of a wire coil wound around a soft-iron core. A pulse of electricity through the coil briefly magnetizes the core, making it able to attract a thin metal strip. As the

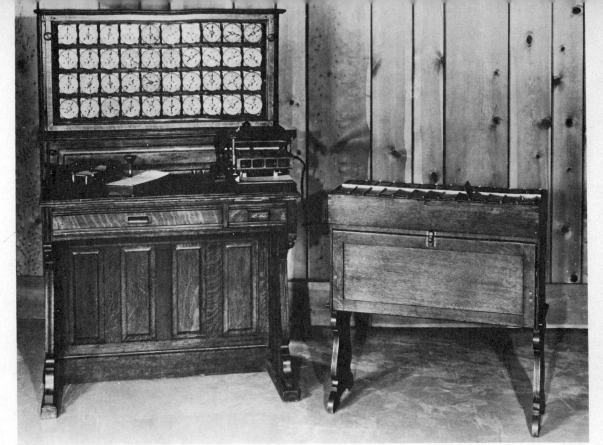

Hollerith's tabulator

(Courtesy of IBM)

metal strip moves from its "normal" position and back again, it opens or closes an electrical circuit. The principle is essentially the same as that of the telegraph key.

As we saw in the Application at the beginning of this chapter, Hollerith's machine was successful in solving the problem of the 1890 census. When its potential usefulness for tabulating and sorting other types of data became apparent, Hollerith formed his own data processing company in 1896. His was the first commercially successful data processing machine. By 1900 he had developed a machine that could sort 300 cards per minute, a card-punch machine, and a semiautomatic tabulator. In 1924 Hollerith merged his company with two others to form the International Business Machines Corporation, now well known as IBM.

For the next 15 years, IBM had only one competitor in punched-card data processing: Remington Rand. The latter had bought the patent rights to data processing machines developed by James Powers, a statistical engineer at the Census Bureau. Then, with the outbreak of World War II, the stage was finally set for the general-purpose machine that Babbage had envisioned a century earlier.

40

Early Developments in Electronic Data Processing

Except for Babbage's analytical engine, all the early machines were essentially single-purpose devices. That is, they were designed to perform a specific task or set of tasks (for example, a machine that did addition could be manipulated so that it would also perform the other three basic arithmetic operations). But a different type of task would require a different type of machine.

The development of a working general-purpose computer was greatly accelerated by World War II. In particular there was a pressing need to develop tables showing in tabular form the ranges and trajectories of new weapons. Many of these weapons fired shells beyond the range of human vision. With firing tables, field commanders could determine targets with accuracy. But without firing tables, such artillery was virtually useless. The mechanical desk calculators of the day were not fast enough for all the calculations involved.

Success came in 1944 with the completion of the Mark I, an electromechanical computer. The first entirely electronic computer—the ENIAC—followed in 1946. Both machines represented the realization of Babbage's dream of a general-purpose machine. But more than a century separated his analytical engine from the Mark I and the ENIAC.

After this long delay there followed almost immediately two of the most important advances in computer technology: the use of binary numbers in computers and the invention of stored programs. Both of these features of modern computers were originally proposed (by John von Neumann in 1945) as modifications of the ENIAC. The first computer to employ binary numbers and a stored program was completed in 1949.

The Mark I.   The official name of the Mark I was Automatic Sequence Controlled Calculator. The longer name was appropriate for the Mark I, for it had taken five years to build and was very large. Howard Aiken of Harvard University, in collaboration with IBM engineers, constructed the Mark I in the years from 1939 to 1944. The result was a computer approximately 50 feet long and 8 feet high. It consisted of some 700,000 moving parts and several hundred miles of wiring. The Mark I could perform the four basic arithmetic operations and could locate information stored in tabular form. It processed numbers up to 23 digits long, and could multiply three eight-digit numbers in 1 second.

The Mark I was—and still is—the largest electromechanical computer ever built. It was also the first automatic general-purpose digital computer. Aiken—who was unaware of the design of Babbage's analytical engine when he started his work—went on to construct a

The Mark I

second relay computer (the Mark II) and two magnetic drum versions (the Mark III and the Mark IV). All, however, were soon overshadowed by the ENIAC.

The ENIAC. The name ENIAC is an acronym for *E*lectronic *Nu*merical *I*ntegrator *A*nd *C*alculator. The proposal for this first completely electronic computer came from a group headed by John W.` Mauchly and J. Presper Eckert at the Moore School of Electrical Engineering of the University of Pennsylvania. As originally conceived, the ENIAC was to be a general-purpose computer. It was subsidized by the U.S. government, however, for the specific purpose of solving ballistics problems for the U.S. Army. The most radical feature of the proposed computer was the use of 18,000 vacuum tubes in its circuitry. (Some experts were convinced that, because vacuum tubes were not sufficiently reliable, any computer with such a large number of them would be unworkable.) The ENIAC also contained 70,000 resistors, 10,000 capacitors, and 7,500 switches. It weighed 30 tons and occupied the entire 15,000 square feet of the Moore School's basement laboratory.

On its test run in February 1946, the ENIAC took only 2 hours to solve a nuclear physics problem that would previously have required 100 years of calculation by a physicist. The ENIAC's speed of calculation was a thousand times faster than the best mechanical calculators. Each of its 20 accumulators could perform 5,000 additions of ten-digit numbers in 1 second. But it could store only 20 ten-digit numbers in its memory at a time. Although within a few years Mauchly and Eckert produced a computer that could outperform it, the ENIAC continued in operation until October 1955, when it was disassembled.

Von Neumann: Binary arithmetic and the stored program. In 1946 the Hungarian-born mathematician John von Neumann proposed a modified version of the ENIAC. The modified version, EDVAC (*E*lectronic *D*iscrete *V*ariable *A*utomatic *C*omputer), would differ from the ENIAC in two profoundly important respects.

First, the EDVAC would employ binary arithmetic. The Mark I and the ENIAC both used decimal arithmetic in all their calculations. Yet both computers possessed switching devices (the vacuum tube and the electrical relay, respectively) that existed in either of two states, "on" or "off." Computer circuitry that could have processed two digits "naturally" had to be designed for 10. Binary notation has only two digits—"0" and "1." These can correspond to the off–on modes of a switch. Von Neumann showed that binary arithmetic would make for much simpler computer circuitry. (Binary arithmetic is discussed further in chapter 5.)

Second, the EDVAC would have *stored-program capability*. The ENIAC had been programmed by plugging in hundreds of wires and setting a smaller number of electrical switches. When a new problem had to be solved, the ENIAC had to be rewired and reset, a process that involved hours of computer inactivity (now called "downtime"). But with the kinds of problems it had to solve, the ENIAC was kept busy for hours or days at a time. Consequently, the amount of time needed for reprogramming was not considered a serious problem. But it certainly would be a handicap for any computer intended for general-purpose operation.

Von Neumann proposed wiring a permanent set of instructions within the computer and placing these operations under a central control. He further proposed that the instruction codes governing the operations be stored in the same way that the data were stored —as binary numbers. Thus the EDVAC would have no need for special instruction wiring. Instead, it would process instructions by the same mechanism and as quickly as it processed data. Moreover, the computer would in effect be self-modifying, since its built-in program could contain a variety of instructions. And since the ma-

43

chine's instructions could be manipulated by arithmetic operations of the kind used in processing data, the programmer would have much greater control and flexibility in giving the computer its instructions.

Because Mauchly and Eckert later modified the ENIAC to operate as though it were a stored-program computer, there is some dispute about whether von Neumann deserves sole credit for the stored-program concept. But there is no question about the revolutionary effect of his ideas on the development of general-purpose machines. Curiously enough, however, the EDVAC was not the first stored-program machine to go into operation. That honor went to an English computer, the EDSAC (*Electronic Delay Storage Automatic Calculator*), in 1949. Its designer had attended a course of lectures on automatic computers at the Moore School, then returned to England to build a machine that had a more accurate memory, albeit with smaller capacity, than the EDVAC.

First-Generation Machines

The demand for many different kinds of computation increased greatly with the beginning of the Korean War in 1950. The appearance of the first commercial computer, the UNIVAC, in 1951, unofficially marked the beginning of the "first generation" of computers. (The term "generation" in this context refers to major developments in electronic data processing [EDP]. In the computer industry, the word "generation" is used as a term of general characterization rather than absolute distinction. Two generations, therefore, may overlap both technologically and chronologically.)

The characteristic feature of first-generation computers was the *vacuum tube*. This device consists of a negative wire electrode (cathode), a positive wire electrode (anode), and a grid between them, all enclosed in a tube from which the air has been removed. The cathode, when heated by an electric current, gives off negatively charged particles, or electrons. When the grid is positively charged, it attracts these electrons and directs them toward the anode. In the vacuum environment, electrons move freely. Most of the electrons will pass through the grid to the anode, thereby completing an electrical circuit. But if the grid is negatively charged, it will not attract the electrons released by the cathode. By varying the charge on the grid, the circuit within the tube can be opened or closed, which makes the vacuum tube also function as an electrical switch.

As was noted earlier, the vacuum tube represented a tremendous advance in computer technology. It was the device that had made the ENIAC so much faster and more powerful than any of its predecessors. And it was the device that made possible the still more powerful UNIVAC and IBM 700 computers.

The UNIVAC, *UNIV*ersal *A*utomatic *C*omputer, was the work of Eckert and Mauchly, who had developed the ENIAC and then left the Moore School to establish their own computer company. The UNIVAC was originally built for the Census Bureau in connection with the 1950 census. There were other customers for the machine, however, and the UNIVAC became the first commercially available computer. Because of financial problems, Eckert and Mauchly merged their own company with Remington Rand, and the UNIVAC became known as the UNIVAC I.

From 1951, when the first working model was delivered to the Census Bureau, to about 1956, the UNIVAC was perhaps the best large-scale data processing computer on the market. But by 1953 it had already become clear that magnetic core memories, then in the development stage, would soon make the UNIVAC I obsolete.

The UNIVAC II had a magnetic core memory, larger than the UNIVAC I memory, and was altogether a more powerful machine. But production problems delayed introduction of the UNIVAC II until 1957. By that time it had lost its commanding position in the computer market to the IBM 705.

In 1953 IBM produced its first Defense Calculator, later called the 701. This machine had a cathode ray tube memory and was considerably faster than the UNIVAC I for purposes of scientific calculation. Earlier, IBM had announced a character-oriented computer for commercial data processing, the 702. But even before its completion, the 702 was recognized as seriously inferior to the UNIVAC I. IBM undertook a crash program to replace the 702. The resulting 705 had a magnetic core memory instead of the unreliable vacuum tube type. It had an access time (the time required to search for a particular location in memory and retrieve a piece of data) of 17 microseconds, or 17 millionths of a second. In the same year that the 705 appeared, IBM also produced a "scientific" computer, the 704, with an access time of 12 microseconds.

The IBM 704 and 705 were among the last of the vacuum tube machines. With all of its great virtues, the vacuum tube also had several great faults. First of all, it was not a long-lived component. The average time between tube failures in the ENIAC was 12 hours. Any machine with more tubes would have required around-the-clock maintenance. Second, vacuum tube machines were extravagant consumers of electrical power: The ENIAC required some 3,500 kilowatts of electricity per day to provide the heat needed to get electrons moving in all of its tubes. Third, and most serious, was the amount of heat produced by such large amounts of power. First-generation computers required air conditioning and special insulation

45

of the tubes to protect the other components of the machine. Fourth, the vacuum tube made it necessary to construct big, bulky machines. The UNIVAC II was substantially smaller than the Mark I, but the dimensions of its central processor were nonetheless quite large: 9 feet high by 10 feet wide by 14 feet long.

The solution to the vacuum tube problems was already known by the time the IBM 704 and 705 appeared in 1956. It had, in fact, been invented eight years earlier. But three more years would pass before it would be used in commercially available computers.

Second-Generation Machines

By 1959 the IBM 705 was established as the leader in the field of large-scale data processing. Having reached this peak of success, the vacuum tube computer began to give way before the sudden emergence of another generation. In these smaller yet more powerful new machines, the problems of the vacuum tube had been solved: The tube was replaced by a very different device, the *transistor.*

A transistor performs the same functions as a vacuum tube, except that electrons move through solid materials instead of through a vacuum. A transistor consists, in general, of three layers of a semiconductor substance (commonly germanium or silicon) that contains trace quantities of other substances, usually phosphorus and boron. The addition of very small amounts of phosphorus to a semiconductor material adds electrons that are able to move in the presence of an electrical current. The addition of very small amounts of boron produces areas that attract electrons known as holes; holes also are able to move in the presence of an electrical charge.

A transistor can be designed like a sandwich, with the outer layers containing phosphorus and the "fillings" containing boron, and be similar to the grid of the vacuum tube. (The positions of the boron- and phosphorus-containing layers can be reversed.) A small voltage difference applied across the central region sets off a flow of charged particles through the central barrier, thereby completing or closing an electrical circuit.

With the invention of the transistor in 1948 came the technology that reduced radios from bigger-than-a-breadbox-size to pocket-size in one human generation. It had the same effect on computers. A transistor is only $1/200$ the size of a vacuum tube, requires much less power, and produces much less heat. It is cheaper to make and cheaper to operate and it is far more reliable.

Practical realization of the transistor's potential, however, did not immediately follow its invention. It took nearly a decade to develop the methods needed to produce transistors in sufficient quantity and

(Courtesy of IBM)

From left to right:
vacuum tube, transistor,
silicon chip

with the necessary precision for commercial application. The first completely transistorized computer was National Cash Register's GE 304, which appeared in 1959. But the GE 304 was slow and had a limited capacity. Later that year IBM brought out its 7090, a transistorized version of the IBM 709, with a memory cycle of only slightly more than 2 microseconds. The 7090 was a great success.

It soon became clear, too, that there was a market for small computers. Transistors and magnetic core memories had made possible smaller computers that compared favorably in speed and power with even the large vacuum tube variety. The next few years saw the development of various series of computers from a number of manufacturers, including the IBM 1400 and 1600, the RCA 301, the CDC 160, the Burroughs 200, the Honeywell 400, the GE 200, and the NCR 300.

Meanwhile, essential accessories such as high-speed card readers and printers were being developed. The *microsecond* was becoming the standard unit for measuring a computer's access to data and instructions. In programming, "natural" languages began to replace machine language. And a few companies were building *supercomputers* for scientific research financed by the U.S. government. The speed of these machines was measured in nanoseconds. Their power was many times greater than that of commercially available ma-

47

chines. Supercomputers depended for their power and abilities on
large numbers of transistors. Where an earlier transistorized computer might have had some 150,000 transistors, their super successors could have a million.

Third-Generation Machines

The most important advance in computer technology in the mid-
1960s was the *integrated circuit*. The vacuum tube and transistor are
only parts of an electrical circuit, which also contains resistors, capacitors, diodes or wires, and other components that start, stop, and
otherwise control the behavior of current. Integrated circuits are produced as single units, containing dozens of components fused together in a single process. (In earlier computers, these components
had been joined together by wiring, one by one.) Integrated circuits
are produced on "chips," thin layers of silicon or germanium so tiny
that a thimble could hold nearly 50,000 of them. The microelectronics industry significantly reduced the distance between components, the time needed for any given operation, and the size of computers. Integrated circuits also proved to be highly reliable and
relatively inexpensive.

Related developments followed rapidly. Because of the faster
speed of operation, more than one program could be run through the
computer at the same time. Because of the small size of chips, more
circuits—and therefore more computing power and more storage—
could be provided. Optical scanning, magnetic ink character recognition, and data displays on a screen were among the newer and faster means of input and output. Greatly increased storage capabilities
—along with the random-access devices that had been developed for
second-generation machines—made possible direct and immediate
access to enormous amounts of stored data. Moreover, these data
could be "accessed" or brought in from a remote terminal thousands
of miles away. The nanosecond became the standard unit for measuring access and processing times.

Parallel with these developments, there began a trend toward standardization in the mid-1960s. The IBM 360 was intended to standardize—within IBM itself—a number of computer characteristics,
including instruction codes, units of information, and arithmetic
modes. The purpose of the 360 series was to replace all previous IBM
series. The 360 represented a major change of direction for IBM and
had a great influence on the computer industry. RCA soon announced the Spectra 70 series, which was highly compatible with
the IBM 360; that is, equipment in the Spectra 70 line could be readily linked up to equipment in the 360 series.

The Honeywell 200 computer took advantage of standardization in a different way. The 200 was basically an improved, faster, and more powerful version of the IBM 1400 series and was compatible with it. Since the IBM 360 would not be a compatible successor to the 1400, those customers who already had 1400 units and did not want to replace all of their equipment could expand their existing systems simply by adding the Honeywell 200. This computer was enormously successful. It was developed into a series, making Honeywell second only to IBM as a manufacturer of computers for business data processing.

Fourth-Generation Machines

The continued development of microelectronics in the 1970s produced yet another new generation of computers. It was a period of active research and development in many areas of computer technology. These included multiprocessing, multiprogramming, program language, time-sharing, miniaturization, and operating speed, among others. One of the more dramatic advances was the increasing application of *virtual storage,* which had first been developed by Burroughs 10 years earlier. The term refers to a means of providing a computer with direct access to external storage devices as though they were part of the computer's own main storage. Virtual storage greatly increased program storage capacity.

The observable results were spectacular. In the early 1960s a widely used general-purpose computer was IBM's 1400 series. Its CPU took up 200 square feet of space, consumed barely 3 kilowatts of electricity a day, and required a one-ton air conditioner to dissipate the heat it generated. It had a processing speed of 3,000 additions (of two eight-digit numbers) every second and a memory capacity of 16,000 bytes. (A byte is a unit of stored data; see chapter 5.) In the early 1970s, computers began to take the form of desktop display-tube terminals connected by telephone lines to a small central processing unit (CPU). By the end of the decade a computer was available with processing and access time speeds ten times faster, and with a memory capacity four times greater, than the CPU of the IBM 1400 system.

The effect that these developments had on the popularity of the computer can be judged from a few statistics. From 1971 to 1976 alone, the number of government-owned computers grew from 6,000 to 10,000, an increase of 67 percent. But in the same period, the percentage of *all* computers in the United States owned by the government *dropped* from over 6 percent to less than 4½ percent. These figures represent an increase in the total number of computers being

49

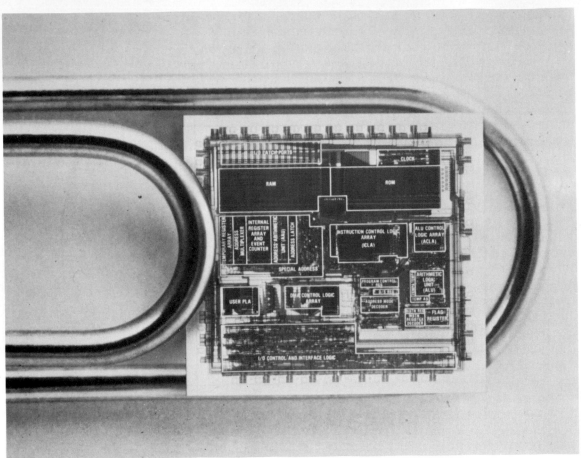

(Bell Labs)

The MAC-4 one-chip computer, designed by Bell Laboratories, compared with a standard paper clip. The various functional areas of the chip are labeled.

used in the United States from fewer than 100,000 in 1971 to 500,000 in 1977!

Without doubt the single most important factor contributing to this tremendous leap in computer use was the development of large-scale integration (*LSI*) of computer circuits. Indeed, without LSI the computer industry would be a different and undoubtedly smaller business today. The increase in computer use has been largely the result of manufacturers' ability to put ever larger numbers of components on a single chip.

When integrated circuits were first introduced in the 1960s, the computer chip carried an average of 10 transistors. In the mid-1970s, microprocessor chips carrying 10,000 to 20,000 transistors became available. Today there are memory chips carrying 200,000 or more transistors. A contemporary microcomputer with about the same number of transistors as the ENIAC can be $1/300,000$ of its size, more than 10,000 times as reliable, consume 56,000 times less power— and directly access eight times as many units of information.

The three factors that have contributed most to the rapid growth of LSI are: (1) improved techniques of "growing" the silicon crystals from which computer chips are made; (2) improved photolithographic methods of "printing" computer circuits on chips; and (3) improved circuitry design that makes more efficient use of the chip area. Other advances and even more densely packed chips are expected. In fact, computer scientists anticipate a thousandfold increase in the number of components that can be printed on a chip. The term associated with the circuits on this more densely "packed" chip is *VLSI* (very large scale integration). It is only a matter of time before VLSI becomes available. Indeed, it is only a matter of time before the fifth generation of computers is delivered.

Fifth- and Sixth-Generation Machines —and Beyond

As we have seen, fourth-generation computers represent the state of the art today. But the fifth generation is on the way. These machines will utilize a variety of recent developments, including *magnetic bubble memories* and *Josephson junctions*.

Magnetic bubbles are microscopic environments of magnetic polarization. Such bubbles can be moved or held at a fixed location, or "station," by exposure to a series of magnetic fields. Consequently, a bubble can be made to travel along a row of fixed stations. In this way, the presence or absence of a bubble at each of the stations can be "read" as data. Magnetic bubble memories are, by their nature, serial in operation (as opposed to random access). But this disadvantage is more than overcome by their primary advantage: They are so minute that they can be packed much more closely together than transistors, resulting in a smaller and/or more powerful machine.

The Josephson junction is a consequence of the phenomenon of superconductivity. When cooled to temperatures near absolute zero, some materials lose all resistance to the passage of an electric current; they are said to become *superconductors*. In effect, supercooling makes it possible for electrons to "tunnel" through a barrier that would otherwise be impassable. The tunnel can be opened or closed by the presence or absence of a small magnetic field. In other words, the electron tunnel can be made to function as an electronic switch or junction. Devices based on Josephson junctions would be supercooled by liquid helium. The cost of the equipment to cool the he-

51

APPLICATION
The 1980 Census

The census of 1980 produced more than three billion separate items of information about some 222 million people. Questionnaires were sent to each of the nation's approximately 80 million households. Most households received a two-page form, but 22 percent of them filled out more detailed forms containing up to eight pages. Each question on the forms was followed by circles to be filled in with pencil according to the answer.

For purposes of the census, the nation was divided into 275,000 enumeration districts, each containing about 800 people. In each enumeration district, the filled-in forms were collected, packed in boxes, and sent by truck to the nearest of three centers for processing.

Processing began as forms from a box were fed, a hundred at a time, onto a conveyor belt in one of 60 automatic microfilmers. Moving along the belt, the forms were photographed on black-and-white film by a 16-millimeter camera at a rate of 130 per minute. The exposure time of 25 microseconds (millionths of a second) allowed the forms to be photographed without stopping. On microfilm, the 28-by-11-inch forms were reduced to $1/26$ of their original size.

The microfilmers were designed to shut down automatically if they encountered a form that had been crumpled or otherwise damaged; human assistance would be needed—but only at that point. Everything else was automatic—including a device to turn the pages of the eight-page forms so they could be photographed in their entirety.

The microfilm was developed immediately and mounted in another special piece of equipment. This was a Film Optical Scanning Device for Input to Computers (FOSDIC), a version of which has been used in censuses since 1960. The microfilm was projected onto a cathode ray tube, like a television screen. FOSDIC scanned the microfilm, noted the darkened circles, and assigned computer-readable numbers to each question answer. Meanwhile a small auxiliary computer recorded whether each question had been answered. FOSDIC "read" 900 short forms a minute, at a rate of 37 microseconds each; it could not read the alphabet, so it ignored the names written on each form, which were retained only on the microfilm.

Next, the data, now in computer-readable form, were sent over high-speed transmission telephone lines to the central computer room in Census Bureau headquarters in Maryland. Here they first went into a small controlling computer, which kept a record of the communities whose census forms had been received and transferred the data to reels of magnetic tape. In this form they would be stored until given additional processing by a UNIVAC 1100 computer.

With the census that will usher in the next millennium in the year 2000, the Census Bureau expects that data collection will no longer depend on pencil and paper. Instead, push-button telephones or other electronic transmission devices located directly in households will be used. But in one respect we may be certain that the census of 2000 will resemble that of 1980 and of Hollerith's day: because suitable equipment will not be available, the Census Bureau will once more have to invent, patent, and even construct many of the components of its data processing system.

lium will make this a very expensive technology. But extremely small amounts of current would be required, thereby reducing the amount of heat generated. The less heat produced, the more closely the junctions can be packed together. And the closer the junctions are, the faster the speed of operation will be.

Computers using bubble memories and Josephson junctions are expected on the market by the mid-1980s. Some devices with bubble memories are already available.

What of future generations? A sixth generation is expected in the mid-1990s. If the present pace continues, integrated circuit chips carrying a *billion* components may be available before 2001! The use of optical communications in computers has tremendous potential. Light waves can carry much more information than radio waves, for example; and many semiconductor materials respond to light just as they respond to electric currents. The technology to produce light-powered devices is now being developed.

It may be that the only limitation on the future development of computer technology will be the human imagination. Physicist Robert Jastrow has speculated that a new form of intelligence will evolve in the form of human−computer partnerships. Someday, perhaps, the only limitation on the future development of computer technology will be a *computer's* imagination!

Summary

The first computerized U.S. census, in 1890, employed a punched-card tabulating and sorting machine invented by Herman Hollerith. His invention marked the beginning of data processing, but the history of computing devices goes back several thousand years.

The world's oldest computing device, the *abacus*, is based on decimal arithmetic and uses *positional notation*. The first mechanical calculator was an "arithmetic engine," invented by the French philosopher-mathematician Blaise Pascal in 1642. In 1694 Gottfried von Leibniz produced a "stepped reckoner," which could add, subtract, multiply, divide, and extract square roots. In 1801 Joseph-Marie Jacquard became the first to produce a machine (a loom) using punched cards both for operation of the machine and for control of its sequence of operations. Charles Babbage conceived his "analytical engine" in 1835, but the design was too advanced to be produced by the technology of his day. These devices, along with Hollerith's tabulator, are classified as the "earliest machines." With the exception of Babbage's analytical engine, these were all special-purpose machines. Babbage was the first to design a general-purpose computer.

53

The first *functioning* general-purpose computer—the electrome-chanical Mark I—went into operation in 1944. It was followed in 1946 by the ENIAC, the first all-electronic computer. At about the same time, John von Neumann proposed two modifications that greatly influenced the development of computers: (1) the use of *binary* numbers in processing, and (2) the *stored program*.

The so-called first generation of computers appeared in the early 1950s. Their characteristic feature was the *vacuum tube*. The UNIVAC became the first computer to be sold commercially. Vacuum tube computers were large, hot, and expensive.

The invention of the *transistor* resulted in smaller, cooler, and cheaper machines—the second generation of computers. The first completely transistorized computer appeared in 1959. The period of the second-generation machines also saw other important developments: high-speed card readers and printers, "natural" languages for programs, and supercomputers. The *microsecond* became an increasingly common unit for measuring computer speeds.

Integrated circuits, the original computer "chips," gave rise to the third generation of machines in the mid-1960s. Thousands of times smaller than the second-generation transistors, these tiny devices significantly reduced the size of computers while greatly increasing their speed. Other developments included multiprogramming, faster methods of input and output, and greatly increased storage capacities. The *nanosecond* became the standard unit for measuring computer speeds. A trend toward standardization of computer components also began at about this time.

The decade of the 1970s saw the emergence of a new generation of computers. It was a period of important advances in many areas of computer technology: multiprocessing and multiprogramming, program language, time-sharing, miniaturization, and operating speed. The two most dramatic developments were *virtual storage* and *large-scale integration (LSI)*. The effect of LSI on computer performance and size was largely responsible for the spectacular growth of computer use in the 1970s. Fourth-generation machines represent the state of the art today.

Fifth-generation machines, which are expected to be available in the mid-1980s, will utilize *magnetic bubble memories* and *Josephson junctions*. A sixth generation, possibly based on advances in silicon technology, is expected in the mid-1990s. Computer chips carrying a billion components may be available in the late 1990s. Optical communications promise to add a new dimension to the capabilities of computers. It may turn out that the only limitation on computer technology will be the human imagination. Or, perhaps someday, a computer's imagination.

abacus
EDP
integrated circuits
Josephson junctions
logarithms

LSI
magnetic bubble
  memories
microsecond
nanosecond

picosecond
transistor
vacuum tube
virtual storage
VLSI

Sources of Additional Information

Abelson, Philip H., and Hammond, Allen L. "The Electronics Revolution." *Science* 195 (1977):1087–91.

Dahl, Aubrey. "The Last of the First." *Datamation*, no. 6 (1978):145–49.

Davis, Ruth M. "Evolution of Computers and Computing." *Science* 195 (1977):1096–1102.

Gleiser, Molly. "Men and Machines before Babbage." *Datamation*, no. 10 (1978):125–30.

———. "Not Altogether Useless Instruments." *Computer Decisions*, no. 5 (1978):76–81.

———. "William S. Burroughs." *Computer Decisions*, no. 3 (1978):34–36.

Goldstine, H. H. *The Computer from Pascal to Von Neumann.* Princeton: Princeton University Press, 1972.

Holton, William C. "The Large-Scale Integration of Microelectronic Circuits." *Scientific American*, March 1977, pp. 82–94.

Huskey, Harry D., and Huskey, Velma R. "Chronology of Computing Devices." *IEEE Transactions on Computers* 25 (1976):1190–99.

Linvill, John G., and Hogan, C. Lester. "Intellectual and Economic Fuel for the Electronics Revolution." *Science* 195 (1977):1107–13.

Reid-Green, Keith S. "The IBM 704." *Byte*, no. 1 (1979):190–92.

Rosen, Saul. "Electronic Computers: A Historical Survey." *Computing Surveys*, no. 1 (1969):7–36.

"Science: The Numbers Game." *Time*, February 20, 1978, pp. 54–58.

Stern, Nancy. "In the Beginning, the ENIAC." *Datamation*, no. 5 (1979): 229–34.

Test Yourself

1. Why are calculating devices needed by human beings? Describe three early (pre-nineteenth century) calculating devices.
2. What two major trends have been apparent throughout the evolution of computers?
3. The circuitry of computers has gone through "generations" of development. What are the distinctive characteristics of each of the four generations?
4. The world's first working general-purpose computer was described but never built. What was the name of the computer, who designed it, and why was it never developed?

5. The development of a working general-purpose computer was accelerated by World War II. What was the reason for this, and what were the first computers?
6. What two new concepts were used in John von Neumann's computer, the EDVAC?
7. The second generation of computers "solved" some of the major problems of the first generation. What were these problems, and how were they dealt with by the new computers?
8. While the fifth generation of computers has not yet arrived, it is expected to use technology that is currently in the developmental stage. What are these new developments?

3 Overview of Computers and Equipment

Drawn by Sandy Dean

"Murder, huh? Well, I'm in for bending, folding, and mutilating a computer card."

APPLICATION

NASA's Microwave Landing System

The National Aeronautics and Space Administration has developed and tested an automatic landing system for conventional aircraft. For years an automatic in-flight system—the autopilot—has routinely been used. Now, sophisticated use of computers has made possible an autoland system. It can fly curved flight paths to bring planes in for a landing under adverse weather conditions, and can also facilitate efficient landing under crowded terminal conditions.

A typical airplane, a Boeing 737, was the test vehicle. On board was a flight-control computer pallet or unit with all the hardware for the microwave landing system (MLS), which controls the curved flight paths necessary for aircraft landing.

The entire process involves a series of computers, some general-purpose, several specialized, communicating with each other to make it all possible. There are three computer units, three memory units, three computer interface units, two different control units, some accessory components, and a display panel. Each computer unit receives inputs, performs computations, and transmits output commands to the appropriate control units that direct the aircraft in flight. Each computer is also able to monitor its own processes through the control units.

The interface units constantly receive such flight data as position, velocity, and rate of acceleration, and automatically convert these inputs to digital format for processing. They then convert the processing results into the different output formats required by the navigation and flight control computers, and transmit these outputs to the appropriate computers, where they show up as figures and symbols printed on the display panel or screen. One control unit monitors the computers, and is able to respond to altered conditions during flight by changing programs as necessary. System status and failures are shown on the display panel.

In flight the pilot monitors the display screen. The navigation system is constantly monitoring the aircraft's position, and when a predetermined position (altitude, latitude, longitude) has been reached, the pilot is able to push buttons on a control panel to switch from standard automatic navigation to MLS. During the 3-nautical-mile final approach on the autoland system, speed, slope, and altitude are continually monitored until, at an appropriate point, flare and touchdown are automatically initiated.

The system is triply redundant, with multiple backups as protection against equipment failure. Obviously, the safety of passengers and crew depends on the dependability of the computers on board. But the pilot is not redundant. The pilot functions as the primary system and as a last-resort backup system. At every stage in the autoland process, the pilot's human judgment is called upon to support or override the program of the computers.

In repeated demonstrations in 1976 and subsequently, the MLS guided the test plane through precision, curved, steep, decelerating, and time-sequenced landing approaches, often under severely adverse weather conditions, including zero visibility. A typical single test flight consisted of five different landing approaches; the system was tested in hundreds of approaches. Tests repeatedly demonstrated the ability of the MLS to fly curved navigation paths with precision. As a result, most new aircraft today incorporate MLS technologies.

WITH GOOD REASON, the computer is often compared with the human brain. Like the brain that devised it, a computer can take in data and process it. It can store the data either in raw form or in the form of processing results, and can deliver the raw or processed data to the outside world on demand.

But there is a very important distinction between the human brain and a computer: the human brain can think and make decisions for itself, while the computer can only perform its feats when it has been instructed, or *programmed*, to do so. And the instructions it receives must be prepared by humans, using the organizing and problem-solving abilities of the human brain.

The computer's storage capacity, or memory, does not yet equal that of the human brain, which was estimated by mathematician John von Neumann to be 10^{20} bits, or items of information. But computer capacity is rapidly increasing, and in the future will undoubtedly exceed the human memory. The computer's clear superiority is in its speed of operation, which today ranges from 100,000 operations per second in a small computer to tens of millions per second in a large system.

As we have seen, computers are not all alike. Just like people, they differ in size, outward appearance, and capability. Also, like people, computers can perform different tasks, but all computers have some basic activities in common. In this chapter we will examine the different classifications of computers, and will describe, in a very general way, how they work and what they do. In subsequent chapters we will deal with the operations of computers in greater detail.

The Basic Functions of Computers

However much they may differ in size, operating mode, and degree of complexity, all computers have four basic functions in common: input, processing, storage, and output. The relationship between these functions is shown in figure 3-1.

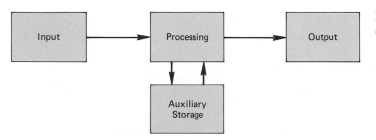

Figure 3-1 The four basic computer functions

The IBM 1419 magnetic character reader. Checks are fed in at the upper right, read as they feed through the compartment to the left, and automatically sorted into one of the small bins according to predetermined features.

Input

The *input,* or data and instructions given to a computer, must be in a form that it can accept and work on. Data for input consist of a mass of raw material that must be organized in a particular way in order to be used by computers.

The first step in preparation of data is capturing it. Data capture refers to the recording and organizing of the basic information to be given to the machine. Raw data appear on forms such as sales receipts, purchase orders, meter readings, or class schedules. The captured data must then be classified (for example, sales data might be classified for inventory according to type of merchandise; class schedules may be classified by department and instructor). Then the captured data must be arranged in a sequence according to the needs of the user.

A major use of computers in business is for the preparation of payrolls. Before it can figure out how much money an employee should receive, the computer must be given certain information: hourly rate of pay, number of hours worked during the pay period, deductions for taxes, and so on. These data must be presented in a form that the machine can recognize and understand.

The earliest computers could understand only the 10 numerals of the decimal system. In order to surpass mechanical calculators not only in speed but also in ~~ability to solve~~ a broader range of problems, computers had to be provided with a more flexible language.

A great advance came when they were designed to deal with letters of the alphabet as well as numerals. These two sets of symbols are the tools that enable us to represent all the things, events, and ideas existing in the world. We use these symbols to communicate with each other.

When we communicate with written language, we are not writing real words as spoken, but symbols that we have agreed upon to represent words. Similarly, numbers are symbols that represent quantities. The great variety of written symbols used to represent numbers and quantities throughout human history and in today's world is evidence of their symbolic nature.

Some of today's computers can recognize both numbers and letters, a combination known as *alphanumeric symbols.* But these machines cannot always read our language symbols; some can read only numbers.

Identify a character set consisting of letters & digits.

"Machine language" is the symbol system in which computer components communicate among themselves. It is very different from the symbols that humans read and understand, because the symbols of machine language must be read electronically. Most computers understand a symbol system known as binary notation, which is explained in chapter 5.

The computer is technologically the most advanced and most efficient device ever to be used in processing data. For millennia, data operations have been and still are performed by hand; for centuries pen and paper have served as recording devices. Electromechanical methods, including typewriters, cash registers, and accounting ma-

(Courtesy of IBM)

Closeup of the IBM 3420 magnetic tape unit. The reel of magnetic tape is mounted on the right, and the take-up reel is permanently mounted at the left. The magnetic tape passes over the read/write heads contained in the black area at the center of the photograph.

61

chines, have been widely used only in the last hundred years or so. Punched-card equipment came into limited use at about the same time. But in most electromechanical systems, a different machine is needed to perform each operation. However, today's computer is often capable of performing most data operations without intermittent human intervention.

Computers may "read" information from special cards, tapes, or disks. Data to be given to a computer in these forms may be converted from human-readable to machine-readable language by keypunching or by some other means (see chapter 4). These punched cards and tapes or magnetic tapes and disks are then put into the computer. Increasingly, though, data can be put into the machine directly by an operator at a terminal. (The preparation of data for input is discussed in greater detail in chapter 5.) The next step after input is *processing*, which involves the steps to output and/or storage.

Processing

At the heart of the computer is its work center, the central processing unit (CPU). It has three components: the arithmetic logic unit (ALU), the control unit, and primary storage. The arithmetic logic unit performs addition, subtraction, multiplication, and division, and is also capable of making logical comparisons. The control unit moves the results of the arithmetic unit's operations either to the outside in a printout or a display on a screen, or into the computer's storage unit or memory. In storage the information is available as a permanent record or as data to be used for further operations commanded by the control unit.

In the preparation of a payroll, for example, it is the arithmetic logic unit of the central processing unit that computes, from the data given to it, the amount of salary or wages due after deductions for taxes. The control unit then moves the results into storage and to an output device such as a printer, producing a paycheck with an attached stub that gives a breakdown of the amount paid and the various tax deductions. In the storage unit, the data are available for future use. For the next pay period, after the arithmetic logic unit computes the amount due and the amounts withheld, the control unit retrieves the stored data so that the arithmetic unit can compute the total amount paid out and the deductions made over a period of time. By repeating this process each pay period, the computer retains a readily available up-to-date record throughout the year of totals paid out and withheld.

The control unit directs operations within the computer, following instructions (in a program or programs) it has been given, In some instances the results of one set of operations determine the next step or steps. For example, the control unit has received instructions in its program for various possibilities. It has been told to complete processing of each employee's paycheck before beginning the next. But perhaps one employee has been on leave for the entire pay period; for "hours worked" there would be only a "0" to enter. The computer has been instructed to stop processing that employee's paycheck and to go on to the next employee.

Storage

After processing, *storage* of data in machine-readable form is most important for the efficient, economical use of computer systems. If data were not readily available, but had to be transcribed from human-readable to machine-readable form each time they were needed, operating time and costs would be huge.

(Courtesy of IBM)

The IBM 2361 core storage. Within each square, horizontal and vertical wires are strung, to form a dense grid. At every juncture, a horizontal and a vertical wire go through a donut-shaped magnetic core.

(Courtesy of IBM)

The IBM 3330 disk storage, allowing data to be stored and accessed directly. Each black rectangle on the photograph contains a single, removable disk pack.

Data are usually stored in machine-readable form on disks or tape in accessory units outside the computer. These supplemental storage units are to the computer what an encyclopedia is to you: readily accessible information that can be referred to when needed, to integrate with existing knowledge.

Instructions that will be in use during the execution of a particular program, as well as data that have been called from auxiliary storage, are held in primary storage. As a program is executing, it calls for additional data, which are brought from auxiliary storage into primary storage as needed, a little bit at a time. This continues until the entire program has been processed. Primary storage contains only those programs, or segments of programs, that are being executed at a given moment, along with the selected items of data called for at that moment by the program.

In the course of payroll preparation, a good deal of data relating to the income and withholding taxes of every employee accumulates during the course of a year. This stored information is then drawn on and processed to provide the forms given to each employee and to the Internal Revenue Service every year. It is not necessary for the data to be reentered and refigured, because this information has remained in the system from one pay period to the next.

Output

After input, processing, and, when necessary, storage, *output* is the final step in computer operation. Output is the form in which we use the results of computer processing. It is the measure of the usefulness of the system and the way in which it works.

Output can be in machine-readable form, suitable to be stored for future use or for immediate use by another system, or it can be in human-readable form. For many purposes the most useful output is a printout on sheets of paper, such as a department store bill or a paycheck, but there are other forms of printouts as well: on rolls of paper, such as stock market ticker tape, which gives a running account of stock prices and the volume of sales compiled by the computer; on a screen, which may be the most useful for some purposes, or which may be preliminary to paper printout. There are also other forms of output for special purposes; these are examined in greater detail in chapter 4.

Classification of Computers

There is an almost bewildering variety of computers, and the number of models available is rapidly growing. To some extent this variety is redundant; many machines are similar in capability. But to a greater extent the variety of computers is related to important differences in capacity and function.

Computers may be classified according to their purpose, according to the kind of processing they do or types of data they use, and also according to the size of the machine and the speed of its internal operations. Speed of operation is often the most important consideration in deciding which equipment to choose for a particular task. With today's machines, it is generally true that the bigger the machine, the faster the operating speed.

Classification by Purpose

In the preceding chapter we saw that the earliest machines were special-purpose machines, built to do a specific task and designed with the capacity to accomplish that task. As technology matured it became possible to design machines with more flexibility. Computers of the second generation were already able to "shift gears" at the insertion of a new program, devoting their circuitry to whatever task was at hand, and then turn to a different task at a subsequent time. The flexibility of general-purpose computers has made them ideal tools for scientific research as well as for industry, and they have been welcomed in particular by organizations and institutions in which many functions are carried on simultaneously by different departments.

General-purpose computers. The discussion in this text will be primarily concerned with *general-purpose computers*. These machines have the capability of dealing with a variety of different problems, and are able to act in response to programs created to meet different needs. In industry, for example, a general-purpose computer can prepare payrolls, handle accounts receivable and accounts payable, keep an inventory of production materials as well as stock on hand, and more, according to the needs of the particular business activity.

In an earlier stage of computer development (and this is still true to some extent today), the general-purpose computer that was standard for commercial use was in marked contrast to the scientific computer. Scientists needed a computer designed, as the commercial computer was not, to remain highly accurate for long and complex sequences of calculations. At the very least, accuracy generally had to be maintained to the equivalent of six decimal digits, and sometimes even more. Reliability was also essential in scientific computers. Then there was the necessity that repairs be kept to a minimum so that the time between breakdowns was far longer than the running time of the longest program. As we saw in chapter 2, this was not possible in the early vacuum tube machines.

 But recent developments have tended to erase the once sharp distinction between commercial and scientific general-purpose computers. Today's machines can handle complex calculations with accuracy and reliability; breakdowns are rare. And the same machine is being used for more than one activity. For example, a large university is both a business and a research organization. The processing of data for both aspects is handled today by the same general-purpose computer.

Special-purpose computers. Special-purpose computers are designed to handle a specific problem, such as the computer designed to land aircraft that was described in the Application at the beginning of this chapter. That computer, as sophisticated as it is, can do nothing else—not even calculate a small payroll. Another such special-purpose computer was designed to do research on ballistic missile defense systems for the U.S. Army. In creating this extremely powerful machine, the designers were not hampered by the need to keep down costs as they would have been in meeting the needs of an industrial client.

Most special-purpose computers have the capability of performing just one task. They are frequently referred to as "dedicated," because of their limitation to the performance of the specific task at hand. Dedicated computers can control processes, such as keeping track of automobile parts during their passage through an assembly line, regulating the temperatures required in industrial chemical operations, or maintaining specified heating and cooling limits in office and apartment buildings.

The variety of applications for special-purpose computers is expanding enormously with the development of microprocessing, which has been made possible by chips. Except in rare instances like that of the very powerful and expensive processor that does research on ballistic missile defense systems, there is generally little point in modifying a single-purpose computer into a multipurpose machine. Advances in technology have greatly reduced the cost of special-purpose computers, because the single program required can now be contained on one very small chip.

The remarkable development of computer chips is bringing special-purpose computers into our daily lives in a way that still sounds like science fiction. Imagine an automobile programmed to avoid collisions; a home thermostat that automatically adjusts heat and humidity; factory tools that assemble components without the mediation of human hands. Already available are computers that control lights and other home appliances, computerized fuel injection systems in cars, computer games, and computerized telephone answering devices. Clearly, the new age of special-purpose computers is upon us.

Classification by Type of Processing

There are essentially two different types of computer processing. Each is made possible by a different kind of electronic circuitry, and each is suitable for different purposes.

Analog computers. The *analog computer* is so called because it provides an analogy or simulation of the object or system it represents. It is especially useful for solving engineering problems that involve relationships between variable quantities in systems that change with time. The analog computer may express those changing relationships in output in the form of graphs. It is able to create such pictures because it responds to changes in electrical voltages that match changes in variable quantities.

A classic example of an analog device is the speedometer in an automobile. The rotation of a shaft is converted into an approximation of the speed of the automobile, which is shown on an indicator in miles or kilometers per hour.

67

A typical problem for an analog computer, illustrating its use in experimental engineering applications, might be to simulate the flight of a rocket fired upward vertically. The computer is programmed by setting up within it electrical circuits with voltages representing each of the variable elements in the problem: the rocket's velocity, its acceleration, and the heights it will reach. The computer will be able to provide voltage curves that show the velocity, acceleration, and height at any given moment.

Analog computers are limited in accuracy, largely because the solution to a typical analog problem involves many sets of connected components. Because there is a small built-in error in each of the many calculations involved in a complex simulation, infinitesimal individual errors accumulate. Generally, for the kinds of problems dealt with by analog computers, an error factor of 0.5 to 1.0 percent can be tolerated. But this error factor makes analog computers unsuitable for business applications. Analog computers are ideally suited for the representation of continually varying data, but they are generally not able to serve the needs of business and industry. A major disadvantage of analog computers is that they cannot represent nonnumeric data.

Digital computers. Essentially, the *digital computer* is a machine that specializes in counting. It operates by counting values that are discrete, or separate and distinct, unlike the continuous quantities that can be measured by the analog computer. The digital computer differs from the analog computer in another way: it may be made increasingly accurate by specifying in the program that additional decimal places must be added to numbers.

The basic operation performed by a digital computer is addition. It can store the sums of addition problems as they accumulate, and can complete a single calculation in a fraction of a nanosecond. For these reasons, by simple rearrangement of other kinds of problems, digital computers are able to subtract, multiply, divide, and compare. And they can be programmed to recognize and manipulate nonnumeric symbols that have been translated into their special machine language (see chapter 5).

The speed and accuracy of digital computers in processing numbers, as well as their capacity to handle nonnumeric data, have found widespread applications in business accounting, billing, and in a wide variety of other uses as well. The memory capacity of the digital computer is also vitally important for such purposes.

Because of its capacity and accuracy, the digital computer has proved its usefulness in statistical analysis and in the control of industrial operations. In controlling industrial processes, digital computers generally perform a supervisory function by evaluating process conditions against desired standards of performance and then determining the changes that are necessary to improve operations.

Digital computers greatly outnumber analog computers today. Because of their widespread use in the business community, digital machines will be the focus of this book.

Hybrid computers. In the late 1950s, hybrid computers, which incorporate in a single device both digital and analog techniques and equipment, were first used to simulate a space mission. It was found advantageous to simulate the motion of the vehicle and its control services by using analog methodology, while a digital device computed the vehicle's trajectory and simulated its navigation system with greater accuracy and precision than an analog computer alone could have done.

Hybrid machines contain special equipment to convert analog voltages into digital voltages, and vice versa. These are special-purpose instruments and are not widely used.

Classification by Size and Speed

For convenience, we can talk of super-, large, mini-, and micro-computers, although the dividing lines between some of these categories are beginning to blur. In computers, size and speed of operation are at present proportionate to each other. Generally, though, recent technology is tending to create smaller machines, making it possible to package equivalent speed and capacity in a smaller format. The supercomputers of tomorrow will be no larger in size than today's microcomputers; the mini- and microcomputers of the future will be no bigger than today's hand-held calculators.

Computer speed is limited by switching delays in circuits and by the size of the machine. Generally, the larger the machine, the longer it takes for electrical signals to travel through its circuits.

Supercomputers. The biggest and fastest machines today are the supercomputers that are used when billions or even trillions of calculations are needed. These machines are essential for applications ranging from nuclear weapon development to accurate weather forecasting.

Because of their size, supercomputers usually sacrifice a certain amount of flexibility. Consequently, they are not ideal for providing a variety of user services. For this reason, supercomputers may need the assistance of a medium-sized general-purpose machine (usually called a front-end processor) to handle minor programs or perform slower-speed or smaller-volume operations.

In view of their inflexibility, there are those who believe that supercomputers will prove to be "dinosaurs." Others just as emphatically predict at least a bright future for them, because they are uniquely qualified to handle important large-volume, high-speed tasks.

The NORC (Naval Ordnance Research Calculator), built by IBM for the U.S. Naval Weapons Laboratory, was one of the first supercomputers. It was begun in 1951 and was delivered four years later. The NORC was designed to perform 15,000 three-address operations per second. (An address is the location of data that must be accessed by the machine; see chapter 6.) Floating-point addition (discussed in chapter 5) took 15 microseconds, and multiplication took 31 microseconds. It had a memory of 2,000 "words" that was provided by an electrostatic tube system. After six years the NORC was given a new and expanded magnetic core memory.

The breathtaking advances in supercomputer design since the completion of the NORC peaked in the CRAY-1. It is the most powerful computer functioning today, equivalent to five or more "large" computers. It can support 138 million floating-point operations per second (MFLOPS) over long periods and as many as 250 MFLOPS in shorter time spans. Its central processing unit consists of 1,056 logic boards—each board is 6 by 8 inches and holds up to 288 integrated circuit chips. The central processing unit's effective cycle time (the time required to complete one operation) is 12.5 nanoseconds. It has a single memory, which is composed of 16 component banks that together have a capacity of more than a million words. The word size of the CRAY-1 memory is 64 bits, or binary units of information.

The cylindrical mainframe consists of 12 wedge-shaped columns and is a model of compactness. To dissipate the heat generated by the CRAY-1, a cooling system was designed to limit the maximum case temperature to 130 degrees Fahrenheit. A refrigerant circulates through aluminum/stainless steel cooling bars that line each section of the mainframe.

Weighing 5.25 tons and costing $8 million to develop, the CRAY-1 has been called "the world's most expensive love seat." The "love seat" consists of benches around the base of the cylindrical mainframe. Each bench is a cabinet that houses one of its power supplies and some plumbing for the cooling system.

The Los Alamos Scientific Laboratory uses a CRAY-1 for nuclear weapon design as well as for nuclear energy programs. The equivalent of one year of the CRAY-1's time may be necessary to design and develop a single nuclear weapon. CRAY-1 systems are also in demand by such large-scale users as the National Center for Atmospheric Research and the European Center for Medium-Range Weather Forecasts. In 1978, a customer spent $4.8 million to acquire the mainframe of a CRAY-1. Supporting hardware and software were extra.

The CRAY-1, faster than any other processor, is named for its designer, Seymour Cray, a founder of Control Data Corporation before he established the firm that bears his name. In January 1981, Control Data Corporation launched its CDC 205, a comparable supercomputer.

Large computers. In contrast to supercomputers, which are used only where maximum speed and power are so important that costs become secondary, *large computers* must prove their cost effectiveness. And they have done this very impressively: as a result of steadily increased capacity and improved performance, the operation of large computers has become a hundred times less expensive since 1960. In the same period the speed of large computers has increased tenfold. (The cost of operating a computer is calculated by dividing the computer's cost by its computing power, measured in millions of operations per second.)

This progress has been made possible by the technology that replaced magnetic core memory elements with semiconductor memory cells in the early 1970s. The integrated semiconductor memory circuits brought about great reductions in costs, as did the integrated logic circuits. In a large mainframe computer today, there may be 100,000 logic circuits and from four to eight million bytes of memory (a *byte* is often eight bits, but may vary according to the computer manufacturer).

These improvements have entrenched the position of large computers with users who must input, store, and output a great deal of information, and then process this data in different ways. Research, academic, and industrial applications depend on these machines. The insurance industry, among others, is very heavily computerized, and this industry alone utilizes a substantial percentage of total electronic data processing capability.

IBM has been a leader in the development of mainframe computers, and its 370 series, introduced in 1971–72, has developed through a succession of models. Until 1977, the smallest was the 370/115, and the largest the 370/168. The central processing unit of the 370/115 has 1,800 logic chips and a cycle time of 480 nanoseconds, while that of the 370/168 has 20,000 logic chips and a cycle time of 80 nanoseconds. The memory capacity of the smallest unit is just below 400,000 bytes, while that of the largest exceeds eight million bytes. The smallest model is 2.5 feet long, and the largest one is five times as long. The costs are, respectively, $175,000 and $4,500,000.

In 1977 IBM introduced a new model in the 370 series, the 3033. It was designed to outstrip in performance and economy the 168 (and

71

(Bill Longcore)

Interior of the mainframe of an IBM computer's main memory, installed. This is the primary storage area; the wiring of the logic boards can be plainly seen. Part of the air conditioner that keeps the computer installation temperature-controlled can be seen below the clock.

its competitors)—and it did. With computing power about 1.6 to 1.8 times greater, the 3033 offered a lower cost per computing unit and occupied less space.

One company that welcomed the new machine was TRW Credit Data, the largest U.S. supplier of automated credit reports to consumer and business credit grantors. It has a data base of more than 70 million consumer and business files and provides information to about 10,000 subscribers. Because of the phenomenal growth of consumer credit, it has had to upgrade its computer system every 18 months.

At the time of the introduction of the IBM 3033, TRW was using a system designed to handle a peak load of about 50,000 reports an hour, with response times at the terminal varying from 3 to 7 seconds. In a test against some components of that system, the IBM 3033 accomplished every task it was given more rapidly than the existing system.

The newest entry from IBM is its H (for "high end") series, designed for large-system users. The new unit will have enormous processing power, perhaps as much as 15 million instructions per second (MIPS), or three times the rating of the 3033. The main memory will also take a huge leap in capacity, from the 16-million-byte maximum of the 3033 to as much as 96 million in the top-of-the-line model of the H series.

The H series is expected eventually to offer a range of processors designed for specific functions. In addition to the top-of-the-line model, the series is likely to include: the smallest unit, with a rating of about three MIPS, a memory of about eight million bytes, at a cost of about $1 million; a second unit with twice the processing power of the smallest unit, or about six MIPS, a memory capacity of 16 to 32 million bytes, at a cost of about $2 million; and a third

The IBM 3033 processor, shown with two terminals and various peripherals.

(Courtesy of IBM)

unit with a 10-MIPS rating, a memory capacity of 24 to 48 million
bytes, and a cost of $3 million to $4 million.

Minicomputers. Technological advances in the 1960s enabled
manufacturers to respond to the growing demand for a smaller
stand-alone machine, the minicomputer, to handle tasks that large
computers could not perform economically.

Minicomputers were at first used mainly for laboratory and process control applications. But within a few years they were being put
to use in a wide variety of commercial operations: airline reservations, car rentals, banking transactions, and inventory control.

Programming software that was developed in the late 1960s made
it possible for users to broaden the application of minicomputers. As
a result, minicomputers are no longer considered "dedicated," as
they originally were, but are now being used as general-purpose
computers. They are increasingly powerful and do almost everything the large computers do, but more slowly and at a much lower
cost. This has put them within reach of small companies that could
never afford the large machines and that do not require the capacity
or speed of the large machines.

A "typical" minicomputer has a 16-bit word length, weighs less
than 50 pounds, and requires no special air conditioning or other
conditions. It consumes less than 500 watts of standard 115-volt
electric power, and can have from 5,000 to 10,000 logic circuits and
from 16,000 to 32,000 bytes of memory. The cost is less than
$50,000.

An example of the minicomputer is the PDP-11/70. Its central processing unit has 600 logic chips and a cycle time of 300 nanoseconds. The memory capacity can exceed four million bytes. The unit
is 21 inches long, 31 inches deep, and stands 6 feet high. It weighs
500 pounds and costs $63,000. It can be classed either as a minicom-
puter or as a small mainframe computer. At the other end of the scale
in this series is the PDP-11/03. It is 19 inches long, 13.5 inches deep,
and only 3.5 inches high. It weighs 35 pounds and costs $2,000.
There are four logic chips in its central processing unit, which has a
cycle time of 3.5 microseconds. The memory capacity is up to 57,000
bytes.

Microcomputers. The developments in microelectronics that
made possible the minicomputer have recently led to the creation of
the microcomputer. Microcomputers take fullest advantage of the
use of large-scale integration on silicon chips. The microprocessors
literally contain a computer on a chip that can pass through the eye
of a needle. The electronic circuitry for an entire program can actually
be burned into a single chip; thus, a special-purpose computer can

be developed in which the "works" would be simply one chip. But today's microcomputers consist of a system of such chips. One chip may contain the central processing unit and its functions, several provide memory, and still others regulate input/output connections to auxiliary equipment.

Originally, microcomputers were designed for hobbyists. Now they are beginning to compete with minicomputers in the marketplace, and are especially attractive to small business operations. The combination of their substantial computational power, low cost, and flexibility make them ideal for applications in which relatively small amounts of data must be handled. They are also finding a market with users of larger computers who have jobs that are too small or specialized to run on the larger machines.

The line of distinction between minicomputers and microcomputers is becoming blurred in regard to physical appearance and size as well as functions. In many cases a microcomputer may be smaller in size than a minicomputer but greater in processing power. A microcomputer might have 1,000 to 2,000 logic circuits and a few hundred to a few thousand bytes of memory and yet cost as little as several hundred dollars.

The TRS-80, a well-known microcomputer with exceptional versatility, is marketed by the Tandy Corporation (Radio Shack). It is being sold as a personal computer that can be expanded by the addition of compatible components.

(Radio Shack, A Division of Tandy Corp.)

The TRS-80 microcomputer system, consisting of a keyboard, display screen, power pack, cassette recorder, and user's manual.

(Radio Shack, A Division of Tandy Corp.)

The TRS-80 32K "Business" System includes a line printer and two disk storage packs.

The basic TRS-80 system includes a 12-inch video-type screen monitor, a keyboard, a battery/AC cassette recorder, and its own power supply. It comes with a user's manual and a two-game cassette tape for playing blackjack or backgammon. Additional software for household, small business, educational, and hobby uses is available on cassettes. The machine can be programmed from prerecorded cassettes or from the keyboard. Blank tapes on which users can record their own programs are also available.

The "brain" of the TRS-80 computer is a Z-80 microprocessor that serves as the central processing unit. Programs are on cassettes; data are on cassettes or can be entered from the keyboard. As program instructions and data are needed, they are transferred to internal memory chips.

The TRS-80 is available in two models; the lower-priced contains 4,096 bytes (4K),* and can be expanded to 16K within the keyboard unit and to 48K by means of an expansion interface with additional memory options. The machine operates on household current. Available components include two kinds of printers, a minidisk sys-

* 1K is equivalent to 1,024 bytes.

tem for even greater memory and programming capacity, and other interface devices that can connect the machine with computers and accessories located at a distance. In this way even the smallest machine can become part of a large computer network.

Trends in Computer Technology

It is impossible to conceive of the world of computers as static. Yesterday's newest model is today's has-been. Today's innovation will be old hat by next year. Already past the drawing board and into early stages of production are the machines that will be commonplace by the end of this decade. And their successors are already gleaming in the eyes of computer designers. As we have seen repeatedly, the trends are moving in three directions at once: reduced size, reduced cost, and increased capacity.

Reduction in size. Minis and micros are the state of the art today, but there is talk of even more compact devices to come. Already some large computers as well as minicomputers are being housed in cabinets larger than necessary for their electronic circuitry. When the cabinet is opened, a lot of empty space can be seen. Manufacturers justify this practice by explaining that customers want to see something substantial and impressive for their money, and that a certain physical appearance is *expected* of such an important and costly device. However, this is likely to change as the public becomes more familiar with the smaller machines and with the technological advances that make them possible.

Reduction in cost. Hand in hand with the reduction in computer size through improved technology has come a reduction in cost, which is the key to rapid expansion. In 1954, just a little more than 25 years ago, when vacuum tubes and later magnetic cores were the switching and memory components of computers, it cost $1.26 to perform 100,000 multiplications. By 1978 the cost had dropped to less than 1 cent. Today a few hundred dollars will buy hardware with a capability equal to that of equipment costing tens of thousands of dollars in the early 1960s.

The chips used in present-day machines may cost no more than $10 each, yet they contain the equivalent of thousands of circuits that formerly had to be laboriously connected with miles of wire at a very high cost for materials and labor.

This is not unlike what happened following the introduction of

77

hand (or pocket) calculators. When they first appeared on the market, they were very expensive. A four-function model, which could add, subtract, multiply, and divide, cost several hundred dollars about a decade ago; today you can buy a four-function calculator for less than $10.

When computers first became commercially available, the hardware was so expensive that vendors sought to encourage sales by giving away the software needed to run the computers. As the hardware has come down in price, the cost of software has increased. Now much of the software must be purchased or leased as a separate item. And some observers forecast a day when all software will have to be purchased, while the computer hardware will be virtually given away.

Increased speed and storage. Perhaps the greatest progress to date in computer development has been in the area of memory. This is a direct result of the advances in chip technology: the more circuitry that can be positioned on a single chip, the more storage capacity that can be given to a computer.

Along with this development there have been marked increases in the speed of computation. The speed of computation depends on switching delays in logic circuits that make up the central processing unit. Logic circuits provide the processing action of the computer; therefore, processing can proceed only as rapidly as a logic circuit can open and close, or switch into action when called on. In the CPU, every logic circuit is constantly on the alert, waiting to be called on as input is changed. Every logic circuit has a small but measurable switching delay, representing the amount of time it takes the circuitry to respond to a change in input. Logic circuits in the vacuum tube of 1959 had a switching delay of 1 *microsecond*. Only a few years later, a printed-circuit card mounted with transistors and other components had a switching delay of 100 *nanoseconds*. But by the end of the 1970s, a single integrated circuit silicon chip contained from five to ten circuits and had switching delays of only 5 nanoseconds. But while the internal CPU speeds are truly astounding, it is important to realize that the speeds of the input and output devices ultimately are controlling factors that determine the productivity of a computer system.

Looking ahead, we can be sure that progress in basic technology—and the economies it brings—will continue. It can be safely predicted that the trends of today will be the reality of the future. But no one can predict the completely new developments, perhaps undreamed of today, that may come along to shape the computer world in the years ahead.

All computers have four basic functions: *input, processing, storage,* and *output.* The input must be transcribed from human-readable to machine-readable form. Computers became much more useful after they were equipped to handle letters of the alphabet as well as numbers. They may "read" information from special cards, tapes, or disks on which data are recorded in machine-readable form by keyboard.

The central processing unit of the computer consists of an arithmetic logic unit, a control unit, and primary storage. The arithmetic logic unit performs addition, subtraction, multiplication, and division, and can make logical comparisons. The control unit directs all internal operations in accordance with its instructions or program. Primary storage contains some data and programs. Additional data and programs can be stored in accessory units outside the machines; this is known as auxiliary storage.

Output, the final step in computer operation, is the measure of any system's usefulness. It must be given, sooner or later, in human-readable form; the most usual forms of output are printed on paper or on a screen.

Computers may be classified according to purpose, according to their type of processing operation, or according to their size and speed.

By purpose: *General-purpose computers* can handle a wide variety of functions. They are, for example, used in scientific research as well as for business data processing. *Special-purpose computers,* sometimes called "dedicated" because they are used for only one specific task, are meeting a growing variety of needs.

By type of processing: The *analog computer* simulates conditions and is used mainly for engineering problems. Because it is limited in accuracy and cannot work with nonnumeric data, it is not widely used. *Digital computers* are highly accurate, can use alphanumeric data, and are more widely used.

By size: *Supercomputers* are important in applications where vast quantities of data must be stored and processed rapidly, such as nuclear weapon development and weather forecasting. Since 1960 the speed of *large computers* has increased tenfold. Large computers are also a hundred times cheaper to operate, and, as a result, have had increasing acceptance throughout the economy, especially in large organizations such as corporations and universities. Increasingly, *minicomputers* have come within reach of small companies that could never afford the large machines. The *microcomputer* is even smaller and is finding applications in small businesses, in education, and more and more for personal and home use.

The present trends toward reduced size, reduced cost, and increased computing speed and storage capacity will bring us smaller and less expensive machines in the not too distant future, machines with substantial capacity that will impinge on more and more aspects of our lives.

Key Terms and Phrases

alphanumeric	hybrid computers	special-purpose
analog computers	input	computers
bits	large computers	storage
bytes	microcomputers	supercomputers
digital computers	minicomputers	
general-purpose	output	
computers	processing	

Sources of Additional Information

Davis, Ruth M. "Evolution of Computers and Computing." *Science* 195 (1977):1096–1102.

Dorr, Fred W. "The Cray-1 at Los Alamos." *Datamation*, no. 10 (1978):113–20.

Lincoln, Neil R. "Supercomputer Development—The Pleasure and the Pain." *Datamation*, no. 5 (1977):221–26.

Pantages, Angeline, and Cashman, Michael W. "The IBM System/370 Model 3033." *Datamation*, no. 5 (1977):235–37.

Reid-Green, Keith S. "The History of Computing: The IBM 7070." *Byte*, no. 6 (1979):148–50.

Rosen, Saul. "Electronic Computers: A Historical Survey." *Computing Surveys*, no. 1 (1969):7–36.

Terman, Lewis M. "The Role of Microelectronics in Data Processing." *Scientific American*, September 1977, pp. 163–77.

Test Yourself

1. The human brain is often compared with a computer. What is an important distinction between the computer and the human brain?
2. List the four basic functions of a computer system.
3. What are alphanumeric symbols?
4. Name the three components of the central processing unit. Describe the function of each.
5. What are the two basic classifications of storage, and what is the purpose of each?
6. Name two forms of computer output.

7. Computers can be classified according to ————. (Hint: there is more than one possible answer.)

8. How have the distinctions between general-purpose and scientific computers changed in recent years? Why?

9. Name the two kinds of computer processing.

10. List the categories of computers according to size. What is a major operating limitation of supercomputers? What features have accounted for the rapid growth of microcomputers?

Unit II
Introduction to Computer Hardware

4 Input and Output Devices

"... God bless you ..."

©Datamation®

APPLICATION
The Bank Teller

Every day millions of people who know nothing about data processing find themselves in direct, or *online*, communication with computers. Equipped with only a small plastic card and a personal identification number, they are able to conduct their regular banking transactions—depositing funds in checking or saving accounts, cashing checks, making withdrawals—at a computer terminal.

Dubbed "anytime tellers" because they are literally available to banking customers around the clock, these terminals require little space and less human care. They might be nicknamed "anywhere tellers" as well, because they bring the most commonly required banking services directly to customers where they are needed most—in shopping centers, on city streets, and even inside supermarkets. The official name for these "cash machines" is automatic teller machine (ATM).

One ATM can handle some 20,000 transactions a month, or approximately the workload of three human tellers. And the ATM is in many ways more efficient than a human teller. For example, when a card is reported lost, the central computer to which the terminals are all connected can instantly put a "hold" on that card. Human tellers would have to telephone every bank branch, where the information would have to be noted by another human teller, generating substantial paperwork in the process. The central computer coordinates all transactions from every ATM that is online to it, and can also keep track of every transaction at each individual terminal. Thus, if an ATM runs short of cash, has had a card jammed into it, or otherwise malfunctions, it immediately "notifies" the central computer.

But ATMs have not quite made human tellers obsolete. Today's human teller is also equipped with a computer terminal, which is operated somewhat like an electric typewriter. The function keys are marked with English letters and abbreviations for ease of operation. Once the passbook or check has been inserted and aligned (some terminals will even do the aligning), the teller then keys in the pertinent information. The terminal prints the entry in the passbook and records the transaction for the data center files. It also displays each phase of the transaction on a screen. Thus the teller can verify each step of the process and correct any errors before the new balance is transmitted to the data files. The time needed for balancing is reduced by more than half. Accuracy is enhanced, customer waiting time is reduced, and the overall volume handled by the bank is greatly increased without additional staff or locations.

The contrast in banking procedures with those of only a few years ago is astonishing! Only a decade ago the bank teller had to go to a file and locate, amid thousands of similar cards, the one card containing each customer's record. The mathematics of the transaction had to be calculated on a hand-cranked adding machine and entered by typewriter—or sometimes by hand—in the bankbook.

Banks traditionally closed early in the afternoon, leading to numerous jokes about "banker's hours." The time was needed, though, for recording the results of the day's, week's, and month's transactions. Today, the widespread use of computer terminals makes possible rapid in-bank accounting, allowing banks to stay open longer and to provide better service to more customers.

N THIS chapter we will examine devices that enter raw data, information, or user questions into computers (input); devices that provide or display data, information, or answers to queries (output); and devices such as terminals that can perform both input and output functions. These combined *input/output (I/O) devices* are what most people have direct contact with when dealing with computers. The savings bank teller who enters data at a terminal, for example, may never see the CPU where the data are processed. A CPU may be several hundred or even thousands of miles from the I/O devices it serves.

The type of data processing used generally determines the type of I/O device. There are two distinct types of processing: *batch* and *online*. In batch processing, data items are collected and sent to the computer in groups, or batches. The data entry mechanism for such systems—keypunch, key-to-tape, or key-to-disk—do not require any computer support to record data. (For that reason they are sometimes called "stand-alone" devices.) The resulting punched cards, disks, or tapes containing the data can then be put on the computer at some later time for processing. Batched data entry is appropriate for any application, such as a payroll processing system that produces paychecks or a credit card billing operation, in which input and/or output occurs at periodic intervals.

In some applications, however, batch processing would be inadequate. In an airline reservations system, for instance, it is imperative that a sold seat be immediately identifiable at all terminals in the system. If this information were batched, it might be hours or even days before airline clerks or travel agents could learn what seats had actually been sold. Computerized reservations systems therefore use online processing, in which data are entered immediately and all users have immediate access to the information. Thus the use of terminals to enter data is appropriate when the system requires constant updating.

Many I/O devices are multifunctional; that is, they can be used both as stand-alone input devices and as terminals. The increasing use of multiple terminals is a relatively new development in data entry equipment. These terminals are "managed" by a controlling processor unit, which in turn has access to the larger central computer.

In recent years the traditional methods of entering data—"card-oriented" methods usually involving data entry at the CPU—have begun to give way to the use of terminals and terminal-like devices. With these devices data are "captured" into the system at their point of entry, instead of being transcribed first onto a card from a source document. Terminals are also being used more often as a means of providing data output, often on a screen. This does not mean that

87

standard output printers are about to be phased out. It does mean that terminals are being used more and more for both input and output. Indeed, the input/output potential of terminals has just begun to be explored.

Input or Data Entry

The primary purpose of an input device is to convert raw data into machine-readable form for processing or storage by the computer. There exists a variety of devices to feed data to computers in machine-readable form. These devices can be classified in three broad categories: keyboarding devices, automatic recognition devices, and what may be called "direct communication" devices.

- Keypunch, key-to-tape, and key-to-disk machines are all devices in which the data to be entered are typed on a keyboard.
- Automatic recognition devices are essentially sophisticated optical scanning or other sensory mechanisms for "recognizing" data items that appear in some kind of printed form. Such data may be printed in magnetic or regular ink or carefully handwritten or penciled in, or they may appear as a bar code.
- Direct communication input methods include the Datapad and voice recognition devices.

Although the mechanics of data entry may vary, the basic principles are always the same. In the conversion of data to machine-readable form in a card-oriented or batch processing system, for example, a source document such as a purchase order is usually filled out by a salesperson. The completed document is then sent to a data entry clerk. If punched media are being used, the data entry clerk is a keypuncher, who transcribes the data onto one of the punched media (cards or tape). To make certain that data have been accurately transcribed, the punched cards or tape are inserted into a machine called a verifier, and another keypuncher reenters the data from the original source documents. If there is a discrepancy, the verifier signals the operator to make a correction.

When verification has been completed, the "clean" data are ready for processing. Key-to-tape and key-to-disk input also require verification, but in these media this procedure is usually performed on the same device that was originally used to enter the data.

With the newest data entry equipment—terminals—a purchase order or other transaction is entered directly on the terminal keyboard, and the computer has been programmed to run an error check to verify the correctness of the data. For example, the computer determines that the customer's name contains no numbers, that the purchased item is correctly identified, that the customer is cleared for credit, and so on. But now the source documents are no longer pieces of paper. Instead they are magnetic "spots" stored on a magnetic medium. Such devices, by eliminating the extra steps of transcription, reduce the probability of error. Every transcription from one medium to another increases the chance of error. But if the data are captured at the point of entry into the system—as by the point-of-sale (POS) devices now used in many retail stores—and directly stored in machine-readable form, there is less opportunity for transcription errors.

These I/O devices offer other advantages as well: The user can update local data, access local files that are kept at a remote site, perform calculations, and generate reports. These and other advantages largely account for the present trend toward terminals and away from card-oriented systems.

Card-Oriented Systems

Punched cards are one feature of data processing with which almost everyone is familiar. In the United States they often appear as payroll checks, telephone bills, magazine subscription cards, and money orders. At present, punched cards are still the most widely used means of entering data into a computer. They have several advantages that explain their long popularity. Punched cards are standardized and thus can be used for transferring data by a variety of data processing machines. Almost every punched card is a "unit record"; that is, it contains the complete record of a single transaction. This means that a punched card can be processed individually if necessary, without affecting the rest of the file. Punched cards are also easy to handle and provide a relatively quick and efficient means of processing data. Another advantage is that the entries are visible. But as we shall see below, they also have certain disadvantages in comparison with other input media.

The 80-column card. The standard punched card is the 80-column, or Hollerith, card. Its dimensions (based on the proportions of the paper currency used in Hollerith's time—see chapter 2) are 18.7 cm by 8.3 cm (7⅜ by 3¼ inches). The card is commonly made of a stiff, heavy-duty paper for durability and ease of handling. It can carry 80 separate items of data in the form of numbers, letters, or special characters. Often all three forms are recorded on the same card.

89

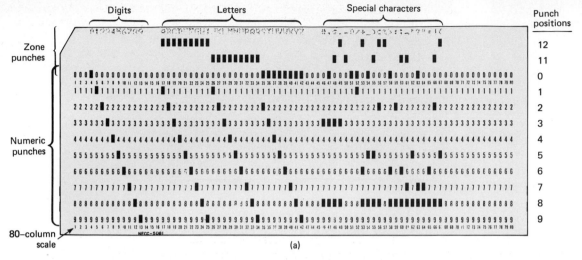

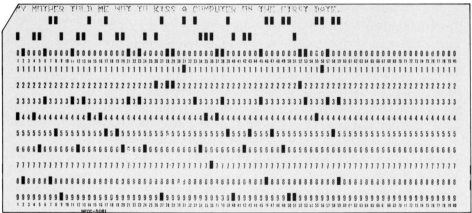

(b)
Data entered on a punched card

Figure 4-1 A punched card showing punch positions (above) and a card punched according to the Hollerith code (below)

The card itself can be thought of as being divided into three sections (see figure 4-1). The lower section consists of 10 rows of numbers. (The two rows of smaller numbers provide column orientation for human card readers.) The bottom row contains 80 "9's"; the next higher row, 80 "8's"; and so on. Because they can be used to represent any digit from 0 to 9, these rows are known as *digit* or *numeric* rows. As figure 4-1 shows, the digit rows are actually printed on the card.

The second section consists of three zone rows, labeled "12," "11," and "0." (Thus the zero row, being in both the numeric and zone sections, can function both as a digit row and as a zone row.) It should be noted, however, that rows 11 and 12 are usually *not* printed on the punched card. Holes punched in the zone rows (ei-

90

Punch 12 plus	Punch 11 plus	Punch 0 plus
1 = A	1 = J	2 = S
2 = B	2 = K	3 = T
3 = C	3 = L	4 = U
4 = D	4 = M	5 = V
5 = E	5 = N	6 = W
6 = F	6 = O	7 = X
7 = G	7 = P	8 = Y
8 = H	8 = Q	9 = Z
9 = I	9 = R	

Table 4-1 The Hollerith punched-card code

ther individually or in combination with digit-row punches in the same column) are used to code for letters and special characters. The third section, located at the top of the card, may be used for human-readable printed display (or "interpretation") of the information coded in the punched holes. The Hollerith code is shown in table 4-1.

Although it is not immediately apparent from the appearance of the card itself, data are recorded on punched cards in areas called *fields*. A field may be a single column, or it may consist of two or more consecutive columns. Its characteristic features are that it contains a particular kind of data and is processed as a single item of information. For example, a punched-card record of a sales transaction might have fields containing the customer's name, an identifying customer code, an invoice number, and so on. The card in figure 4-1 has three fields.

The 96-column card. A second type of punched card was introduced a little more than a decade ago by IBM for use with its Sys-

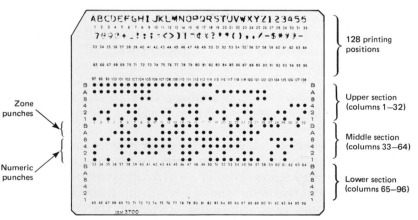

Figure 4-2 The 96-column punched card used in the IBM System/3

91

tem/3 series of business computers. This card has a 96-column format and therefore can carry 20 percent more data; it is also roughly one-third the size of the Hollerith card. The card consists of two sections—an interpretation, or print area, at the top and a punched section below (see figure 4-2). The latter consists of three tiers of 32 columns. Each tier has six rows of punch positions, two zone and four digit: B, A, 8, 4, 2, and 1. The newer card requires fewer rows because it makes greater use of the possible combinations of punches that can be made in a single column. The print area contains three lines, each one corresponding to a tier of the punch area.

Card Processing Devices

The keypunch. The device for recording information from source documents in the form of holes punched in cards is the *card punch,* more commonly known as the *keypunch.* The keypunch operator transcribes data onto punched cards by pressing keys on a keyboard, much as a typist does on a typewriter. Depending on the keyboard, the operator is able to record numerical or alphabetical information, or both. The machine automatically feeds blank cards from a hopper onto a card bed that moves them through the punching machinery one column at a time. The machine stacks the cards as they are completed.

Keypunch machines also have several features that increase the speed of the keypunch operation. These include a *skip key* for moving quickly from one field to another; a *duplicating key* to produce duplicate cards or sections of cards; and a *program card* that provides for automatic skipping, duplicating, and shifting from alphabetic to numeric symbols throughout a batch. However, even with these automatic features, keypunching is a slow and costly process. One reason is that it must be repeated for verification.

The verifying machine or verifier. Because keypunch operators are human, the possibility of error is always present. It is particularly important to avoid mistakes in punching, since even one mistake will cause errors in the subsequent processing of data throughout the system. Moreover, it is much less costly to correct a mistake before processing than afterward. Error detection and correction are performed by means of a *verifier.*

A verifier is very much like a keypunch machine except that it "reads" holes instead of punching them. The verifier operator proceeds just as a keypunch operator would and types from the same source documents that were used in keypunching the cards. If a data item typed on the verifier does not agree with the corresponding

(Courtesy of IBM)

An IBM 129 verifying punch. This machine allows an operator to keypunch cards from a source document and perform subsequent verifying without having to transfer the cards to another machine.

item on the punched card, an "error" light comes on. If a second verification attempt fails, the machine punches a notch over the column containing the error. Such cards are easily identified and rejected by the machine as it groups the correct cards for further processing. The inaccurate cards are then replaced by correctly punched revisions. If no error is found, a notch is made on the right side of the card.

One variation of the verifier is a machine called the *verifying punch*. This device is essentially a keypunch with a memory. The operator types in the data to be punched, but the verifying punch stores the information in its memory without punching any cards. The operator then keys the same source data a second time. If the data items keyed the second time agree with those held in the memory, the cards are punched. If there is a discrepancy, the operator simply reenters the correct data. (See figure 4-3.) There are other combination machines as well.

93

Figure 4-3 Data entry and correction on one type of keypunch-verifier

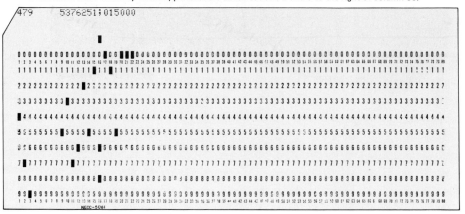

(a)

If data have been correctly entered, punches are added to rows 2 and 3 to the right of column 80.

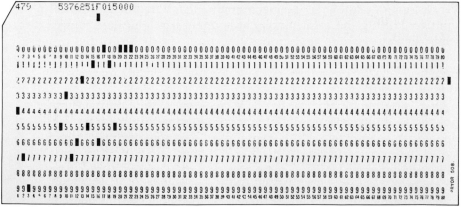

(b)

If a card has been punched incorrectly, the correction is held in memory while the error-carrying card is ejected from the machine. This card contains no punches to the right of column 80.

(c)

A new blank card is inserted and data are entered from memory; a punch entered only in row 2 to the right of column 80 indicates that this card is a corrected duplicate.

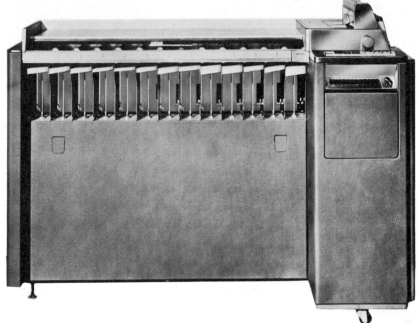

(Courtesy of IBM)

A typical card sorter. The cards are fed in at the upper right, read one column at a time, and sorted according to punches in that column.

The sorter, reproducer, interpreter, and collator. One advantage of punched cards in data processing is that they are usually unit records. Because each card may carry a complete record of a transaction such as a sale, it can be added, sorted, rearranged, or removed individually, without affecting the data content of other cards. This particular feature is the essential requirement of many data processing systems. Usually such unit record systems consist of several different devices for processing punched cards in various ways. The most common of these are the *sorter*, the *reproducer*, the *interpreter*, and the *collator*.

The *sorter* arranges cards in a predetermined order for input and processing. Sorting is usually performed before any other processing.

The *reproducer* transfers data from one card to another, but not necessarily to the same field or fields as on the original card. Thus the device reproduces the data but not always the position of the data on the card. This is necessary when some of the data are to be used for another purpose or in a different system. Sales data, for example, could be transferred from a billing system to an inventory control system in this way. The reproducer can also *gangpunch*, or transfer a single data item from one master file card to a number of other cards.

95

The *interpreter* prints—in a form readable by human operators —all or part of the data coded in the card columns. As we saw in figures 4-1 and 4-2, the printed data may appear at or near the top of a card. Print may appear elsewhere on the card as well. The printed "translation" makes possible the human use of punched cards.

A *collator* can perform a variety of functions, including checking for correct sequence of cards, combining two files into a single file (merging), comparing cards from different files and extracting those that do not match (matching), and extracting individual cards from a file without changing the file organization (selecting).

Disadvantages of punched cards. Despite their considerable advantages, data processing systems that use punched cards have a variety of handicaps. First of all, the amount of data a punched card can contain is limited to the coding of the 80 or 96 columns. A more extensive data record will require two or more cards, while a shorter record means wasted space. Second, punched cards are not reusable. Updating of information requires punching a new card, verifying it, and so on.

Third, card processing is slow compared to other forms of data input. Cards must be moved manually for storage or from one machine to another for processing. Keypunching, verification, and cor-

An interpreter. Punched cards without text are fed into the interpreter at the upper right. The machine automatically reads the punched code and prints the appropriate text across the top of each card.

(Courtesy of IBM)

(Courtesy of IBM)

A collator. A deck of
punched cards is placed
on the slanting platform.
One by one, cards are
read by the collator and
automatically added to
the appropriate stack.

rection are time-consuming procedures. Cards must be processed sequentially, and the various data devices cannot process cards at
speeds higher than from 500 to 3,000 cards per minute. Such limitations become especially acute when large volumes of data must be
processed. Fourth, cards are bulky and require considerable storage
space. And fifth, cards necessarily receive a great deal of handling by
human operators. A sizable staff, requiring a sizable payroll, may be
necessary. And the cards can be lost or damaged and may also become jammed in machines.

Key-to-Tape and Key-to-Disk Input

Punched paper tape represents some advance over punched cards.
Information is entered in eight rows, or channels, running the length

97

Figure 4-4 Punched paper tape showing the eight-channel code

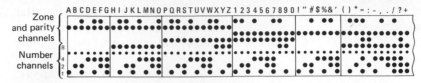

Frames running across the tape are analogous to the columns on punched cards, and represent letters, numbers, and various special characters. Channels running the length of the tape are analogous to the rows on punched cards. The four channels at the bottom of the tape represent the numbers 1, 2, 4, and 8. All number values can be expressed as one or a combination of these number channels. (Between channels 4 and 8 are sprocket holes by means of which the tape runs through the machine; they are not part of the code.) The four upper channels contain parity and zone punches. The zone punches are similar to those in cards, combining with punches in the number channels to form various characters.

of the tape in a sequence similar to that of the Hollerith code (see figure 4-4). Ten characters can be contained in 1 inch of tape. Thus a strip of paper tape that is 1 inch wide and 8 inches long can contain as much data as an 80-column card. Data records of different lengths are readily accommodated on a continuous tape. Also, tape receives much less handling by human operators. On the other hand, paper tape is not an easily correctable medium, is fragile, and therefore has a short life span. The relatively slow processing speeds also make it less feasible to use paper tape with large computers.

Punched paper tape represents a transitional development between punched cards and magnetic input media. *Key-to-tape* and *key-to-disk* devices are, in a sense, extensions of the keypunch machine. The keyboards of magnetic tape and disk machines resemble those of keypunch machines but record data on different media instead of punching holes in cards or tapes. These newer devices record data as magnetized "spots" on tape reels, cartridges, cassettes, or disks. The recording media are similar in some respects to those used in sound recording.

In most of today's key-to-tape and key-to-disk machines, the recorded data appear on a display screen as they are entered. This feature allows for easy verification and correction by the keyboard operator. When an error is detected, the operator simply backspaces (as on a typewriter) and rekeys the correct data. The tape can also be rewound and the original data retyped to provide a second verification check.

In the latest key-to-disk machines, the data are stored, checked, and edited by a minicomputer before being finally recorded on a magnetic disk. When errors are detected, the system alerts the operator and "waits" until the error is corrected. The magnetic disk usually serves only as temporary storage. After editing and correction, the data are automatically transferred as input into the main computer.

Data entry systems that use magnetic tapes and disks have several advantages over punched-card input devices. First, as with paper tape, record lengths are no longer limited to 80 or 96 characters. Second, magnetic tapes and disks do not have to be replaced when they are corrected or updated. In other words, they are reusable. Third, tape and disk devices work electronically rather than mechanically, so they are faster (and quieter) than keypunch entry systems. Fourth, tape and disk storage is much more compact than card storage. For example, an inch of magnetic tape can hold from 800 to 6,250 characters of stored data.

Although these advantages are considerable, (they are also expensive.) Consequently, key-to-tape and key-to-disk systems are most efficient when used to prepare large volumes of data for processing by medium and large computers.

Automatic Input Data Recognition

Every day banks in the United States process many millions of checks. They are able to do so because these checks carry certain information printed in a special type and printed with a special ink. Numerals and symbols in MICR form are shown in figure 4-5. The books of check blanks supplied by banks to their customers carry an identifying bank code and customer account number—printed in magnetic ink—on each check. The special ink contains tiny metal particles that can be magnetized for rapid recognition by a special reading device.

Magnetic ink character recognition (MICR). Processing a check begins after it has been cashed or deposited with a bank. Using a special keyboard device known as a *magnetic ink encoder,* the operator types or encodes the amount of the check on the check itself. The check now carries four items of information printed in magnetic ink: the code of the issuing bank, the check number, the account on which the check is drawn, and the amount of money involved in the transaction. Figure 4-6 shows an MICR-encoded check.

Next, a *magnetic ink character reader* reads all the encoded information, translates it into computer-readable code, verifies it, and either enters it directly into the computer or encodes it on a magnetic tape for later entry into the computer.

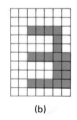

Numbers

ₐ₁ Amount symbol

Dash symbol

Transit symbol

"On-us" symbol

(a)

(b)

Detailed definition of an MICR character

Figure 4-5 Numbers and symbols used in magnetic ink character recognition (MICR) devices

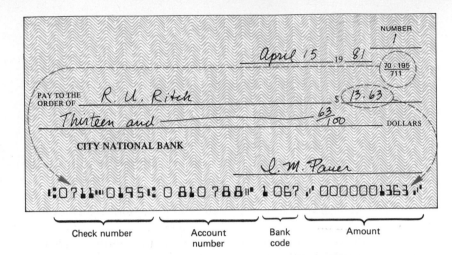

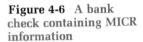

Figure 4-6 A bank
check containing MICR
information

Check number   Account number   Bank code   Amount

Perhaps the greatest advantage of MICR is that the information on the source documents (for example, checks) does not have to be copied or punched on another input medium. In other words, the source documents can be read both by humans and by machines. The elimination of a copying step greatly minimizes the possibility of costly human errors. The result is a largely automatic input system that is much faster than any keypunch system.

MICR, however, does have its own drawbacks. Only some data are preprinted, while other data must be entered by a human operator, thereby increasing the potential for error. Also, the magnetic code consists of only ten digits and four special symbols. The type of information that can be encoded, therefore, is greatly limited. Finally, the magnetic reader can read *only* magnetic ink characters. It ignores everything else that appears on the check. This limitation makes the system vulnerable to abuse. In one documented case, for example, an individual substituted several thousand blank deposit slips, all bearing the number of his account in magnetic ink, for those supplied at several branches of a bank; $250,000 was unwittingly deposited to his account before the blank deposit slips were removed.

A B C D E F G H I J
K L M N O P Q R S T
U V W X Y Z
0 1 2 3 4 5 6 7 8 9
⌐ : ⌐ = + / ≠ * ⌐ &
' — { } % ?

Figure 4-7 Letters, numbers, and symbols for optical character recognition (OCR) devices

Optical character recognition (OCR). Optical character recognition is an input method in which light and photoelectric cells scan printed data. Although the data to be scanned may take a variety of forms, there is a standard set of printed characters that can be read by an OCR reader. These include all 26 characters of the alphabet (both upper and lower case), the 10 digits of the decimal number system, and a dozen or more special symbols (shown in figure 4-7). The slightly angular and somewhat stylized characters of the OCR type-

100

face commonly appear on utility bills, retail price tags, credit cards, and a variety of other media.

Other, more expensive OCR reading devices can cope fairly reliably with typewritten characters and even with characters printed by hand—if they are printed carefully! The reliability of OCR readers, however, depends very much on the clarity of the characters being read. Unlike an MICR reader (which ignores everything not printed in magnetic ink), an OCR reader may misinterpret data that are smudged, are not dark enough, have grease spots on them, or appear on wrinkled paper. Any one of these conditions may also cause the reader to simply reject the document.

A standard OCR reader/sorter can validate and process OCR-imprinted material at a rate of 400 documents per minute. Validated data are recorded on magnetic tapes or disks or entered directly into the computer. The reader can also sort the documents into separate "reject" and "validated" stacks.

A different kind of OCR reading device employs a *light pen* or *wand*. This instrument is operated by hand and can be moved at a speed of up to 10 inches per second (the equivalent of 100 cps, or characters per second) across a document. Like the standard reader, the wand can read the OCR typeface, typewritten characters, and handwritten numerals.

The basic operation of OCR reading devices involves shining a light on the material to be read as it passes under an array of photoelectric cells. Light reflected from the ink is detected by the photoelectric cells and converted into electrical impulses. These in turn are analyzed by a "recognition unit."

The great advantage of OCR is that it completely eliminates manual keyboarding and the reading of data by a human operator. In these respects it is superior to MICR. But while an OCR reader can also recognize a greater variety of characters and symbols than the MICR reader, it is nonetheless restricted to a very limited document format. Moreover, equipment costs and rejection and error rates all tend to be higher than those of many other input media. Clearly, more research and development are needed in this area of input/output technology. It should also be clear that the potential of OCR is very great.

Mark-sense input. Anyone who has taken a computer-graded examination has used a mark-sense form (see figure 4-8). A mark-sense reader will read the marks made in well-defined areas of a form. On a computer-graded exam, for example, these areas are often indicated by pairs of broken lines or circles. The person taking the exam uses a special pencil to fill in such areas. The reader senses the presence of

101

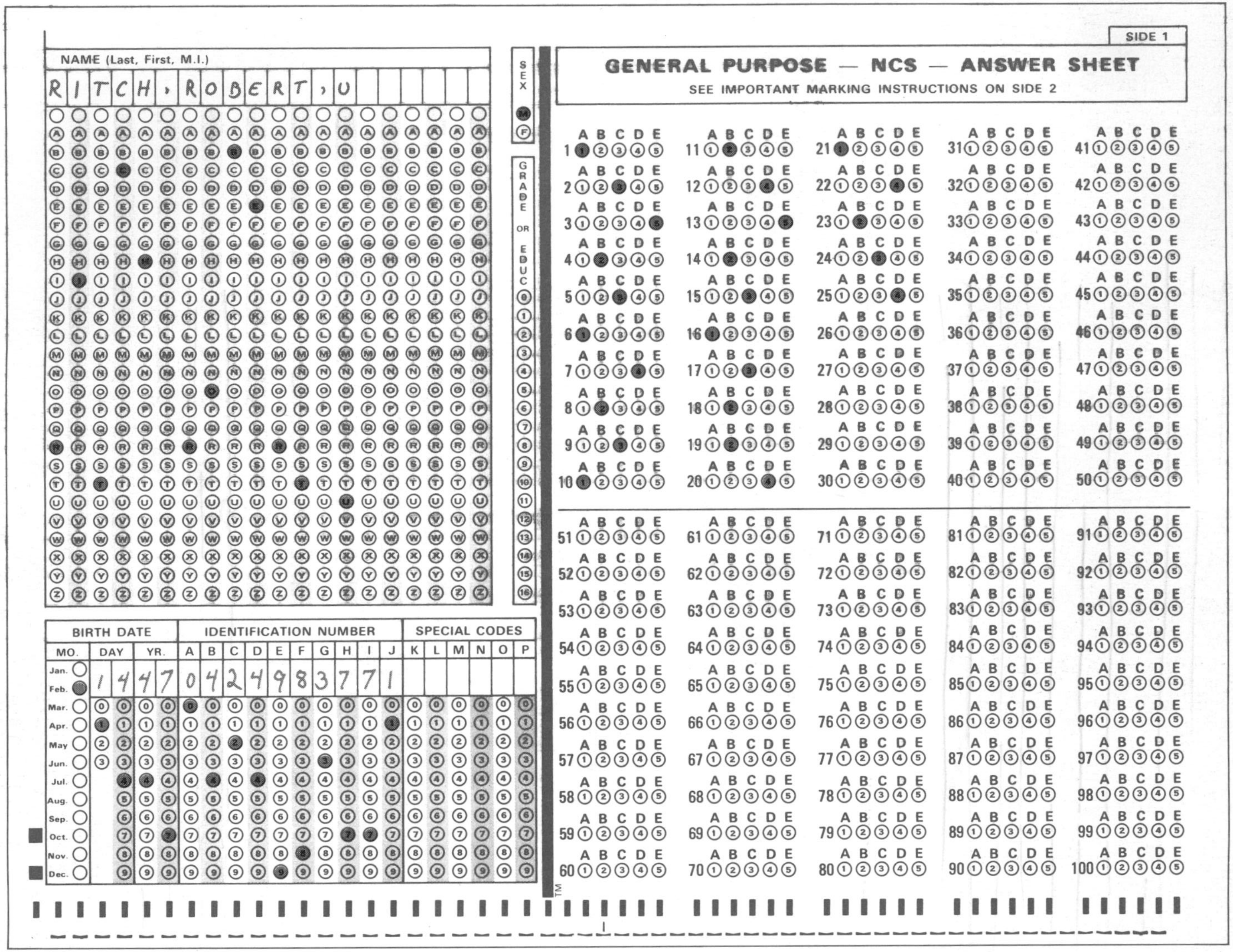

Figure 4-8 General-purpose answer sheet for mark-sense reading

Grocery packaging includes the Universal Product Code (UPC) designed to be read by a scanning device at the checkout counter for automatic inventory control.

pencil marks, and the computer analyzes them to determine their significance. This method of testing may well be the most practical way of handling grading for a large number of individuals.

Mark sensing is also used in surveys and other questionnaires where cost considerations are a factor or where the number of responding individuals makes multiple-choice questions necessary. An improved form of mark sensing is *Optical Mark Read* (OMR), which permits the use of any black pencil. OMR made possible the rapid processing of vast quantities of data in the 1980 census (see chapter 2).

A mark-sense input, like that of MICR and OCR, provides direct entry of data into the computer, without any intermediate copying step. OCR/OMR devices may also produce cards or tape for input into the CPU.

Bar codes. A *bar code* is a series of parallel lines or bars of different widths (and sometimes colors). A bar-code reader passes light over the code and "reads" the light reflected from the lines, translating it into numeric and alphanumeric characters for the computer.

The IBM 3660 supermarket system. Lasers read the Universal Product Code as an employee passes the product over the read station at the checkout counter.

The thickness and sequence of the lines contain the coded information.

Perhaps the most commonly encountered bar code is the one found on most packaged items in grocery stores and supermarkets. This code—known as the Universal Product Code (UPC)—was first used in 1976. Today, UPC readers are found at many checkout counters. Using a laser beam to read the code, a UPC scanner can "ring up" sales much faster than a human cashier. And because the system reads the code and rings up the price automatically, the bar-code system is much more accurate than a cashier. At the same time, the system is constantly recording changes in product inventory. An up-to-date inventory for any item in stock is instantly available to management, thereby increasing a supermarket's efficiency and improving its service to customers.

Not surprisingly, bar-code systems are becoming increasingly popular for rapid and accurate input of data. Railroads, credit card companies, and various industries have begun to use bar codes instead of keyboard entry when up-to-date record keeping is essential.

APPLICATION

Optacon for the Blind

All the automatic recognition devices described in the preceding section have one feature in common: they all translate into machine-readable form the visual data that have been printed, written, or "blocked out" in some kind of pattern. Remarkable as these devices are, the computer's ability to translate one type of information into another has begun to produce even more remarkable applications.

Perhaps the most unusual application developed to date is a sensory aid for the blind known as *Optacon*. Essentially, Optacon is a direct translation reading device that converts visual images into tactile stimuli. The visual images are printed characters on the pages of a book, magazine, or newspaper. A camera, held by the user over the reading material, focuses the image on an integrated array of phototransistors. The output from this array is then electronically processed and converted into tactile stimuli. The output device is a field of tiny, electronically controlled pins protruding through perforations in a plastic plate. With one hand resting on the plate, the Optacon user receives an exact tactile facsimile of the printed character "observed" by the camera held in the other hand.

Several thousand Optacons are presently in use in the United States. There are also devices that can read a text and convert it to audio output. Scientists are working to develop other sensory aids for the handicapped. Among the most promising of these prosthetic devices are an auditory prosthesis that can be implanted in the inner ear of deaf individuals, and a visual prosthesis that would provide direct visual input to the brain. The bionic human may be closer to reality than we imagine.

The *terminal* is both an input and output (I/O) device. Because a terminal is in direct communication with a CPU, the keyboard input can elicit an instantaneous response that is output on either paper or a CRT screen. The interaction between input and output in such systems is so immediate that it is virtually impossible to separate them. However, some terminals may be used strictly for input, others strictly for output, and others for both functions. Terminals also make it possible to communicate with the CPU.

Terminals have had a tremendous impact on data entry. The more traditional methods of data entry—keypunch, key-to-tape, and key-to-disk—are usually performed at a central location. The trend now, however, is toward decentralized (or "distributed") input of data. Terminals can be scattered at various locations, and yet all are communicating with the same CPU. A familiar example of such a distributed system is the network of cash registers, or point-of-sale (POS) terminals, in a department store, all of which are online to a CPU in another office, building, and/or city. Less familiar is the system of the Library of Congress, in which some 1,500 terminals located in congressional offices, the Patent Office, and the library itself are connected to a single data processing center.

Data entry at such terminals is by keyboard or by an automatic recognition device, such as an OCR reader. These terminals provide additional functions; for example, a terminal user is able to edit data, access local files stored at a remote site, and even perform some remote-site processing. Indeed, the potential of terminals is developing so fast that they are becoming more and more like full-fledged computers.

Other Data Entry Devices

The automatic recognition devices discussed above partially or completely eliminate the intermediate steps of copying or processing that characterize keyboarding devices. Recent technology is responsible for several new directions in data entry equipment.

The Datapad. A device that enters data items directly on magnetic tape as they are being generated by the user is known as the Datapad. This new input medium consists essentially of a pressure-sensitive pad. The user first places a fill-in-the-blanks form on the pad and then hand-prints the data to be entered in the appropriate spaces. In this respect, the Datapad resembles mark-sense input. However, the mechanism by which it works is different. A sensing

105

device underneath the pad produces electrical signals that can be processed digitally. The data are displayed on a CRT screen for immediate verification, are available for processing, and are also entered on magnetic tape for storage. As with automatic recognition devices, one very important advantage of the Datapad is the reduced chance for error during data entry. This can produce substantial savings in time and money.

Voice recognition devices. For many years, science fiction writers have been imagining voice communication between computers and human beings. Today, the use of the human voice for data input is no longer a science fiction dream but a computer capability waiting to be fully developed and utilized.

Human voice input has obvious advantages: it can be used by operators who do not know how to type, permits the operator to move about, and frees the hands for other tasks. A voice recognition system was installed in the Missouri offices of the Monsanto Chemical Company, which had to absorb some 25,000 pieces of interoffice mail every day. Letter-sized mail was handled by an electronic sorter, but until that time larger mail had to be sorted manually. Now the mail sorter, who wears a microphone headset, simply reads aloud the initial of the addressee's name and the first four letters of the surname. A small CRT screen displays the addressee's name and the department or building to which the package should be sent. If two or more employees have the same first initial and first four letters in their surnames, the screen displays the full names of these employees so that the sorter can select the appropriate addressee. According to one official, this system doubled the rate at which oversized mail was processed.

Clearly, voice input is especially appropriate when the operator needs to have both hands free while entering data. It has many potential applications in manufacturing, such as for quality control, shipping and receiving, and various types of inspection. Such a system of data entry eliminates the need for the operator to stop and record data by writing down or keying it in. The time thus saved may itself pay for the cost of the system. In addition there are all the costs saved by not having to write, keypunch, or verify data input.

Output

The results of data processing operations performed by a computer are known as *output*. There exist a number of different kinds of devices for displaying these results to the user. Most output devices produce some form of print—on paper, cards, film, or screen. This very broad category of printers consists of both *hard-copy* devices, which produce printing on cards, paper, or some other tangible format, and *soft-copy* devices, in which printed output appears in transient form, as on a CRT screen. The overwhelming majority of print output devices produce hard copy.

There are a number of nonprint output devices as well. These may produce punched cards, microfilm, or graphic representations, or may record data on disks, in data cells, or on magnetic tape. Some of the newest output devices simulate the human voice.

The choice of which output device to use with which computer system is largely determined by the needs of the user and the characteristics of the system. Six factors are of particular importance in the choice of an output device:

(Bill Longcore)

In this computer installation, the operator stands in front of one printer; a printing terminal is in the foreground.

1. *Speed.* The printing speeds of print output devices range from 10 characters per second (cps) to 45,000 lines per minute (lpm). (In comparison, an expert typist may type 80 words per minute—about 7 characters per second or 9 lines per minute.) The choice of printer speed is usually related to the volume of output required and the amount of data generated by the computer system. Very high speed printers (4,000 lpm and up) are generally used for high-volume printing with large computer systems. High-speed printers (1,000 to 2,000 lpm) are usually associated with either medium- or large-scale computers. Low-speed printers (120 cps to 200 lpm) usually accompany minicomputers, small business systems, and terminals. Very low speed printers (10 to 100 cps) are seldom used for volume output. Rather, they are commonly used with terminals as console printers or for word processing.

2. *Print quality.* The clarity of print can be as important as speed in the choice of output devices. Depending on the device, print clarity ranges from letter quality to barely legible. A number of factors determine print quality, including the technology involved, quality and type of paper, and number of copies required. The use for which output is intended determines the clarity and legibility required.

3. *Direction of print.* Many output devices print in one direction only, from left to right. In recent years, however, several models have appeared that print in both directions (that is, one line left to right, the next line right to left). This two-directional ability increases printing speed.

(Courtesy of IBM)

The IBM 3211 high-speed printer

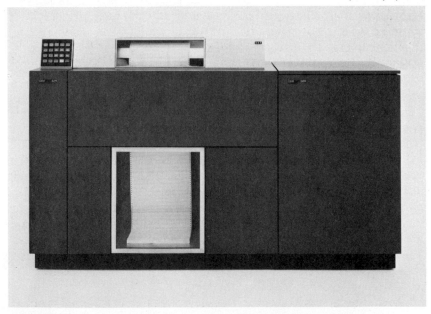

4. *Paper.* The quality and cost of paper are related factors that must also be considered. Paper quality influences the legibility of print. Also, the needs of the user will affect the choice of paper. Some hard-copy printers can make multiple carbon copies, whereas others print only one copy. Then there are some output printers that use ordinary paper, while others require specially treated paper. And either kind may or may not require additional "treatment," such as the use of special inks or specialized equipment. Printers usually are limited in the size and format of paper as well.

5. *Printer/terminal relationship.* Some of the output printing methods discussed in the following pages can be used with stand-alone devices as well as with terminals. This fact also plays a part in determining the choice of output device.

6. *Cost.* The initial purchase price of a printer may be anywhere from $500 to $300,000. In addition, operating costs must be taken into account. These include maintenance, consumables such as ink or ribbon, paper (plain, preprinted, or chemically treated), and additional printheads (which contain the type).

Hard-Copy Printers

The two major types of hard-copy devices are *impact* and *nonimpact* printers. Generally, impact printers work on much the same principle as a typewriter: an image of a character is made to strike against a printing medium such as paper, and an inked ribbon between the image and the paper reproduces the image as a printed character on the paper. In contrast, nonimpact printers use heat or chemical means to produce characters on specially treated paper. The application of heat or of a laser beam may transfer print to heat-sensitive paper. Metallic ink may be used on an electrostatic surface, or a jet of ink may be "sprayed" onto paper.

Hard-copy printers are also distinguished by the way in which a single character image is printed and/or by the way in which a whole line is printed.

A printed character may be either a *shaped* or a *dot matrix* character (see figure 4-9). A shaped character, like that produced by a standard typewriter, is a whole letter made up of solid lines. In dot matrix printing, by contrast, each individual printed character is actually composed of a group of dots. Often the dots are clearly visible, but some devices produce dots that are so fine and close together that the resulting printed characters are almost indistinguishable from the shaped variety. Either type of printing may be produced by impact or nonimpact devices.

A line of type may be printed character by character, or all at once.

(a)

(b)

These characters are formed on a 35-dot matrix.

Figure 4-9 Shaped characters (a) and dot matrix characters (b)

109

Character-by-character printing is called *serial* printing if the letters are formed in series, or sequentially. *Line* printers print an entire line of type all at once. In actuality, this distinction between line and serial printing is partly illusion. A line printer starts printing a line only after it has been given the full text of that line. It can then print the line sequentially, one or several characters at a time. But it prints so rapidly that it appears that the line is being typed all at one time.

Impact printers. Impact printing devices have in common that they produce characters on a print medium such as paper by means

Table 4-2 Key Features of Impact Printer Technologies

Technology	Type	Speed	Advantages	Limitations	Price Range
Cylinder	Serial	10 cps	Low cost	Slow speed, low reliability, low print quality, noisy	$1,000 to $2,000
Ball	Serial	to 15 cps	Excellent print quality, large character set, interchangeable fonts, low cost	Slow speed, relatively noisy	$2,000 to $5,000
Daisy wheel	Serial	30 to 55 cps	Good reliability, good print quality, interchangeable fonts, higher speed than ball	Slower speed than matrix	$1,400 to $7,000
Impact matrix	Serial or line	30 to 330 cps (serial), to 600 lpm (line)	High resolution with dense matrix, ROM changeable fonts, graphics capability, medium speed	Low reliability with high-duty cycles, low resolution with sparse dot matrix	$1,000 to $10,000
Drum	Line	300 to 2,000 lpm	High reliability, good medium- to high-duty cycle	Limited character fonts, slight vertical misregistration	$10,000 to $60,000
Chain or train	Line	300 to 2,000 lpm	Good print quality, interchangeable character sets, up to 128 characters	Chain or train track wear	$10,000 to $112,000
Band or belt	Line	30 cps to 3,000 lpm	Interchangeable fonts, good print quality, high reliability	Belt and drive wear, entire band replacement for individual worn character	$3,000 to $87,000

Reprinted by permission from *Computer Design* magazine. © Computer Design Publishing Corp., January 1979.

of mechanical or electromechanical technology. Within this category, though, there are a number of distinctive printing methods. Table 4-2 summarizes the key features of impact printers.

Dot matrix printers. The dots that constitute a printed matrix character are commonly produced by a set of needles or wires. In the device that makes the impression on the paper, usually called the printhead, the needles or wires are arranged in a vertical column or columns. As the printhead moves across a page, the needles are selectively pressed against the paper (and an intervening ribbon) to produce the desired printed characters. In serial printers, each movement of the printhead across the page produces one line of print. In line printers, the needles or wires are mounted on a horizontal bar, or "comb." The printhead prints one row of character dots at a time, and complete characters are formed as the paper moves up one row at a time. Impact serial matrix printers range in speed from 30 to 330 cps; line matrix printers, up to 600 lpm.

A matrix is the array of dots (columns of wires or needles) used to form a single character. Dot matrix arrays range in size from 35 dots (a 5-by-7-dot matrix) up to 1,500 dots (a 30-by-50-dot matrix). A matrix array that is from 1 to 8 vertical dots deep can print both above and below the line. That is, it can print superscripts, subscripts, and letters that ascend above or descend below the line, such as "d" and "p." In matrices of fewer than about 100 dots, the individual dots of each character are clearly visible. A matrix of 200 dots or more can produce letters more or less indistinguishable from shaped characters.

One of the great advantages of matrix printing is its flexibility in "setting" different typefaces. Changing from one font, style, or number of characters to another usually requires no more than substituting one read-only-memory (ROM) chip for another. The general price range of impact matrix printers is from as little as $1,000 to as much as $10,000.

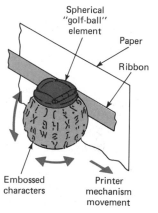

Figure 4-10 **A ball printer**
A ball or sphere rotates on its axis to move selected embossed characters into position against an inked ribbon. The character pushes the ribbon against the paper to print.

Reprinted by permission from Computer Design magazine. © *Computer Design Publishing Corp., January 1979.*

Serial character printers. As the name indicates, serial character printers will print characters one at a time in sequence across a page. Although some serial character printers have speeds of up to 120 cps, most print at speeds of 10 to 30 cps. A variety of impact and nonimpact devices employ serial character printing. Of the impact serial character printers, the best known are the *ball, daisy wheel,* and *cylinder.* Nonimpact printers are discussed on pages 115–21.

A *ball* printer employs a spherical printhead (the "ball") with a set of characters embossed on or slightly raised above its surface. (A well-known example is used on the IBM Selectric typewriter.) The ball rotates on its axis to move a selected character into position. The

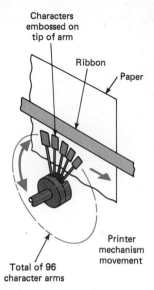

Characters embossed on tip of arm

Ribbon

Paper

Printer mechanism movement

Total of 96 character arms

Figure 4-11 A daisy wheel printer
A set of spokes, each having a single character embossed on its end, radiates from a central wheel, or hub. The hub rotates to bring the selected character into position, where a hammer mechanism pushes it against the inked ribbon and the paper.

© Computer Design Publishing Corp.

Figure 4-12 A cylinder printer
Characters are embossed in a series of rings around a cylindrical printhead. The cylinder is rotated and shifted up and down on its axis to move the selected character into position. As a hammer strikes the cylinder, the character is pushed against the inked ribbon and the paper.

© Computer Design Publishing Corp.

ball itself strikes the paper (with the ribbon between them). A movement mechanism shifts the ball horizontally to print a line while the paper remains stationary. (See figure 4-10.)

Ball printers have speeds up to 15 cps. Such low print speeds are a major limitation of ball printers, which also tend to be relatively noisy. In their favor, however, is the fact that they can produce excellent quality print at low cost. The character sets are large and interchangeable. Changing a font is simply a matter of changing the ball printhead. The general price range of ball printers is between $2,000 and $5,000.

The *daisy wheel* printhead consists of a set of 96 "spokes" radiating from a hub. (The appearance of this device led to its name, but it is something of a misnomer, since the "wheel" has no rim.) Each spoke has on its end a tiny plate or tab with a single character embossed on it. The hub rotates to move the selected character into position: a hammer mechanism strikes the tab, impressing it against the ribbon and paper. As with ball printers, the printhead moves horizontally while the paper remains stationary. (See figure 4-11.)

Daisy wheel printers have speeds of 30 to 55 cps. Their advantages include good print quality, interchangeable fonts, and reliability. They are faster than ball printers but slower than matrix printers. They range in price from about $1,500 to $7,000.

Cylinder impact printers employ a cylindrical printhead with characters embossed in a series of rings. To move a character into place, the cylinder can shift up or down as well as rotate. A character is impressed on the ribbon and paper by a hammer striking the cylinder. A movement mechanism shifts the cylinder horizontally as it prints a line. (See figure 4-12.)

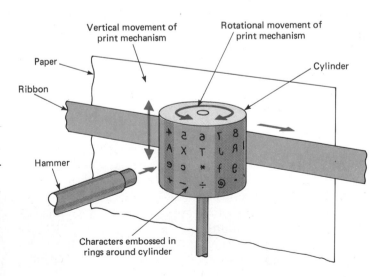

Vertical movement of print mechanism

Rotational movement of print mechanism

Paper

Cylinder

Ribbon

Hammer

Characters embossed in rings around cylinder

Cylinder impact printers are very slow, with a standard speed of 10 cps. Other limitations include poor print quality, noisiness, and low reliability. Their great advantage is low cost. Cylinder printers range in price from about $1,000 to $2,000.

Line printers. Line printers can be both impact and nonimpact devices. Because line printers print a whole line at a time, it is not surprising that they are generally much faster than serial printers. Overall, line speeds range from as slow as 30 cps to about 3,000 lpm for impact printers, and as high as 45,000 lpm for generally high-speed nonimpact printers. Printers with speeds of less than 300 lpm are usually rated as having low speeds. Medium-speed printers produce between 300 and 600 lpm. Anything above 600 lpm is considered high speed. Line printers are not only faster, but they are also technologically more complex, and therefore more expensive, than serial printers. Nonimpact line printers (those that employ electronic and xerographic techniques) can cost as much as $300,000. Impact line printers are generally less costly, ranging in price from $3,000 to over $100,000. The best known and most widely used of the impact line printers are *chain*, *band*, and *drum*.

In *chain*, or train, printers, the printhead is a series of metal slugs with characters embossed on them. The slugs are either connected to pull one another along a horizontal track (chain), or they are unconnected and push one another along (train). Opposite the horizontal array of character slugs is an array of hammers, with one hammer for each print position in the line. When a selected character is in place, the corresponding hammer strikes, pressing the paper and ribbon against the character slug. (See figure 4-13.)

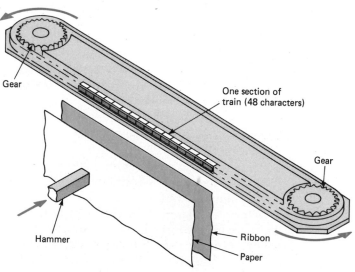

Gear

One section of train (48 characters)

Gear

Hammer

Ribbon

Paper

Figure 4-13 **A chain or train printer**
Paper is inserted between a horizontally moving array of character slugs and a set of hammers. There is one hammer for each print position, and each selected hammer pushes the paper against the appropriate character as it is rotated into position.

© Computer Design Publishing Corp.

113

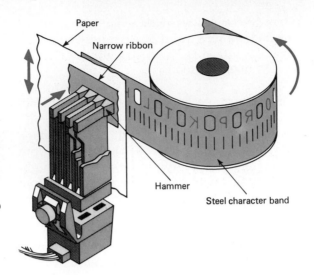

Paper

Narrow ribbon

Hammer

Steel character band

Figure 4-14 A band or belt printer
A band of embossed characters (or a belt of character slugs) moves past the paper and inked ribbon. The appropriate characters are moved into position as the hammers are activated.

© *Computer Design Publishing Corp.*

Chain and train printers range in speed from 300 to 2,000 lpm. They produce good quality print and have interchangeable fonts of up to 128 characters. Their chief limitation is wear and tear on the track carrying the chain or train. They range in price from $10,000 to more than $100,000.

Band, or belt, printers are similar to chain printers except that their characters are embossed on a metal band, or belt. (One variant uses a polyurethane belt with metal slugs.) Again, as with chain printers, the band moves past an array of hammers. When a hammer strikes, it presses the paper and ribbon against the character. (See figure 4-14.)

Band printer speeds range from as low as 30 cps to as high as 3,000 lpm. Their major advantages include good print quality, interchangeable fonts, and high reliability. Their greatest limitations are vulnerability to wear at speeds above 600 lpm and the necessity of replacing the entire band when a single character becomes worn. Prices range from $3,000 to $90,000.

The operating principle of *drum* printers is much like that of chain and band printers. Characters, arranged in rings of 64, are embossed on a cylindrical rotating drum. As the drum turns on its long axis, the various characters pass an array of hammers. The stroke of a hammer drives the paper and ribbon against a particular character on the drum. (See figure 4-15.)

The range of printing speeds for drum printers is from 300 to 2,000 lpm. They are highly reliable and wear better than either chain or band printers, and are generally used in association with medium- or large-scale computers. Their character fonts are limited,

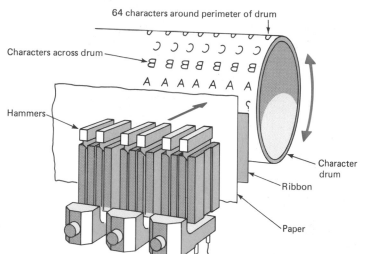

64 characters around perimeter of drum

Characters across drum

Hammers

Character drum

Ribbon

Paper

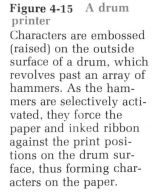

Figure 4-15 A drum printer
Characters are embossed (raised) on the outside surface of a drum, which revolves past an array of hammers. As the hammers are selectively activated, they force the paper and inked ribbon against the print positions on the drum surface, thus forming characters on the paper.

© *Computer Design Publishing Corp.*

however, and they have a tendency to print a slightly uneven line. Drum printers range in price from $10,000 to $60,000.

Nonimpact printers. While the impact devices just discussed generally involve mechanical or electromechanical technologies, nonimpact printing employs a wide variety of technologies. Nonim-

(UPI)

A technician placing a font strip on the wheel of a computerized typesetter at Compugraphic Corporation. The font strip is a photographic negative containing complete sets of characters in different typefaces. As the wheel turns at 1,500 revolutions per minute, light is beamed through the negative to produce character images on paper. The speed of this nonimpact print makes phototypesetting feasible for small businesses and publications.

115

Table 4-3 Key Features of Nonimpact Printer Technologies

Technology	Type	Speed	Advantages	Limitations	Price Range
Thermal matrix	Serial	30 to 120 cps	Low cost, low noise	Slow speed, special paper, no preprinted forms	$1,000 to $5,000
Electro-sensitive	Serial	160 to 2,200 cps	Low cost, medium speed	Special paper, wrinkles easily, attracts fingerprints, low print quality	$400 to $3,000
Electro-static	Line	300 to 18,000 lpm	Graphics capability, versatile fonts, high speed	Special paper, wet toner	$5,000 to $165,000
Xerographic	Line	4,000 to 14,000 lpm	High speed, high resolution, quiet, multiple character sets, 132-column wide data, eliminates preprinted forms	High cost, high maintenance, high-volume applications	$145,000 to $310,000
Ink-jet	Serial or line	30 cps to 45,000 lpm	Plain paper, forms flexibility including envelopes, quiet, high resolution at low speeds	Reduced print quality at high speeds, reduced reliability	$2,500 to $25,000 $5,800/month

Note: All nonimpact printers have matrix-generated type fonts, and all are limited to single-copy output.
Reprinted by permission from *Computer Design* magazine. © Computer Design Publishing Corp., January 1979.

pact printers have a number of advantages in common when compared with impact printers, but they are generally two to ten times faster, much more flexible in their ability to produce different page layouts, and much quieter, a feature that can be important to potential users.

The major disadvantage of nonimpact printers in comparison with the impact variety is that every document they produce is an original; they cannot make multiple or carbon copies. This limitation has, in particular, prevented the use of some nonimpact printers with computer terminals. Nonimpact printers are also generally more expensive than impact printers, with some devices costing more than $300,000. Table 4-3 summarizes the key features of nonimpact printers.

One way to categorize nonimpact printers is by their use of plain or specially treated paper. For instance, thermal matrix, electrostatic, and electrosensitive printing techniques all make use of specially treated paper. Xerographic and ink-jet printing both employ plain paper. The following is a brief survey of the most important nonimpact printing techniques: *thermal matrix, laser, electronic, xerographic,* and *ink-jet.*

Thermal matrix printers take their name from the type of printhead they use. It consists of an array of printing elements with tiny rods coated with silicon or some other material that acts like an electrical resistor. A small current passing through an element heats each rod. When the printhead is moved over a special heat-sensitive paper, the result is a pattern of dots, depending on which elements in the printhead have been heated. The thermal paper contains a very thin coating of particles of two heat-sensitive substances. Wherever heat is applied, the coating fuses and the two substances flow together, producing a colored image. Blue and black are the usual print colors. Most thermal matrix printers use a printhead with a 5-by-7 array of dot elements. Characters are printed either by moving the printhead across the paper or by moving the paper past a full-width printhead. (See figure 4-16.)

Thermal matrix devices are serial and have printing speeds of 30 to 120 cps. Despite such low speeds, however, thermal matrix printers are more widely used than any other kind of nonimpact printer. The reasons for their popularity are fairly simple. They are relatively inexpensive—in the $1,000 to $5,000 range. More important, they are mechanically simpler, with no hammers, ribbons, chains, or belts, and are thus less vulnerable to wear than many other devices. Moreover, thermal printers are quiet, clean, and compact. These three features make them ideal for use with desktop computers and terminals. But there are drawbacks as well. These include the cost of

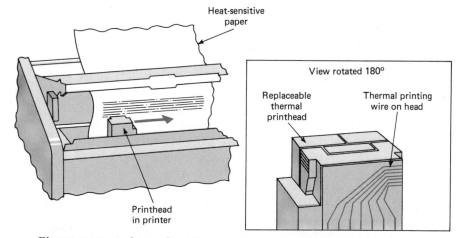

Figure 4-16   A thermal matrix printer
Characters are formed by a selectively heated printhead as it moves across the printing surface. The heat-sensitive paper changes color where heat has been applied.

thermal paper, which is significantly higher than that of plain paper. In addition, thermal paper remains somewhat sensitive to sunlight and heat after it has been printed. Consequently, the printed images are less permanent (and potentially harder to copy) than those produced by impact printing. Finally, like other nonimpact printers, the thermal type cannot produce multiple copies.

Technologically, *laser* printers are much more advanced than thermal output devices. They are correspondingly faster and more expensive. In this type of printing, a low-power laser beam exposes selected areas of the light-sensitive surface of a rotating drum. A dry, powderlike ink is applied to the drum as it turns. This ink adheres only to areas that have been exposed to laser beams, and is then transferred to plain paper to produce printed characters. The dot matrix used in laser printers is extremely fine and usually consists of about 45,000 dots. (See figure 4-17.)

One of the great advantages of laser printers is their speed. The popular IBM 3800 prints over 13,000 lpm; but several other models have speeds of more than 20,000 lpm. Another great advantage is the almost unlimited flexibility in choice of typeface and page format. Laser printers also have fewer moving parts and therefore are more reliable. They can also print on any kind of paper.

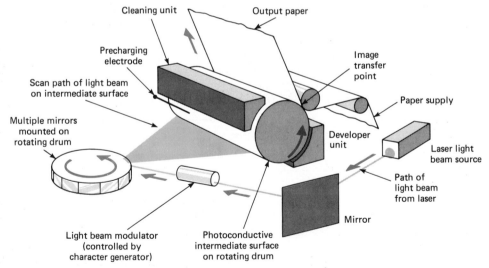

Figure 4-17   A laser or xerographic printer
The basic design of both laser and xerographic printers is similar. In both technologies, a light source produces an image on an intermediate photo-sensitive surface that is coated with an ink powder; the image is electro-statically transferred to the output paper.

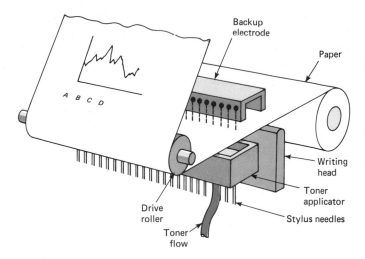

Backup electrode

Paper

A B C D

Writing head

Toner applicator

Stylus needles

Drive roller

Toner flow

Figure 4-18 **An electrostatic printer**
Specially coated paper is passed over an array of stylus needles. When electric current is applied to selected needles, characters are formed on the paper as electrically charged spots. The paper then passes through toner and the charged areas develop into black print.

© *Computer Design Publishing Corp.*

Despite these considerable advantages, laser printers have several important limitations. They require a flat paper surface for printing, and they can print only one sheet at a time. In both respects they are more restricting than ink-jet printers (see below).

The price range for laser printers is quite broad, from $25,000 to $325,000.

Electronic printers are of two different kinds, both requiring an electrical charge and special paper. In *electrostatic* printers the printhead is a stationary array of stylus needles to which voltages can be selectively applied. The specially coated paper used is dielectric; that is, it can build up and hold an electric charge. As the paper passes over the printhead, the charged stylus needles produce electrically charged spots on the paper. The paper then passes through a toner, which adheres to the charged spots and thereby forms the printed characters. (See figure 4-18.)

Electrostatic printers have a speed range from 300 to 18,000 lpm. They are flexible in choice of font and can produce graphics. But their chief advantage is their relatively low cost when compared to impact printers with similar speeds. Even so, some models are quite expensive; prices range from $5,000 to $165,000. The main disadvantages of electrostatic printers are that they require special paper and a wet toner.

The printhead of *electrosensitive* printers is movable rather than stationary. The paper has a thin metallic coating and a black underlayer. Voltage can be selectively applied to the stylus matrix in the printhead. As it passes over the paper, the matrix head selectively "burns" away the metallic coating, thereby exposing the black underlayer, which appears as printed characters. (See figure 4-19.)

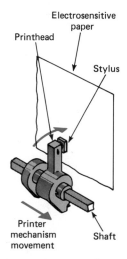

Electrosensitive paper

Printhead

Stylus

Printer mechanism movement

Shaft

Figure 4-19 **An electrosensitive printer**
Electric current is selectively applied to the printhead as it moves across specially coated paper. The current burns away the coating, exposing the underlayer that forms the characters.

© *Computer Design Publishing Corp.*

119

Electrosensitive printers are serial and are considerably slower than the electrostatic variety, with speeds ranging from 160 to 2,200 cps. They have an important advantage in their very low cost. Prices range from as low as $400 to $3,000. Their main disadvantages are the special paper required, which wrinkles and smudges, and the low print quality.

Xerographic printing, also known as electrophotographic printing, is an electrostatic process very much like that first used in Xerox copying machines. The technology depends on the photoconductive properties of materials such as selenium, which can hold an electrical charge but loses it when exposed to light. In xerographic printing, a selenium-coated plate or drum is first electrically charged. The image to be printed is then projected on the surface through a lens or by laser beams. In effect, the charged surface is exposed to light except for those areas where the image is to appear. When negatively charged toner is applied to the surface, it adheres only to the positively charged areas. Then the paper to be printed is placed over the surface and given a positive electric charge. As a result, the dry ink remaining on the plate or drum is attracted to the paper. The image is made permanent by the application of heat, which fuses the ink to the paper. The mechanism is similar to that of laser printers; see figure 4-17.

Xerographic printers have speeds ranging from 4,000 to 14,000 lpm. Their chief advantages are high speed and high resolution. But they also have a variety of fonts and are quiet. At the same time, their maintenance requirements are high, and they are expensive—prices range from $145,000 to over $300,000. They are most cost-efficient when used for high-volume applications.

Ink-jet printing is exactly what its name suggests: A tiny stream of charged ink droplets is jet-sprayed onto paper or some other print

Figure 4-20 An ink-jet printer
Ink injection chambers, when set in motion by an electric charge, spray ink to form matrix-type characters on the print surface.

© *Computer Design Publishing Corp.*

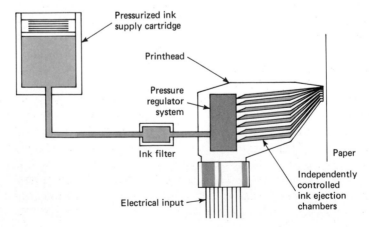

Pressurized ink supply cartridge

Printhead

Pressure regulator system

Ink filter

Electrical input

Paper

Independently controlled ink ejection chambers

medium to form the desired character image. Because the ink stream passes through an electric or magnetic field, it can be deflected to the appropriate spots on the print medium. The characters printed are matrix images. An ink-jet printer, in effect, spray-paints the characters on the print medium. (See figure 4-20.)

Ink-jet devices may be serial or line. Accordingly, their print-speed range is very broad, going from 30 cps at the low end to 45,000 lpm at the high end. The IBM 3890 check processor is a specialized ink-jet device. It prints numbers in a unique sequence on checks that pass by its ink jets at a rate of almost 31 feet per second, spraying 130,000 droplets of ink per second, to imprint as many as 40 checks per minute.

Perhaps the greatest advantage of ink-jet printers is the ability to print on almost any surface, from envelopes and boxes to tin cans and even fruit (for example, the name "Sunkist" on oranges). They are quiet and have excellent print quality at low speeds. At higher speeds, however, both printer reliability and print quality are reduced. Prices range from $2,500 to $25,000.

Soft-Copy Printers

Any discussion of soft-copy printers is necessarily a discussion of terminals with CRT display screens. (Terminals are discussed in detail on page 125.) Here we will briefly survey some of the capabilities and uses of the most visible part of soft-copy printers, the display screen.

Terminals with CRT display screens are now the most common type of terminal. Anyone who has operated such a system, or watched someone else operate it, can easily appreciate both their appeal and their potential. The terminals described in the application at the beginning of this chapter, widely used in banking, are a familiar example. The copy displayed on a CRT screen can be edited to varying degrees and, depending on the system, may be presented in a variety of formats. Indeed, the terminal/CRT combination has capabilities for revising copy that are simply not available with hard-copy printers.

To cite one of the most important applications, many newspapers and magazines in the United States today have their copy set at a terminal keyboard and edited on CRT screens. All stories are stored in memory. To edit a particular news item or story, an editor simply "calls it up" and the first 15 or 20 lines appear on the screen. A "forward" key allows the editor to read successive lines as the computer scans them. Another key reverses this progression; still another produces a quick "jump" from the last line of copy to the beginning,

121

instead of following the slower process of backtracking. The editor can stop at any point along the way and revise a letter, a line, or an entire paragraph. Such editing is done with the aid of a cursor, which usually appears as a small, bright rectangle, or "blip," on the screen. The cursor can be moved to any part of the screen where the editor wants to make a revision. After any change, the computer automatically adjusts the lengths of all successive lines.

Some systems have a split-screen capability, in which old and revised versions of the same story can be viewed side by side. Many such systems also provide a variety of formats and will calculate the amount of space that an item will take up in, say, one width of column as compared with another. It is also possible to determine the amount of space required for a story that starts in one column width and is continued in a different column width. And the most sophisticated systems can display—two facing pages at a time—the actual final format as it will appear when printed, including the space for pictures and advertisements! Finally, some systems allow the operator to do a certain amount of programming in advance—for example, by storing a set of editing instructions in the computer.

These are only a few common examples of what is being done today with CRT display systems. The potential of this kind of soft-copy printing is clear. One of the more remarkable recent applications to develop is computer graphics—the capability of displaying computer-generated drawings and illustrations. Some CRT screens display graphics in color. Computer graphics is a young but expanding area. Full utilization of computer graphics is still a number of years in the future.

Other Forms of Output

Hard-copy and soft-copy printing are by no means the only forms of output available. There are at least five others worth noting: *card-punch; microfilm* and *microfiche; plotter;* and *voice.* Some of these, such as card-punch output, have been in use for a relatively long time. Others, such as voice output, have yet to be fully developed.

Card-punch output. Card-punching devices receive output data from the computer and translate the information into holes punched in cards. These devices usually have a "reading" mechanism as well, to verify that the newly punched code is the correct one. The punched cards are the familiar 80- or 96-column types used for data input. As output, punched cards have much the same advantages and disadvantages that they do as input. They are readable by humans, are usually unit records, and are inexpensive. On the other hand, they cannot be read rapidly. Reading speeds for output data from punched cards range from 100 to 1,000 cards per minute. Magnetic tape data can be read a hundred times faster. Also, punched cards cannot be reused and are bulky. For example, the data density of punched cards is one-thousandth that of magnetic tape.

Micrographics. One of the most serious problems facing the computer industry today is a problem of its own making—the mountains of paper generated each day by computers. One solution to this problem is to reduce computer output documents to a much smaller size by means of *micrographics*. This term refers to two methods of recording data on film—*microfiche* and *microfilm*.

In the microfiche process, a large number of documents can be recorded on a single strip of 105-mm film (4 by 6 inches is a common size) that typically contains 200 frames or pages of content. The advantages of microfiche include the ability to record on unused portions of the film at any time and the fact that the film can be randomly accessed. In the older and more familiar microfilm process, documents are recorded sequentially on a spool of film. Documents are also updated and retrieved sequentially. Both types of film can be read easily on desktop viewers.

An important recent advance in micrographic processes is *computer output microfilm* (COM) recording of data. COM recorders are flexible and can provide computer output in either microfiche or microfilm form. Some can produce both 16-mm and 35-mm film in both black and white and color. Moreover, the output speeds are high—between 5,000 and 30,000 lpm. These speeds compare very favorably with the high-speed nonimpact printers now available. And the average cost of a COM printer is less than half that of the nonimpact type.

Graphic plotting. *Plotters* are printing devices that use matrix technology to plot data graphically at a density of 100 dots per inch. Plotting technology, when combined with color graphics and print capability, has numerous applications in such fields as industrial design, advertising, marketing, architecture, and more. This is as yet an expensive system, which has limited applications thus far.

Voice output. All the various forms of output discussed thus far are visual. They must be read. For some purposes, however, it would be more convenient and more effective if the output could be listened to rather than read, especially if the output took the form of words spoken by a human voice. We have already seen some of the advantages of being able to enter data by means of voice input. How much more advantageous the human/computer interaction would be if the computer could talk back. The idea of "conversations" between humans and computers is certainly a fascinating one. But what is more interesting is that not only does the technology for such voice communication exist—it is actually being used in a variety of applications.

For example, one area making increased use of *voice output* is that of specialized call-in services, such as "banking by phone" or "banking from home," which some banks now provide. The state of Illinois recently installed what is believed to be the first computerized credit card telecommunications system with both voice input and output. In making a credit card call, the user speaks directly with the host computer, which can ask questions and give instructions. With a communications system already available in the telephone system, other applications for voice output are not hard to find. Reservations systems, merchandise ordering, and inventory checking are only a few of the possibilities.

A relatively new development on the computer market is the voice synthesizer module, such as the one designed for the TRS-80 computer. This device, the size of a small hi-fi speaker, can produce almost any word in the English language and many foreign words as well. Words are produced by synthesizing separate speech units, or phonemes; the TRS-80 accessory, for example, produces 62 electronic phonemes that can be electronically combined into word sequences. It may serve as a vocal supplement to the video display or printer and repeat what has been printed, or it may be used alone.

The capability for verbalizing computer output has almost endless potential. Possible applications include games, computer-aided instruction, alarm systems, and terminals for blind users. It is also obvious that such a capability will eliminate the need for terminals in many applications. Banking by phone, for example, would make a keyboard and CRT unnecessary. It has been predicted that voice output will become as important in the future as hard-copy and CRT output are now.

Future Developments in Output

Computer technology has been characterized by such rapid development and a variety of equipment and applications that it is difficult to foresee the next developments in data output. Nonetheless, several trends that are quite clearly established at present are expected to continue for some time and can give us a reliable glimpse especially of the not-too-distant future.

We can expect to see further cost reductions, especially where electronic output technologies are concerned. Computer systems will be increasingly adapted to xerographic, micrographic, and graphic output and to providing output on request. As these media are increasingly utilized, there will be a corresponding decrease in the use of preprinted forms as an output medium. This will be possible because the newer technologies provide greater flexibility in choice of font and page layout. Output formats will be more and more determined by the user, and will be controlled by software as needed.

The trend toward user-designed output will combine with extended use of online terminals to accelerate two other trends: increasing decentralization and greater availability to a larger number of users. As communications between user and computer advance, the user will be able to operate a computer from remote sites. Conversely, the expansion of remote-site access will provide increased availability to a variety of users. The day of individual computers is fast approaching.

Terminals as I/O Devices

The development of terminals has been so rapid in the past few years that one could examine a different model every day and not have seen them all by the end of a year. The increase in the number of terminal models has been paralleled by an increasing sophistication in terminal capability. It is now possible, and even necessary, to distinguish *dumb* from *smart* terminals and to distinguish both from *intelligent* terminals. These categories are not strictly exclusive and have nothing to do with IQ. Instead, they describe the general capabilities of terminals.

"Dumb" is now the accepted term for CRT terminals that have *minimum* capabilities. In its most basic form, a dumb terminal consists of a keyboard, a CRT display screen, and a communication line to a CPU. In use it serves as a simple input/output device. The demand for dumb terminals has grown, however, and manufacturers have added other features accordingly. These include upper- and lower-case type; a numeric pad (like the number keys on a calculator); and a cursor or other form of on-screen locating device. These terminals now cost less than $1,000.

A "smart" terminal has all the features of a dumb terminal plus others, up to—but not including—user programmability. For example, the visual capabilities include *blinking* (to draw attention to a particular type of data item on the screen), *underlining*, and *dual intensity* (the highlighting of some section of the display to distin-

125

guish it from the other parts). Other important features include improved transmission, formatting, and communications, as well as editing functions. Smart terminals range in price from $1,000 to $5,000 and are especially useful for word processing applications.

Smart terminals also have read-only memories (ROM). That is what distinguishes them from "intelligent" terminals, which have random-access memories (RAM). Intelligent terminals have many of the features to be found in smart terminals, but they also have a processor as well as a RAM and can "make decisions." Some compare favorably with minicomputers in terms of general capability. The cost of intelligent terminals starts at about $25,000.

The terminal—dumb, smart, or intelligent—is rapidly becoming the most visible piece of computer hardware. For example, point-of-sale terminals have just about replaced the electromechanical cash register. Among the advantages of such terminal applications is accuracy of sales data, rapid reporting of inventory and sales information to management, and more legible bills and receipts for the customer. Department store chains, hospitals that have to bill for Medicare reimbursements, and airlines wishing to improve or expand their reservation systems—all have found that terminals pay for themselves many times over.

These applications are only the beginning, however. Terminals already can provide hard- or soft-copy output. But one now available has a bubble memory printer! The next step is a bubble memory CRT. As microprocessors in terminals decrease the cost of these devices, and as communications improve and decentralization increases, the distinction between terminal and computer will become more and more hazy. The unmistakable trend is in the direction of terminals so powerful that they will be practically indistinguishable from small computer systems.

Summary

Input devices enter raw information or user questions into computers. *Output* devices take the processed data of a computer and provide or display this output in the form of data, information, or answers. Devices called *terminals* perform both input and output functions and are often referred to as I/O (input/output) devices. Some terminals are multifunctional devices—they can serve both as "stand-alone" input devices (with no computer involvement) and as terminals.

The choice of input/output device is determined by the intended system application. One important consideration is whether data items should be processed only after being collected in groups, or batches (*batch processing*), or be processed individually as they are entered (*online processing*). In applications requiring constant and immediate updating, such as reservations systems, online processing is the obvious choice. Where such updating is not required, as in payroll check processing, batch processing might be preferable.

Input *keyboarding devices* include three types: keypunch, key-to-tape, and key-to-disk mechanisms. *Automatic recognition devices* include magnetic ink character recognition (MICR), optical character recognition (OCR), mark sensing, Optical Mark Read (OMR), and bar-code readers, each of which "recognizes" specially printed material. Direct communication devices include the pressure-sensitive Datapad and voice recognition machines.

Card punching is still the most widely used method of data entry. Punched cards are a unit record medium (that is, they carry a complete record of a transaction) and can be processed individually. The standard 80-column card represents the Hollerith code, consisting of 10 digit or numeric rows (0 through 9) and three zone rows (12, 11, and 10), with an interpretation in the print area at the top. Punched cards may be divided into information fields of one or more columns. The more recent 96-column card is about one-third as large as the Hollerith card and can hold 20 percent more data.

The *keypunch*, or *card punch*, transcribes input from source documents by punching holes in cards according to the Hollerith code. The accuracy of transcription must then be verified. Other devices used in processing cards include: the *verifier, verifying punch, sorter, reproducer, interpreter,* and *collator.*

Punched cards have several drawbacks as an input medium: they have limited record content, are not reusable, are relatively slow, require considerable storage space, and are vulnerable to damage by human operators and by machines.

Key-to-tape and key-to-disk input systems resemble keypunch devices but record data in the form of magnetic "spots." Verification can usually be performed on the input device itself. When compared with key-punch systems, the magnetic media are reusable, can hold more data, are faster for transcription, data input, and accessing, and require less storage space.

Other input methods reduce or eliminate the copying step between the source document and data entry, but are limited in the kinds of input they can receive. MICR devices can transcribe data printed in magnetic ink. OCR devices can "read" a special typeface and some printed and handwritten characters. Mark-sense devices "read" pencil marks made in specific areas on a printed form. A bar code, usually the Universal Product Code (UPC) on packaged grocery items, is also computer-readable. The Datapad and voice recognition are two other input techniques. Most important and increasingly prevalent is the terminal keyboard.

Output may be hard copy, soft copy, or in some other form. Hard-copy devices include impact and nonimpact printers. Impact printers are designed on the same basic principle as a typewriter: a key is struck against a printing medium, such as paper, to produce a printed character. Nonimpact printers achieve the same effect by a variety of means, including "burning" and "spraying" the image on the paper. These printers may produce *shaped* (that is, whole) or *dot matrix* characters. They may also be *serial* (that is, character by character) or *line printers*.

The major advantage of impact printers is the ability to produce multiple copies; that of nonimpact, their generally greater speed.

The major types of impact printers are: (1) *dot matrix*; (2) *serial character* (the *ball, daisy wheel,* and *cylinder*); and (3) *line printers* (*chain, band,* and *drum*).

The major types of nonimpact printers are: (1) *thermal matrix*; (2) *laser*; (3) *electronic* (electrostatic, electrosensitive); (4) *xerographic*; and (5) *ink-jet*.

Soft-copy printers produce images on a display screen such as a CRT. This kind of display always appears in association with a terminal.

Other forms of output include: *card-punch output; microfiche, microfilm,* and *computer output microfilm (COM); plotters;* and *voice output*.

Dumb terminals have minimum capabilities. *Smart terminals* have additional capabilities such as editing but cannot be user-programmed. *Intelligent terminals* can be programmed by the user.

Key Terms and Phrases

ball printer	dot matrix	intelligent terminals
band printer	character	interpreter
bar codes	drum printer	keypunch
batch processing	dumb terminals	key-to-disk devices
card-punch output	electronic printer	key-to-tape devices
chain printer	field	laser printer
collator	hard-copy printers	line printer
computer output	impact printers	magnetic ink
microfilm (COM)	ink-jet printer	character recognition (MICR)
cylinder printer	input/output (I/O)	
daisy wheel printer	devices	mark-sense input

microfiche
microfilm
nonimpact printers
online processing
optical character
   recognition (OCR)
Optical Mark
   Read (OMR)

plotters
reproducer
serial printer
shaped character
smart terminals
soft-copy printers
sorter
terminal

thermal matrix
   printer
verifier
verifying punch
voice output
xerographic
   printer

Feidelman, Lawrence. "The New Look of Data Entry." *Infosystems*, no. 12 (1977):46−51.

Gargagliano, Tim, and Fons, Kathryn. "The TRS-80 Speaks." *Byte*, no. 10 (1970):113−22.

Hansen, John R. "Retail Terminals Mind the Store." *Infosystems*, no. 3 (1979):54−58.

Kelley, Neil D. "What's Happening in Terminals." *Infosystems*, no. 3 (1978):82−84.

Kuhn, Larry, and Myers, Robert A. "Ink-Jet Printing." *Scientific American*, April 1979, pp. 162−77.

Lusa, John M. "Going to the Source." *Infosystems*, no. 4 (1979):52−56.

Miller, Frederick W. "Computer Talk." *Infosystems*, no. 8 (1979):68−69.

Myers, Ware. "Interactive Computer Graphics: Part I." *Computer*, no. 7 (1979):8−15.

Stiefel, Malcom L. "Line Printers." *Mini-Micro Systems*, no. 1 (1979):40−52.

———. "Non-programmable CRT Terminals." *Mini-Micro Systems*, no. 7 (1979):78−91.

Strassmann, Paul A., and Willard, Charles F. "The Evolution of the Page Printer." *Datamation*, no. 5 (1978):167−70.

Wieselman, Irving L. "Trends in Computer Printer Technology." *Computer Design*, no. 1 (1979):107−15.

Sources of Additional Information

Test Yourself

1. The type of I/O device used with a computer system depends on the type of processing employed. What are the two types of processing?
2. It is essential that only correct data be entered into a computer system. What is the process of "cleaning" data called?
3. Describe two types of punched media used with computers.
4. Name two types of magnetic media used with computers.

5. List the four devices often used with punched-card processing, and describe the functions of each.
6. What are the major advantages of key-to-tape and key-to-disk devices as compared with punched cards for data entry?
7. Name and describe two types of optical recognition input.
8. What are the two major categories of hard-copy printers? Explain the differences between them.
9. Soft-copy printers are most often found in association with what type of device?
10. List four forms of nonprint output.
11. What are the distinguishing features of "dumb" and "smart" terminals?

5 The Central Processing Unit

© Booth
The Drawing Board Greeting Cards, Inc.

**"Every year accounting requires more
and more little bitty fingers and toes."**

APPLICATION
Computerized Weather Forecasting

Each day weather data from all over the world are transmitted to Suitland, Maryland, just outside of Washington, D.C. There a cluster of nearly 30 computers perform the very complex, high-speed data processing necessary for predicting weather patterns. The resulting output is in the form of hundreds of charts, maps, photographs, and reports distributed to government and commercial offices world-wide. The part that most of us are familiar with, which becomes only a minute or so of broadcast time, is just the tip of the iceberg.

The process of data collecting is continuous and goes through two cycles a day, every day of the year. At midnight and at noon Greenwich mean time, more than 800 weather stations throughout the world record a variety of weather factors—temperature, humidity, wind direction, wind speed, and air pressure. Many of the measurements are taken at ground level; others are recorded at altitudes of 100,000 feet and higher. Still other sources provide additional data at periodic intervals throughout the day. In all, 1,200 observations are made from aircraft every 6 hours; data are sent in four times daily from more than 5,000 weather stations and 2,500 ships worldwide, and even more often from weather satellites.

The computer facility is one of two operated by the National Oceanic and Atmospheric Administration (NOAA). (The other, devoted chiefly to research, is located in Princeton, New Jersey.) At the Maryland center three IBM 360/195s and some two dozen other small and medium-sized computers complete two input/processing/output cycles every day. Each cycle takes over 10 hours of processing. The scheduling is tight, and it leaves little room for failure—human or computer.

Every processing cycle involves running data through at least four, and sometimes five, different weather "models." The first run starts only 75 minutes after the first data for that cycle are recorded (that is, when it is 1:15 A.M. or 1:15 P.M. in Greenwich, England). The first model divides the northern hemisphere into a grid of 381-kilometer squares (about 235 miles), and divides the atmosphere horizontally into two layers. The simulation is crude, but it makes possible a broad, 48-hour forecast of trends developing in the atmosphere.

The second model offers greater precision for a smaller area. It covers only North America, uses a finer grid, subdivides the atmosphere into six layers, and is the major source of 48-hour weather information for domestic forecasting. A third model covers the northern hemisphere, providing forecasts for ships and aircraft. A fourth model, with a very fine grid and a 10-layer atmosphere, can focus on a particular meteorological event such as a hurricane. The fifth model, the last to run in every processing cycle, is global.

The output of each processing cycle includes 500 weather charts and some 2,000 digitized satellite photos. These and other types of weather information are distributed both domestically and worldwide—west to Tokyo and east to Moscow, north to Oslo and south to Buenos Aires.

But even today's supercomputers are not super enough to handle such future needs as an accurate 14-day forecast. The more data that go into the weather model, the more powerful must be the computer—which implies the CPU—that will process them.

T IS NOT an exaggeration to call the central processing unit (CPU) the "brain" of the computer. It is the *only* component of the computer that can *process* data. A computer without a CPU would be analogous to a human body without a brain.

Although there are some variations from one type of computer to another, all CPUs consist of three major components: *primary storage*, an *arithmetic logic unit*, and a *control unit*. The basic functions of the CPU are directly related to these three components. Primary storage is often referred to as "primary memory" or "main memory"; the terms are interchangeable. During processing, primary storage functions as the *working* storage or memory unit. It holds the program instructions and data that the computer needs in order to perform a given processing task.

The arithmetic logic unit (ALU) performs addition, subtraction, multiplication, and division, and makes logical comparisons. The ALU does not store the results of any of its arithmetic or logic operations. Instead, these are sent to primary storage, as directed by the control unit. The control unit directs and coordinates all the operations of a computer, including those of the CPU components themselves. These major components and operations of the CPU will be discussed in greater detail below.

The CPU, especially in the most recent computers, can do an enormous amount of work. But it cannot perform all the tasks associated with computers. For this reason, additional or peripheral components are connected to the CPU through one kind of communications channel or another. (Computer communications are discussed in chapter 7.) *Peripherals* include such devices as terminals and printers; this hardware was discussed in chapter 4.

The term *online* is commonly applied to an operating component (such as a terminal or disk drive) that is in direct communication with the CPU. By definition, any online component is immediately accessible by the CPU. Card readers and printers are online compo-

(U.S. Census Bureau)

Tabulating the U.S. census. An operator at a console is able to interact with, and override if necessary, the entire computer system, in a real-time environment. In the background, several magnetic tape drives and other peripherals can be seen.

133

nents. A keypunch, on the other hand, functions independently of the main computer system and is therefore classified as an offline device.

Real time refers to the immediate response of the computer (or CPU) to input and the production of output for the user quickly enough to affect ongoing activities. The term "real time," then, refers to the short period of time during which the CPU is actually processing data (that is, without the delays involved in batch processing) between input and output. A system operating in real time must be online; however, not all online systems are in real time.

Data/Number Coding

Human users of computers communicate with their machines by means of *special numbering systems*. The output of computers is so varied that it is easy to lose sight of what they are really doing. But what computers are really doing is: computing. That is, they work with numbers to generate other numbers. Their natural language is a number system. But because computers are electronic devices, the number system most natural to them (machine language) is very different from the number system with which most of us are familiar. There are, in fact, many possible number systems. All will give the "right answers" to a problem, too. But some are better suited to special purposes than others. In this section we shall discuss three such systems: one "human" system—*decimal*—and two "machine-oriented" systems—*binary* and *hexadecimal*.

The Decimal System

The decimal, or base-10, number system is the most widely used number system. There may be several reasons why humans over the centuries have tended to select this system in preference to others. The most likely reason sounds almost too simple: humans have 10 fingers. (But not all humans count by tens. In some cultures twos, fives, and twenties are the way to figure; the Babylonians used a base-60 system.)

Because we count by tens, every position or place in a decimal number has a value equal to *10 times* that of the next position, or place, to the right. For example, in the number 8,764, the 4 is in the ones column, 6 in the tens column, 7 in the hundreds column, and 8 in the thousands column. (When the value of a digit depends on its position, the system is said to use *positional notation*.) Thus, the

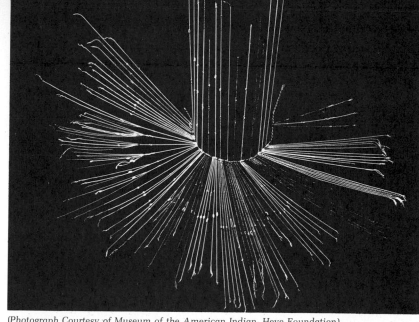

An Inca *quipu,* or counting string, of woven llama wool. In this elaborate astronomical record from ancient Peru, each string and knot has a definite significance that varies according to its size, position, and other factors.

(Photograph Courtesy of Museum of the American Indian, Heye Foundation)

number 8,764 can be broken down into the addition of four numbers —8 thousands, 7 hundreds, 6 tens, and 4 ones:

$$(8 \times 1,000) + (7 \times 100) + (6 \times 10) + (4 \times 1)$$
or, $8,000 \quad + \quad 700 \quad + \quad 60 \quad + \quad 4$

But this does not fully explain why decimal counting is described as counting by tens. The actual reason is that each position (or column) can be represented by a *power* of ten. The mathematical concept of *power* is important for understanding the binary system and therefore of importance to programmers. Thus, 10 "raised" to the 0 (*zero*) power, or 10^0, is equal to 1. (Any base number raised to the zero power equals 1.) The value 10 can be represented by 10 raised to the *first* power, or 10^1. (Any base number raised to the first power is equal to that number; for example, $2^1 = 2$, $18^1 = 18$, and so on.) Correspondingly, 10^2 (that is, 10×10) equals 100; 1,000 is 10^3 (that is, $10 \times 10 \times 10 = 1,000$); and so on. (See figure 5-1.) We can then write our original number, 8,764, as:

$$\underset{8 \times 10^3}{\underline{\text{thousands}}} + \underset{7 \times 10^2}{\underline{\text{hundreds}}} + \underset{6 \times 10^1}{\underline{\text{tens}}} + \underset{4 \times 10^0}{\underline{\text{ones}}}$$

So far we have been discussing whole numbers, such as 8,764. These are generally called *fixed-point* numbers—there are no fractions and the decimal point always follows the last (rightmost) digit

Figure 5-1 Place values in the decimal number system

10^5	10^4	10^3	10^2	10^1	10^0	10^{-1}	10^{-2}
100,000	10,000	1,000	100	10	1	.1	.01

(that is, it is fixed). But we also use numbers with fractions, expressed as digits to the right of the decimal point. These fractional, or *floating-point*, numbers can also be represented by a power of 10 —a negative power, such as 10^{-1} (10 to the minus 1). For example, the number 32.56 is 3 tens, 2 ones, 5 tenths, and 6 hundredths:

$$\underset{\text{tens}}{3 \times 10^1} + \underset{\text{ones}}{2 \times 10^0} + \underset{\text{tenths}}{5 \times 10^{-1}} + \underset{\text{hundredths}}{6 \times 10^{-2}}$$

(Note that 10^{-1} equals $1/10^1$, or .1; and 10^{-2} equals $1/10^2$, or $1/100$, or .01.)

It should be noted that the decimal point is not actually stored in the computer. Instead, the computer has information that tells it where the decimal point *should* go. With this information it can process different numbers accurately.

Computers and the Need for Coding

The first two general-purpose computers—the Mark I and the ENIAC—employed decimal arithmetic in all their computations. This required a great deal of complex circuitry, for the decimal system that seems so "natural" to us is anything but natural to devices that use electrical switching to perform calculations.

Because electrical switches are either "on" or "off," a "natural" number system for electronic computing devices would use only two digits. A two-digit, or base-2, number system is a *binary* system. The two digits, "1" and "0," readily represent the "on" and "off" states, respectively. Binary representation results in much longer strings of numerals than the decimal system. One of John von Neumann's greatest contributions to computer science was the demonstration that the use of binary arithmetic would—despite this drawback—greatly simplify the computer circuitry required.

Nonetheless, human beings continue to think in decimal numbering. Consequently, the binary system can be viewed as a *code* into which *our* number system must be translated. The "on" and "off" can represent much more than the binary digits 1 and 0. In appropriate combinations they can be used to code all other numerals, as well as letters and special symbols. But before we examine how this type of coding is done, we need to understand some simple binary arithmetic.

2^8	2^7	2^6	2^5	2^4	2^3	2^2	2^1	2^0
256	128	64	32	16	8	4	2	1

Figure 5-2 Place values in the binary number system

The Binary or Base-2 Number System

Like decimal arithmetic, the binary system uses positional notation. Also, just as in the decimal system, a given position or column represents the power to which a base number is raised. In binary, this base number is 2 (instead of 10). In other words, instead of positions that represent powers of 10, we have positions that represent powers of 2. The first or rightmost column is 2^0, or 1; next is 2^1, or 2. Moving to the left again the columns represent 2^2, or 4; 2^3, or 8; and so on. (See figure 5-2.) It is easy to see that the unit value of each succeeding column to the left is double that of the preceding column. The decimal number 215 is represented in binary as 11010111. This number breaks down as follows:

128's col.	64's col.	32's col.	16's col.	8's col.	4's col.	2's col.	1's col.
1×2^7 +	1×2^6 +	0×2^5 +	1×2^4 +	0×2^3 +	1×2^2 +	1×2^1 +	1×2^0

Only 1's and 0's are used, and only positions containing a 1 are added. In decimal notation (say, 207), a "0" in a given column represents the power of 10 for that column multiplied by 0 (zero), which equals 0. Similarly, in binary notation a "0" in a given column represents the power of 2 for that column multiplied by 0. Thus, 11010111 is $128 + 64 + 0 + 16 + 0 + 4 + 2 + 1 = 215$. (This example stops at the 128's column, but obviously it could have extended indefinitely, to the 256's and 512's columns and beyond.)

Binary notation is rather cumbersome from our decimal perspective. But from the computer's "point of view" it is the only logical system to use, because it directly corresponds to the two states— "on" and "off." Because computers contain multiple circuits, they can handle on—off switches extremely rapidly. For example, the Cray-1 can perform *100 million* calculations per second. That is the same as adding $1 + 1 + 1 + 1 \ldots$ all the way up to 100,000,000— and doing it in a single second. Even the slowest computers are very much faster than the best mechanical calculators using decimal notation. And the speed of the slowest computer more than compensates for the extra-long strings of numerals it has to process.

It is obvious that binary notation can represent any integer, or *fixed-point* number. (See table 5-1.) Binary can also represent fractions, or *floating-point* numbers. But here the notation runs into some

137

Table 5-1 Binary Equivalents of Decimal Numbers

	Binary									Binary							
Decimal	128	64	32	16	8	4	2	1	Decimal	128	64	32	16	8	4	2	1
1	0	0	0	0	0	0	0	1	35	0	0	1	0	0	0	1	1
2	0	0	0	0	0	0	1	0	·								
3	0	0	0	0	0	0	1	1	·								
4	0	0	0	0	0	1	0	0	40	0	0	1	0	1	0	0	0
5	0	0	0	0	0	1	0	1	·								
6	0	0	0	0	0	1	1	0	·								
7	0	0	0	0	0	1	1	1	·								
8	0	0	0	0	1	0	0	0	45	0	0	1	0	1	1	0	1
9	0	0	0	0	1	0	0	1	·								
10	0	0	0	0	1	0	1	0	·								
11	0	0	0	0	1	0	1	1	50	0	0	1	1	0	0	1	0
12	0	0	0	0	1	1	0	0	·								
13	0	0	0	0	1	1	0	1	·								
14	0	0	0	0	1	1	1	0	·								
15	0	0	0	0	1	1	1	1	60	0	0	1	1	1	0	0	0
16	0	0	0	1	0	0	0	0	·								
17	0	0	0	1	0	0	0	1	·								
18	0	0	0	1	0	0	1	0	70	0	1	0	0	0	1	1	0
19	0	0	0	1	0	0	1	1	·								
20	0	0	0	1	0	1	0	0	·								
·									80	0	1	0	1	0	0	0	0
·									·								
25	0	0	0	1	1	0	0	1	·								
·									90	0	1	0	1	1	0	1	0
·									·								
30	0	0	0	1	1	1	1	0	·								
·									100	0	1	1	0	0	1	0	0

problems. Take, for example, the binary number 00001001.0101. Since the first four values are zero, they can be eliminated from the calculation. That leaves us with the following:

8's col.		4's col.		2's col.		1's col.			1/2's col.		1/4's col.		1/8's col.		1/16's col.
1×2^3	$+$	0×2^2	$+$	0×2^1	$+$	1×2^0	$(.)$	0×2^{-1}	$+$	1×2^{-2}	$+$	0×2^{-3}	$+$	1×2^{-4}
8	$+$	0	$+$	0	$+$	1	$\cdot$	0	$+$	1/4	$+$	0	$+$	1/16

This floating-point number, in decimal fraction form, is 9 5/16. Obviously 9 5/16 presents no problem for binary notation. There are, however, floating-point numbers that cannot be precisely represented. For instance, an exact binary equivalent of the decimal fraction $\frac{1}{10}$ (.1) simply does not exist. That may be difficult to understand, since any whole number can be represented. But consider the problem of representing this fraction in binary. The first three places after the point represent values that are too large: $1 \times 2^{-1} = \frac{1}{2}$ or .5; $1 \times 2^{-2} = \frac{1}{4}$ or .25; and $1 \times 2^{-3} = \frac{1}{8}$ or .125. The fourth position represents a value that is too small: $1 \times 2^{-4} = \frac{1}{16}$ or .0625. Since the values of the digits in a number are additive, it may be possible to represent $\frac{1}{10}$ with a multidigit fraction. Thus, you must start with $\frac{1}{16}$, since $\frac{1}{8}$ is larger than $\frac{1}{10}$. Then you add the next smaller fraction that can be represented by an additional binary position: (.)00011. This floating-point number is equal to $(1 \times 2^{-4}) + (1 \times 2^{-5})$, or $\frac{1}{16} + \frac{1}{32} = \frac{3}{32}$. The fraction is closer to $\frac{1}{10}$ but not yet equal to it. Adding another 1 in the next binary position gives you (.)000111, or $\frac{3}{32} + \frac{1}{64} = \frac{7}{64}$. This is larger than $\frac{1}{10}$. In fact, you could continue adding a string of 0's and 1's to the binary form of this number and get closer and closer to $\frac{1}{10}$ without ever reaching it. (In a string of 1's, each added fraction is smaller than the preceding one, by a factor of 2.)

One way of resolving this type of difficulty is to use coded representations such as *binary coded decimal.*

Computer Codes

Computer systems process binary numbers in groups of several digits, not digit by digit. These units are the building blocks of all codes used by a computer.

Bits and bytes. The most basic unit of information in machine language is the *bit,* or a single *binary digit.* Thus 1 and 0 are both bits. Probably because of the association with electrical switching, 1's are often called "turned-on bits," and 0's are often known as "turned-off bits."

Bits are grouped together to form *bytes.* A byte is usually a sequence of eight bits, but not always. An eight-bit byte includes eight binary columns:

128's	64's	32's	16's	8's	4's	2's	1's
col.	col.	col.	col.	col.	col.	col.	col.
bit	bit	bit	bit	bit	bit	bit	bit

Remember that each bit can be turned either on or off, depending on whether a "1" or a "0" is called for in that column.

For programming purposes, the bits that make up an eight-bit byte are numbered consecutively left to right from 0 to 7. In addition, one or more "check" bits (generated automatically by the computer) are

Figure 5-3 **The difference in binary and BCD bit configurations**

Note that there is a difference in the bit configurations used to represent a number in binary and in binary coded decimal (BCD). In BCD every four bits stores one decimal digit. Using two eight-bit bytes, the number 999 would be represented in BCD as:

9				9				9				+ or − sign			
8	4	2	1	8	4	2	1	8	4	2	1	8	4	2	1
1	0	0	1	1	0	0	1	1	0	0	1				

Using the same number of bits and bytes, the binary representation of 999 is:

32,768	16,384	8,192	4,096	2,048	1,024	512	256	128	64	32	16	8	4	2	1
0	0	0	0	0	0	1	1	1	1	1	0	0	1	1	1

transmitted with each byte or group of bytes. A group of bytes, or *field*, may consist of two consecutive bytes (a *halfword*), four (a *word*), or eight (a *doubleword*). Halfwords are the basic building blocks of program instructions.

Binary coded decimal (BCD). Binary coded decimal, or BCD, is a code for storing numbers that uses only four bits instead of eight or more. Four bits are quite sufficient for the task, since four bits are able to code all 10 decimal system values 0 through 9. It also provides a solution to troublesome fractions like .1.

As we saw above, computers have no problem processing whole, or fixed-point, numbers but can only approximate certain decimal fractions such as .1. This limitation would make it necessary to use rounded values. Such a lack of precision might not be a handicap in some scientific calculations, where accurate approximations are acceptable, but in business and financial applications, accuracy to the last penny is essential. To represent $12.10 as the sum of $1/16 + 1/32 + 1/64$ . . . or "$12 and *almost* 10 cents" would not be very useful.

The use of BCD makes it possible to circumvent this problem. (See figure 5-3.) Each numeral can be stored as a unique and independent whole number, that is, without a decimal point. In fact, computers do much better without decimal points. They can process numbers faster and store more of them. What the computer must know, however, is *where* the decimal point is supposed to be so that it can align numerals properly. For example, consider the sum:

$$
\begin{array}{r}
1.23 \\
+\,22.45 \\
\hline
23.68
\end{array}
$$

Placing the decimal point elsewhere could produce

$$
\begin{array}{r}
.123 \\
+\ 2.245 \\
\hline
2.368
\end{array}
$$

The same decimal digits are produced for the sum 2,368, but the *location* of the decimal point, and therefore the *value* of the sum, has changed. Consequently, the computer never actually converts .1 to binary form but stores it as the decimal system number 1, using four bits: 0001. The decimal point is inserted on the printout. (Thus the decimal is said to *float*, since it is not "fixed" until it is printed.)

Extended binary coded decimal interchange code (EBCDIC). In addition to the decimal system digits 0 through 9, computers often deal with alphabetical characters (both upper and lower case), specific control characters, and special characters such as &, (), %, $, #, and @. The use of certain bit configurations (that is, series of 1's and 0's) to represent various characters has become well established in the form of the extended binary coded decimal interchange code, more commonly referred to as EBCDIC. Some EBCDIC characters and corresponding bit configurations are listed in table 5-2. Because

CAN STORE MORE DATA IN SAME AMT. SPACE

Table 5-2 Extended Binary Coded Decimal Interchange Code (EBCDIC) and American Standard Code for Information Interchange (ASCII)

Character	EBCDIC 8-Bit Configuration		ASCII 8-Bit Representation		Character	EBCDIC 8-Bit Configuration		ASCII 8-Bit Representation	
A	1100	0001	0101	0001	S	1110	0010	1011	0011
B	1100	0010	1010	0010	T	1110	0011	1011	0100
C	1100	0011	1010	0011	U	1110	0100	1011	0101
D	1100	0100	1010	0100	V	1110	0101	1011	0110
E	1100	0101	1010	0101	W	1110	0110	1011	0111
F	1100	0110	1010	0110	X	1110	0111	1011	1000
G	1100	0111	1010	0111	Y	1110	1000	1011	1001
H	1100	1000	1010	1000	Z	1110	1001	1011	1010
I	1100	1001	1010	1001	0	1111	0000	0101	0000
J	1101	0001	1010	1010	1	1111	0001	0101	0001
K	1101	0010	1010	1011	2	1111	0010	0101	0010
L	1101	0011	1010	1100	3	1111	0011	0101	0011
M	1101	0100	1010	1101	4	1111	0100	0101	0100
N	1101	0101	1010	1110	5	1111	0101	0101	0101
O	1101	0110	1010	1111	6	1111	0110	0101	0110
P	1101	0111	1011	0000	7	1111	0111	0101	0111
Q	1101	1000	1011	0001	8	1111	1000	0101	1000
R	1101	1001	1011	0010	9	1111	1001	0101	1001

there are 256 possible eight-bit configurations, EBCDIC also makes possible the representation of lower-case letters, special symbols, and many special abbreviations.

American Standard Code for Information Interchange (*ASCII*). The *American Standard Code for Information Interchange*, originally based on a seven-bit configuration, was later modified to an eight-bit standard to be compatible with more recent equipment. ASCII-8 is similar to EBCDIC in format, but uses a different series of eight-bit configurations (see table 5-2). It contains a total of 128 characters, including 94 alphanumeric and other characters and 34 control symbols.

The Hexadecimal Number System

As we have seen, a four-bit binary sequence (BCD) can be used to represent the 10 decimal system digits. But BCD only uses a portion of the total number of combinations possible with a four-bit sequence composed of two different digits (0 and 1). There are actually 4^2, or 16, different possible configurations. This has led to another numbering system. the hexadecimal or base-16 system.

Considering that computers work with binary numbers, and humans with decimal numbers, it might be supposed that another number system would only add confusion. But hexadecimal is convenient for a very specific and important purpose—the detection of errors. When programmers "debug" programs (that is, hunt out and correct errors), they often obtain a complete printout or "dump" of the computer's memory. A dump printed in binary would appear as a mass of 0's and 1's. Imagine trying to check for errors in a program that prints out 720 lines of 0's and 1's, with each line 132 positions long. The use of hexadecimal numbering makes it possible to reduce the same printout to a more manageable 180 lines. For the human programmer, hexadecimal is easier to read than binary or decimal. And it is easier for the computer to convert from binary to hexadecimal than from binary to decimal.

The hexadecimal system uses positional notation and has 16 as a base number. Thus the unit value of each position or column is a power of 16—1, 16, 256, 4,096, and so on. Table 5-3 lists the first 16 integers in all three systems. Note that one hexadecimal number can represent the information contained in four binary bits. Hexadecimal represents the decimal numbers 0 to 15; for efficiency it is coded as the 10 decimal system digits and the first six letters of the alphabet—0 to 9 and A to F. For example, decimal number "10" is hexadecimal "A," and decimal "15" is hexadecimal "F."

Table 5-3 Hexadecimal
Equivalents of
Decimal and Binary
Values

Hexadecimal Equivalent	Decimal Equivalent	Binary System (Place Values)			
		8	4	2	1
0	0	0	0	0	0
1	1	0	0	0	1
2	2	0	0	1	0
3	3	0	0	1	1
4	4	0	1	0	0
5	5	0	1	0	1
6	6	0	1	1	0
7	7	0	1	1	1
8	8	1	0	0	0
9	9	1	0	0	1
A	10	1	0	1	0
B	11	1	0	1	1
C	12	1	1	0	0
D	13	1	1	0	1
E	14	1	1	1	0
F	15	1	1	1	1

The comparison of equivalent values in table 5-3 does not fully demonstrate how very compact the hexadecimal system is. For example, the decimal number 42,436 requires *five* decimal positions. The binary representation of this number requires 16 positions:

1010010111000100

Hexadecimal can represent the same number much more simply as A5C4:

$$\begin{array}{cccc} 4,096\text{'s} & 256\text{'s} & 16\text{'s} & 1\text{'s} \\ \hline A \times 16^3 + & 5 \times 16^2 + & C \times 16^1 + & 4 \times 16^0 \end{array}$$

or, $\quad 10 \times 16^3 + 5 \times 16^2 + 12 \times 16^1 + 4 \times 16^0$

$\quad\quad 40,960 \;+\; 1,280 \;+\;\quad 192 \;\;+\;\quad 4$

These four numbers add up to 42,436. Since hexadecimal uses positional notation, all that is necessary now is to substitute hexadecimal numbers for *10* ($\times 16^3$), *5* ($\times 16^2$), *12* ($\times 16^1$), and *4* ($\times 16^0$). (See figure 5-4.) The result is A5C4. Compare that to the binary version or even to 42,436. Moreover, the larger the original decimal system number, the greater the saving provided by the use of hexadecimal numbers.

16^4	16^3	16^2	16^1	16^0
65,536	4,096	256	16	1

Figure 5-4 Place values in the hexadecimal number system

If human beings had to translate decimal numbers into hexadecimal, there would be no advantage to its use. Fortunately, all the work is done in the CPU under the control of the program. Thus input is in decimal form. One program converts this input to binary in the CPU. The CPU then processes the binary information. For purposes of error detection, the CPU converts the binary data to hexadecimal form, but output is in decimal. The conversion is performed by translation tables. It all takes place in the CPU.

Parity: Another Check on Computer Accuracy

In the course of processing, the CPU moves data from and to various components, in addition to performing a variety of operations on them. With all of this "back and forth," there is always the possibility that data will be lost or added through some kind of electronic mishap. To ensure that the data initially read into the system are (and continue to be) transmitted correctly to all components, most computers incorporate what is known as a *parity check*.

The parity check is usually a *ninth* bit added to an eight-bit byte. (Sometimes it is an eighth bit added to a seven-bit byte.) The principle involved is quite simple: Depending on the number of "1" bits in a byte configuration, that byte can be classified as odd or even. Accordingly, a "0" or "1" bit can be added to make the total even or odd. Depending on the machine, then, the parity bit is chosen to make all bytes odd or even.

To understand how this principle works in practice, consider the following configuration: 11110101 ( ). The parentheses represent the space for the parity bit. In the configuration, six bits have been "turned on," as indicated by the number of 1's. That is, the byte is even. Let us assume that the computer in question uses a system of *odd* parity. (It could use *even* parity as well, but of course not both.) In that case, the computer will add a "1" to the configuration, making the total number of 1's odd: 11110101 (1). Conversely, if the byte contained an odd number of 1's, the computer would make the parity bit 0: 11110100 (0). Consequently, in an odd-parity computer, a value detected as 11110110 (0) would cause the machine to indicate the existence of an error.

In effect, parity enables a computer to run its own check on every number it processes. The computer adds the parity bit automatically, and this bit cannot be affected by the program being processed. Of course this kind of parity cannot detect errors involving the loss (or addition) of two bits in a single byte, or of one loss and one addition. There are, however, other parity systems for dealing with such errors.

Computer-generated models are derived from vast quantities of data about weather conditions worldwide. Weather forecasts for the general public and for specialized purposes are the result.

(NOAA Photo)

Functions of the Central Processing Unit

All data processing is performed in and by the CPU, through the interactions of its three basic components. The functions of the CPU are:

1. *Storage* of data and programs needed for a given processing task. This primary storage, or main memory, is "internal" and immediately accessible, in contrast to storage of data in "external" files.
2. *Arithmetic logic operations,* which constitute the major type of processing performed on individual data items.
3. *Control,* the function of what might be called the "executive" unit of the CPU that directs and issues instructions for the performance of all components of the computer system.

The Processing Sequence or Execution Cycle

During processing, all three major components of the CPU work together to execute a program. The following sequence gives a brief, general description of what actually occurs during the execution of a program and also how the three main CPU components function and interact.

1. Before a program can be executed, it must be translated from a programming language (for example, BASIC, COBOL, or FOR-TRAN) into the machine language (binary) that the computer can "understand." The translation is performed automatically by a

145

Control panel of the mainframe of the Sperry-Univac 1100/80 CPU, showing lights, buttons, and dials. The control panel provides the means by which humans interface with large computers; it should not be confused with the control unit inside the CPU itself.

(Sperry-Univac/U.S. Census Bureau)

compiler program or *compiler*. The translated, machine-language program—usually called the *object program* or *object module*—is now ready for execution. It can be stored outside the computer (for example, on a magnetic disk) for future processing, or it can begin executing immediately.

2. Execution of an object program begins when it is placed in primary storage. The program then takes control of the computer (through the control unit) to perform the tasks specified in the original program.

3. The control unit fetches the first instruction of the program from primary storage and "interprets" it; that is, the control unit determines what processing step(s) must be carried out to execute the instruction.

4. Next, the control unit converts the "interpreted" instruction into electronic impulses that the rest of the CPU "understands." The control unit may issue any of a number of instructions. It can direct which data in primary storage are to be used, ask for more data input, direct the transfer of data to the ALU, specify which operations are to be performed there on particular data, return the results of such operations to locations that it specifies in primary storage, and so on.

5. The control unit continues to fetch instructions—one by one—from the primary storage, interpret them, and issue appropriate directions to other components of the computer system.

6. During execution of the program, instructions direct the control unit to direct primary storage to transfer the results to an output device.

Multiprocessing

It often seems as though a computer is performing many operations at the same time. But as the above description of the processing sequence indicates, the CPU executes a program *one instruction at a time*. It appears to be performing a variety of operations simultaneously because it executes each instruction so rapidly. Thus the capacity of a CPU is a function of its speed. In the same way, the capacity of a computer system is a function of the CPU. When one CPU is employed, the computer system can handle only as much as that one CPU can process. The computer system's capacity can be enlarged only by increasing the CPU speed or increasing the number of CPUs. The use of more than one CPU within a given machine is known as *multiprocessing*. This should not be confused with multiprogramming, which implies the processing of more than one program at a time by one CPU; this will be discussed in greater detail in chapter 8.

Storage (Memory) Locations—Addresses

To direct the processing of data, the control unit must be able to find each data item and program instruction in primary storage. It does so by means of an *address* system. Each storage location in primary memory is assigned a number, starting with 0 and continuing consecutively to the last location. Some primary memories have many millions of such addressed locations.

The amount of information that a location can hold varies with the type of computer. In many computers, each memory location holds one byte, or (usually) eight binary bits. An information item larger than one byte would require two or more storage locations, each holding a part of the item. Specialized programs provided by the computer manufacturer are designed to keep track of the contents of the storage locations being used in a program.

It is important to remember, particularly in programming, that the address of a location and its contents are two different things. The set of storage locations in a primary memory is often likened to the array of individual mailboxes at a post office. These boxes have unique identifying numbers (addresses), and each box contains whatever mail (stored data) has been sent to it. Thus program instructions do not say "multiply x by y" when the programmer wants to compute the amount of tax on an item. The instruction is instead expressed in terms of the locations where x and y are stored. For example, suppose the price of an item is $20.00 and the sales tax is 6 percent. Assume that the address of PRICE in this example is 141, and that of TAX is 148. The programmer writes an instruction telling the computer to multiply 141 by 148. But the computer does not produce 20,868 ($= 141 \times 148$) as the answer. Rather, it interprets the instruction to mean that the contents of location 141 are to be multiplied by the contents of location 148. Consequently it multiplies $20.00 by 6 percent to get $1.20. (See figure 5-5.)

Temporary Storage Registers

When combined with the program's instructions, the data called for at any given time during the execution of a program could easily fill the main memory of the CPU. Moreover, it is not really necessary to keep everything at the ready. *Registers* function as subsidiary and temporary storage (memory) devices in the CPU. They are not part of primary storage but serve to facilitate the execution of instructions by receiving, holding, and transferring data according to the instructions they receive from the control unit. Some registers also perform intermediate calculations on data.

In the past a variety of registers were used to perform specific func-

Address	0141	0142	0143	0144	0145	0146
Amount	20.00	29.00	40.00	13.00	1.25	469.82
Address	0147	0148	0149	0150	0151	0152
Amount	.0001	.06	'Item'	62.48	3.821	
Address	0153	0154	0155	0156	0157	0158
Amount	'Total'	.22	423.982	'Help'	88.43	1980.00
Address	0159	0160	0161	0162	0163	0164
Amount	'Hello'	0.00	'Searching'	'Subtotal'	'Working'	18826.29
Address	0165	0166	0167	0168	0169	0170
Amount	'Bye'	43.22	9884.		.6621	0.6992
Address	0171	0172	0173	0174	0175	0176
Amount	0.01	'System'	22.24	'Failure'	699.27	888.00

(a)

Address	0141	0142	0143	0144	0145	0146
Amount	20.00	29.00	40.00	13.00	1.25	469.82
Address	0147	0148	0149	0150	0151	0152
Amount	.0001	.06	'Item'	62.48	3.821	1.20
Address	0153	0154	0155	0156	0157	0158
Amount	'Total'	.22	423.982	'Help'	88.43	1980.00
Address	0159	0160	0161	0162	0163	0164
Amount	'Hello'	0.00	'Searching'	'Subtotal'	'Working'	18826.29
Address	0165	0166	0167	0168	0169	0170
Amount	'Bye'	43.22	9884.		.6621	0.6992
Address	0171	0172	0173	0174	0175	0176
Amount	0.01	'System'	22.24	'Failure'	699.27	888.00

(b)

Address	0141	0142	0143	0144	0145	0146
Amount	20.00	29.00	40.00	13.00	1.25	469.82
Address	0147	0148	0149	0150	0151	0152
Amount	.0001	.06	'Item'	62.48	3.821	1.20
Address	0153	0154	1055	0156	0157	0158
Amount	'Total'	.22	423.982	'Help'	88.43	1980.00
Address	0159	0160	0161	0162	0163	0164
Amount	'Hello'	0.00	'Searching'	'Subtotal'	'Working'	18826.29
Address	0165	0166	0167	0168	0169	0170
Amount	'Bye'	43.22	9884.	21.20	.6621	0.6992
Address	0171	0172	0173	0174	0175	0176
Amount	0.01	'System'	22.24	'Failure'	699.27	888.00

(c)

Figure 5-5 How a computer executes a program
Three stages in the execution of of a program are shown as they take place in the same section of memory: (a) A sale of $20.00 has been entered as a subtotal, along with the sales tax rate of 6 percent (.06). (b) The subtotal has been multiplied by the tax rate, and the result of the multiplication, the amount of the sales tax, is shown. (c) The sales tax has been added to the subtotal, and the final total is shown.

Figure 5-6 Organization of the central processing unit

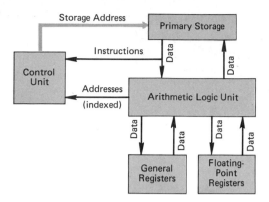

tions. Most common was the *accumulator*, which accumulates the results of a series of computations. An *address register* holds the address of a data item that is called for in an instruction. During the execution of a program, each instruction is transferred to an *instruction register*. While held in this register, the instruction is decoded by the control unit. *Storage registers* hold information that has been taken from or will be sent to primary storage.

Today, a wide variety of functions, including fixed-point arithmetic operations and addressing, are performed by *general registers*. Such registers are programmable and are accessible to the control program. Two other types of programmable registers common to most computers are *floating-point registers*, which are used exclusively for arithmetic operations involving fractional numbers, and *control registers*, which facilitate the handling of information and instructions used to control certain operations.

The number, size, and types of registers used with any given computer system will vary according to the functions and requirements of that particular system. The relationship between some registers in the CPU of a given system is diagrammed in figure 5-6.

Other Features of CPUs

The capability and value of a CPU are frequently described in terms of certain features, such as the amount of information it can process, the speed and "permanence" of its memory, and its cost.

Processor capacity. The amount of information a CPU can handle is largely a function of the capacity of its primary memory. Memory capacity is commonly measured in units of K (from the Greek combining form *kilo-*, or "thousand"), which may mean either 1,000 or 1,024 (that is, 2^{10}). For example, a typical minicomputer memory has a capacity of 65,536 eight-bit bytes, and is described as a 64K memory because it consists of 64 1K memory units: $64 \times 1,024 = 65,536$. So one must use the term with care.

Speed. The speed of a computer is determined by two related factors. *Access time* is the time it takes to bring, or *access*, a data item from an internal or external storage location or to enter (store) it in that location. *Cycle time* is the time that elapses before the next data item can be entered or accessed. Access times are usually shorter than cycle times. A typical access time for a magnetic core memory is 300 nanoseconds, and a typical cycle time is 750 nanoseconds. For semiconductor memories, access and cycle times are both of the order of 300 nanoseconds. For certain, very fast read-only memories, access and cycle times can be as rapid as 7 nanoseconds. (A discussion of the different kinds of memories follows.)

Refreshing. In some kinds of random-access memories (RAM) that are made of semiconductor material, stored data items must be accessed periodically to prevent them from dissipating. The process by which this information is renewed is known as *refreshing*. Dynamic RAM storage requires such refreshing. Static memories do not. Of course, both types lose their storage contents when the power is shut off.

Cost. The cost of memory is commonly expressed in cents per bit. For core memory, the usual cost is in the neighborhood of 1 cent per bit. RAM semiconductor chips are about five times cheaper. Bubble memories promise to lower the cost still further, perhaps by a factor of 10.

Components of the CPU

Regardless of how greatly computers differ from one another, their CPUs all have the same three components: a primary memory or storage unit (sometimes called main memory), an arithmetic logic unit, and a control unit.

CPU Storage (Memory)

From a computer perspective, the word "storage" has the same meaning as the word "memory." Memory within the CPU can be of two kinds: primary memory (also called primary storage and main memory) and other or add-on memory. An add-on memory may either replace an existing main memory or add to the computer's main storage capacity. Add-on memories are generally connected directly to the CPU by communications channels but remain external to the computer. Add-on memories that are incorporated into the computer housing itself are sometimes called *add-ins*. But whether the electronic component is physically within or external to the actual computer structure is immaterial; what counts is its direct association with the CPU.

The basic structural units of memories in CPUs in use today are the magnetic core and the semiconductor chip. Although magnetic core memories remain important, semiconductor chips have been the predominant technology since the late 1970s.

Random-access memory. Primary or main memory is usually *random-access memory* (RAM), and is always involved in the program currently being processed. Thus RAMs are memories involved in and needed for the execution of programs. The term itself refers to the fact that access time is independent of the position of the storage location being accessed. The circuitry is arranged in such a way that the location of each individual binary bit is uniquely specified by a row-and-column address (similar in principle to the letter and number arrangement used to locate cars in a large parking lot). An address decoder in the CPU simply selects the correct row and column specified by the binary address. The access times of RAMs are commonly of the order of 45 nanoseconds, though some have even faster access times of less than 10 nanoseconds. In serial-access memories, by contrast, the computer must hunt through its main memory by following a given sequence, location by location, until it finds the one wanted. Consequently, access time for any given item is a function of the position of that item in the search sequence; a data item near the beginning of the sequence will be accessed in less time than an item further along. (This would seem to be more time-consuming overall; however, the extremely rapid circuitry of bubble memories, for example, which function only as serial-access devices, will make the time factor negligible.)

RAMs can both "read" and "write" when they access a location. That is, they can simply "report" the contents of a location (*read*), or they can store new information (*write*). Read-only memories (ROM), on the other hand, cannot write in new data (see below).

Memory Technologies

The first electronic memories were serial access. Although these first computer memories were economical, they suffered from a limi-

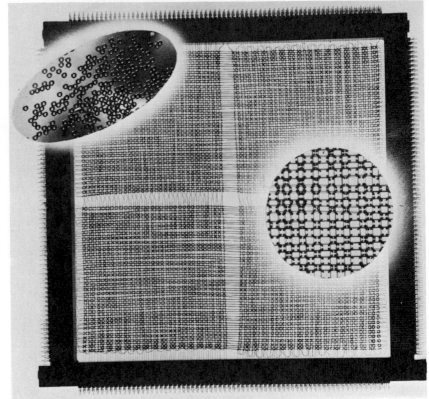

(Courtesy of IBM)

The wiring behind core memory. Magnetic cores, shown in close-up in upper left, are strung at the intersections of wires on a grid (close-up at right).

tation that is inherent in serial-access memory: the larger the memory capacity became, the longer was the average time required to access a given item. With the development of random-access memories this problem was eliminated. Also, by giving the computer complete freedom of access to all storage locations, RAMs made possible the development of branching, the computer's ability to follow one part or another of a program (see chapter 12).

Magnetic cores. The first RAMs were electrostatic storage tubes. This type of memory, however, quickly gave way to *core memories,* which first appeared in the late 1950s. Core memory was so successful that the term almost lost its technical meaning and was frequently used as if it were synonymous with central storage. Today the technical meaning predominates and refers to the actual electronic device from which such memories are constructed.

A magnetic core is a tiny, doughnut-shaped piece of magnetizable material. Information can be stored in a core because the core can be magnetized in one of two possible directions. To understand how

Figure 5-7   Magnetizing a core
Inducing a magnetic field in a core according to the right-hand rule: Imagine that the wire passing through the core is grasped by your right hand. Your thumb points in the direction in which current is flowing through the wire, while your fingers indicate the direction of the induced magnetic field.

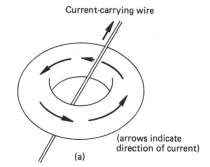

Current-carrying wire

(arrows indicate direction of current)

(a)

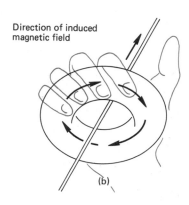

Direction of induced magnetic field

(b)

this is done, imagine a single core with an electric wire passing through, as illustrated in figure 5-7a. An electric current passed briefly through this wire will magnetize the core; that is, it will give the core its own magnetic field. This field is circular and has a direction (which is another way of saying that it acts like a magnet). The direction of the core's magnetic field is determined by the direction of the electric current according to the "right-hand rule." To illustrate, hold your right hand with the four fingers curled into the palm and the thumb extended (as you would if hitchhiking). Now your thumb indicates the direction of the electric current in the wire, and the curve of your fingers indicates the direction of the magnetic field that forms around its core. (See figure 5-7b.)

A core memory consists of an array of cores strung on fine wires. Two wires capable of carrying current pass through the center of each core at right angles to one another (see figure 5-8). The current passed through each wire is only one-half the amount needed to magnetize it (or change its direction of magnetization). Thus, only when current is sent through both wires can the core be magnetized. The arrangement is, in principle, the same as the rows-and-columns arrangement described earlier, and makes certain that only the target

(Courtesy of IBM)

In this close-up of magnetic cores, the crossed wires passing through each core can be clearly seen.

core is being magnetized. The two possible directions of the magnetic field are used to represent 0 and 1.

This all happens very rapidly, and so core memories typically have access and cycle times of less than 1 microsecond. Typical core memories have a capacity of one million words, with between 30 and 60 bits per word. Some larger core memories have capacities on the order of 100 million words. And they are nonvolatile, or permanent; a power failure will not erase any data in the memory.

Figure 5-8 Selecting a magnetic core
A magnetic core is selected by passing one-half the current through each of two wires at right angles. (Does the right-hand rule still work? Try it!)

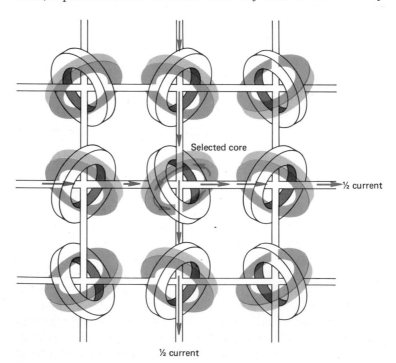

Selected core

½ current

½ current

Some of the drawbacks of core memories became apparent only as newer and more efficient semiconductor technology replaced them. Cores are, for example, larger than comparable semiconductor memories, and are from 50 to 100 percent more expensive per bit. Also, a computer with a core memory requires a large number of additional circuits in order to extract information from the memory. For example, a "sensing wire" is needed to detect the change in magnetization caused by accessing. If the control signal is simply a "read" instruction, then another signal must be generated for restoring the core to its original state. Thus, except for certain special applications, core memories are gradually being overtaken by newer technology.

Semiconductor memories. Semiconductor memories are smaller, have faster access times, and require less power than core memories. These advantages result from the fact that the circuitry of a semiconductor memory can be "printed" on a silicon chip. One chip the size of a magnetic core (about 1 mm in diameter) can carry the equivalent of thousands of cores. Because they are cheaper as well, semiconductor memories have largely replaced the core variety and are expected to continue dominating the market, at least until they are replaced in turn by even smaller and faster devices (see below).

Semiconductor devices work on the same on/off principle as core memories but in a somewhat different manner. A semiconductor is "on" if a current can pass through it, and is "off" if it cannot. Thus, it acts as an electrical switch. The actual switching mechanism is a transistor. Essentially, this is a small area on a silicon chip divided into electrically positive (or p) and electrically negative (or n) zones. The passage of an electrical current between two n zones can be controlled if these two zones are separated from one another by a p zone. A small voltage applied across the p zone determines whether or not an electrical current can flow from one n zone to the other. Consequently, such an arrangement acts as an electronic switch, or transistor. The opposite arrangement—two p zones separated by an n zone —works the same way and is also used. Thousands of these tiny switching devices can be incorporated into a single chip.

One advantage of the semiconductor transistor over the magnetic core is that the information it contains (that is, "on" or "off") does not have to be restored after the transistor has been read. Thus, there is no need for the additional circuitry required by core memories. One important disadvantage of semiconductor memories, however, is volatility, or vulnerability, to power failure: all stored data are lost if the power goes off. (Of course, ways to compensate for this shortcoming have been developed.) Core memories, as was noted before, are permanent. But the greatest advantage of semiconductors is the versatility of the material itself, which has made possible the development of integrated circuits.

Integrated circuits. The first silicon chips with transistorized memories could store only a limited amount of information. As late as 1972, the standard semiconductor memory held no more than a thousand bits, and was not yet a threat to the domination of core memories. Today, a ¼-inch square silicon chip can carry more electronic elements than the ENIAC. And in addition to having a larger memory and being thousands of times more reliable, semiconductor devices are at least 20 times faster, consume considerably less power, are 30,000 times smaller, and cost 10,000 times less than core memories. This tremendous increase in power is a direct result of the development of *integrated circuits* (ICs).

The first IC memories appeared in the early 1960s, only a few years after the first transistorized memories. Several important technological advances contributed to this development: (1) The use of photolithographic techniques to "print" circuits on silicon chips; (2) the use of new (solid-state diffusion) techniques to produce the *p* and *n* regions in a silicon chip; and (3) the batch production of chips, in which several hundred chips are first printed on a single silicon wafer and then cut into individual units. The result of these developments was the rapid and efficient production of large quantities of chips containing a larger number of complete circuits (complete circuits consist of transistors, resistors, capacitors, and amplifiers).

The development of large-scale integration (LSI) in the late 1960s represented a tremendous increase in the power and capacity of integrated circuit devices. Now circuits with separate functions can be incorporated together on a single silicon chip. This meant that the electronic circuitry of an entire CPU could be put on one chip. As LSI technology developed, the capacity of IC chips quickly increased to 16,000 bits and then to 64,000 bits.

Integrated circuits have drastically reduced the size of computer components (particularly primary memory), have made them very much smaller and faster, and have greatly reduced their cost. Thus it is not surprising that most of the world's present electronic devices employ IC technology.

Bubble memories. "Bubbles" are tiny cylindrical domains of magnetization in a thin film made from a material that is amorphous, or noncrystalline, in structure. (Silicon chips, on the other hand, are crystalline.) These tiny domains are generally from 2 to 20 microns in diameter, but bubble sizes are being reduced—Bell Laboratories has succeeded in producing bubbles that are 1 micron in diameter. Under a microscope these magnetized areas appear as circles, or

Magnetic bubbles (the large white dots) move along a track—a circuit —on an iron-containing sheet. Each bubble is four-thousandths of an inch in diameter. In the computers of the future, counting, switching, memory, and logic functions will all be contained in one solid magnetic material.

(Bell Labs)

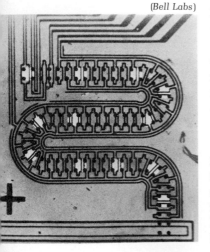

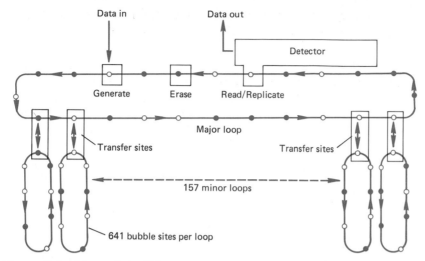

Figure 5-9   Magnetic bubble memory
This diagram of a magnetic bubble memory shows the pattern of circulation in the 100,637-bit memory. The major loop holds a single data block, consisting of 1's and 0's (bubbles or no bubbles) that are being written into the memory, read out, replicated, or erased. In this particular device the data block contains 157 bits. In the writing cycle the 157 bits first enter the major loop, from which they are transferred simultaneously, at a signal, to the 157 minor loops, one bit per loop. Each minor loop in turn provides sites for 641 bubbles. Thus the total capacity of the device is 157×641, or 100,637, bits. In the read cycle 157 bits are transferred simultaneously, at a signal, from the minor loops into the major loop, which carries them past the read head.

bubbles—from which they get their name. They are produced by applying a magnetic field of specified intensity to the film. The film itself is already magnetized, and the bubbles appear with opposite magnetization. If the intensity of the applied field is increased beyond a certain critical value, however, the bubbles disappear.

The ability to create and erase magnetic bubbles in this fashion is the basis for using them to represent information in binary form. The presence of a bubble stands for a binary 1, and its absence for a binary 0. A series of bubbles and no-bubble spaces can be moved by the application of small magnetic fields. The bubbles move around a track or a memory "loop," and the data are read by a combination detector/replicator at a fixed point, or station, in the loop. When a bubble passes this station, it is replicated, producing two bubbles. One of the bubbles continues to circulate in the memory loop while the other enters the detector, where it is read. (See figure 5-9.) Access to stored data is therefore serial.

Because they are so tiny, bubbles can be packed into a very small area. Chips carrying one million bubbles are now available, and chips with densities of one billion bubbles per square inch are due in the near future.

Bubble memories have several important characteristics that, in some respects, make them superior to core, semiconductor, and IC memories. As we have seen, a serious limitation of core memories is the amount of electrical wiring required. Even the highest-quality wire resists the flow of current to some extent, and the longer the wire, the greater the resistance. Thus, there is a built-in limitation on the speed of core memories. Semiconductor and IC memories, which have no wires connecting the components on a chip, eliminated this difficulty altogether. Bubble memories are also "wireless," and have the added advantage that their manufacture is even simpler and involves fewer steps than does the production of semiconductor and IC devices. As a result, they are easier to miniaturize and therefore capable of holding even more memory per unit area of chip.

Furthermore, bubbles provide a nonvolatile medium for information storage. That is, information is not erased when the power is turned off, as happens with semiconductor and IC memories. Also, the reading operation in bubble memories does not destroy the stored data. Unlike core memories, then, they do not have to restore information after reading it. Bubble memories require almost no maintenance and use even less electricity than comparable semiconductor memories. However, because they are serial-access devices, bubble memories are better suited for use in fast auxiliary memories and mass-storage devices (see chapter 6) than in large primary memories.

Charge-coupled devices. Packets, or concentrations, of electrical charge can function in much the same way as magnetic bubbles. Charge-coupled devices (CCDs) make use of this principle. Their circuitry is printed on semiconductor silicon chips. Access to data is serial, as with bubble memories. The electrical charges can be manipulated by controlling the voltage of the current. In this way CCDs are made to circulate in a memory loop. The charges (and uncharged spaces) are read as they pass a reading station in the loop. CCDs have access times that are approximately 10 times faster than bubble memories and transfer data about 10 times as fast.

The most serious drawback of CCDs, when compared with bubble devices, is the volatile nature of the memory. As with all semiconductor-based memories, stored data are erased whenever the power fails or is shut off. Also, the data must be refreshed periodically.

CCDs are well suited to applications that can take advantage of serial accessing and where long-term retention of data is not important, such as signal processing and solid-state TV cameras. Compared with integrated circuit RAMs, CCDs have both advantages and disadvantages. The density of bits on a CCD chip is higher—by a factor of about two—than that of the standard RAM chip. This higher density results, in part, from the fact that CCD memory requires less supporting circuitry. On a typical CCD chip, 30 percent of the area is given over to auxiliary circuitry, while the corresponding figure for a RAM chip is 50 percent. On the other hand, as serial-access devices, CCDs are inherently slower than RAMs. This disadvantage holds even when the information is stored in *blocks* that can be randomly accessed. For while the CCD has random access to all the information in a block, it must nonetheless access the blocks serially.

Josephson junctions. Of all the recent developments in computer technology, the Josephson junction promises the most dramatic improvement in memory capacity and speed. This device is an electronic switch based on the phenomenon of superconductivity: At extremely low temperatures (usually at −273.15° C., or −459.67° F., a few degrees above absolute zero), some materials lose virtually all resistance to the flow of electric current. They become superconducting. Under this condition, the flow of current can be stopped by a small change in a local magnetic field.

Such a device can operate at speeds 10 to 100 times faster than any semiconductor, and the amount of power required is 100 to 1,000 times less. This much smaller power demand means that much less heat is generated, so Josephson junctions can be packed very close together.

Other Types of Memory

The functions of a computer can be incorporated in the software or the hardware of the system. Software functions are stored in the random-access memory of primary storage. Software has the advantage of being flexible—it can be changed without rewiring the computer. It also has the disadvantage of being vulnerable to human error. By contrast, hardware has the limitation of being inflexible (it cannot be reprogrammed), and has the advantage of being reliable (it is hardwired into the circuitry).

Functions that are part of the hardware of a computer (that is, hard-wired) may be placed in a *read-only memory,* or ROM. As the name indicates, information can be accessed (read) from this type of memory, but new information cannot be stored (written) in it. The information in a ROM is permanent and generally cannot be altered.

159

What ROMs do store are *microprograms,* or sets of instructions (logic), for specific functions (for example, calculating the square roots of numbers). If new instructions are required, then a new ROM must be developed. Only by physically replacing one ROM chip with another can the program or fixed data be changed. By means of interchangeable ROMs, though, the basic operations of a computer can be tailored to meet the requirements of the user.

Although ROMs are individually inflexible and are generally programmed by the manufacturer, some ROMs can be programmed by the user to meet specific needs. Such programmable chips are known as *programmable read-only memories,* or PROMs. A user can therefore burn the logic for a new program onto a blank PROM chip.

Another variant with more flexibility is provided by *erasable programmable read-only memories,* or EPROMs. The programs on these chips can be erased by exposure to ultraviolet light, making them available for new programs. These chips may be erased and reprogrammed any number of times. An *electrically alterable read-only memory,* or EAROM, can be programmed electrically without being removed from the computer circuit. EAROM reprogramming can be complete or partial, since selective alterations can be made without erasing the remaining stored information.

The Arithmetic Logic Unit (ALU)

The arithmetic logic unit performs a variety of arithmetic and logical operations. These operations can be divided into four distinct categories: decimal arithmetic, fixed-point arithmetic, floating-point arithmetic, and logical operations.

The ALU often performs operations on decimal data in what is called storage-to-storage processing. In this type of processing, the data are accessed from main storage, processed, and returned to main storage without passing through any general registers. Decimal arithmetic processing is used mainly in commercial applications.

Fixed-point arithmetic is employed in operations on data and on storage addresses. Floating-point arithmetic is used mainly in scientific applications. This type of operation greatly increases the precision, efficiency, and speed of computations. Values that the ALU can process in floating-point arithmetic commonly range from about 10^{-76} to 10^{76}.

The logical operations that an ALU can perform include comparison, translation of characters, editing (for example, punctuation), and transfer of logical data. In a typical comparison, for example, the program might instruct the ALU to see if the result of a calculation was the same as, greater than, or less than a particular data item. These logical operations make programming possible (see chapter 12).

The Control Unit

The control unit interprets the instructions specified in a program stored in the primary memory. Taking these instructions one by one from main storage, the control unit generates electronic impulses that instruct other components of the computer to execute the program instructions. These electric impulses also activate a set of timing mechanisms or clocks. These clocks control and synchronize the various activities of the computer as well as keep track of data and the time of day. When the computer is turned off, the time-of-day clock goes off as well and must be reset when the machine becomes operational again. In a system with more than one CPU, each CPU may have its own time-of-day clock or may share it with another CPU.

The control unit also directs and coordinates operations within the CPU itself. For example, the control unit issues the electronic commands directing an input medium (for example, a magnetic disk or tape drive) where to store data in the primary memory (that is, tells it to what addresses data items should be sent). In addition, the control unit generates the commands that tell the input device the sequence in which the data items are to be entered.

The control unit also tells the ALU the locations in primary storage of the data needed for processing, the specific operations to be performed on those data, and to what addresses in primary storage the results are to be sent. Finally, the control unit is responsible for initiating the transfer of data from primary storage to the appropriate output device.

How It All Works

Earlier in this chapter there was a brief and very general description of how a computer executes a program. What follows is a more detailed account of how a computer executes a specific type of program. The example is that of a clerk at a POS terminal about to calculate the sales tax on several items of merchandise to get the total cost to the consumer. This example assumes that a program to perform this task is already in primary storage and in the process of being executed. (See figure 5-5 on page 148.)

A clerk rings up a sale, calculates sales tax and total charges, and keeps a running tally of inventory by using an IBM 3653 point-of-sale (POS) terminal.

1. The control unit fetches the next instruction from primary storage.
2. It "decodes" the instruction and determines that *subtotal* (the total of the prices of the individual items purchased) is to be multiplied by *sales tax rate*, and the answer is to be stored as *sales tax*.
3. The control unit then locates the address of *subtotal* in primary storage and directs that the amount stored there be transferred to a register associated with the ALU. (Assume *subtotal* = 20.00.)
4. The control unit locates the address of *sales tax rate* in primary storage and directs that this amount be transferred to a register associated with the ALU. (Assume *sales tax rate* = .06.)
5. The control unit directs the ALU to multiply *subtotal* by *sales tax rate* and to send the result to the address associated with *sales tax* in primary storage. At this point:

$$subtotal = 20.00$$
$$sales\ tax\ rate = 0.06$$
$$sales\ tax = 1.20$$

6. The control unit now fetches the next instruction from primary storage.
7. It decodes the instruction and determines that *subtotal* is to be added to *sales tax*, and the result is to be stored as *total sale*.
8. The control unit then locates the address of *subtotal* in primary storage and directs that this amount be transferred to a register associated with the ALU.
9. Next the control unit locates the address of *sales tax* in primary storage and directs that this amount be transferred to a register associated with the ALU.
10. The control unit then directs the ALU to add *subtotal* and *sales tax* and to send the result to an address associated with *total sale*. At this point:

    subtotal = 20.00
    sales tax =   1.20
    total sale = 21.20

11. The control unit now fetches the next instruction from primary storage.
12. It decodes the instruction and determines that the value associated with *total sale* is to be displayed on the cash register.
13. The control unit now directs the register (output) to display the value of *total sale*:

    total sale: $21.20

Certainly this looks like a cumbersome and time-consuming series of steps. But it is no exaggeration to say that the time required to list (or read) this series of steps is *millions* of times longer than it takes a computer to perform them. Even the few seconds it would take you to do the calculations yourself—far less than the time it took you to read this—is millions of times longer than it would take the CPU to do the job. After all, some computers can perform a million such steps in just 1 second. As you probably know from your own experiences as a customer, the most time-consuming part of ringing up a sale is the entry of data into the POS terminal.

Summary

The "brain" of the computer is the *central processing unit*, or *CPU*. All the processing performed by a computer is done in and by the CPU. All CPUs have three major components: *primary storage (primary memory* or *main memory*), an *arithmetic logic unit* (ALU), and a *control unit.* Primary storage is the internal memory used during processing. It holds the program instructions and data needed for a given task. The ALU performs arithmetic and logical operations on data but does not store them. The control unit directs and coordinates the operations of the computer.

Peripheral devices, or *peripherals,* are components connected to the CPU by a communications channel. Some peripherals have direct, or *online,* communication with the computer. Processing that is done when both input and output devices are online is said to be *real-time* processing (that is, output is not delayed as in batch processing).

Computers commonly deal with three number systems: decimal, binary, and hexadecimal. *Decimal,* used for input of data, is a base-10 system. Decimal system input is translated by a *compiler* into binary form. *Binary* is a base-2 system in which numbers are constructed from two digits (0 and 1) representing *powers of 2* and corresponding to the on—off switching of electronics. Binary is used by the CPU in all of its processing. *Hexadecimal,* a base-16 system, is more compact than binary or decimal and is used to check for errors.

Binary cannot represent certain *floating-point,* or fractional, numbers such as .1. These numbers are therefore stored in *binary coded decimal* (BCD) as whole numbers, and the decimal point is added to output in the appropriate place by the computer. *Extended binary coded decimal interchange code* (EBCDIC) has been developed to represent alphabetical characters and special symbols in the 1's and 0's of binary terminology. ASCII is another code.

The most basic unit of information in the computer's binary language is the binary digit, or *bit.* Bits are often grouped together in sets of eight to form *bytes.* Larger units include *halfwords, words,* and *doublewords* of two, four, and eight bytes, respectively. To ensure that data are not lost or added during processing, the computer automatically adds a *parity bit* to each byte.

In executing a program, the computer executes one instruction at a time until the program has been completed. Computers appear to perform a number of functions at the same time only because they execute individual instructions so rapidly. The capacity of the computer is only the capacity of the CPU. One way to increase a computer system's capacity is to increase the number of CPUs. The use of more than one CPU in a system is known as *multiprocessing.*

Storage locations in primary memory are assigned an identifying number or *address.* The address of a location is not to be confused with its contents.

Registers are temporary storage devices in the CPU that facilitate the execution of instructions. Some registers are associated with only one specific task (for example, storage addressing). *General* registers can perform several different functions. *General, floating-point,* and *control registers* are also programmable.

The capacity of a CPU is frequently described in terms of its memory capacity, speed (*access time* and *cycle time*), the permanence of its memory (that is, whether stored data need *refreshing* periodically), and cost per bit.

The two main types of memory are *primary* (or *main*) memory, stored directly in the CPU, and *add-on* memory, connected to the CPU by a communications channel. Primary memory is often *random-access memory,* or *RAM.* Such memories can both *read* (access) and *write* (store) data.

Read-only memories, or *ROMs,* cannot write. ROMs may be *programmable (PROMs), erasable programmable (EPROMs),* or *electrically alterable (EAROMs).*

Magnetic core memories have been dominant until very recently. Most electronic devices in use today are based on *semiconductor* and *integrated circuit* technology. These RAMs are printed on silicon chips and are smaller, faster, and cheaper than the core variety.

Key Terms and Phrases

access
access time
accumulator
add-on memory
address
address register
American Standard Code
  for Information Interchange (ASCII)
arithmetic logic unit (ALU)
binary coded decimal (BCD)
binary number system
control register
control unit
core memories
cycle time
decimal system
electrically alterable read-only memory (EAROM)
erasable programmable read-only memory (EPROM)
extended binary coded decimal interchange code (EBCDIC)

fixed-point numbers
floating-point numbers
floating-point register
general register
hexadecimal number system
instruction register
microprograms
multiprocessing
online
peripherals
primary storage
programmable read-only memory (PROM)
random-access memory (RAM)
read
real time
refreshing
registers
semiconductor memories
storage register
write

165

Sources of Additional Information

"Bubbling Up Some Memory Devices." *Data Management*, no. 8 (1977):12–15.

Hodges, David A. "Microelectronic Memories." *Scientific American*, September 1977, pp. 130–45.

Holton, William C. "The Large-Scale Integration of Microelectronic Circuits." *Scientific American*, September 1977, pp. 82–94.

Lecht, Charles P. "Tsunami/In Depth." *Computerworld*, May 7, 1979, pp. 1–15.

Noyce, Robert N. "Microelectronics." *Scientific American*, September 1977, pp. 63–69.

Rajchman, Jan. "New Memory Technologies." *Science* 195 (1977):1223–29.

"Science: The Numbers Game," *Time*, February 20, 1978, pp. 54–58.

Theis, Douglas J. "An Overview of Memory Technologies." *Datamation*, no. 1 (1978):113–31.

Toong, Hoo-Min D. "Microprocessors." *Scientific American*, September 1977, pp. 146–61.

Withington, Frederic G. "IBM's Future Large Computers." *Datamation*, no. 7 (1978):115–20.

Test Yourself

1. What are the three major components of the CPU? What is the primary function of each?
2. In the decimal number system, what are the positional values to the left and right of the decimal point?
3. What digits are used in the decimal number system? In a binary number system?
4. Determine the binary equivalent of the following decimal numbers: (a) 47; (b) .75; (c) 3.25.
5. Determine the decimal equivalent of the following binary numbers: (a) 1101; (b) .1101; (c) 110.011.
6. If a computer's memory can store 1,024 bits, how many bytes, halfwords, words, or doublewords can it store?
7. How would the decimal number 569 be represented in a four-digit binary coded decimal system?
8. What is the difference between BCD and EBCDIC?
9. What is the BCD representation of the hexadecimal number A3F7? What is the decimal equivalent?
10. Explain how a parity check can find an error in a binary number.
11. What is the purpose of a compiler?
12. What is the difference between a location (or group of locations) in primary storage and a register?
13. What is the difference between RAM and ROM?
14. What is an advantage of core memory over semiconductor memory? Of semiconductor memory over core memory?
15. Why is the binary number system used in the computer rather than the decimal number system?

6 Auxiliary Storage

© Computerworld

"I've just invented the wheel."

APPLICATION

The IBM 3850 Mass Storage System

Every day, the Ohio National Bank, like others of its size, receives nearly half a million checks and other documents. The data contained in these pieces of paper have to be stored for months and kept available for ready reference.

Before being filed for storage, however, the data have to be processed. Incoming checks must be sent to the banks on which they were drawn, and customers' accounts must be appropriately debited or credited. For such routine processing, conventional automated systems are quite adequate. But some items must be traced back because of processing errors or questions. In a traditional system, millions of pieces of paper would have been stored in file drawers, organized by date and account number, and searched for manually as needed.

This situation is a perfect application for a mass storage system such as the IBM 3850. With all incoming check data online, and with display terminals to retrieve information, a bank employee using a keyboard can answer any question in seconds. Here's how it is done:

As each check comes in, it is put through a special check processor that reads the magnetic ink data encoded on it, assigns it a transaction identity number, imprints on it certain batch codes that will facilitate retrieval, and feeds the data into the archive retrieval system. The day-to-day records accumulated in this way are kept in accessible storage for at least two months.

The actual data are stored in data cartridges, each of which has its own storage cell. The controller in the system's CPU assigns a position to incoming data, retrieves the cartridge from that position, and enters the data on a magnetic disk for high-speed transfer to the CPU. After further processing as necessary, the data are returned to the storage cartridge. One cylindrical cartridge the size of a vitamin bottle has a 50-million character capacity and can store 400,000 item records. Two such cylinders can store a day's supply of incoming checks—with space to spare.

One of the most important benefits of a mass storage system is the reduced time required to handle an inquiry or an adjustment. With the 3850 system, finding the needed items is easy, because the archive data base has an index to the precise location of the information. Under the system previously used, it was not cost-efficient to search for items involving $50 or less: employee time was more valuable. But the speed and efficiency of the new system makes it feasible to follow up every adjustment inquiry, no matter how small the amount.

The IBM 3850 has also been installed at Dun & Bradstreet, which provides numerous credit and marketing services to the business community throughout the nation. The new equipment reduced D & B's tape library by about one-third, and made it possible to issue frequently updated reports directly from the stored data. The director of computer operations for D & B, estimating that hundreds of employee hours per month have been saved, praises the system for making possible "important gains in performance and quality, significant cost savings and a real assist in internal operations."*

* Robert Porowski, quoted in "3850 Simplifies Life at Dun & Bradstreet," *Data Management*, no. 8 (1977):5.

DATA PROCESSING in a business environment implies that large data files—accounts payable and receivable, inventories, credit records, and so on—are stored and updated constantly. To retain this mass of data in the CPU's main memory, even if there were room, would be much too costly. For this reason, auxiliary storage devices are used.

Auxiliary storage devices are accessory units that are physically separate from but in contact with and controlled by the CPU. After input, data in machine-readable binary language are transferred from main memory to an auxiliary device for storage on magnetic tape, disks, or drums or in mass storage cartridges.

There are two significant advantages of auxiliary memories: reduced cost and increased storage capacity. The cost per bit of information stored on magnetic tape or disks can be as little as $1/10,000$ that of electronic storage in a CPU. With proper handling, data stored on such physical media will not be lost or erased, whereas electronically stored data might well be erased if the computer's power supply should fail. Vast quantities of data can be accommodated by auxiliary storage devices. Using auxiliary storage, files that are used infrequently do not have to occupy facilities that could be devoted to data used regularly, and may even be kept at remote locations.

It may, however, be more time-consuming to retrieve data from auxiliary storage than from main memory. However, this drawback can be minimized by the selection of a system of data storage appropriate to the needs of the business organization and to the type of processing being done. The key consideration in determining the type of auxiliary storage to use is the method by which the stored data will be accessed.

The access method is simply the way in which the records in a data file can be retrieved by the computer. Files may be accessed sequentially or directly. In *sequential-access* media, stored data can be retrieved only in the order in which they were stored. In *direct-access* media, however, the computer can retrieve a stored data item independently of any other. For example, if the letters of the alphabet were stored in a sequential device, and printout only of vowels was desired, the CPU would select A, then have to search through B, C, and D before locating E, then through F, G, and H before reaching I, and so on. But if the same data file was stored in a direct-access device, the five vowels could be located independently of the 21 consonants. That would, obviously, produce the same output more rapidly.

Magnetic tapes and punched cards are sequential-access media, while magnetic disks and drums provide direct access. In this chapter we will examine the variety of auxiliary storage devices in greater detail, and will also take a look at the future forms of auxiliary storage.

Sequential-Access Devices

In sequential-access devices, the records in a data file are arranged in physical rather than in logical sequence. Although sequential access may be too time-consuming or cumbersome for many purposes, there are some applications for which it is ideally suited. For example, sequential accessing is commonly used for storage of a master file against which input transactions will be batch-processed. In batch processing, all input transactions are sorted by the CPU and arranged in the same sequence as the master file. When a certain time limit or batch size is reached, the whole batch is processed together. This type of operation is inexpensive and is often used for applications like inventory records, sales receipts, and employee payroll transactions.

The major limitation on the use of sequential-access storage is that in order to find a particular record, the entire file must be searched from the beginning until the desired item is found. If we wanted the computer to retrieve the letters and print out the word "HELLO" from the master file containing the alphabet, the file would have to be searched from A to each letter, a total of five times. On the average, half a sequential file must be searched before any particular record can be found. This can be time-consuming, especially for larger files.

Moreover, sequential files cannot be added to or updated by simply substituting new data for existing items. Instead, the entire file must be rewritten from beginning to end. In a system for which updating is frequently necessary, sequential-access storage would be inefficient.

Punched Sequential Media

Sequential-access devices use either punched or magnetic media to store records. Punched media include cards and paper tape on which data are stored in code form by punched holes in the proper places (see chapter 4).

Once punched, the cards or paper tape can be stored until the data they contain are needed. However, these media take up considerable space and must be stored and handled very carefully because they are paper. Data retrieval from paper is relatively slow compared with that from magnetic media.

Magnetic Sequential Media

As soon as it was introduced, magnetic tape became a popular medium for sequential-access storage. The tape itself and the tape drive that operates it have some resemblance to an ordinary reel-to-reel tape recording system. Computer tape is made of a nonmagnetic material, usually ½-inch-wide plastic ribbon, coated with a thin magnetic film. Tapes are available in standard lengths from 50 to 3,600 feet, although most tapes now in use are 2,400 feet long. The tape is divided horizontally into seven or nine channels. Positions on the channels are coded in much the same way as positions in punched paper tape. (See figure 6-1.) Information is stored vertically by placing magnetized spots called bits in the channels. Each vertical column of seven or nine bits is a byte that represents one alphabetic or numeric character or other symbol.

The storage capacity of a magnetic tape depends on the number of

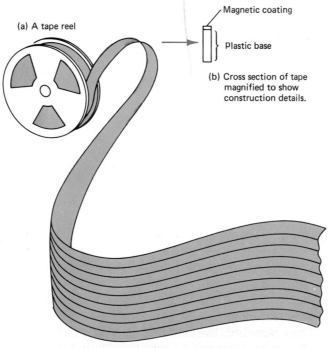

(a) A tape reel

Magnetic coating

Plastic base

(b) Cross section of tape magnified to show construction details.

(c) Nine-track tape includes eight EBCDIC tracks and one parity track.

Figure 6-1 Magnetic tape

171

(Teresa Zabala/The New York Times)

The magnetic tape storage facility of the U.S. Census Bureau.

bytes per inch (BPI) it can store. This parameter is known as *tape density*; standard densities are 800 to 1,600 BPI. A 2,400-foot tape with a density of 1,600 BPI can store the data equivalent of 400,000 punched cards on a reel about the size of a long-playing record. For applications where even larger storage capacities are required, high-density tapes of 6,250 BPI have been developed.

The tape drive is the mechanism that pulls the magnetic tape into position past the read/write head. (See figure 6-2.) This head, an electromagnet, converts the magnetized bits it "sees" on the tape into electrical pulses and transmits them to the CPU. When data are being written onto the tape, the read/write head magnetizes the appropriate areas and simultaneously erases any information previously stored in that location. The rate at which data are transferred to or from a storage location is called the *data transfer rate*. Tape must pass the read/write head at a precise speed in order for the data to be transferred properly.

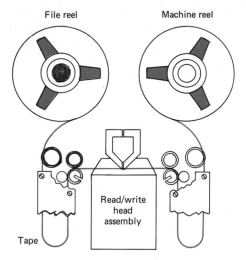

File reel   Machine reel

Read/write
head
assembly

Tape

Schematic diagram of the tape-drive mechanism

(a)

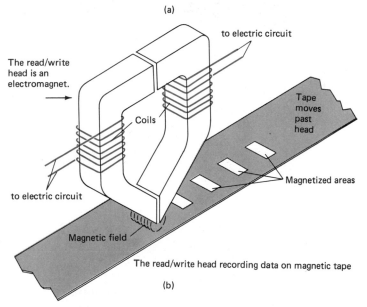

to electric circuit

The read/write
head is an
electromagnet.

Coils

Tape
moves
past
head

to electric circuit

Magnetized areas

Magnetic field

The read/write head recording data on magnetic tape

(b)

Figure 6-2   Reading magnetic tape

Characters are grouped on the magnetic tape in clusters called a *record*. Each record is physically separated from the next by a blank space called an *interblock gap* (IBG). This blank may be ½- to ¾-inch wide, depending on the tape system used, and contains no data. (See figure 6-3.) The IBG serves three purposes: (1) it separates individual records; (2) it allows space for the tape drive to reach its operating speed; and (3) it allows space for the tape drive to decelerate after a read or write operation. It takes about half an IBG to get the tape to the read/write speed.

173

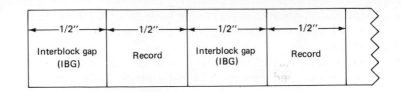

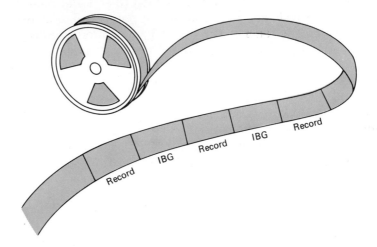

Figure 6-3 Unblocked
records
The space between each
record can also be called
the interrecord gap (IRG).

Figure 6-4 Records
with a blocking factor
of 5

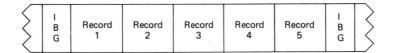

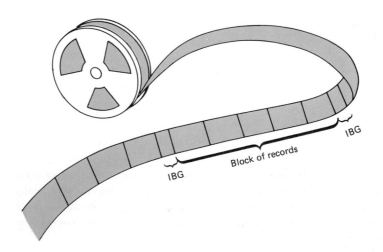

174

Magnetic tape also contains a signal to the tape drive to stop at the end of a file or reel. These are known, respectively, as *end-of-file* and *end-of-reel* markers.

For more economical use of tape space, records that have some logical relation are grouped together to form a block. This block is treated as one storage location, and the records in the block are read together. The number of records stored between two IBGs is known as a *blocking factor.* When the blocking factor is 1 (that is, one record to the block), the records are often considered *unblocked,* and the space between records is sometimes referred to as an *interrecord gap* (IRG). The records diagrammed in figure 6-4 have a blocking factor of 5.

Magnetic tape has been in use for several years. More recently, less expensive tape cartridges or cassettes were introduced, primarily for use with mini- and microcomputers. These are generally smaller than standard tape reels and have lower storage capacities as well as slower access times. One cassette is capable of storing from 10^6 to 10^7 bits, with access times ranging from 10 to 100 seconds. This medium is particularly suited to small business and personal computing applications.

Magnetic media are nonvolatile; that is, the information stored will remain unchanged unless it is altered by an external magnetic field. This makes magnetic tape a safe storage medium for important files or when long-term storage is desired. However, improper handling can cause accidental erasure, not only by operator error, but also from poor storage and transportation practices. The presence of dust, ashes, food particles, or even a hair on the tape surface can cause the loss of data bits. It is also important to avoid touching the tape surface, since skin oils and body salts on the tape can collect debris.

The temperature and humidity of storage areas must be considered when storing tapes and other magnetic media. These media perform most reliably when subjected to only small environmental changes. The ideal temperature range is from 45° to 85° F., with a maximum humidity of 60 percent.

Direct-Access Devices

In direct-access storage, each physical record is not just another step in a sequence—it can be reached independently at its own discrete location. Each location is identified by an address; if the address of any record is known, that record can be accessed without searching the entire file.

(Courtesy of IBM)

The IBM 3370 direct-access storage device (DASD). A nonremovable pack of six disks is contained in each unit.

Direct-access storage devices (DASD) are usually used with online processing. Unlike batching, where data are grouped or arranged prior to processing, data processed online enter the system immediately without being sorted or edited. Input transactions are not processed in any particular sequence, but rather in the order in which they enter the system. With online processing and direct-access storage, data can be processed by a program that refers to more than one file at a time, and unscheduled transactions may be performed during a regular program run.

One important advantage of a directly accessed storage file is that it enables the user to make inquiries of the system at any time. Since a direct-access file is always up to date, any information can be accessed without interruption to the program being run. Data in a sequential file cannot be accessed by one program while another program is operating. Only after the program is complete and all data have been updated can individual data items be accessed.

One very common example of the usefulness of prompt response is illustrated thousands of times each day at any bank branch. At any time during banking hours, a teller can determine the current balance, make a deposit or withdrawal transaction, and reenter the new balance in any account by accessing it directly from the master file.

File Organization for Direct-Access Devices

The characteristics described above give direct-access storage much greater flexibility than sequential access. This is also true of the way in which data may be organized in a direct-access device.

Four types of file organization are available: (1) sequential, (2) indexed sequential-access method (ISAM), (3) direct, and (4) virtual storage access method (VSAM).

Sequential organization. In sequential organization, records are written on the storage medium one after the other. The actual location of the records in the file is the basis of organization. Records in a sequential file are usually arranged in either ascending or descending sequential order according to some predetermined value in the record. For example, in a payroll file, the records in the file may be stored in ascending sequential order according to employee number. Records are arranged in the desired sequence before being entered into the file. (See figure 6-5.)

Records in a sequential file must be accessed and read in the same order, or sequence, in which they appear in the file. If it is desired to access the 250th record in the file for updating or other processing, each of the previous 249 records must have at least been read first and in the order that they appear in the file. It is therefore time-consuming to access individual records out of sequence. Furthermore, if records are to be added to or deleted from a file, the entire file must be rewritten.

Sequential organization might seem to make the special capabilities of direct-access devices unnecessary, but the combination of sequential organization and direct accessing is useful in specific situations. It makes possible more rapid processing of larger files, and is typically used when most of the records in the file are to be processed in some manner at the same time. For example, the time cards turned in by employees of a company must be arranged in ascending sequential order according to employee number, just as the master payroll file is. The time cards are accumulated, or

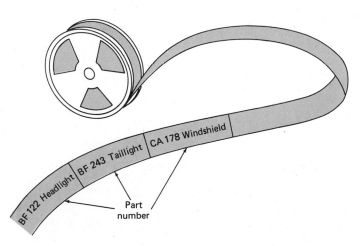

Figure 6-5 Sequentially filed inventory records

177

batched, for processing as a group at a specified time. During processing, they are matched by employee number as the file is accessed in sequence.

Sequential organization of data on a direct-access device is used primarily for tables of information and for intermediate storage. Intermediate storage allows certain transactions that do not have to be processed immediately to accumulate for processing when computer time is available. This ensures the most efficient use of computer time.

Indexed sequential-access method (ISAM). In an ISAM file, records can be accessed sequentially as well as individually out of sequence. This is possible because as each record is filed it is accompanied by its own unique key. The key is a user-oriented identifying code. It may be a name or a number, such as the number of a savings bank account. An ISAM file contains an index to the keys of all the records it contains. The index enables the user to access the filed records by sequential arrangement or by key number. For example, when a customer initiates a transaction against her/his bank account, the account number could serve as the key associated with the record of that account. The teller would enter the account number, and the computer would be able immediately to access the information pertaining to that account. The same file can be accessed sequentially at the end of the banking day to determine various transaction totals. One such total might be the total of savings account deposits. The computer can easily scan all the accounts sequentially to find the sum of all deposits. It would be far more time-consuming to have to supply all the keys necessary to access each record. ISAM file organization permits this "dual" access.

An ISAM file contains three distinct areas. The *index* is a logical chart that relates the keys of the filed records to the addresses in the prime areas where each record is stored. Each entry in the index gives the range of key numbers on a particular track of the direct-access storage device (see figure 6-6). By searching the index, the track containing the desired record can be found. Although this track must then be searched sequentially to find the record, sequential search of a single track takes a very short time.

The *prime area* is the portion of the storage medium where the actual data records are written. Records in an ISAM file must have key numbers and must be stored in key sequence, at least initially.

The *overflow area* allows additions to be made to the ISAM file without extensive rewriting. This area is initially empty; when a new record is added to its proper place in the prime area, each existing record is moved up one location, and any extra records are "bumped" into the overflow area. Although the records in the over-

178

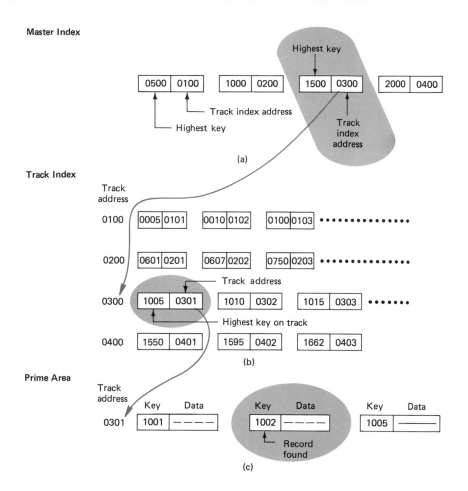

Master Index

(a)

Track Index

(b)

Prime Area

(c)

Figure 6-6   Accessing a record in an ISAM file
This figure illustrates the process by which a computer would locate a file
record whose key is 1002. (a) The computer reads the first record in the
master index, which refers to records with key values between 0001 and
0500. Since 1002 is greater than 0500, the computer looks at the next
index record; but this refers to file records with key numbers between
0501 and 1000. Then the machine checks the next master index record,
which contains information about file record keys 1001 to 1500, and
therefore includes 1002, the record key we are looking for. The computer
reads in the index that the next level of the index associated with this record is on track 0300. (b) So the computer goes to track 0300 and starts to
read the records on that track. The first record indicates that it has information pertaining to records 1001 to 1005. Since 1002 is within this
range, the computer notes that the record being sought is on track 0301 in
the prime area. (c) The computer goes to track 0301, searches sequentially
until it finds record 1002, and retrieves the record called for. All this takes
place in a fraction of a second.

179

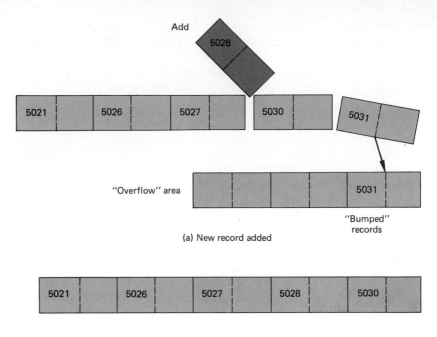

Add

5028

5021 | 5026 | 5027 | 5030 | 5031

"Overflow" area | | | | 5031

"Bumped" records

(a) New record added

5021 | 5026 | 5027 | 5028 | 5030

(b) Revised file

Figure 6-7 Adding a record to an ISAM file

flow area are not physically in key sequence like those in the prime area, they can be accessed in key sequence through the index (see figure 6-7).

Direct organization. In a directly organized file, there is a definite relationship between the key of a record and its address. This type of organization serves the same purpose as ISAM without having to devote valuable storage space to an index. By a simple calculation, the CPU can determine from the numeric key of a record exactly where on the magnetic disk or drum that record is stored. The read/write head can then be moved directly to that location to access the data.

Direct organization is recommended when a short access time is critical. It is especially useful for low-activity processing, where a large master file is kept but only a small percentage of input transactions are processed during each run. Direct organization shares with ISAM the advantage that changes and additions can be entered in the file without the necessity for extensive rewriting of the file.

Virtual storage access method (VSAM). In some computer systems, the maximum size of any application program is limited by the capacity of primary storage. However, a virtual storage system makes possible an application program bigger than main memory and "virtually" as big as all direct-access storage available. In a virtual

180

storage system, the machine is able to bring a portion of a program into primary storage in the CPU when needed; the remainder of the program resides in virtual storage until the CPU "requests" it. In VSAM, the software that operates the system exists in virtual storage alongside the application programs that use it. A portion of the operating system, along with the relevant application programs, can be quickly accessed as needed, while the program segments that have been completed are returned to virtual storage.

VSAM was developed to make the most efficient use of data retrieval systems. It is dependent on specific IBM equipment and software; with these, it is a flexible system that can be used with data sets filed in any of the three ways we have previously discussed: entry-sequenced data sets (sequential access), key-sequenced data sets (ISAM), and relative record data sets (direct access).

Magnetic Disks

In order to store a data file that is organized according to one of the methods we have discussed, a direct-access storage medium must be used; magnetic disks are one such medium. There are several varieties of disks.

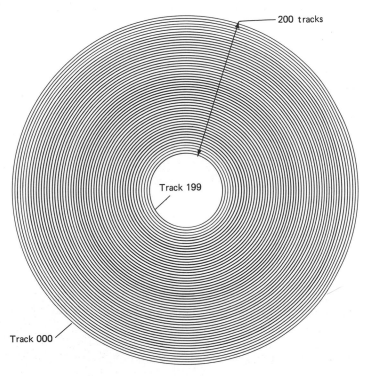

200 tracks

Track 199

Track 000

Figure 6-8 Surface of a magnetic disk containing 200 concentric tracks

181

The IBM 3336 disk pack

(Courtesy of IBM)

Rigid disks are aluminum platters, 14 inches in diameter and covered with iron oxide, a ferromagnetic material. The upper and lower surface of each disk is divided into tracks. Disk tracks differ from the grooves of a phonograph record in that they are concentric, not spiral (see figure 6-8). The width of each track is approximately 10^{-3} inches, and there may be as many as 800 or even more tracks on a single side of one disk.

Often, several disks are grouped into a disk pack and mounted at

Figure 6-9 Side view of a disk pack
This disk pack contains 11 disks with 20 recording surfaces and 10 access arms, each with two read/write heads.

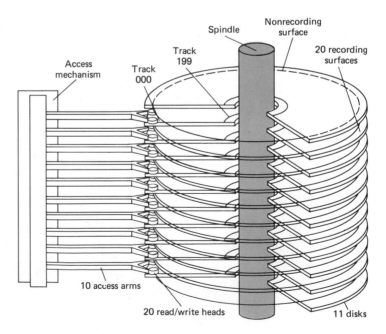

182

equal intervals on a vertical spindle. Data are stored on all surfaces of a disk pack except the upper surface of the top disk and the lower surface of the bottom disk. These surfaces are exposed and therefore highly susceptible to damage. A typical disk pack with 11 disks will thus have $2 \times 11 - 2$, or 20, data-recording surfaces. Storage and retrieval of data from magnetic disks are done by read/write heads similar to those used for magnetic tape. However, because a disk pack has several surfaces as opposed to a tape's single surface, several heads are needed, one for each disk surface to be read. An access arm containing two read/write heads extends between every set of adjacent disk surfaces. Each data-recording surface has its own read/write head, as shown in figure 6-9.

Data records are stored on a track serially bit by bit, eight bits per byte. Records can be blocked and are separated by IBGs just as on magnetic tape (see figure 6-10). The capacity of a disk surface depends on the number of *bits per inch* (bpi) of track length, called the linear packing density, and the number of *tracks per inch* (tpi) of disk radius. Increases in these two factors, as well as an increase in the number of disks per pack, can double or triple the number of bytes of storage without a significant increase in cost. Loss of reliability at higher packing densities, however, limits the amount of data that can be stored on one disk. At present, packing densities range from 1,000 bpi for lower-performance drives to 6,000 bpi and greater for Winchester drives (these are discussed below).

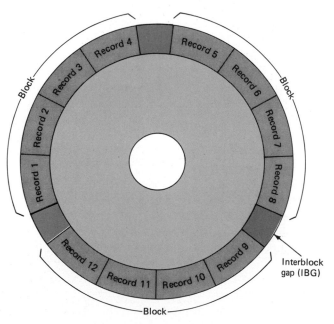

Figure 6-10 Blocked data on a magnetic disk track

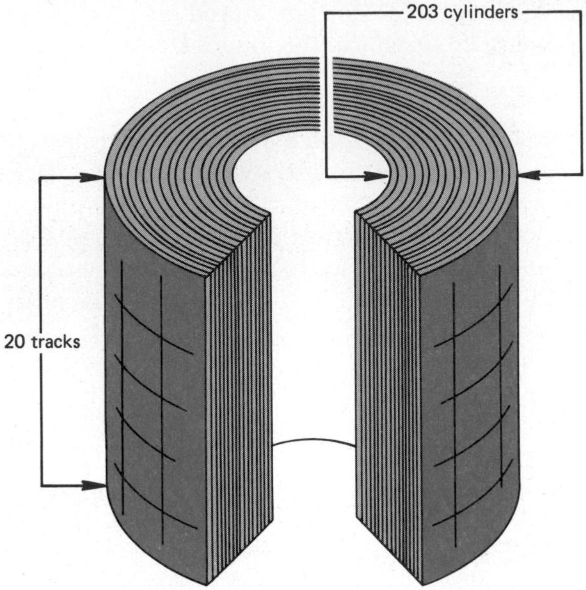

Figure 6-11 Cross-sectional diagram of a disk pack
This cross-sectional diagram of a disk pack illustrates the concept of the cylinder as a unit of data storage.
(*Courtesy of IBM*)

Although a disk pack is physically made up of a number of separate horizontal surfaces, it consists, from an access point of view, of concentric cylinders equal to the number of tracks per surface. If there are 400 tracks per surface, there will be 400 cylinders, each of them one track wide. In a disk pack of 20 such recording surfaces, then, each of the 400 cylinders will be 20 tracks high (see figure 6-11).

The *cylinder* is an important concept, because one positioning of the access arm will enable all the read/write heads to reach data stored on the several tracks in a cylinder. By definition, a cylinder of data is the amount that is accessible by one positioning of the access head. A large amount of data stored in a single cylinder means that fewer movements of the access mechanism will be needed to read or write data.

There are two different types of read/write mechanisms: a movable-head type is usually used with removable disk packs, while a fixed-head type is usually used with fixed disk packs.

A typical movable-head or comb-type access mechanism consists of a group of access arms mounted on an assembly. One arm extends between every two adjacent disks; each arm has two heads, one for the upper and one for the lower disk surface. The entire access assembly is able to move horizontally from the outermost to the innermost cylinder and back. At the same time, the disk pack rotates on its spindle. In this way the read/write heads are positioned at the proper sector of the cylinder containing the data to be accessed. The head

Close-up view of the IBM 2316 disk unit showing read/write heads and access arms between adjacent disk surfaces.

(Courtesy of IBM)

that is in position over the data is then switched on electronically; only one head may read or write data at any time.

The speed with which data can be read or written by a movable-head mechanism depends on two factors. The *access or seek time* is the time it takes for the access mechanism to move to the cylinder

(Courtesy of IBM)

The IBM 2305 fixed-head storage facility

185

where the necessary data are stored. This time depends on the number of cylinders the mechanism has to cross before it reaches the desired one. The *rotational delay* is the time spent in rotating the disk pack to the correct position. In today's technology, these times are expressed in milliseconds.

Fixed-head access mechanisms do not have read/write heads that move. Instead, a head is provided for each track. Access times are much faster, since seek time is eliminated and there is only rotational delay. Although higher in cost, fixed-head mechanisms are often used for applications where speedy data retrieval is essential.

In one type of fixed-head access mechanism, a disk is subdivided into addressable recording tracks. An addressable track is half of a full track and consists of two logical track segments—one on the top surface of the disk and one on the bottom. A pair of read/write heads is provided for each addressable track. Data are recorded serially by bit, but in parallel by byte. This means that every even byte is recorded on the lower segment and every odd byte on the upper one. It takes two read/write heads working together to access any one data record.

Since an addressable track is a 180-degree arc, it only takes half a rotation to read or write data. On the average, a quarter of a turn will be needed to locate any particular record. This decreases the rotational delay.

In another type of fixed-head device, four mechanisms are positioned around the disks, each able to access a quarter of the tracks on each surface. In other words, one mechanism will access the data on tracks 1, 5, 9, 13 . . . on every surface; a second mechanism will access the data on tracks 2, 6, 10, 14 . . .; a third mechanism will access tracks 3, 7, 11, 15 . . .; and a fourth mechanism will access the remaining tracks.

This type of mechanism stores data serially bit by bit and byte by byte. Since it has only one head per track and twice as many recording tracks per surface, it can store twice as many bytes of data as the first type of fixed-head mechanism discussed above.

Disk Drives

All of these components—the disk media, access mechanism, and read/write heads—are combined in a subsystem known as the *disk drive*. A disk drive may combine a movable-head access mechanism with disk media packaged in a removable pack, or a fixed-head access mechanism with rigid disk media fixed within the drive. Single-disk cartridges are also available for use with movable-head mechanisms and in several hybrid drives. The most recent development in disk drive technology is the data module, which contains the disks, spindle, read/write heads, and access arms, all in one sealed cartridge.

The performance of a disk drive depends on several parameters, most of which should be familiar to us by now: storage capacity, bit density, disk rotational speed, access times, and reliability.

The older drives that are still in use have the smallest capacities. Their disk tracks are fairly wide—.0038 to .005 inches—compared with those of the newer disk surfaces. Also, their bit densities are lower—1,000 to 4,000 bpi—compared with those of the newer units that have densities of 6,000 bpi or more. Older drive models also have slower rotational speeds and higher access times, because many of them are the movable-head type. The newer fixed-head drives are improving in all these parameters; in addition, they boast higher reliability than removable-disk types.

Winchester Disk Drives

Because the disk surface travels at speeds exceeding 100 miles per hour during read/write operations, any direct contact with the read/write head would destroy the magnetic coating. Therefore, these heads are designed to float or "fly" on the rotating film of air that adheres to the disk surface. The correct spacing between head and surface is maintained by applying a load on the head assembly. This spacing, called the "flying height," is significant in that the farther away from the surface the head is when it writes, the larger will be the area of each bit. The reason for this has to do with the special

(BASF Wyandotte Corporation)

A Winchester disk module containing disk access arms, read/write heads, and disks. The entire module is completely sealed to avoid contamination by dust particles, fingerprints, and other hazards that tend to cause "head crash" in open disk packs.

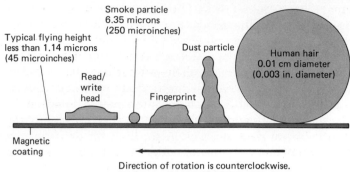

Figure 6-12 How contamination of track surface affects flying height

Adapted from Mini-Micro Systems, February 1979. © 1979 Cahners Publishing Company.

characteristics of magnetic charges. The lower the flying height, the more bits per inch can be written on a disk track. Typically, a read/write head flies less than 45 microinches above the track surface.

Occasionally the read/write head comes in contact with, or "crashes" into, minute foreign matter on the disk. This is known as "head crash," and the most frequent cause is the presence of human hair (about 3,000 microinches or millionths of an inch in diameter), smoke particles (250 microinches), and dust on the disk surface. Hitting this debris can seriously affect the operation of the read/write head. (Figure 6-12 shows the relationship between flying height and various kinds of debris.)

Special technologies have been developed to overcome this and

In mid-1980, BASF introduced its 6170 series Winchester-type data storage systems featuring high-storage-capacity fixed disks in a lower-cost, floppy-sized package. The hard disks are enclosed in a pack with a filtered air system to prevent data errors due to dust, smoke, and other contaminants, and require no maintenance. The Winchester-type head is less sensitive to shock and vibration than other types of disk heads.

(BASF Wyandotte Corporation)

other problems. One such device is the Winchester disk drive, in which magnetic disks, read/write heads, and a head actuator are all packaged together in a module that is sealed from outside air and is nonremovable. A small amount of air circulates through the drive for cooling purposes; it is filtered to eliminate all particles 0.3 microns or larger. Because the disk module is impervious to contaminants, head crash caused by dust and dirt particles are virtually eliminated. This allows lower flying heights, and therefore more compact data storage, than ever before possible.

During the read/write/seek operations, the Winchester head flies only 20 microinches above the disk surface. Because of the head's lightweight design, it is able to rest on a silicon-lubricated landing zone during starts and stops without disrupting its recording ability. This is another feature that helps eliminate head crashes.

Because of the improved head design, more precisely defined bits and higher bit densities—above 6,000 bpi—are attainable. Track widths are also much narrower—0.001 inch as opposed to 0.0023 inch for the most advanced unsealed model. Reliability of the Winchester drive is also noticeably better. It boasts mean-time-between-failure rates of 6,000 hours, compared with less than 3,000 hours for removable disk packs.

Winchester disk drives have the lowest cost per stored byte, highest storage capacity, and lowest cost of movable-head rigid magnetic disk drives. They also have the lowest cost per processing transaction or function, primarily because of their faster rates of data transfer. Rates now range from 156,000 bytes per second to over one million bytes per second. With higher storage capacities, Winchester disks are smaller—8 inches as compared with the 14-inch aluminum disk. In the future we should expect to see even smaller disks, probably about 5 inches in diameter, with the same storage capacity.

Floppy Disks

Floppy disks, floppies, or flexible disks, also called diskettes, are used primarily for minicomputers as inexpensive random-access storage devices. The 8-inch-diameter disks are made of polyester film covered with an iron oxide compound. The disk is permanently sealed inside a protective jacket that prevents data loss and damage to the surface. When set on its spindle, the floppy is able to rotate freely within this jacket.

A floppy disk is divided into 77 tracks similar to those on rigid disks. Only 74 of these are used for actual data storage; the remaining tracks contain the operating system and the names and addresses of all the files in storage. The tracks are divided into sectors, or wedge-shaped sections. Data may be stored sequentially or by sector allocation.

In sequential storage, the new file is placed on the disk in the empty sectors following the last file entered on the disk. If a file is deleted, its space remains empty until there is no more room at the end of the last file stored. Then a special program shifts all the files on the disk to take up the unused space. This is called compressing or packing the disk.

With sector allocation, one track of the diskette contains a bit map. This is similar to a file index. On the bit map, each sector on the diskette is represented by one bit. The bit map indicates which sectors are in use and which are empty. As new files are entered into the empty sectors, a program adjusts the bit map to show the new arrangement. When a file is deleted, the bit map is similarly adjusted to show that new space is available.

Floppy disks have capacities of 800,000 bytes for single-sided and 1.6 million bytes for double-sided double-density diskette drives. They are a relatively inexpensive means of obtaining direct-access capabilities for mini- and microcomputers, and so are becoming more and more common.

Magnetic Drums

A magnetic drum is a metal cylinder covered with a thin layer of iron oxide. The drum rotates past read/write heads located tangentially to the drum surface. Like magnetic disks, magnetic drums are a relatively fast auxiliary memory, having access times from eight- to 200-thousandths of a second. Storage and retrieval of data from the magnetic drum are done in much the same way as magnetic disks, except that the drum rotates around a horizontal axis past the fixed read/write heads.

Mass Storage Systems

The ability to store data files in the order of 100 billion bytes or more may seem like a fantasy. However, government agencies, large manufacturing companies, retailers, publishers, automotive manufacturers, and several other kinds of organizations that require mass storage have already installed such systems.

The most inconvenient aspects of storing large data files are the actual handling of tape reels and disk packs and the physical storage space needed for them. Mass storage systems eliminate these woes by absorbing the storage and handling into the system itself. Data are

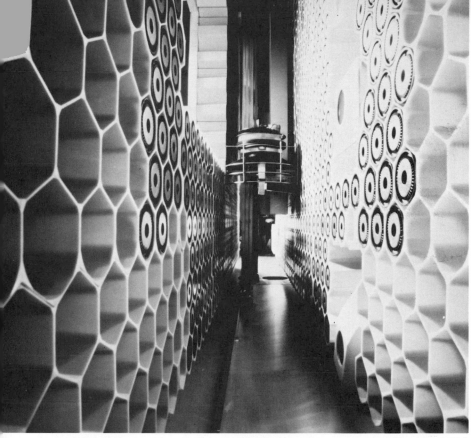

The IBM 3850 mass storage system showing nested "honeycomb" compartments and movable access mechanism.

(Courtesy of IBM)

(Courtesy of IBM)

Close-up of access mechanism and mass storage cartridges in the IBM 3850 mass storage system.

191

recorded on magnetic tape enclosed in small cartridges. Each cartridge is stored in its own cell, which is nested into a honeycomb-like arrangement. A cartridge can be automatically retrieved by the system when it is required for read or write operations. Retrieval rates are from 250 to 275 picks per hour in a typical system, much quicker than an operator mounting and dismounting tape reels manually.

The reliability of most commercially available mass storage systems is good. Since the tapes are enclosed in cartridges, many of the problems associated with tape damage or with accidental erasure are eliminated. Many applications of mass storage, however, may require backup data files; this is not easily accomplished, either outside the system or within the system itself.

The IBM 3850 is a mass storage system that can store 472 billion bytes or characters. Since there are approximately four billion people in the world, a 3850 could store a 100-character record for every man, woman, and child on this planet! Of course, that would only account for 400 billion characters; 72 billion would be left over—just enough to store the contents of the Manhattan telephone directory.

Criteria for File Selection

There is no one best method of storing data. The program selected or specific user requirements will usually determine the file organization technique. User requirements are determined by such factors as response time, file activity, file volatility, file size, and cost.

Response time is the interval between a request for information from the system and the receipt of an answer from the system. If, for example, a manager requests the total sales for the previous month, and does not need the actual data until one or two days later, then the file that stores those data could be sequential. If, however, as in an airline reservation system, an immediate response is desired, then direct-access file organization would be necessary.

File activity is the ratio of the number of records required for processing compared with the total number of records in the file. In a file of 10,000 payroll records, almost all the records in the file are processed every time the payroll is prepared. Only data for those individuals who for some reason are not getting checks for a given period would not be processed. If, therefore, 9,990 records were processed out of 10,000 total records, the file activity would be 0.999. Such a high file activity would lend itself to sequential processing. According to a data processing rule of thumb, file activity of 0.3 (30 out of 100) or higher requires sequential organization. If, however, file activity is lower than 0.3, direct-access organization should be chosen. Although a single direct-access record can be retrieved rapidly, there is inevitably some time involved in finding that one record. When a substantial number of records are to be accessed, then the time required on a direct-access file to retrieve and process all the transactions might be greater than that required to process an *entire* sequential file.

File volatility is a measure of the number of records added to or deleted from a file within a specific period of time. In sequential file organization, the only major concern would be the physical size of the file. But for an ISAM or direct-access file, additional factors must be considered. Adding records to an ISAM file would cause records to be "bumped" to an overflow area and thus require additional time to search for a given record. In ISAM and direct-access files, deleted records are not actually physically removed. They are simply "tagged" as having been deleted, but held in the storage medium until the entire file is revised. Consequently, such files tend to accumulate deleted records that occupy space. This wastes file storage space, requires the development of new keys (otherwise new records would occupy the locations of the deleted records), and ultimately results in an increase in search time.

The *size* of the data file is an important consideration in file organization selection. Some very large files must be stored sequentially on magnetic tape, simply because there is not enough storage available on disks. Small sequential files, however, could be stored on magnetic disks.

Cost is often the ultimate decision criterion. It is much less expensive to store data on sequential file media, such as magnetic tape, than on direct-access storage media, such as magnetic disks.

But each of these criteria must be considered in conjunction with the others.

Tomorrow's Technology

The auxiliary storage devices now in use are mechanical in nature. That is, the data-containing component is moved physically into a particular position and then past the read/write component. Although electronics makes these mechanical movements possible, the data are not contained in the electronics of the system. This will change in the future.

Magnetic bubble memory avoids all mechanical motion involved in read/write operations while retaining many advantages of mechanical auxiliary storage, including high speed, high capacity, and nonvolatility of data. Magnetic bubbles (see chapters 2 and 5) can be made to move when exposed to a magnetic field. Data bits are thus transferred within the bubble memory without any mechanical assistance. Bubble components are already being produced.

Other technologies that show great promise are still in various stages of development. Electron-beam memories have been developed on a principle reminiscent of the vacuum tube memories of the very first computer. In these memories, data are written on a storage chip or target inside a tube or configuration of tubes. The target stores data as a positive charge; readout is accomplished by the use of an electron beam of a lower energy level than that used to write the data. Depending on whether a 1 or a 0 is stored, this beam causes a high or lower current to flow off the target. This type of memory is nonvolatile but semidestructive; data must be rewritten after several read operations.

Laser photochemical storage, an optical memory, produces an image called a hologram in a pattern that functions as a data record. Josephson junction memory cells are the most promising development in energy economy for quantity data storage. A large number of such cells can be mounted on a single chip. This technology, too, is beginning to move from the developmental stages, and devices incorporating Josephson cells will be available in a few years.

Such high-capacity, high-speed capabilities will make possible the storage of greater amounts of data within primary storage. Increasingly, the demarcation line between main memory and auxiliary storage will become blurred as these developments are incorporated into the computers of the future.

Summary

Large data files accumulate in business data processing and require auxiliary storage systems that are flexible and inexpensive and can be accessed quickly. Of course, compromises must be made when selecting a particular system. Sequential-access storage devices such as magnetic tape are inexpensive, but they lack flexibility and speed. Direct-access devices, while more costly, provide a greater number of options for file organization and data processing.

Direct-access files may be organized in four ways: sequential, indexed sequential, direct, and virtual storage access. Each has advantages in certain applications. The direct-access storage devices (DASD) in which files may be stored by these methods are: rigid magnetic disks, magnetic floppy disks, Winchester disks, and magnetic drums.

In mass storage systems, tape cartridges that store up to 472 billion bytes of information can be directly, and rapidly, accessed. Such systems are increasingly employed where great masses of data must be entered and processed rapidly.

In the future, auxiliary storage will move toward elimination of most or all of the mechanics involved with such storage media as tapes and disks. Solid-state or optical-based information systems now being developed will blend primary and auxiliary storage, as it becomes possible to store greater quantities of data more efficiently in bubble, laser, and Josephson junction memories.

Key Terms and Phrases

bits per inch (bpi)
bytes per inch (BPI)
blocking factor
cylinder
data transfer rate
direct-access devices
disk drive
end-of-file marker
end-of-reel marker
file activity
file volatility
floppy disks
index
indexed sequential-access method (ISAM)

interblock gap (IBG)
interrecord gap (IRG)
overflow area
prime area
record
response time
rotational delay
seek time
sequential-access devices
tape density
tracks per inch (tpi)
unblocked
virtual storage access method (VSAM)

Sources of Additional Information

Blair, Donald. "The Care and Maintenance of Disk Media." *Mini-Micro Systems,* no. 10 (1979):81–83.

Bowers, Dan M. "The Rough Road to Today's Technology." *Datamation,* no. 9 (1977):69–74.

"Bubbling Up Some Memory Devices." *Data Management,* no. 8 (1977): 12–15.

Halsema, A. I. "Bubble Memories: A Short Tutorial." *Byte,* no. 6 (1979): 166–67.

Hasler, Alfred S. "8-Inch Disks Come of Age." *Mini-Micro Systems,* no. 7 (1979):73–76.

Hodges, David A. "Microelectronic Memories." *Scientific American,* September 1977, pp. 130–45.

Juliessen, J. Egil. "Where Bubble Memory Will Find a Niche." *Mini-Micro Systems,* no. 7 (1979):48–61.

Theis, Douglas J. "An Overview of Memory Technologies." *Datamation,* no. 1 (1978):113–31.

Yasaki, Edward K. "Peripherals: A Very Difficult Birth." *Datamation,* no. 1 (1979):52–54.

1. What is the function of an auxiliary storage device in a computer system?

2. What is meant by the phrase "access method" when referring to an auxiliary storage device?

3. Name and briefly describe the major access methods that may be used by the computer system to locate and retrieve data and/or records from an auxiliary storage device.

4. Why would you *not* choose to use the sequential-access storage method for processing in an information system?

5. You currently have a master file, on magnetic tape, with information on 10,000 customer charge accounts. The records have been stored on the tape as single entities, separated from each other by IBGs. When a file update is performed, the process is very time-consuming and cumbersome. How can the existing file be restructured to expedite the update process? Explain.

6. The entries on the employee payroll deductions file are in employee number sequence. You have been given a group of transaction records that must be added to and deleted from the master file. The addition and deletion records are in random order. When you attempted to apply these records against the deductions file, most of the records were rejected as not matching. Why? Explain your answer.

7. If there is no room on a direct-access storage device for a new record, what will happen to that record?

8. If you were to simulate manually the action of a computer system, how would you locate this page, within this chapter, using first the sequential-access method and then the direct-access method?

9. If you were asked to establish a chart for comparison of the disk media produced and/or marketed by various vendors, what parameters should be included?

10. What is a "head crash"?

11. Why is a sequential file inefficient for random processing purposes?

12. The president of your company recently read an article in a business magazine about diskettes. She questions whether or not we could utilize the diskettes with our large-scale computer as auxiliary storage. How would you respond?

13. What are some of the advantages of a mass storage device?

14. Punched cards and punched paper tape are considered to be forms of auxiliary storage. Compare these two media with magnetic tape. How are they similar? How do they differ?

15. What is unique about a Winchester disk?

7 Data Communications

© Computerworld

"Hello, Operator, I just wanted to hear a human voice."

APPLICATION
Electronic Funds Transfer

Using her Touch-Tone home telephone, the benefits administrator of a large corporation dials a special number, which puts her in communication with a computer at her bank. Again using the Touch-Tone phone, she keys in her own account number, then the bank account code for her local telephone company, her telephone number, and the dollar amount of her phone bill. The computer debits her account, and credits payment to the telephone company. She is not concerned about her bank account balance because she received verification of the balance after her take-home pay was deposited directly to her account. Later in the day she will need cash. Going to an electronic teller terminal at a nearby branch of her bank, she will insert her identification card, key in the amount, and receive a package of money that has been debited to her account.

The benefits administrator is employed at the main office of a company that has 14 subsidiary branches in five states on both the east and west coasts. By prior arrangement with cooperating banks, the main office has arranged for its own bank to receive income directly. At predetermined intervals, payments transferred by wire from wherever business transactions take place are credited to the company's account. This arrangement has reduced from two or more weeks to one day the time needed to clear funds from distant locations. This speedup has significantly improved the company's cash flow.

This is the world of electronic funds transfer, or EFT. EFT has been in the news for over a decade. It is made possible by a new mix of data communications equipment, carrier networks, private industry, and banks. Originally heralded as the arrival of a "checkless society," EFT for the consumer has come more slowly than expected. But business applications have rapidly expanded, under pressure from various industries to speed up transfer payments. Fortunately, these pressures increased at the same time as the technology to accomplish the task was being developed.

In advance of the checkless society, however, consumers are experiencing limited applications of EFT. In addition to those suggested above, transfer payments from the Social Security Administration and paychecks from many corporations can already be deposited directly into individuals' accounts in cooperating banks. But, because of consumer and legislative fears about privacy, safeguards, and guarantees, a truly checkless society for the consumer is not much closer than it was a decade ago.

On the other hand, EFT has had a major impact in the business sector because it provides a big advantage: By accelerating the receipt of accounts receivable, EFT makes more cash available to a business or organization in a given time. On the other hand, individual banks may lose the use of funds that move out too quickly, and are not able to retain their customers' money for as long as they did previously.

OVER 250 BILLION data transactions a day are currently transmitted or received by computers in the United States. These transactions move through channels, which may be of copper wire (such as conventional cable and telephone lines) or may be microwave links or modern glass fiber cable. Telecommunications channels—domestic and international telephone and telegraph wires, radio and television wavelengths, and such specialized media as telecommunication satellites—constitute a vast industry. The developing technology has crossed state, national, and international borders, and is responsible for many new and accelerated transaction capabilities—and many new considerations about data integrity.

A communications channel forms a pathway between sending and receiving (input and output) devices. A channel can be intracomputer (that is, between a CPU and an auxiliary or other input/output device); or it may be extracomputer or remote (that is, between two or more computers or between terminals and computer). The user terminals can be thousands of miles apart or separated by only a few feet.

The technology for directly linking a computer to auxiliary equipment in close proximity is relatively simple. Data between computer components flow along cables that are the property of the equipment user. The cables, which in effect link the equipment together, are analogous to the cables linking a high-fidelity receiver to its associated speakers and reproduction equipment. The organization of channels or pathways is limited to the computer system that they serve.

However, where computers and terminals are separated by larger distances, the channels along which data are transmitted belong to common carriers. A common carrier is a company engaged in the transportation of goods and services for the public. Railroads and airlines are common carriers, but our concern here is with carriers of telecommunications, specifically the telephone and broadcasting industries. These carriers are regulated by the Federal Communications Commission (FCC).

Until 1968, telephone companies had a monopoly of communications channels. But in that year, the FCC allowed new private carriers to compete for the lines owned by the telephone companies, and also allowed users to interconnect private equipment with telephone company lines. Users now have a variety of companies from which to choose, each providing different cable accommodations at different costs. That ruling vastly increased cable services, and resulted also in the production of special equipment to meet the demand for speeding up and controlling data communications.

Several broad aspects of data communications are the subject of this chapter: the data pathways, or channels, within a computer, as well as those to nearby storage and peripheral devices and to remote communications equipment. We will look also at the equipment most often used to transmit and receive data over common channels, at the various communications channels in use, and at some of the methods used to speed up and condition data so that more information can be "packed" onto a channel for transmission in a given time period. Finally, different data processing methods in relation to their communications needs will be described.

Intracomputer Communications

When a program is being executed in primary storage in the CPU, data stored on associated tape or disk media are usually needed. The executing program itself informs the CPU of its need for specific data items, and instructs the CPU where the required data are stored so that the correct address in the storage device may be accessed. The CPU then sets up a connection between itself and the storage device. Because data are transmitted electronically, they must be carried along a pathway capable of conducting an electric current. The pathways for electrical transmission between two or more points are known as *channels*; the terms *circuit, line,* and *link* are also often used.

A data channel, then, is an electrical circuit. Every time the CPU requires information, and again when the revised information is returned to auxiliary storage, a data channel must be set up.

Primary storage is used most efficiently to hold executing programs. If it also had to direct the traffic flow, its processing capacity would be decreased. Moreover, since the CPU operates much more rapidly than its peripherals, it would often be idle between execution of programmed instructions.

To overcome these problems, an input/output (I/O) control unit is used, which relieves the CPU of its "traffic cop" functions. Directed by the operating system, the control unit organizes the data channels between the equipment units. (Figure 7-1 shows a typical data processing installation with several tape and disk storage devices and other peripherals attached to a CPU via I/O control units.) The I/O control unit also displays program status information, so the computer operator is aware at all times of which peripherals are being used.

An I/O control unit is designed as part of a particular data processing system. As a result, different installations contain I/O control devices that may serve somewhat different functions. Generally, an

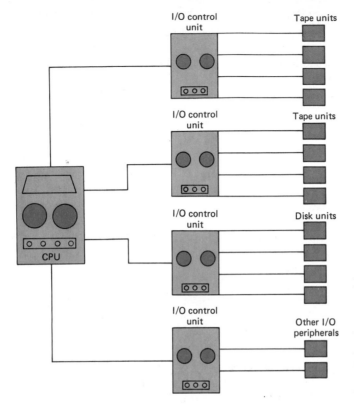

Figure 7-1 I/O control units
The I/O control unit serves as an interface between the CPU and auxiliary storage and other peripheral devices, directing inputs and outputs between them.

I/O control unit will, under the control of the program, organize, connect, and direct the data channels between a CPU and its peripheral equipment. It will monitor status between the CPU and each piece of equipment, and will determine whether a data transfer is occurring, or has been completed. It can usually validate message content and determine whether a transfer error has occurred.

An I/O control unit also acts as a buffer, storing information from each peripheral device until the CPU can accept it, and can usually accumulate data input from several sources simultaneously. However, because the CPU can execute only one command at a time, the I/O control unit will switch its accumulation of data into the CPU in whatever sequence is requested by the CPU. Thus, CPU processing efficiency is maintained at high levels.

I/O control units are important, too, in their role as "translators." They provide any necessary codes to convert data as received from a storage device, and may reconvert data when placing new information back into the tape or disk storage device. They can also convert inputs from punched cards, magnetic card readers, and remote terminals into computer code.

Handwritten margin notes:

I/O CONTROL UNIT

1. ORGANIZE, CONNECT, & DIRECT data channels

2. MONITOR STATUS of CPU & EQUIPMENT

3. deterMINE IF a data tRANSFER IS OCCURING

4. CAN VALIDATE MESSAGE CONTENT to SEE IF tRANSFER ERROR HAS OCCURED

5. StOReS data FOR CPU

6. ASSIST IN CONVERSION OF DATA

201

Remote Communications

Not too long ago, computer power could be accessed only by a user who was physically present at the computer site, and information had to be physically transported from one site to another. However, communications capabilities today have made it possible for computers and their users to be at geographically dispersed locations.

When a CPU is at a great distance from user terminals and displays, or from other computers with which it may be communicating, data must be transmitted over lines owned by common and specialized carriers. These telecommunications lines are organized into networks that can connect equipment located in different buildings, cities, states, nations, and even continents. Centralized controls coordinate the flow of data through channels linking one site to an-

(Ray Trozzc, Communication/Design, Citibank, N.A.)

Making a deposit at a branch bank terminal. Computer communications make it possible to verify the bank card and account number and to credit or debit the account. Instructions can be given to the user in any of several languages—here they are in Spanish.

other. Typically, the branches of a bank or department store, or the various factory locations of a single manufacturer, would use such remote communications connections to a central CPU.

Common carrier networks facilitate data transactions in many ways. They make it possible for intracomputer communications to occur at the same time as intercomputer communications. With these channels, data can be processed in *real time*, so that the resulting output becomes available almost immediately to all users in the system.

(handwritten marginalia): NETWORKS MAKE able REAl time processing so data available immediatly to All USERS

Use of common carrier cables solves some problems but involves others. Cables are limited by their frequency and bandwidth in the amount of information they can handle. (Bandwidth refers to the range of frequencies over which a device operates.) Accidental damage from various sources poses a hazard to switching equipment and cables installed over a wide area. In some cases, computer links and other equipment attached to the communications lines can be a source of accidental damage.

Because the carrier networks are geographically far-flung, they are subject to deliberate violation from a variety of sources as well. Ensuring the security of data entrusted to these channels is an ongoing concern. Special devices are required that can provide a safe interface between the computers and end-use equipment in the system and the common carrier cables, and that can transmit data with maximum efficiency. Before describing these devices, however, we will examine some characteristics of the data transmission channels themselves.

Data Transmission

The common carriers utilize several operating media to accommodate domestic, national, and international traffic. Ordinary telephone and telegraph wire and cable are used by telephone companies for local installation at each site. For longer links and higher traffic densities, however, special transmission cables are required. Very-high-frequency (microwave) radio links between earth stations and communications satellites are also available.

Media for data transmission. Most people today are familiar with the concepts of frequency and bandwidth from their experience with AM and FM radio. They know, for example, that a radio with a range of from 20 Hz (hertz) to 20,000 Hz will receive signals sent at every frequency within this range or bandwidth. They may not know, though, that this corresponds to the range of frequencies that can be heard by the human ear.

(handwritten marginalia): AM/FM & HUMAN EAR 20 - 20,000 Hz.

Frequency and bandwidth are the determinants in using and choosing the various channel media available. A telephone line has a bandwidth of approximately 3,000 Hz, operating at audible frequencies from 300 Hz to 3,300 Hz. Higher-frequency ranges are provided by different channel media. Microwave links, for example, can transmit frequencies in millions of hertz. Higher-frequency ranges permit broader bandwidths, and thus can accommodate many more, and broader, channels simultaneously.

In older telephone installations, in which all wires were strung aboveground between telephone poles, *open wire pairs* carried the transmitted signals. These wires were open; that is, they were not insulated. They were separated from each other (and grounded to prevent injury and escape of current) by insulation on the poles themselves. Except in older rural areas where there is not enough traffic to justify conversion, or under specific geographic conditions, open wire pairs are no longer in use.

Ordinary telephone lines in widest use today consist of *wire cable*, usually two wires, each with its own insulated coating. The insulation makes it possible to pack the wires closely together. Each wire pair can carry one telephone channel operating at human-voice frequency. The bundle of wires forming a cable is protected by an outer cable jacket. In most telephone cables, the insulation covering the wires is color-coded to connectors in the telephone or terminal box. Cables from separate locations meet and are joined together at large terminal blocks in basements and under roads and streets. Thus the cable from one telephone becomes linked with hundreds, and then thousands, of others in a vast network running underground. These cables provide the channels to switching equipment at the nearest telephone company exchange center; from there, incoming calls are routed—by computer in most cases today—to their destinations.

Instead of two separate wires, *coaxial cable* consists of an outer cylinder of copper wire surrounding a single inner conducting wire, but is separated from the inner wire by spaced insulators. A protective wrapping surrounds the outer conductor. There is less signal loss over long distances with coaxial cable than with plain wire pairs. Coaxial cables can also operate at higher frequencies and bandwidths, and therefore can accommodate several hundred simultaneous calls on one cable. In addition, coaxial cables can be bundled together—20 of them can handle 18,740 telephone calls at the same time. Like wire cable, coaxial cables are joined into larger and larger bundles underground and can form complex networks. Telephone companies and specialized carrier networks use this medium for larger communications installations and for transmitting large volumes of data.

Submarine cables are basically coaxial in design and are laid along ocean floors. They can accommodate several hundred simultaneous channels. The outer jacket of the cable is designed to withstand the rigors of deep ocean pressure. Prior to the introduction of satellites, submarine cable was the only reliable link between continents. Submarine cable does not have the capacity to serve today's voice and data customers, and the technology and labor required to lay it have become prohibitively expensive.

Extremely high radio transmission frequencies are known as microwaves. FM and television signals are transmitted along the lower microwave bands; radar travels along the higher bands. Microwave signals are carried, without wire or cable, through the earth's atmosphere in a straight line between sending/receiving towers. These tall structures are necessary because microwaves travel in a straight line; the microwave transmitter must "see" its receiver along a line-of-sight path. The earth's curvature limits efficient transmission paths to about 25 miles over flat terrain; transmission lengths can increase across mountainous areas, depending on peak heights. At each receiving site, prior to retransmission, the signals are usually restored and boosted, or amplified; this happens in fractions of a second. Despite the disadvantages imposed by the need for transmission towers at frequent intervals, microwave transmission has two key advantages. First, many thousands of narrow band channels can be carried simultaneously along the relatively broad microwave bandwidths. Second, the carrier network saves the cost of stringing or laying additional cable.

Communications satellites are similar in concept to the repeating links provided by microwave towers. Placed in a fixed orbit above the earth, with their circular orbit speed matching that of the earth's rotation, satellites provide permanent line-of-sight transmission links. They can receive signals from, and retransmit them to, numerous microwave sending/receiving stations. Circuits in the satellites are designed to accept, store, or forward communications signals. Depending on the overall communications requirements, signals can be forwarded in real time, or they can be stored for later "dumping" at preselected times. Satellites, which can accommodate many thousands of channels simultaneously, have not only vastly increased the number of communications channels available, but also have shortened connecting times between continents and countries and increased the accuracy (fidelity) of long-distance communications.

Fiber-optic cables are constructed of lightweight and infinitesimally thin glass fibers. The glass fibers are light-conducting, and receive and transmit light signals controlled by laser or by light-emitting diode (LED) switching mechanisms. These are high-frequency light sources that can code light into an analog of the on/off code

205

Dish-shaped antennas receive signals and transmit signals between an orbiting communications satellite and its earth station. Shown here is the South Mountain Earth Station of RCA American Communications in Somis, California.

(Courtesy of RCA)

(Courtesy of RCA)

Inside an earth station, which controls communications satellites. Shown here is the RCA Americom station at Vernon Valley, New Jersey, which also provides voice, data, and video communications services to the New York area. The communications console, including television signal monitoring equipment, is at the left.

206

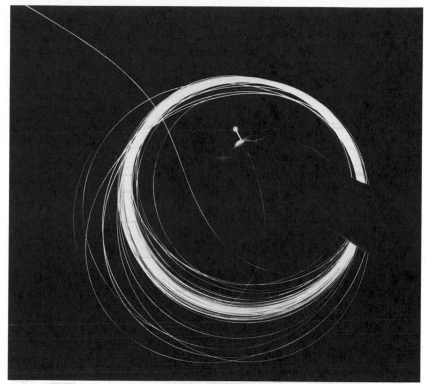

(Bell Labs)

Loops of hair-thin glass
fiber, illuminated by
laser light, are the
transmission medium for
lightwave communi-
cations systems.
Typically, 12 glass fibers
are embedded between
two strips of plastic in a
flat ribbon; up to 12
ribbons are stacked in a
cable that can transmit
more than 40,000 two-
way voice and/or data
channels.

provided by electrical signals; the light transmissions are then decoded at the receiving end. Glass fiber has certain advantages over
conventional copper wire or wire-based cable. It is immune to wire-
tapping, and greater distances between signal amplifiers are possible. Glass fiber cables are much thinner than copper cable, and can
replace conventional cable in existing ducts. They also weigh about
0.015 percent that of conventional cable. Because they are switched
at very high frequencies, they offer both broader bandwidths to accommodate high-speed data communications and more channels in
proportion to cable diameter. Currently, design limitations in the
technology for the light sources (the laser or the LED) are still preventing full-scale use. Several experimental systems have been
tested in large cities, with great success. Plans are now under way by
the common carriers for many large-scale installations in major
urban areas.

High-frequency radio and waveguides are used much less frequently. In particularly remote parts of the world, high-frequency
radio may be used for transmission of computer data. Because it operates relatively slowly, has a high rate of transmission error, and requires very large antennas to carry the signals, high-frequency radio
has few computer-related applications. Waveguides are hollow,

[Handwritten marginalia:]
ADVANTAGES of
FIBER OPTICS

1. immune to wire
   tapping
2. greater distances
   between applifiers
3. lighter than wire
4. broader band widths

207

open-ended containers (tubes or rectangles) through which high-frequency radio waves can be concentrated. Although they can carry 100,000 or more voice lines simultaneously, their use is limited to applications in which data must move over relatively short distances—for example, to link radar or microwave tower antennas within a few thousand feet of each other.

Types of data transmission. A transmission channel consists of all the equipment and carrier media that provide the electrical linkage between a transmitter and a receiver. The most usual carrier medium consists of telephone cable. Most links use two-wire cable, and some applications require four-wire cable; the difference between two- and four-wire use depends on the data requirements of the computer installation.

There are three basic types of transmission in relation to channel wiring. In *simplex* transmission, communication takes place in one direction only. The direction is fixed at all times and cannot be reversed. *Half-duplex* transmission provides for two-way transmission, although not simultaneously. Data are transmitted first in one direction, and then in the reverse direction. In *full duplex* transmission, simultaneous two-way communication is possible. (See figure 7-2.)

Simplex and half-duplex communication require only a two-wire circuit. However, full duplex transmission requires a four-wire circuit, with one pair of wires dedicated to each channel direction.

Modes for data transmission. The characters making up a data item are generally transmitted serially, or one following the other, until transmission of an entire record is complete. The receiver must at all times operate in synchronization with the transmitter, or the received signal will be garbled. There are two general modes for data transmission.

In *asynchronous (or nonsynchronous) transmission,* each character is preceded by a "start" bit and is followed by one or two "stop" bits. These instructional bits alert the receiver to recognize each character according to a predetermined code format, and keep the receiver and transmitter terminals aligned as each character is sent.

Figure 7-2 Modes of transmission

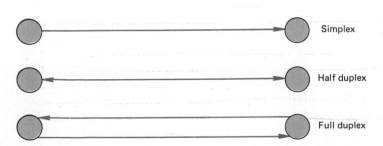

Simplex

Half duplex

Full duplex

(A.T.&T. Co. Photo/Graphics Center)

Equipment for data
transmission. The VuSet
with an alphanumeric
keyboard operates
synchronously over both
switched and private
line networks.

It is not necessary for characters to be sent at any particular intervals;
often, there may be wait periods of several seconds between characters. Asynchronous transmission is sometimes referred to as "start-
and-stop" transmission for this reason.

In *synchronous transmission,* several blocks of characters that are
several thousand bits in length may be transmitted without a break.
Under this scheme, the receiver counts bits as they arrive to form
characters, and forwards each character to the CPU. Synchronization
takes place just prior to the start of transmission, and is reestablished
during wait intervals. This approach permits high-speed data transmission, and is more efficient.

There are advantages and disadvantages to each transmission
method. Messages sent asynchronously are not subject to gross dis-
tortion; an interruption in transmission would destroy only a single
character on an asynchronous line during a break interval. Under the
same circumstances, though, the message content of an entire synchronous data stream would be lost. Although slower than synchronous transmission, the equipment and line media for start-and-stop
operations are simpler to design and less expensive to purchase and
maintain. Moreover, lines and equipment can be used efficiently.
Synchronous transmission requires more sophisticated equipment
and lines, and is used where greater data amounts and the need for
greater speed justify the additional expense.

209

Error detection. Errors may enter data communications systems from various sources. The primary source of errors is in the carrier cables, which are susceptible to certain interferences. A smaller error source is in the communications equipment. Error control, though, can be critical for dependable operation.

The severity of problems resulting from transmission error may depend on whether the data transmitted are alphabetic or numeric. Completely verbal messages, for instance, can contain a few missing or substituted letters and still be understood by the ultimate human reader. But numerical—dollars and cents—applications cannot afford inaccurate data reception.

Telephone line errors may be due to unwanted electrical signals or "impulse" noise, which is generated by lightning and thunder, or may be caused by telephone company switching equipment. Impulse noise is random and transient in nature, and lasts about $1/100$ of a second. Power outages can be disastrous, causing substantial loss of data. Other sources of error are cross talk (conversations or signals on one line that are induced into an adjacent line), signal attenuation, and line echoes. The error rate increases as transmission distance increases. On the average, there is an error rate of about one character per 10,000 characters transmitted over telephone lines. Unfortunately, errors usually are not evenly distributed, but are likely to occur in bursts that affect a sequence of bits, perhaps as many as 50 to 100 bits.

Errors may be ignored, as for a completely verbal transmission. More often, it is necessary to detect them and either request retransmission or automatically correct them upon detection.

Retransmission requires relatively little in additional storage and software. The synchronizing information in the asynchronous and synchronous transmission methods described above can automatically trigger circuits that request retransmission upon error detection, and also alert the operator to the error. Error-detection methods depend on coding schemes that alert receiving equipment to out-of-order bit sequences or the number of odd and even bits (parity checking) in the character. Another method of error detection applies complex mathematical equations to data as they are sent and again as they are received; if the results of the procedures do not match, the equipment is alerted to the need for retransmission.

The more error-detection bits are added to data, the more readily errors can be detected. If enough extra bits are programmed in, the data transmission may contain enough information to correct itself. One Bell Telephone error-correcting code provides 12 check bits for every 48 data bits, or 25 percent redundancy. Codes of up to 100 percent redundancy exist.

Error control can be provided in software or in hardware, and at the input or output levels, or both. In very large installations, error controls are designed into the input and output control equipment. Separate hardware that can be added to existing equipment in most installations is available from various manufacturers.

Encryption. Concern about assuring the privacy and integrity of data stored in the computer or transmitted over open channels has led to the development of protective devices. In the brief life span of computer communications, there has been ample evidence of the vulnerability of data to loss and alteration through direct tampering, surreptitious eavesdropping (spying), and theft through unauthorized entry into a computer system.

The earliest protective measures limited access to the computer installation to select personnel. Another early safeguard involved designing passwords into the software: this is still a popular method. Operators and programmers can gain access to the computer only after they key in an identifying code, which also restricts users to their own program section. But password codes can be broken by intelligent systems analysis and programming knowledge. For this reason, safer methods were sought.

Securing digital data sent by remote communications channels has been a particular concern of governments and the military. They have led in the search for an unbreakable code, since secrecy of technological knowledge is vital to national security and strategic planning.

Encryption, the application of complex coding techniques, has been the result. Cryptography, used for communications since ancient times, was especially developed for military and government applications during and after the Second World War. The derivation of cryptographic systems requires considerable mathematical application and the use of coding (encryption) and decoding (decryption) equipment. There is a subtle distinction between a code and a cipher. A code bears no regular or predictable relationship to the original message, or *plaintext* (see table 7-1). A cipher depends on a key, which alters the data in a consistent manner throughout. The example below is a relatively simple cipher, in which the ciphertext alphabet is written underneath the plaintext alphabet. The ciphertext alphabet is arrived at by the use of a keyword. In this cipher, the keyword is "Patricia Zlotnik," and it is followed by the unused letters of the alphabet in order; no letter is allowed to repeat.*

A B C D E F G H I J K L M N O P Q R S T U V W X Y Z
P A T R I C Z L O N K B D E F G H J M Q S U V W X Y

* Adapted from John P. Costas, "Cryptography in the Field; Part 1: An Overview." *Byte*, no. 3 (1979):57.

Table 7-1 A Simple
Two-Part Code

Encoding		Decoding	
Plaintext	*Codetext*	*Codetext*	*Plaintext*
BALANCE	17599	17590	AFTERBURNER
BALANCE SHEET	43987	17591	DETACHED
BALL	15638	17592	UNLIKELY
BALLAST	28457	17593	(NULL)
BALLISTIC	12953	17594	JAMMING
BALLISTIC	57465	17595	STATUTE OF
BALLISTIC			LIMITATIONS
MISSILE	72589	17596	BALLOON
BALLOON	17596	17597	ARBITRARY
....		17598	(NULL)
NULLS	17593	17599	BALANCE
	43874		
	12958		
	17598		
	54355		

Note: The encoding portion is arranged alphabetically, and the decoding portion
numerically. To frustrate the efforts of someone intercepting the message, nulls are
frequently used (a null is a portion of the codetext that has no plaintext equivalent),
and some plaintext terms have more than one codetext equivalent.

Source: Adapted from John P. Costas, "Cryptography in the Field; Part I: An Overview," *Byte*, no. 3 (1979):56.

Encryption:
3 ways

Computer applications have helped design more complex ciphers,
but the computer is also a very powerful tool that can be used to
break ciphers.

Today's encryption techniques use one of three methods. The
symbols in the text may be transposed or scrambled, new symbols
may be substituted for the original symbols, or transposition and
substitution methods may be combined. This latter approach is the
basis of the Data Encryption Standard (DES), which was adopted by
the federal government in 1977 for its business applications (that is,
where national security is not involved). A complex key acts on the
bits of the data to be transmitted, transposing and substituting the
bits in the data stream.

Encryption is applied to computer communications in three ways.
In link-by-link encryption, stand-alone devices transform data at
both ends of a communications channel. Node-by-node encryption
is used when data are sent over a line containing several links; software at each node, or connecting point between links in a line, re-
codes or reciphers the data during transmission. Data text will be
coded to the first station, then decoded and recoded for transmission
to the second station, and so on. The data may thus undergo several

transformations before arriving at their final destination. Decoding can be part of the programming software, or stand-alone equipment can be used. In end-to-end encryption, a data message can be encrypted and sent through many stations with no change in the key. This method is not only simpler than the prior one, but also affords the best security since the message is not decrypted, as it is at each way station in the node-by-node method, until transmission is completed.

Auxiliary Hardware

Special equipment is needed to send, code, amplify, and receive the signals transmitted through the various communications channels. Devices that interface with telecommunications channels include modems, processors, multiplexers, and concentrators. Each has a different function, but all enhance the safety and maximize the efficiency of the data transmission network.

Modems. Modem is an acronym for modulator/demodulator, which is an electronic device capable of changing or converting information-bearing electrical signals from one form to another in data communications. For communications involving digital data and telephone lines, the modulator portion of the modem converts the digital pulses (bits), originated by computer or terminal equipment, to a wavelike (analog) signal acceptable for transmission over telephone lines. The demodulator portion reverses the process at the receiving end, converting the analog signal back into a bit sequence acceptable to the computer or terminal. (See figure 7-3.)

Just as the bit is the unit of digital information, a *baud* is the unit of signalling speed on a communications line. The speed of a modem, the rate at which it transforms data being transmitted, is expressed as bauds per second (bps). A baud is by definition equal to

Figure 7-3 The use of modems in converting data
The figure below shows how modems are used to convert binary data to analog frequencies and then reconvert analog frequencies to binary data.

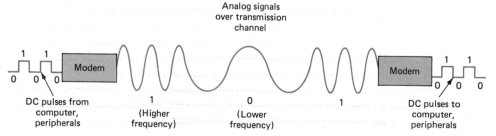

Modems:

low speed - under 1200 bps

medium   1200 - 2400 bps

High   over 2400 bps

the number of discrete conditions or signal events per second; it is not to be confused with a bit. Baud refers to the number of times a line condition changes each second. If a computer supplying data at a rate of 1,000 bits per second were teamed with a modem designed for transmission at 1,000 bauds per second, the data rate and baud rate would be equal.

Modems are generally classified as low speed (under 1,200 bps), medium speed (1,200 to 2,400 bps), and high speed (over 2,400 bps to 4,800 and 9,600 bps). Depending on computer volume and the type of transmission line used, a modem that matches data speed to line signalling speed capability should be selected.

Modems are additionally classified as: simplex, using one telephone wire pair and able to transmit in one direction only; half duplex, also using one wire pair but able to transmit or receive at any given time; and full duplex, using two wire pairs (four wires) and able to transmit and receive simultaneously.

Acoustic couplers. One kind of temporary modem installation depends on acoustic coupling. An *acoustic coupler* is a telephone handset that is placed in a special cradle on a terminal. The cradle contains microphones and circuitry that, when put into operation, convert the digital signals into analog acoustic tones for transmission, and reconvert analog signals back to digital form for reception. This method is often used where remote communications are intermittent and where speed of transmission is not an important factor. Acoustic couplers are relatively inexpensive devices that permit use of conventional voice-grade telephone lines on a dial-up basis, without the purchase or leasing of more costly equipment.

Front-end processors. Typically, a data communications system comprises a number of different types of terminals, along with a variety of peripherals, a number of modems, and other electronic control devices. They will be operating at different rates and times and possibly with different languages and codes. In such a system, streams of bits from different sources are constantly entering the CPU. Usually, bits from the different components follow each other in no particular order. Sorting the data requires CPU memory, software, and execution time. Moreover, the CPU may have frequent idle intervals, because the CPU accepts data input more rapidly than data can be transmitted over telephone lines.

A front-end processor is often used between the CPU and terminating equipment in high-traffic, multiterminal installations to relieve the CPU of the sort-and-wait burden (figure 7-4). A front-end processor is able to accept all the bits as they come in, and sort and store them for later transfer to the CPU. The data are organized and

A typical telecommunications installation for connection of a host computer to remote terminals. Modems are contained in the center of the unit shown, and multiplexers are at the top and bottom. The equipment is manufactured by General Datacom Industries.

(Bill Longcore)

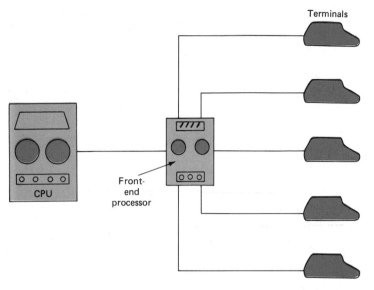

Terminals

Figure 7-4 A computer configuration using a front-end processor

recoded, and then given to the CPU, which can now process the information more efficiently.

Although some front-end processors are fixed-program devices, most applications today use processors that are really programmable minicomputers. The additional cost of such a processor can be more than offset by the saving of additional CPU memory, storage, and execution time.

In addition to restructuring all incoming data, front-end processors continually poll all input and output devices in the system to determine which have a message to send or are in a state to receive. This monitoring provides for efficient use of all equipment in the system. The processor can be programmed to use different polling sequences at different times, depending on anticipated traffic.

Front-end processors can also monitor incoming data to determine whether errors are present, and reject messages or call for retransmission if an error is found. They can also be used to direct traffic within the network, switching messages between terminals if necessary, without using the CPU.

Multiplexers. As we have seen, the common carrier telecommunications channels are not capable of handling high-volume traffic. Telephone line costs can be prohibitively expensive when long amounts of time are used. A *multiplexer* improves efficient use of telephone lines by concentrating data from a number of sources simultaneously. It shortens transmission time by making it possible for one higher-speed link to accommodate the same amount of traffic as several slower links. (See figure 7-5.)

215

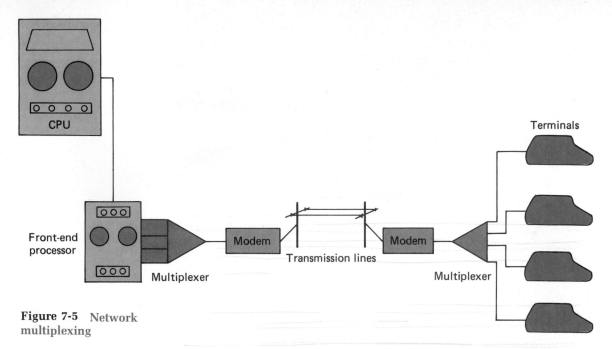

Figure 7-5 Network
multiplexing

A multiplexer is able to subdivide a typical voice-grade line into narrower bandwidths, each of which becomes a separate channel. The multiplexer assigns each channel to a designated terminal, codes data for transmission, and decodes and reroutes at the receiving end. This method is known as frequency division multiplex (FDM).

Another kind of multiplexing procedure takes advantage of the time gaps between streams of data transmission. By weaving several slow data streams into one continuous high-rate stream or "bursts," more efficient use of receiving equipment is made possible. This is known as time division multiplex (TDM).

Multiplexing therefore makes it possible for users to improve upon the limitations of the carrier networks. It is also used by carriers within their own networks to increase message density. In long-distance communications, several tiers of signal concentration may be involved.

Concentrators. Concentrators may be thought of as super multiplexers, which are made so by the addition of a small special-purpose CPU. In addition to being able to concentrate traffic through predetermined channels, they are programmed to make certain decisions relating to communication procedures. Concentrators can temporarily store messages until time is available on a channel, change message formats, and route or reroute messages. Concentrators are

(Bell Labs)

The Lightwave Terminating Multiplex Assembly, used in conjunction with glass fiber transmission, shown at Bell Laboratories at Holmdel, New Jersey. This terminal equipment combines signal multiplexing and terminating functions previously performed by separate units of equipment.

generally used only in very high traffic networks, where their additional cost is justified by the saving in volume and time. They are more likely to be used by a carrier than by the end user.

Types of Processing Systems

A basic principle of data processing is that different applications require different kinds of systems. There are three processing systems or modes: batch, online, and distributed data processing (DDP). All of these systems may have an array of hardware, including

217

input/output devices, CPUs, auxiliary storage devices, and other equipment. The amounts and kinds of equipment utilized depend on the size of the system and its desired capabilities. The type of processing used is a function of the information requirements of the user. Three determining requirements are "turnaround time" (the time that may elapse between a request for information and the output of the information to the user), the kinds of input data and the ways in which they are accumulated for entry, and the physical locations of the users of the system.

Batch Processing

Batch processing is used in applications where current up-to-the-minute information is not needed for operations. Information is typically accumulated on punched cards, magnetic cards and disks, and magnetic tapes. When sufficient information is accumulated, or the computer schedule calls for the data, the operator sets up the program to process that batch of data. Typically, batch processing is appropriate for accounting applications. (See figure 7-6.) Incoming accounts receivable (A/R) information is held for a specified period of time, then incorporated into the master A/R file, and held until the next scheduled batch processing. Typical accounting schedules would be weekly, biweekly, or monthly, depending on the particular application. Payrolls might be prepared biweekly, inventory analyzed weekly, and accounts receivable summarized monthly. Sequential access is the most practical and economical method of organizing files for batch processing.

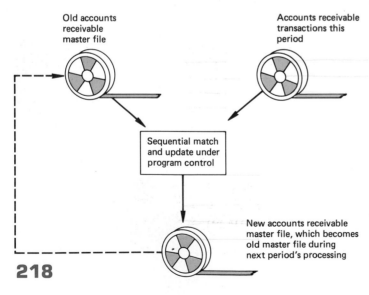

Old accounts receivable master file

Accounts receivable transactions this period

Sequential match and update under program control

New accounts receivable master file, which becomes old master file during next period's processing

Figure 7-6 Batch processing
Interim accounts receivable (A/R) information is matched to the existing master A/R file, which is updated by the CPU. A new A/R master file is generated to be held until the next scheduled batch processing. In this figure, magnetic tapes represent both the input data (transaction file) and the master file. This is because batch processing usually involves sequential files. In an accounts receivable system, for example, data are usually sorted into ascending or descending sequential order according to a key, such as customer number. Similarly, an inventory control system might be organized sequentially according to numbers assigned to individual products or parts.

218

(Courtesy of IBM)

The IBM 1401, a limited batch processing system. A card reader and punch is at the left, the computer is in the center, and the printer is at the right.

Batch processing can be either local or remote. In local batch processing, data are accumulated in their original physical form (time cards, invoices), and forwarded periodically to the data processing center for computer updating of files and any other necessary processing. A printed report or other output is generated. Turnaround time can be several or more days.

In remote batch processing, usually called remote job entry (RJE), data are transferred to the computer periodically over communica-

Figure 7-7 Expanded batch processing In this computer configuration capable of supporting a batch operation, the card reader is used to input the accumulated data. The CPU updates the master file on tape, which is then printed out. The new tape contains revised information. The punched cards will be kept separately for a period of time in storage files, in case record reconstruction is necessary.

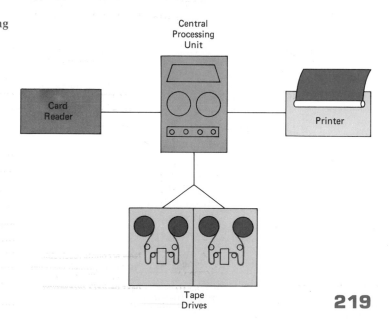

Central Processing Unit

Card Reader

Printer

Tape Drives

219

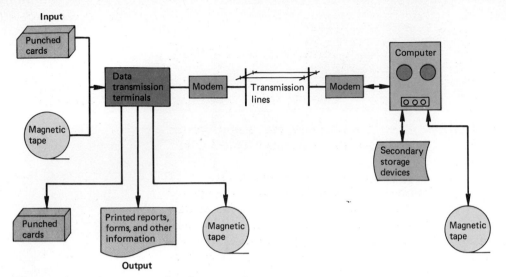

Figure 7-8 Online remote batch processing
The above online configuration can support remote job entry batch processing. In this configuration, information is accumulated locally on card-to-tape storage media. The data are periodically transmitted to the CPU. The CPU will update the master files and retransmit the revised data back to the originating station for report generation. Printed reports are generally taken directly off the line as they are transmitted.

tions channels from various locations. The data can be transmitted offline (that is, to an auxiliary storage unit) and held for input to the computer at the scheduled time. Offline batch processing is a comparatively inexpensive method of processing, requiring very little in the way of additional control devices and terminals, and is practical for many uncomplicated and routine applications (see figure 7-7). Data can also be transferred online, or entered into the computer as they are received, to be held for subsequent batch processing (see figure 7-8).

Online Real-Time Processing

In *online* systems, one or more terminals are in direct contact with the central processing unit, to which additional devices may also be attached. A user at any terminal in the system can query the CPU and see the answers immediately displayed. This immediate response is usually referred to as *real time*.

Online real-time (OLRT) systems are called for when information is needed continuously or when data in information files must be continuously updated as new information becomes available. Retail

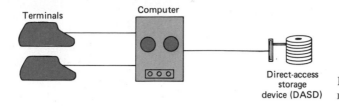

Figure 7-9 Online
real-time processing

inventory control, airline ticket reservations, and manufacturing processes are some applications that require constant updating and immediate reporting.

Because of the demands for information, direct-access storage is required by online real-time systems. The advent of disk storage and terminals has permitted the rapid expansion of this mode of data processing. In a typical disk storage system supporting online processing, one permanent disk may contain the programs, and replaceable disks may contain the master files. OLRT systems are also interactive. Data can be entered from any terminal in the system. The user receives output in the form of confirmation of the input transaction and/or in any other form as desired. Once entered, the data can be accessed from any terminal in the system. (See figure 7-9.)

Online real-time processing makes *time-sharing* possible. A CPU that is online to several terminals will accept and operate on any one input at a time. The operating system allows the CPU to query each of its online terminals at frequent intervals to determine which is ready to communicate. Because CPU execution time is much faster than terminal operator reaction time, the user generally does not notice any response delays. Effectively, it is as if the terminal operator has sole access to the computer. In larger time-sharing installations, CPU organization becomes very sophisticated. The CPU will sequentially sample hundreds of users, and those users will generally not be aware of any delays. The CPU can be programmed to allocate queries according to the relative needs of its different terminals, and to assign its time proportionately among all users.

Terminals connecting to such interactive systems can be physically located virtually anywhere. Connection can be made on a permanent basis by using plug-in cables, or the connections can be made via common lines from remote locations.

Distributed Data Processing

In large-scale real-time installations, a single computer may be performing tasks for hundreds of users online at individual terminals (see figure 7-10). However, if the computer fails, the entire line comes to a halt. *Distributed data processing* (DDP) comprises several

221

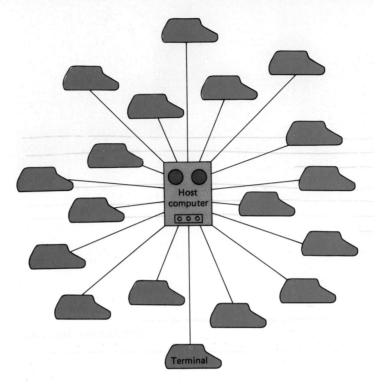

Figure 7-10 Large-scale
configuration of basic
online real-time
processing

alternative arrangements of a number of computers and peripherals
to circumvent this hazard.

DDP evolved, first, because of the need for large interactive installations with a high degree of reliability and, second, because the development of minicomputers made it economical to use more than
one computer in a network. Computer configurations offering great
flexibility to meet varied user requirements became possible. In a
large retailing organization, a computer at each branch online to a
computer at the main office may solve information problems at several levels of management.

In a typical business application, each branch of the organization
may require its own current sales information, inventory control, automatic reorder from a central warehouse, accounting information,
and so on. At the same time, the headquarters unit may require up-
to-date sales information from all branches, combined current inventory status from all warehouses, accounting information from all
branches and on a consolidated level, and so on.

DDP puts computational power where it is needed, at each location where data entry and computation take place. In a DDP configuration, computer failure at any one branch would not affect any
other branch, and computer failure at headquarters does not affect
branch operations.

(Photo by Irene Springer)

The main computer installation in a distributed data processing network. Two large computers serve as backups for one another in this facility. Both are online to some 50 other CRTs on several floors of the same building and to another installation several miles away, serving the order and warehousing departments of a major publisher.

Additional advantages accrue to users of DDP networks. DDP has the computational power of very large central computers, but each separate installation requires much less software and thus lowers the overall cost. DDP provides a degree of autonomy to local users, giving them some real-time control over local events. It provides information to the data source as well as to upper management. Operational management becomes more efficient as a consequence of the informational flexibility provided by the system.

DDP network configurations can be designed to fit the needs of every user. The type of DDP installation is determined by the size, locations, overall economics, and informational needs of the users. There are several standard network designs.

Point-to-point network. In the point-to-point network (see figure 7-11), each computer is online to another. Typically, two computers form the network. Each can be used for specific functions, since each can give information to the user of the other. For example, one can

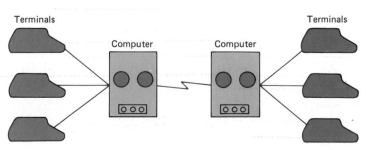

Terminals   Computer   Computer   Terminals

Figure 7-11 Point-to-point network

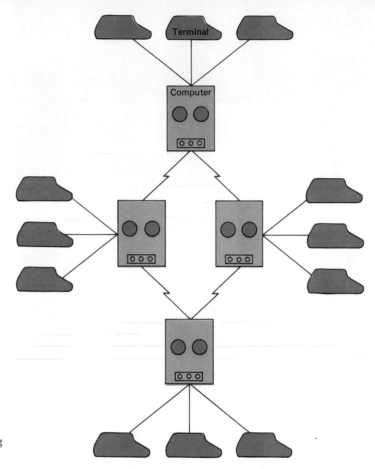

Figure 7-12 Loop or ring network

be devoted to data processing, while the second can assume I/O con-trol functions, including buffering and message routing. This would permit limited operation while a malfunctioning computer is being repaired. If sufficient memory and storage are allocated, each could theoretically parallel the other, but the expense might not be justi-fied by operational savings.

Loop or ring network. In a loop or ring network (see figure 7-12), which is analogous to a number of people standing in a circle hold-ing hands, each computer is serially linked to its nearest adjacent computers. In case of computer malfunction, the adjacent computer or computers have the ability to assume some of that computer's op-erational functions. Each computer must have additional storage and memory capability to serve the dual functions. If one computer needs information from another not linked directly to it, it must ob-tain the information via the intermediate computer(s).

224

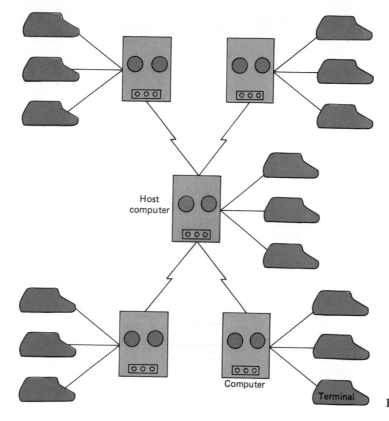

Figure 7-13 Star network

Star network. In the star network, each of several minicomputers is connected by a separate line to a central computer (see figure 7-13). This is the typical configuration wherever a central source of information controls common information flowing to several branch nodes. Information flows in two directions: the branch minicomputers can perform all local operations independently of the central computer, while the central computer controls combined operations and supplies centralized data as required. Typical applications include centralized inventory control and availability, airline reservations, ticketing for shows, and similar operations where a central information source is needed.

In very extensive star installations, every computer in the network is cross-linked to every other computer. Each computer node will contain all the information in the remaining nodes, and parallels the others during operation (see figure 7-14). Thus there is no one central computer, and each computer node can act as the "star" for the remaining nodes. The cross-linking circumvents any breakdown in communications anywhere in the system.

The star network is generally restricted to a specific geographic

225

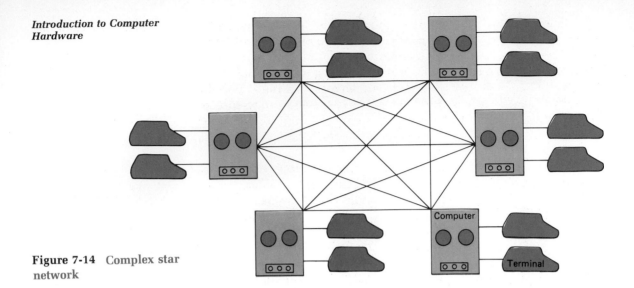

Figure 7-14 Complex star
network

area: the cost of communications lines for a very far-flung network can be prohibitive. In complex installations, independent star networks at different geographic locations can be assigned to interact with one computer in each star location. This one computer is then configured more powerfully to accept the additional remote data from the other affiliated networks.

Summary

Data communications require an electronic pathway between the communicating devices. The electrical pathways are usually referred to as *channels*, but the terms *circuit*, *line*, and *link* are also used.

Intracomputer communication involves the circuits set up within the machine. An input/output (I/O) control unit is often attached to the line connecting a CPU to peripheral devices and in-computer areas. The I/O device organizes the data channels between units of equipment and directs program operation, thus leaving the CPU free to work on the actual program execution.

In remote data communications, the common carrier networks— telephone and broadcasting—that link communities and countries are the electronic media of transmission. These channels must be adapted by means of specialized equipment to be able to transmit vast amounts of data at the high-speed requirements of computers.

A *modem* (modulator/demodulator) converts the digital signals of computers to analog frequencies that can be transmitted over channels designed for voice-frequency ranges. *Acoustic couplers* are a specialized kind of modem and consist of a telephone handset linked to a terminal; they are relatively inexpensive devices that are useful for intermittent data communications over telephone lines. *Multiplexers* and *concentrators* provide varying means of subdividing a single channel into several data channels, making it possible for more data to be transmitted at a time. *Front-end processors* are computers that can sort and organize incoming data in a complex system; they store and, if necessary, decode and recode the data before transmission to the CPU.

Other media for data transmission include microwave radio frequencies, communications satellites, and fiber-optic cables.

Channel wiring allows three basic modes of data transmission. In simplex transmission, communication travels in one direction only. Half-duplex transmission makes possible two-directional communication, although not at the same time. And full duplex transmission allows simultaneous two-way data communication.

Data may be transmitted asynchronously, or at irregular intervals; asynchronous transmission is sometimes referred to as "start-and-stop" transmission. In synchronous transmission, long streams· of uninterrupted data are sent, with computer software at both the sending and receiving terminals synchronizing the data bits to form the characters of the message; this requires more complex equipment but makes possible faster transmission of greater quantities of data.

Errors may enter data transmission systems through transmission media, communications equipment, or human agency. Means of detecting and correcting errors are provided in applications programs, systems software, and hardware. The need to assure privacy and integrity of data has led to the development of *encryption*, or "secret code" techniques, for computer-transmitted information.

Three general types of data processing systems are batch, online, and distributed data processing (DDP). The type of processing system chosen depends on the application and information requirements of the user. Important factors to consider include turnaround time, kinds of input data and how they will be accumulated, and the physical locations of the system's users in relation to one another.

Batch processing is used where input data typically accumulate for periodic processing and where constant updating and output are not requirements of the user. Batch processing can be local or remote. Remote batch processing is usually called remote job entry (RJE) and involves periodic input of data to a central computer from various locations.

In *online systems*, one or more terminals are in direct contact with the central processing unit, and users at any terminal can input data and query the system at any time. This immediate response is referred to as *real time. Online real-time* (OLRT) systems are required for applications that need constant updating and frequent accurate output. OLRT makes *time-sharing* possible; a single CPU can operate so quickly that it can handle the input and output requirements of several users.

Distributed data processing connects several computers and their peripherals, and was developed as a means of enhancing system reliability to suit the requirements of individual users. Generally, DDP networks are based on one of several standard computer configurations: point-to-point, loop or ring, star, or complex star.

Key Terms and Phrases

acoustic couplers
asynchronous transmission
baud
channel
concentrators
distributed data processing (DDP)
encryption
full duplex transmission

half-duplex transmission
modems
multiplexers
online real-time (OLRT) systems
plaintext
simplex transmission
synchronous transmission
time-sharing

Sources of Additional Information

Bach, Gabriel G. F. "International Data Flow and Protection Regulations." *Telecommunications*, no. 5 (1979):89–92.

Costas, John P. "Cryptography in the Field: Part I. An Overview." *Byte*, no. 3 (1979):56–64.

Crispin, Howard. "Satellite Communications and the Growth of Earth Stations." *Telecommunications*, no. 4 (1979):25–29.

Dick, George M. "The Lowly Modem." *Datamation*, no. 3 (1977):69–73.

Gantz, John. "The Secret and Promise of Fiber Optics." *Computerworld*, October 8, 1979, pp. 1–10.

Hiltz, Starr Roxanne, and Turoff, Murray. *The Network Nation: Human Communication Via Computer.* Reading, Mass.: Addison-Wesley, 1978.

Kahn, David. *The Codebreakers.* New York: New American Library, 1973.

Karjian, Ronald. "Encryption Techniques Make Data Secure." *Telecommunications—International Edition*, no. 1 (1979):21–24.

Kinnucan, Paul. "Data Encryption Gurus: Tuchman and Meyer." *Mini-Micro Systems*, no. 9 (1978):54–60.

Miller, Frederick W. "Checkless Society Gets Closer." *Infosystems*, no. 3 (1979):48–52.

Solomon, Arthur H. "The Merging of Telecommunications and Information Processing: The Technological Underpinnings." *Computerworld*, January 21, 1980, pp. 1–17.

Yeh, Leang P. "Fibre-Optic Communications Systems." *Telecommunications—International Edition*, no. 9 (1978):33–38.

1. How does the use of data communications by banks affect the way you keep track of the status of your checking account?
2. How can data communications be used to improve the inventory control procedures for a retail store chain?
3. Some telecommunications systems are so complex that we often wonder how they function with any reliability at all. Name some points in a telecommunications system where problems can arise to interfere with accurate transmission.
4. You are in charge of setting up an online reservation system for a hotel chain. How will concerns for data security affect your planning of the system?
5. Draw a diagram of a hypothetical data communications system, including as much as possible the hardware described in the chapter.
6. Develop a simple encryption scheme that could be used in data transmission.
7. What is electronic mail? What stake does the Postal Service have in the progress being made toward its development in the U.S.?
8. Through what kind of communications channels can ships at sea be a part of a telecommunications network?
9. The ASCII code is a standard code for data transmission. Describe an ASCII representation of a character.
10. (a) If you bought a home computer, what hardware would you need in order to tie in to a data communications network? (b) How is telecommunications technology being used to bring the information resources of the world into your home?
11. Point-of-sale systems are spreading throughout every branch of retailing. What advantages of telecommunications technology have contributed to the increased use of POS systems?
12. In what ways has the life-style of private citizens been affected by the growth of data communications? Your answer should include both the positive and negative factors.
13. Should government be involved in regulating data communications? If so, in what way? If not, state your reasons.

Unit III
Introduction to Computer Software

8 Systems and Applications Software

"Have you noticed that as these things work faster and faster, we finish our day's work earlier and earlier?"

APPLICATION
A Microcomputer Learns to Drive

Increasingly strict standards for exhaust emissions, coupled with sharply rising fuel costs, have left automobile designers with a dilemma: How to design a car with low exhaust emissions and high fuel economy without sacrificing driveability. The design must meet economy and emissions standards while operating over a wide range of conditions: hot, cold, or normal starting; high- or low-altitude, hot-environment, urban, and highway driving; and maximum power.

To build an engine control system with the flexibility to handle these variations, one car manufacturer turned to microcomputer technology. The result was a three-level microcomputerized distributed data processing system mounted within the car's engine, controlling the basic engine subsystem.

In the emissions control subsystem, for example, partially uncombusted gases are recirculated back from the car's exhaust system to the carburetor for mixture with the primary air intake and fuel. This prevents unburned fuel from reaching the atmosphere. And in the electronic engine control subsystem, seven sensors continuously monitor engine function, sending signals to the electronic control assembly. The microcomputer determines the correct ignition timing and monitors both the exhaust gas recirculation flow rate and the secondary air flow rate. It then sends commands to the various sensor modules to make any necessary adjustments, which are made at the rate of about 20 times per second.

Programming a computer to do all this required the cooperation of numerous individuals with specialized skills over an extended period of time. The hardware already existed. The question was how to get it to operate in the internal environment of an automobile engine.

First, systems engineers had to define the engine parameters to be controlled, determine the mathematical relationships between input and output values and express them as equations, and establish the control ranges within which the input and output values must be maintained for proper vehicle operation. Then software engineers joined the team to design a practical computer program within the limits of the microcomputer's memory and speed. Next, this program must be coded in assembly language by components engineers, who also enter it into the disk storage files of a large computer system. Within this system the program is translated from assembly to binary machine language. The computer system emulates the binary code for design verification. The engineers run tests of the program design by simulating the operating conditions of the microcomputer on a larger computer. Thus they are able to see how the microcomputer will behave during operation.

Finally, to detect errors in accuracy or logic, the engine control system program is run, using special test cases. These cases simulate various combinations of inputs to determine the corresponding range of outputs. Once all the bugs, or problems, have been discovered and corrected, the electronic engine control system is ready to be tested in an actual car. If it passes that test, it can be incorporated into a prototype line of automobiles. But only a track record of safe and efficient performance and consumer acceptance will determine whether all the work was really successful.

N THE preceding unit, computers were considered as pieces of mechanical equipment, or hardware, electrically connected to form a system. But this is only part of the whole picture. The computer hardware—the CPUs, card readers, magnetic tape drives, printers, storage devices, and other peripherals—cannot do anything useful without a *program,* or set of logical instructions, to follow. Programs written for the computer are referred to as *software,* and are a critical part of the total computer system.

In this unit we will be examining the software that tells the hardware what to do. In the chapters that follow, we will look at the data on which computer programs operate, the structure and organization of the computer environment, the use of flowcharts, the essential steps in program preparation, and the languages used by and for computers. First, however, we will survey the kinds of software that make computers "go."

Computer programs may be classified as either *application programs or system software.* Application programs direct computer hardware to perform specific operations such as those involved in billing, payroll, or inventory control. Such programs are often written in-house, that is, by the computer user's own staff. They may also be purchased from the hardware vendor or from a software consultant. Application programs are usually written in a high-level language, such as BASIC, COBOL, or PL/I. These languages are quasi-English and easy to understand (after a few lessons in programming, that is).

System Software

System software directs all the internal operations of the computer. These operations include job input and output, scheduling of jobs waiting to be processed, location of data needed to process a job, and termination of a job when an illegal (incorrect) instruction is encountered. System software is often provided by the hardware vendor. Once it has been programmed into the computer, the user usually does not have to be concerned with internal operations. This allows for efficient utilization of computer time.

The most important piece of system software is the *operating system.* This is a series of interrelated programs that supervise the processing of an application program from the time it is read into the computer until the final output. The operating system is the connecting link between the computer hardware and the application program.

In addition to the operating system, system software includes

(Marc Anderson)

Programs are the software that tells the computer hardware what to do.

compilers to translate application programs into machine-readable language, *linkage editors* to collect the subroutines needed for program execution, and *I/O programs* to control the input/output hardware. Certain ready-made utility programs are also available to perform routine functions like copying, sorting, and combining data.

Throughout this chapter, terms like compiler and linkage editor will be used as if they were physical units. It should be understood, though, that these terms are simply convenient names referring to self-contained lists of instructions, not to pieces of hardware.

The Operating System: Computerized Self-Control

Modern computers are capable of executing millions of instructions per second. Control of such high-speed operations requires quick decisions about job priority, job termination, data storage, and other functions. The only entity capable of making these decisions is the computer itself. However, the computer cannot think independently; it can only follow directions. It must be programmed to make these decisions according to the needs of the computer user. Such a program is the operating system; when executed, it controls the operation of the computer.

The operating system consists of several subsidiary programs, called *routines*, that perform three basic control functions: job management, data management, and task management.

Job management routines. A program that is waiting to be processed is called a *job.* Job management refers to the operating system routines that control the initiation, or start of processing, of all application programs read into the computer. Job management routines keep track of the status of all jobs, making sure that they are initiated according to the user's priority list. They also assume that when a program is initiated it has access to all necessary data sets and I/O devices. For this reason a job management routine is often referred to as a *scheduler*. Finally, the scheduler temporarily records on a disk the output of a program in process, for printing or punching when processing is complete.

Data management routines. Software designed for efficient control of the enormous amounts of data frequently needed for program processing is known as *data management routines*. These programs control all operations associated with I/O devices; they allocate storage space, assign titles to and catalog data sets, move data between main and auxiliary storage, and handle errors incurred during input/output.

Task management routines. After a program (or a job) has begun executing, it is referred to as a *task*. *Task management* assures all tasks an appropriate share of CPU time by controlling the allocation and use of the CPU, virtual and real storage, and programming resources. The routines comprising task management are referred to collectively as the *supervisor* or *monitor*, and are usually stored permanently in the computer's main memory.

To avoid wasting expensive computer time, modern large computers execute several programs simultaneously. It is the supervisor's function to see that these programs are kept separate and that one does not read or write data into a space allocated for another. The supervisor also interrupts the execution of a program whenever an error or illegal statement is encountered; if the error cannot be corrected, the offending program is terminated without interfering with the execution of other programs. When a program's execution must be suspended while data are being accessed from auxiliary storage or read in by an I/O device, the supervisor allocates this CPU time to another program.

Evolution of System Software

The operating system as we know it today did not come about all at once. Rather, it evolved in response to the needs of programmers and users, as well as to the needs of computers. Computers were first employed in the mechanization of manual operations such as those

237

of basic accounting and record keeping. It was not long, however, before computers entered a more challenging phase. Information retrieval and management information systems, inventory control systems, and a host of other business-oriented applications were devised. The modern operating system developed to provide the efficient control required for these complex operations.

Early system software. The first stage of development came about because of the language barrier between the computer and its users. The numerical language that the computer understood was time-consuming and tedious for human beings to read and write and required great precision. A miniscule mistake could trigger a whole chain of errors when the program was executed. Numerical language also required a large staff of programmers to work mainly on translations.

The development of compilers solved this problem. Compilers are programs that translate standard terms and phrases of a given language into the binary code needed for processing.

A number of codelike machine-oriented languages were the first to appear. These were soon followed by more conversational types using familiar English words and phrases, such as FORTRAN and the business-oriented COBOL.

Another difficulty associated with early computers was the discrepancy between the relatively slow I/O devices and the much faster data processing capabilities of the CPU. Because of this, I/O operations and processing could not be carried on simultaneously, and early CPUs had to remain idle for long periods of time while data were transferred between I/O devices and main memory. This wasted time was eliminated when computing systems were developed to coordinate the performance of input, output, and data processing operations for several programs at the same time. However, it was necessary to synchronize I/O and processing operations. The CPU could not process data until they had been read into main storage, nor could it destroy processed data before they were transferred to an output device.

To prevent such problems, an I/O control system was devised. With such a control routine loaded into main storage, a programmer could call it into action simply by issuing a "READ" or "GET" instruction. Then the I/O control system picked up the instruction, and initiated and controlled the transfer of the correct block of data to or from main storage. In the meantime, the CPU could continue to process data. To transfer to an output device, the programmer merely had to issue a "WRITE" or "PUT" instruction. The I/O control system would automatically pick up and consolidate the appropriate records into a block and then transfer it to an output device.

System development: The second stage. The second stage of operating system development began, like the first, because of problems encountered when hardware resources interacted with human resources. Actually, the human resource, the operator, was too much involved in the mechanics of data processing. The operator could not match the speed and reliability of the computer, which often sat idle while a job was being set up for processing. As the speeds of the newer computing systems increased, this setup time accounted for ever-larger proportions of total response time.

The solution to this dilemma was obvious: utilize the fast hardware resources of the computer to reduce the data processing activities of the operator. This was done by integrating the compiler and I/O control components already in use with several other automatic control routines. The result was the operating system.

The control program of the early operating system consisted of two parts. The nucleus, or basic monitor, remained in main storage while a series of jobs were processed. It provided for communication between the operator, the control program, and each routine that was part of the operating system. The nucleus also contained the supervisory routines that coordinated and controlled all I/O operations.

The transitional monitor, unlike the nucleus, occupied main storage only during the interval between one job step and another. Its main function was to read and interpret the control statement for each job step and to transfer control of the CPU to the appropriate subsystem or program. Once this transfer was completed, the main storage space occupied by the transitional monitor became available for use in performing the job step. After the step was completed, the transitional monitor again entered main storage to initiate the next job step.

Operating systems today. The development of general-purpose systems to increase the range of a computer's application and its overall productivity represents the third and current stage in the evolution of operating systems. This is accomplished by combining several techniques, including new ways of designing programs and managing jobs and data. The goal is a computer system adaptable to the needs of a variety of users.

The Programming Process: An Illustration

The interaction of a modern operating system and the other elements of computer operation can best be understood by a step-by-step description of the program execution process.

239

SOURCE - BEFORE

OBJECT - AFTER

TRANSLATED

Job entry. When the application program is read into the computer by an input device such as a card reader, the job management segment of the operating system immediately detects that a job has entered the system. From information that was input with the job on a job control card (see below), the operating system identifies the language in which the program is written. In most business applications, the language used is COBOL. The operating system then signals the COBOL compiler to translate the program into binary machine language. Before the application program is translated, it is called a *source program.* After translation, and if the compiler finds no syntax errors, it becomes an *object module.*

When the compiler has finished translation, the operating system calls the I/O supervisor to temporarily store the object module on a disk. All reading and writing operations during the execution of a program are controlled by the I/O supervisor.

Subroutines. In most application programs, one or more sets of instructions or sequence of steps will be called for repeatedly. An example would be the mathematical equations calculating the present value of a stream of future cash payments. Such a sequence of program instructions can be stored together as a *subroutine.* When a user wants to include these calculations in a program, it is necessary only to write an instruction directing the operating system to "CALL" the subroutine out of storage.

In a given program the operating system may be directed to access several subroutines. But the program may not specify where these subroutines are stored. Since a program cannot be executed until all of its parts are completely defined, the operating system will ask the linkage editor to locate the appropriate subroutines. The linkage editor is a segment of data management software that keeps track of the location of all subroutines in storage. Subroutines are generally held in sections of auxiliary storage called *libraries.* When the linkage editor finds the subroutines called for by a particular program, it makes this information available to the operating system. The operating system then calls a utility program to copy the subroutines and stores them in the proper order on the disk with the object module. It is now called a load module. (Complicated? Certainly. And remember, all this takes only milliseconds!)

Executing. Now that all the information needed by a particular program has been found, the load module is ready to be loaded into main storage. This process is controlled by the part of the operating system called, appropriately, the *loader.* Once this is done, the load module, which is now called a task, begins executing.

When all of the steps in the program have been completed and the data stored temporarily on a disk, the operating system will turn over control to the I/O supervisor. The I/O supervisor prints out the desired data according to the instructions included with the original program.

Interrupt handling routines. Sometimes an error is encountered during the processing of a program. Depending on what caused the error, control of the CPU is relinquished to one of several interrupt handling routines. The routine given control must try to find out what went wrong and correct the malfunction. If this is accomplished, control of the CPU is given back to the program being executed. But if the error cannot be located or corrected, the interrupt routine will inform the operating system, which then terminates execution of the program. Errors may be caused by the violation of a program rule, the malfunction of the machine itself, or the violation of an external restriction such as a time limit.

But interrupt handling routines have an even more important function than dealing with error situations. They act as an interface between the task and supervisory routines. For instance, while an I/O supervisor is reading in data for task A, CPU control is given to task B so that the CPU is not idle. When task A input is complete, the I/O interrupt handling routine takes over. It determines whether the input operation has been successfully completed. If it has, the I/O interrupt handling routine sends a request to the task management system to stop work on task B and restart task A. But if input has not been completed properly, the interrupt handling routine tries to correct the malfunction.

Although we have discussed only I/O interrupt handling routines, there are several similar operating components. In fact, for every supervisory routine that may take control of a task at some stage of processing, there is an interrupt handling routine.

Multiprogramming

As the preceding discussion of the programming process makes clear, today's CPUs can switch from one task to another—they can execute one task while data for another are being inputted, and can resume execution of one task without losing their "place" in another. But operations of this complexity were not possible until the advent of multiprogramming.

This term *multiprogramming* denotes the execution at the same time of two or more application programs by one CPU. This is accomplished by compartmentalizing main storage. In the simplest multiprogramming system, only three jobs can be active at any time.

241

One copies input data onto a disk or another auxiliary storage medium for jobs to be processed. Another actually executes a job, reading its input from the disk and sending its output back to the disk. The third copies data generated by previously executed user programs onto paper or some other form of output. In larger systems, several user jobs may be active simultaneously, in addition to the input and output jobs.

Fixed - operating
              system

dynamic - Application
              programs

Main storage for a multiprogramming system is divided into two parts: fixed and dynamic. The fixed part is devoted entirely to the storage of operating system routines; the dynamic part is shared among application programs. In one kind of system, the dynamic part may be divided into partitions, each containing only one task, or program that is executing. The partitions of dynamic storage can be any size, as long as the total number of bytes does not exceed the number of available bytes in the dynamic part of main storage.

In more sophisticated multiprogramming systems, there are no rigid partitions, and application programs may be stored wherever there are enough bytes of storage available next to one another. The amount of storage allocated to an application program in these systems is called a region. All partitions in a partitioned system have to be large enough to accommodate the largest task expected, even though smaller tasks are usually stored there. The number and size of the partitions can be changed by the operator, but that is a time-consuming procedure. Regions of dynamic storage permit greater freedom in programming. Sometimes, however, the new program being stored does not fill all the contiguous bytes of a single empty region. The result—many areas of unusable main storage—is known as *fragmentation.* Though fragmentation can be minimized by competent operators, it cannot be entirely eliminated, and often cannot be reduced at all. Some waste of main storage, then, is inevitable.

Virtual Storage

In the early days of computer data processing, a program with 25,000 addresses (you will recall that an address represents the storage location of a byte of data) was considered gigantic. As data processing problems became more complex, however, programs became larger—now there are programs with a million addresses.

Because today's computer can assemble and execute millions of instructions in seconds, writing a program with several million bytes presents no real difficulty. But a problem does arise when a multimillion-address program is to be executed as a single load module. Remember that the loader is the part of the operating system that takes the load module from a disk in temporary storage and brings it into main storage. The loader must assign an address to each byte in the program, and then place each byte into the main storage location with the assigned address. If an addressable main storage byte is not available that corresponds to each byte of a program, execution cannot proceed.

Multiprogramming offers one solution to this problem. A large program can be divided into smaller components that will be executed in the proper sequence. This method is time-consuming, however.

Another solution is segmentation, in which a large program is divided into small load modules for processing. As processing proceeds, a transaction analysis load module determines which processing modules are required and loads them into main storage immediately prior to their use. In this way, only data about to be processed are in main storage at any moment. This technique, while slightly superior to executing several sequential programs, is still time-consuming.

The most recent solution to this space problem is *virtual storage*. This requires the connection of the CPU hardware to a direct-access storage device (DASD). With this additional hardware, a 10-million byte program can be executed with only a few thousand bytes of main storage. The virtual storage system accomplishes this feat by setting up a storage hierarchy—small amounts of expensive main storage backed up by large amounts of relatively less expensive disk or drum storage. Data are automatically transferred between auxiliary and main storage, requiring no interference by the operator or special instructions from the programmer.

Virtual storage can best be understood by examining an application program as it is loaded and executed. First, each byte of the program is assigned an address, called a *virtual address*, and placed in storage on the DASD. Groupings of bytes ready for loading into virtual storage are known as *pages*. A page may contain 4,000 bytes. As each page is loaded onto the DASD, its virtual address and its actual location on the DASD are listed on an *external page table*. Data bytes are also assigned *real addresses* that represent the actual locations they will occupy in real, or main, storage during program execution. A *page table* is generated to show the real addresses assigned to each page. Each page table corresponds to an external page table.

Since there are fewer bytes of main storage than data to be stored, the same real addresses will be assigned to several pages. To show which page is actually in a real address location at any given time, an identifier called the *invalid bit* is used. This bit is stored with each page table entry. When the invalid bit is 0, the page is in real

243

O = REAL STORAGE
1 = EXTERNAL STORAGE

storage; when the invalid bit is 1, the page is in a slot of external page storage.

When execution begins, one or more of the program's pages are loaded into main storage. A segment of main storage that can hold a page is called a *frame.* The special direct-address feature of the DASD translates the virtual address of each data byte into its real address. When the program references an instruction that is not in real storage, a condition called a *page fault* occurs. The supervisory routine, called the paging supervisor, then begins what is known as the *page-in-operation.* This system: (1) locates in external page storage the page containing the referenced instruction; (2) selects a frame of real storage to hold the page; (3) moves a copy of the page from its slot in external page storage to the page frame in real storage; (4) updates the invalid bit in the page table entry to show that the page is now resident in real storage; (5) completes the virtual address translation; and (6) resumes program execution. This entire operation is known as demand paging, and it all takes place automatically and in fractions of a second.

Although it may not be immediately apparent, demand paging is much less time-consuming than the previously discussed method in which a transaction analysis module controls the loading of processing modules. This is because less time is required to assign addresses to data bytes every time a transaction analysis module loads a processing module into main storage. With virtual storage, the assignment of addresses is done only once; thereafter, the special DASD hardware translates virtual addresses into real addresses. This translation takes place at a much higher speed than the storage of addresses and data.

With a typical virtual storage system, 16 million virtual addresses are available for use. If they were divided into 10 regions or partitions, more than one million addresses would still be available for each region. This would seem to be enough for almost any program. But as many as 10 million addresses are needed by some of today's more sophisticated programs. The technique of subdividing these massive programs into smaller modules could be used in addition, but this would require repeating the loading operation. *Multiple virtual storage* was devised to accommodate such large programs efficiently.

In a multiple virtual storage system, some 10 million virtual addresses are available to the user; the rest are set aside for storage of the operating system software. The collection of user addresses is called an address space. A multiple virtual system may have as many as 20 or 30 initiated programs in the system at one time, giving a user an apparent or "virtual" address space of 10 million addresses for each program. The CPU and its translators are available to only one user's address space at a time. Also, each user's address space has its own set of page tables, and a supervisory routine makes sure that only one set of page tables is active at a time.

Multiprocessing

The systems described up to this point handle as many programs and as large a program as necessary, but still consist of only a single CPU and associated I/O devices. These are called *uniprocessor systems*. At installations where two or more uniprocessors were operating, the workload was frequently not shared equally among the systems. Because users' needs over a short period of time were often unpredictable, it was difficult to schedule the systems' time more efficiently.

The obvious solution to this problem was to find a way to join uniprocessor systems together for greater efficiency. In multiprocessing, each user's resources are placed in a pool from which each member can choose. This also allows some of the redundant resources to be eliminated. Of course, there are drawbacks: a particular user might not have access to a required resource immediately, as would be possible with an individual system. Also, there must be an overall administrative structure to keep track of all requests for resources and the status of all resources at all times.

Single data processing systems can be coupled tightly or loosely. In a *tightly coupled multiprocessing system,* one operating system with a common storage facility controls two CPUs, each with full I/O capability. It is also possible for one operating system to control two CPUs, only one of which has I/O capability. There are several types of *loosely coupled multiprocessing systems.* One is asymmetric multiprocessing, in which a special collection of job management routines makes it possible for two or more CPUs, each with its own operating system, to work together to process a single input program.

Applications Software: Developing a Program

The system software discussed thus far in this chapter is an essential part of any computer system. However, the application program bears as much weight as the system software in deciding whether or not the system output will be satisfactory. It is conceivable that a program may be input and executed without an error, and yet may output data that are totally useless as a solution to the problem at hand. As a matter of fact, it happens so frequently that programmers have created an expression for it: garbage in—garbage out, or GIGO.

The development of a useful application program requires two basic steps. First, a mathematical or logical model must be set up that correctly defines the problems to be solved. The problem's parameters must be defined, a meaningful output requested, and the appropriate data collected for input. Modeling and defining problems for computer input, the province of the *systems analyst*, require highly specialized skills. The second step is the actual step-by-step writing of the program, in an appropriate high-level language. This is the province of the *application programmer*. FORTRAN, one such language, was specifically designed to make computer programming easier for mathematicians and scientists. COBOL allows the programming of a problem in the language of the business world. No matter which language is used, it is necessary to inform the computer, in an exact and logical manner, what is required of it. Failure to do so results in errors, wasted computer time, increased costs, and a lot of human frustration. (For more about the languages used by people and computers, see chapter 13.)

In order to make the computer work for them, application programmers do not need an in-depth understanding of computer science. They do, however, have to know the general capabilities and limitations of computers, as well as the particular programming language to be used. The tools of programming—comprising the process of systems analysis and including design, implementation, and

(Joseph L. Sardinas, Jr.)

Graduate students at a university have developed software packages to assist them in their courses; here they review one of their programs.

evaluation, as well as an overview of flowcharting and programming languages—will be discussed at greater length in the chapters that follow. This will give a broad base of background information to future computer users in the business world, no matter what their area of interest may be.

Job Control Language: The Computer's Road Map

An application program may be written in one of several languages, which is then translated by the operating system into machine language in order to execute instructions. One very important feature of the operating system that remains to be discussed here is *job control language* (JCL). This is the language in which a user tells the computer where a job, or a collection of related problem programs, begins and ends and what must be done with it. Statements in job control language specify such information as: which system program to load and execute, where to find the input data for the program, and where to place the output from the program.

Job control language acts as an interface between the operating system and the application program. Job control language is machine-dependent; that is, the computers made by one vendor will generally respond to a job control language that is different from the language for another vendor's computers. For this reason, a comprehensive description of job control language is impossible. Through one example, though, a clearer understanding will become possible.

We saw above that when an application program is read into the system, the job management routines of the operating system detect that a job has been entered. The presence of a job control statement makes possible the detection of a job that is ready for processing. This statement may be in the form of a job card placed at the head of the deck of input cards. A typical job card contains the user's name and some sort of identification code. The second card in the deck may tell the operating system which compiler is needed to translate the program. For an application program written in COBOL, the job control card will read //EXEC COBOL (that is, get the COBOL compiler to translate a COBOL program). This card will be followed by others describing the I/O requirements of the compiler and the COBOL source statements to be compiled.

When the compiler has finished its translation and stored the output on a disk, another job control card calls on the linkage editor to merge all of the subroutines needed in the program. This card is followed by still other I/O description cards.

Finally, when the linkage editor has finished creating the load module version of the program, the load module's title must be given to the job management routine so that it can be scheduled for execution. Job management routines also have to be informed of the load module's I/O requirements. Additional job control cards provide for these steps.

The newly created load module is the GO step. The job entry has thus required three steps: compile, linkedit, GO.

The above is the general sequence usually found in some form in input card decks. But not all job control languages are exactly the same as this example. However, although the job control statements may differ, the purpose of the job control statements in any machine remains the same—to coordinate the operating system software with the application program of a job that is ready for execution.

Microprogramming: More Orderly Control

As we have seen throughout this chapter, a set of software programs, when executed, controls the operation of the computer hardware. To understand how a list of logical instructions relates to the actual hardware, we will focus on the part of a CPU's hardware that is concerned with control. (For purposes of this example, we will not consider the hardware that performs the arithmetic and logic operations.)

The control element of the CPU consists of a network of electronic switches, sometimes called gates. These switches, when either on or off, represent logical decisions such as "either A or B," "A and B," and "if A then B." The operating system instructions are also stored in main memory by on/off switching. (An "on" condition represents a 1 in binary language, and an "off" condition represents a 0.) When the computer is instructed to make a logical decision, the conditions represented by activated electronic signals ("on," or "1") are tested, gate by gate. Because an instruction is interpreted by the logical network gate by gate, this system is known as random logic. As a rule, the more random, or general-purpose, the computer hardware is, the more numerous and detailed will be the instructions required to program it—and the more detailed will be the programming and the more time will be needed for the execution of a program.

To eliminate the randomness of control logic and thus save valuable execution time, microprogramming was devised. In this process, a set of *microinstructions* is executed from a separate control memory of the computer to govern the operation of the control unit. The microprogram is thus a sort of "computer within a computer."

Microprogramming is *not*, despite the name, programming for microcomputers, and confusion between these concepts should be avoided. The name is derived from its reference to a part, or microcosm, of a larger program.

In a microprogrammed machine, execution of an instruction does not follow a random path through the control logic. Instead, it is mapped to its corresponding microprogram, which guides it through, so to speak. The microprograms are stored in a read-only memory (ROM) in main storage.

Microprogramming made possible another development, known as *emulation.* This allows for one computer to simulate another. Microprogramming techniques are used to provide one computer with a ROM that could make it behave as if it were another model with the same basic machine language but with a different internal organization. The computer doing the emulation is usually referred to as the *host machine,* while the computer being emulated is called the *target machine.*

Originally, microprogramming techniques were considered the tools of the computer designer, not the user. Users were not able to modify or extend the microprogramming capabilities of ROMs; this required the design of a new or modified ROM. But then the *writable control store,* a control memory with a write as well as a read capability, was introduced. This gave programmers and users, as well as designers, a role in microprogramming. Recently, computers that are fully microprogrammable have begun to appear. These machines employ extensive or exclusive writable control store. They can be microprogrammed to emulate a variety of different target machines or accomplish a variety of tasks. The trend is toward the design of a universal host machine, which could be microprogrammed to emulate any target machine desired. It is not yet available, but probably will be in the not-too-distant future.

Firmware

A microprogram residing in a ROM has many of the attributes of conventional software, but in some ways it is merely an extension of the hardware. To describe this dual status, the term *firmware* is used. Conventional software programs usually remain in main memory or on a direct-access storage device while they are executing. Firmware, on the other hand, consists of a program whose logic has been "burned" into a silicon chip; that is, the electronic circuits for a specific program are contained on a single chip. This chip is "plugged" into the computer; when the program is executing, the machine only has to go to the chip to locate and execute the microinstructions. This usually results in a faster execution of the program than if a software package were directing the process.

249

There are several advantages to the use of firmware as a software replacement. Firmware costs are decreasing, as are hardware costs, while the cost of software is remaining fairly constant. Also, firmware can be standardized more easily than software, and it is more portable (that is, adaptable to a variety of machines). Some proponents of firmware feel that the low cost of mass-produced firmware would discourage illegal program copying.

The Elements of Programming

Software or programs are the product of the systems analyst, who identifies the needs of a particular user, defines the problems or objectives, and develops plans to meet these needs and objectives. None of these steps is less important than the others. Ultimately, one plan is selected; this becomes the design of the system.

Once the system is designed, actual programming expertise is needed to convert the system into programming language for the computer. Here the programmer takes over, working from a flowchart developed by the systems analyst. A flowchart is an illustration of the steps, or flow, of the logic in the designed system. The program translates that logic into an application program, ready to be entered into the computer for execution. Different languages have been developed to convert the steps of a program, developed by human beings to meet human needs, into instructions to be understood by machines that can only distinguish "on" from "off."

In the next chapter, our examination of computer software continues with descriptions of data bases and the management systems that make them accessible to computers and human users. These are important considerations, since even the most carefully constructed program can do nothing unless it is supported by appropriate data.

Summary

The term *software* refers to all programs written for the computer. Software may be classified as either *application programs*, which instruct the computer to perform specific operations, or *system software*, which controls the computer's internal operations.

The *operating system* is the series of system software routines that takes charge of application programs from input to output. It controls all peripheral I/O devices, the transfers of data to and from auxiliary storage, and all CPU operations.

To accommodate the ever-increasing size of application programs, the concepts of multiprogramming, virtual storage, and multiprocessing have been developed.

Multiprogramming is the execution of two or more programs by one CPU. It allows execution time to be used by another program while the first one is reading in data from an I/O device or auxiliary storage. The operating system controls the scheduling of the CPU so that different programs do not conflict with each other.

Virtual storage allows multimillion-byte programs to be loaded into the computer. When stored on a direct-access device, data for large programs can be transferred from their virtual addresses in auxiliary storage to their real addresses in main storage as needed. This transfer is automatic and allows a virtually limitless address space for data storage.

Multiprocessing is the joining together of two or more CPUs and their associated devices to form one system. This allows several users to take advantage of combined computer resources.

Job control language is a machine-oriented language that interfaces the application program with the operating system. It contains the instructions that enable the operating system to call on compilers, linkage editors, and I/O devices to provide necessary data and to detect the beginning and end of a job. Job control languages differ according to the particular type of computer that is in use; they are said to be machine-dependent.

Microprogramming uses a set of microinstructions to govern the control unit of the CPU. A microprogram is a "computer within a computer."

Firmware is a hybrid of software and hardware. It is the result of writing a logic program permanently on a silicon memory chip, which is then "plugged" into the computer. When the program is executing, the machine goes to the chip to execute the microinstructions.

Key Terms and Phrases

application programmer
application programs
compilers
data management routines
demand paging
emulation
external page table
firmware
fragmentation
frame
host machine
interrupt handling routines
invalid bit
I/O programs

job
job control language (JCL)
job management
libraries
linkage editors
loader
loosely coupled multiprocessing
  system
microinstructions
microprogramming
monitor
multiple virtual storage
multiprogramming
object module

251

operating system
page fault
page-in-operation
pages
real addresses
region
routines
scheduler
source program
subroutine
supervisor

system software
systems analyst
target machine
task
task management
tightly coupled multiprocess-
    ing system
uniprocessor systems
virtual address
writable control store

Sources of Additional Information

Computerworld Extra, September 17, 1980, entire issue.

D'Angelo, Joseph. "A Primer on Virtual Memory." *Mini-Micro Systems,* no. 3 (1979):39–45.

Gear, C. William. *Introduction to Computers, Structured Programming, and Applications.* Palo Alto, Calif.: Science Research Associates, 1978.

Salisbury, Alan B. *Microprogrammable Computer Architecture.* New York: Elsevier, 1976.

Test Yourself

1. What is a program?
2. What is an operating system?
3. List the three basic control functions of the operating system.
4. What is the difference between a source program and its object module?
5. What is the difference between multiprogramming and multiprocessing?
6. What is the main purpose of virtual storage?
7. What is a subroutine, and why is it useful?
8. What is the purpose of job control language?
9. Explain the difference between firmware, software, and hardware.
10. Describe the functions of the linkage editor.
11. Explain the difference between applications programs and systems software.
12. Explain the role of the interrupt handling routine in the response of a computer to errors.
13. What is emulation?
14. Describe the steps in the development of an application program.

9 Data Base Management

"True, we don't give out personal information, but every once in a while the computer takes it upon itself to spill the beans."

APPLICATION
A Data Base for Citibank

In the late 1960s and early 1970s, Citibank of New York expanded, providing more services to a much larger customer base. Staff and clerical operations increased to support Citibank's growing financial, trade, and other operations. But at the same time, staff productivity began to decrease. Consequently, operating expenses rose while customer satisfaction declined. Citibank responded by decentralizing its operations. It created separate marketing groups and corresponding operations groups for its various activities. These groups were further subdivided into divisions and departments, many with their own computers and support staffs.

Different divisions used different computer systems, yet the growing decentralization increased the need for an exchange of information between departments. Meanwhile, the quantity of information about customers, income and outflow, and internal operations was increasing. So was the number of distinct information systems, all separate from Citibank's main accounting systems. The loss of efficiency in information flow became apparent.

To integrate management and accounting information, Citibank developed its Integrated Accounting and Management Information System (IAMIS). IAMIS was designed to coordinate data capture, editing, validation, and transmission to other systems. It thus made possible the construction of a data base that would satisfy many of Citibank's varied information and data processing needs.

The data capture system for IAMIS, called Citiproof, ensures that the various decentralized groups and departments feed the same categories of data to both the management and the accounting systems. The Citiproof network of some 50 computers and 200 CRTs receives data directly from CRTs and from data tapes produced by other systems. It processes these to produce accounting reports and a "raw" transactions file (RTF). These reports and the detailed RTF data are then processed by IAMIS in two subsystems. The subsystem that processes transactions is able to add customer, product, and other information to the RTF data, thus producing a very detailed data base. This data base supports accounting and management analyses within each of the separate banking groups, and can be used to generate a variety of reports (for example, reports by customer, product, or type of business involved).

The other subsystem processes customer balances and management information services (MIS) data. This subsystem edits and validates the daily customer balance and other MIS data, such as loans, time deposits, and foreign exchange, and then transmits the accumulated data directly to the main data base. Finally, IAMIS also receives the general ledger account balances each day.

The IAMIS consolidated data base makes it possible to reconcile individual customer balances with the proper general ledger accounts. Any discrepancies can be identified and referred to the appropriate group. IAMIS also provides data for its customers' auditors, supports a variety of smaller functions requiring a centralized data base, and can be used to develop specialized, one-time reports as the need arises. IAMIS is an excellent example of one of the most important recent developments in data processing—*data base management*.

HISTORICALLY, computer data have been organized and maintained according to the applications for which they were needed. That is, each application has had its own file. For scientific applications, data organization and storage are generally simple. In such applications, relatively few separate data items are processed by sophisticated software that may involve many equations and models. In business data processing, on the other hand, the situation is usually the reverse. Here the actual processing is generally simple, but the number of data items is often very large. For example, keeping track of all policies issued by an insurance company may require thousands of reels of magnetic tape.

That a large mass of computer data organized according to the needs of individual applications can create problems for the user is clear from the example of Citibank discussed in the Application. For this reason, more and more businesses today are turning to *data base management systems* (DBMS) to organize and store all their computer data. Such systems store data in, and retrieve data from, a single, comprehensive collection of records known as the *data base*. To form a data base, separate computer file sets, each designed for a particular application, are reorganized into a single set of nonrepetitive files to support a variety of applications. A data base reduces repetition of data, makes the data easier to update and control, giving the user greater flexibility in utilizing the information contained in it.

The term "data base" is sometimes used to refer to any grouping of data, including that organized by separate application. Moreover, the term "data file" is sometimes used to describe a *small* data base, while "data bank" may be used to describe a *large* data base. Properly, however, the term "data base" should be used to refer to *all* organized collections of information.

A data base management system consists of programs designed to maintain and manage the data in a data base. Data base software is beginning to influence hardware design as the demand for greater processing flexibility and efficiency grows. In the data base computers now in research and development, data base management information will be built into the hardware, thus making CPU main memory more available for actual data and speeding up processing time. Incorporated into hardware, DBMS would be much easier to test and less likely to produce errors than the complex software systems required at present.

The Application Data Base

When computers first became available to businesses and corporations, they were used almost exclusively for clerical and accounting operations, such as processing payrolls, invoices, accounts receivable, and accounts payable and for general ledger preparation. The standard 80-column punched card was a natural medium for these applications, because it was a unit record. By using fixed-length fields and code numbers in place of written information, it allowed early business computers to perform the same operations that accounting machines had previously performed, only much, much faster. And computers were able to process massive amounts of punched card data.

A simple business typically organizes information about its activities in a number of different categories, such as accounts payable, accounts receivable, cost accounts, employees, general ledgers, inventory, and invoices—and even more. The information in each of these categories is a *file*. Each of these files is used for a different purpose or *application;* however, the data they contain are related, and more than one file may be required for a single application. For example, invoice processing requires names and other information

Figure 9-1 Application data bases

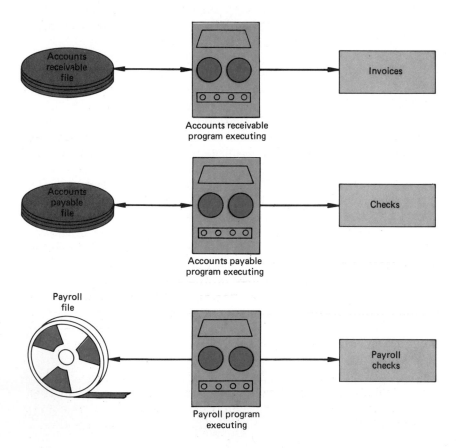

from the customer file as well as information from the invoice file. The different types of data used in the operation of an organization are inevitably related to varying extents. Application files must reflect relationships to be of any use.

Organizing and coordinating separate application files so that the computer system produces the required information is the responsibility of application programmers. Traditionally, application programmers have treated each application as a separate and distinct job for the computer. The customary approach to development of a computer application—sometimes called the *process approach* —can be summarized as follows:

1. Identify the computer's processing requirements and the data needed for each program to be used in the application.
2. Construct files for the application.
3. Write a program (or programs) that will define the specific application for the computer to execute.

PROCESS APPROACH

The collection of all of these application-oriented files constitutes a data base. It is known as the *application data base* because all of the files are specific to an application. (See figure 9-1.)

Problems of Application Data Bases

A significant characteristic of the early business use of computers was the large number of applications programs and the many files required to support these programs. The emphasis on single applications, without reference to the overall information needs of the organization, resulted in efficient individual programs. But these same programs represented an inefficient use of the total information resource system to which they belonged. Every new application requested by management required sorting and merging of existing files to create a new one to satisfy the requirements of the new application program. Application files proliferated. Often they were incompatible, having been reformatted to meet the needs of different program requirements. To alter these highly specific applications and files was costly and time-consuming. In fact, it was often more cost- and time-efficient to create a new program and file than to revise an old one.

But the most wasteful aspect of files is data *redundancy*. This occurs when some of the data in one file is also contained in another. The primary customer file, for example, may duplicate some data in the invoice file. When data must be updated, a separate program is

257

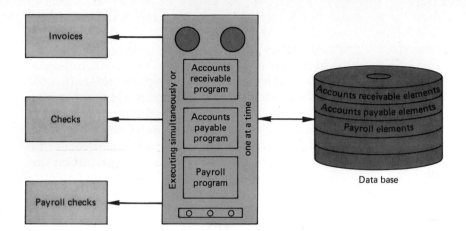

Figure 9-2 A data base management system

required to revise *each* file. Customer purchases, for example, must be entered into the invoice, inventory, and sales files, and perhaps several others as well. If a given data item is updated in some files but not others, the various reports derived from the different files will not agree. Thus updating becomes a difficult, error-prone process. Moreover, redundant data requires additional storage space, at greater cost, while denying that same space to other data.

Related problems arise when the data in auxiliary storage must be revised. Because business records must be current, data must often be added and old data deleted. Certain changes will be relatively easy. But some changes may necessitate a change in the record format itself. Perhaps the company is dealing with several new suppliers; the field for supplier codes has to be enlarged. Not only will the file need to be reorganized, but all programs drawing on that file will need to be changed. The format of records in a file is specified in the program. The computer will not execute the program if the record format in the program specification does not agree with the format of the records stored in the file. The need to change programs in accordance with changes in data represents a major maintenance problem in many data processing systems.

Still another problem involves the incompatibility of an "old" system with new hardware and software. This problem has surfaced with the development of faster, more capacious, and less expensive storage devices. To take advantage of them means transferring records from the old to the new devices. And that, in turn, may mean changing the programs. Thus application programs may be hardware-dependent as well as format-dependent.

The need to resolve these and other data storage problems has given rise to the development of data base management systems.

The most important feature of a *data base management system* (DBMS) is that it processes an organization's data as an integrated whole. (See figure 9-2.) Today, the term "data base" refers to a collection of interrelated data items that can be accessed by *one or more* application programs. A modern data base is not merely an accumulation of separate files; it is, rather, a collection of related items of information arranged for minimal redundancy of data. Because the data are related, a data base cuts across lines of organization and function. It thus becomes an organizational resource.

Components of DBMS

A data base management system can be viewed in terms of three components: (1) the user's needs, expressed through an application

Using query language, the data administrator can directly access the data base from a terminal in his office.

(Joseph L. Sardinas, Jr.)

Figure 9-3 General relationship between components of a DBMS

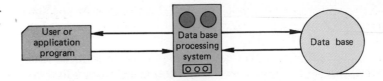

program; (2) the processing component, often referred to as the data base processing system or just the data base system; and (3) the actual data base. (See figure 9-3.)

The user. Users generally interact with a DBMS indirectly through an application program. The application program in turn interacts with the processing component via a program language, such as COBOL. The user can, however, interact directly with the processing component via a *query language* for a one-time, or *ad hoc*, application; that is, an application that is called for so seldom that a written program could not be justified. A query language also makes the data base accessible to users who do not know how to write programs.

The data base processing system. The data base processing system is the functional link between the user (or application program) and the data base itself. This component of a DBMS is a set of com-

Figure 9-4 Schematic diagram showing the relationship between the data base, DBMS, and CPU

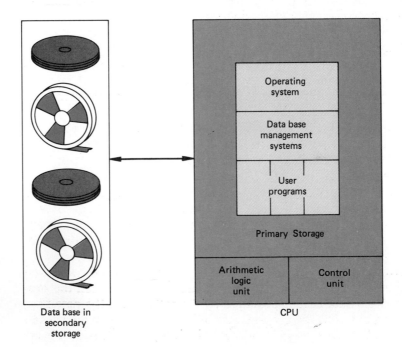

Data base in secondary storage

CPU

260

puter programs that translates the commands of the user or application program into computer operations to be performed on the data base contents.

There is some confusion in the terminology used to refer to such systems. Some computer professionals use the term "data base processing system" to include all three components of the DBMS, while others use the term "data management system" as a synonym for DBMS. To avoid confusion, therefore, this text uses DBMS to refer to all three components as a functional whole, that is, an information management system based on an integrated data base. We will use the term "data base processing system" to refer to the second component of such a system as described here.

The actual data base. The data base, of course, is the collected data used to fill the information requests of the user. The data base also contains information about the format of the data and about the relationships between different data items.

Schema and subschema. To understand the organization of a data base and how it provides data for specific requests, we need to consider the concepts of *data schema* and *data subschema*. A data schema is a complete description of all the data (and their logical interrelationships) contained in a data base. A schema, then, is the "universe" of data items available in a data base. By definition, an individual data base is defined by one, and only one, schema. A set of data items required for a specific application program is a subschema. A schema may contain several overlapping subschemas. This happens when two or more applications have overlapping data requirements. The subschemas for payroll and personnel applications, for example, will overlap to some extent, since they both require employee names and numbers. (See figure 9-5.)

The data base of a DBMS can be accessed in two ways: First, through the host, or high-level, language generally used for programming, such as COBOL; and second, through a modified high-level language built into the DBMS operating system. These simplified languages—really glossaries of special terms and phrases—were developed to permit wider access to data bases. The *data manipulation language* (DML), also known as the "data base command language," controls the transfer of data between the application program and the data base.

In writing a DBMS program, the programmer defines the required data in terms of a subschema. The functional link between the program and the data base is provided by the software in the data base processing system. The programmer does not have to be concerned about the physical storage locations of specific data in the data base.

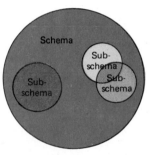

Figure 9-5 Schema and subschemas

Thus, a DML statement is actually a combination of host-language instructions—for example, in COBOL—and special instructions contained in the data base processing system and in the data base.

Data Base Management Systems: Pros and Cons

One major advantage of a data base management system is that it provides greater security for the data. This is because the data base can be accessed only through the data base processing system software. Only that part of a data base called for by a given program can be accessed at a time; data cannot be accessed from other programs.

Another important advantage is that the data items are, by definition, compatible; that is, they are so organized that less response time is needed and more information is available. There is a "rule of thumb" that the greater the compatibility, the greater the amount of information that can be extracted from a given quantity of stored data.

Still another advantage is the reduction of costly and wasteful data redundancy. The elimination of duplication not only saves storage space but also can simplify the processing operation.

Generally, data base processing makes for more economical management of information. Data can be centralized and managed from one department. This is more efficient and less expensive than having several separate staffs managing a portion of the same data. Moreover, an improvement made in the data base processing system for processing one application will also become available for use in processing other applications.

Efficiency also results because changes in the content of a data base do not affect the programs that access it. Updating or even reorganizing a data base only requires changes in the data base processing system. It does not require rewriting the application programs that the data base supports. In a DBMS, the data fields can be readily expanded or cancelled; the only changes needed will be in the logical definitions of the information in the data base. Thus, the data base can constantly grow without having to be reorganized.

For some users, these considerable advantages may be outweighed by some disadvantages. First, a DBMS is expensive. Depending on the needs of the user and the quantities of data to be organized and processed, the system itself can cost as much as $100,000 or even more. Moreover, the purchase of new hardware—additional memory, a more powerful computer, or other devices—may be necessary. The cost of converting existing equipment can be very high. And processing costs may be higher as well, since a DBMS is not designed for simple and economical sequential processing.

Second, data base processing is, by its nature, quite complex. The data base contains large quantities of data in various formats. That means more complex programming, which means more sophisticated designs and systems and more skilled programmers.

Perhaps the greatest disadvantage of a DBMS is its vulnerability to the failure of any part of the system. Because a DBMS can be accessed by several users at the same time, a failure in one program creates problems for others. If program X fails after modifying several records, program Y (reading the same data right after modification) may use invalid data. It also may be difficult to determine the correct data content of the data base just prior to program failure. And a hardware failure in any component may bring the entire system to a halt.

Until now, installation of data base management systems was feasible only for large computer facilities. However, recent advances in software technology have made available data base management systems with limited capabilities for use with both mini- and microcomputers, at a cost of under $1,000.

Data Base Management Capabilities

The concept of data base management clearly implies certain operations. For example, not only must a data base be created—usually from existing records—but it must be maintained as well, by such operations as data deletion and updating. An ideally functioning DBMS should also have the following capabilities or characteristics: (1) data independence, (2) data relatability, (3) data nonredundancy, (4) data integrity, (5) data compression, (6) data security, and (7) system auditability.

Data independence. Storage and retrieval of data in a DBMS are not restricted by the format of the data; that is, the data are independent of the data format and, therefore, independent of the program that accesses it. For example, FORTRAN programs usually include *format statements* that specify the kind of data to be accessed and the form in which they are stored.

A format statement may inform the computer that a particular data item is a "real" (that is, decimal) number containing a maximum of five digits and two decimal places. The format in this case would be F5.2. On the other hand, a five-figure integer might have the format I5, and an alphabetic character variable five bytes long might have the format A5. Thus, the computer "knows" the difference between the format of an employee's salary, social security number, and last

263

name, even though all of these items of information may be stored together on a disk track.

Changes in data content do not affect programs in a DBMS. But changes in the storage *format* of data can mean a change in the program or programs accessing them. Such changes can be extremely expensive in an information system consisting of application data bases. In a DBMS, the programming needed to enable the data base processing unit to deal with format differences is considerable. Attempts to make data independent even of accessing programs are being made through program languages such as PL/I. As application programs become independent of changes in stored data and storage format, the cost of maintaining and updating data will decrease and the flexibility of the data base will increase even more.

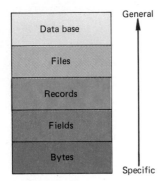

Figure 9-6 Schematic diagram showing the relationship of levels of information to a data base

Data relatability. Relatability refers to the logical relations between data items. This includes relationships between data items in different records as well as relationships between different items in the same record. It would be illogical to store the name, address, and social security number of an employee and other relevant information in widely separated byte positions, or to have a sequence that listed salary and tax rates in between the street address and the zip code.

To make data contained in different records relatable requires the use of special filing/storing/addressing techniques. These enable a user to access records with similar types of information without having to search the entire data base. The greater the relatability of data, the greater the potential efficiency of the programs accessing them and the less time required to process them.

Data nonredundancy. Redundant data leads to inefficient data processing. This redundancy also makes data difficult to update and wastes storage space. However, the creation of an integrated data base does not, *by itself,* do anything to reduce data redundancy. It is the responsibility of the data manager to create and maintain an integrated data base that minimizes the duplication of data items. Redundant entries must be removed when the data are being organized and integrated into the new DBMS.

Data integrity. A data base with perfect data integrity would be error-free. But practically speaking, an error-free data base is unattainable. By its very nature, an integrated data base has many users. Errors may be introduced when new data are captured as well as when stored data are updated. A variety of techniques for error reduction, including check bits and field-size validation, have been devised to reduce data "pollution" as much as possible.

Data compression. One of the more interesting recent developments in data processing is the data compressor. In hardware or software form, a compressor reduces the record length of a given item of input. For example, the field used for storing an individual's last name may have space for 14 characters. But if the last name has only six characters (Ritsch, for example), eight storage spaces will be unoccupied. A compressor will store this name as "RITSCH6," using seven spaces, a saving of 50 percent of storage space. Multiplied by the many entries in a large data base, data compression can lead to impressive savings. In actuality, compression takes place at the bit level and is more complex than this example would suggest.

Data security. No data security system can guarantee complete safety from unauthorized access and improper use, theft, or hazards such as fire and flood. But simply because it is centralized, a DBMS permits greater control and tends to impose limitations on access to data unrelated to a user's application.

System auditability. In any business, auditors must be able to verify the accuracy of transaction and accounting records. Because integrated data bases are vulnerable to accident and malfunction, most DBMS are designed with safety features to secure data integrity. They usually have, for example, built-in logging and journaling procedures to restore data that might be accidentally destroyed. Auditors can make use of these procedures and records to ensure that all operations have been performed properly.

Data Base Models

The term *data base model* refers to the *logical* arrangement of data elements in the data base. Logical arrangement should not be confused with the actual or physical arrangement of data items. Because the organizing relationships are logical rather than physical, systems incorporating such models are often referred to as logical DBMS. Among several possible models of logical organization, the three most important are the *hierarchical, network,* and *relational* data models.

In the *hierarchical data model,* data records are organized by levels. Records at one level carry the addresses of records in the next related level. (See figure 9-7.) The hierarchical model is often said to be "treelike," or similar to a family tree. Thus, most records will have a *parent* (a record in the next level above) and one or more *children* (records in the next level below).

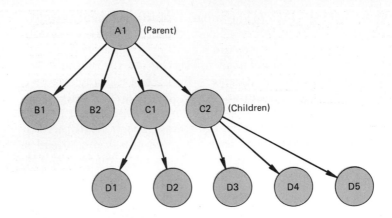

Figure 9-7 A hierarchical data model

Because the structure of most businesses and other institutions is hierarchical, this type of data arrangement can be thought of as natural for visualizing the logical relationships between various types of organizational data. However, the organizational relationships are usually of the one-to-many type (such as superior to subordinates); one group of records must arbitrarily be "parents," and the other group "children."

The structure of the *network data model* is derived from set theory, and so is the terminology that describes this model. In the hierarchical model, each logical child has exactly *one* logical parent. In the network data model, this limitation is removed, so that a data "child" may have two or more "parents." Network data are organized in *sets*, each with an *owner* and several *members*. Data elements are joined by *pointers*. (See figure 9-8.)

The *relational data model* is much simpler than the other two. Hi-

Figure 9-8 A network data model

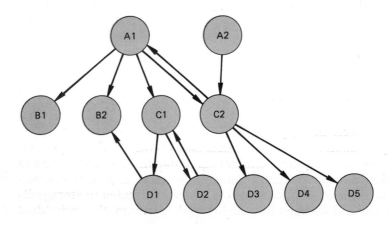

STUDENT NAME	ADDRESS	OTHER
DAVOS, L.	OAKLAND	••••••••
JONES, B.	SEATTLE	••••••••
PAUER, I.	PORTLAND	••••••••
RITCH, R.	WINNIPEG	••••••••
THOMAS, M.	LONG BEACH	••••••••

a. Table listing students

STUDENT NAME	COURSE	OTHER
DAVOS, L.	ACCOUNTING	••••••••
DAVOS, L.	STATISTICS	••••••••
JONES, B.	ACCOUNTING	••••••••
PAUER, I.	AUDITING	••••••••
RITCH, R.	COMPUTERS	••••••••
RITCH, R.	MANAGEMENT	••••••••

b. Table showing relationship
between students and courses

Figure 9-9 A relational data model
showing structure of a data base

COURSE TITLE	COURSE NUMBER	OTHER
ACCOUNTING	B101	••••••••
AUDITING	B107	••••••••
COMPUTERS	B110	••••••••
MANAGEMENT	B112	••••••••
STATISTICS	B113	••••••••

c. Table representing courses

erarchical and network data elements are linked in "chains" and
sometimes "rings." Even for a few data elements, the linkage can become quite complex. But the relational model organizes data relationships in terms of two-dimensional tables. (See figure 9-9.) This
gives the user a very clear view of the data. Many-to-many relationships can be seen as clearly as one-to-many relationships. The relational model is very flexible and offers several advantages in terms
of greater data security. Some computer experts believe that the
relational model will largely replace others in organizing data
bases.

Distributed Data Bases

In distributed data processing (see chapter 7), computers at physically separate locations can all have access to the same data base.
Often, however, the application needs of each computer location
may require somewhat different data bases. This would be true, for
example, of the computer installations of the different branches of a
bank. The branches constitute a distributed data processing network, but for practical purposes each bank maintains in storage its
own customer data base. In a distributed data base, the individual

data bases of all branches would follow the same format and be available online to terminals at all other branches.

In this way, distributed data processing is supported by an integrated, not isolated, data base. The logical relationships within the data base are maintained, but those elements most relevant to a particular computer facility in the distributed data processing network are physically located at that facility. At the same time, every computer installation within the network has access to the entire distributed data base when needed. The sophisticated software that will support distributed data bases is now being developed.

Setting Up a Data Base

A well-designed data base management system can be a tremendously valuable resource for the management of any organization. It is a powerful aid in organizing information and making relevant data available promptly when needed, in usable formats. A DBMS can also improve the quality of information available to management, thus providing a more reliable foundation for decision making. However, a poorly designed DBMS can be an expensive hindrance that creates more problems than it solves.

Whether a DBMS helps or hinders an organization is often determined in the very first stages, and depends on how the data base component of the system is developed. For this reason, data base design and the process by which data bases are generated have become important subjects to computer users and professionals.

Until very recently, data base construction was often seen as a problem in what was commonly called "file conversion." This view tended to focus on organizing data rather than on how the data were to be used. A DBMS produced from this viewpoint often became a highly elaborate access system that ultimately was not relevant to user applications.

Four Steps to a Data Base

Construction of an effective DBMS requires a focus on the needs of its users. There are four steps in the design of a flexible and practical data base: (1) Identify the data needs of the organization, (2) identify the processing requirements (applications) involved, (3) generate the data base schema and subschemas, and (4) produce software to convert the data to a form and organization that is usable by a DBMS.

268

Data needs. Everything depends on an accurate understanding of the data requirements of the users. In most organizations, several component units will use the data base. Data output requirements of all departments and individuals must be determined. This is most accurately done by means of interviews and often with questionnaires as well, which are directed to the appropriate personnel of the various user departments.

Important questions include: What are the objects or relationships (often called *entities*) of interest to each department? What is the appropriate identifying name for each entity? What *attributes* of an entity are important to each user department(s)?

The result of such questions will be a list of entities and attributes of major concern to all departments and staff using the DBMS. With this list, the data base designers will be able to establish the data relationships between entities. They will resolve conflicts between entity names, and will also develop detailed descriptions of the data base and its organization. These descriptions will serve as a guide for creating the data base schema and subschema.

Identifying data processing requirements. The data processing requirements of an organization include the ability to process and produce data for various transactions. They also include the need to enter revised and updated information into the data base at selected intervals. Questions that might be asked include: What kind of transactions are handled by each department? What is the frequency of each type of transaction? What are the processing priorities of each type of transaction? The result is a list of transactions and their attributes, which helps to identify redundant functions. The list also clarifies the relationships of data transactions to entities, and helps in identifying formats needed by the various departments of the organization. These conclusions will also form part of the DBMS schema and subschemas.

Creating the schema and subschemas. The data base schema and subschemas should be derived from a thorough and careful analysis of the needs of the organization as determined in the two preceding stages. The schema and subschema should not be developed by adapting the software of an existing DBMS; that would lead to inefficiency.

Existing data, on the other hand, must be related to the schema. The data description of all the data and relationships involved in the schema and subschema must be written. Existing and new data must be loaded onto the system according to the specifications of the schema. We will examine the steps in the production of software in the following chapters.

APPLICATION

A Data Base Gone Astray

In the early 1970s, Montgomery County, Maryland, decided to replace its second-generation computer system with one that would support multiprogramming and data communications. A DBMS was clearly called for. The county government was especially interested in developing a data base that used *geographic coding* ("geocoding") to relate demographic information to land use. Geocoding would enable county officials to determine the population of a census tract or a specific city block and then relate that information to the need for library facilities, to demands for different county services, and to police calls, among other kinds of information.

Initially, county officials and the systems supplier decided that two primary data bases were needed—one for people and one for property. The people data base would contain information about voters, property holders, merchants, permit holders, liquor license holders, and individuals who had been arrested. The property data base would contain information about land parcels and government property inventories (cars, office furniture, library books, and so on). It would also contain street directory information for the police and fire departments. Use of these two data bases was expected to eliminate data redundancy and updating problems caused by redundancy.

The system was intended to answer such information requests as: (1) List all county employees of a specified service grade (or higher) who are county residents, property owners, and registered Democrats (or Republicans); or (2) provide the population densities of the areas in which construction of public buildings has been proposed.

But six years after the decision to convert to a DBMS was made, all the people and property data bases existed separately or were about to be separated, and the geographic reference file was of little use. What had gone wrong?

Basically, the project was ahead of its time. It used one of the first data base management systems on the market, in which data maintenance was both tedious and error-prone. But data relationships and collection were as big a problem. The logical connections between other data items were difficult to integrate with geocoding, which needed a schema to describe a huge amount of possible data relationships. In addition, there was no single source of all the geocoding data called for in the plan, or for the entire county. Then, too, there was much overlap and as many gaps and discrepancies in files of the same data collected and stored by different departments. Also, the system planners had not considered the implications of including, for example, information about library cardholders and people with an arrest record in a single file.

Despite these and other difficulties, Montgomery County finally did install a system with important improvements over the previous system. Among its achievements are applications programs largely independent of the stored data, and backup and recovery procedures that improved data integrity and security. But the new system bears only a distant resemblance to that envisioned by the original planners. Without a doubt, the original plan was too comprehensive. But a thorough analysis of actual data needs at the very beginning would have produced a plan that was both more realistic and easier to implement.

Computer data have traditionally been organized and stored as files to conform with the specific applications they support. As these files have proliferated, data managers have encountered serious problems of data redundancy, updating, and integrity. Consequently, computer users today are turning to *data base management systems* (DBMS).

These information management systems are characterized by a single, comprehensive, nonrepetitive set of data elements called a *data base.* The collection of all application-oriented files is known as an *application data base.* An integrated data base minimizes data repetition, makes data easier to update and maintain, and provides greater flexibility in use of the DBMS for various applications. (The term "data base" is properly applied to all information bases, including application data bases and the kind that characterize a DBMS.)

A DBMS has three components: (1) The user and/or application program by which the user interacts with the DBMS; (2) the data base processing system—a set of computer programs that provides the functional link between the user or application program and the data base; and (3) the data base itself, the collection of stored data that provides the information to be processed by the DBMS. The data base also contains information about the format in which the various data elements are stored and about the logical relationships between data elements.

The organization of the data elements in a data base are described in terms of a *schema* and its *subschemas.* A schema is a description of all the data elements in the data base and their logical interrelationships. By definition, a data base has only one schema but may have any number of subschemas. Subschemas may intersect or overlap. Programs accessing the data base, however, are written in what is known as *data manipulation language* (usually controlled by a higher-level language such as COBOL).

The important capabilities of DBMS include data *independence, relatability, nonredundancy, integrity, compression, security,* and *auditability.*

The three main models for organizing data base information are the *hierarchical, network,* and *relational.* The hierarchical model categorizes data in terms of levels (specifically, *parents* and *children*). The network model permits a data "child" to have more than one data "parent"; the logical relationships, however, are described in terms of *sets, owners,* and *members.* The relational model organizes data in "tables." This type of model is the simplest of the three discussed, and it is expected to replace all others eventually.

Setting up a data base requires thorough and careful planning, and should focus in particular on the needs of the user rather than on the processing requirements of the system.

**Key Terms
and Phrases**

application
application data base
data base
data base management system
  (DBMS)
data base model
data manipulation language
  (DML)
file

hierarchical data model
maintenance
network data model
pointers
process approach
query language
redundancy
relational data model

**Sources of
Additional
Information**

Burch, John G., Jr., and Sardinas, Joseph L., Jr. *Computer Control and Audit:
A Total Systems Approach.* New York: Wiley, 1978.

Davis, Gordon B. *Management Information Systems: Conceptual Foundations, Structure, and Development.* New York: McGraw-Hill, 1974.

Holland, Robert H. "DBMS: Developing User Views." *Datamation*, no. 2
(1980):141–44.

Hsiao, David K. "Data Base Machines Are Coming, Data Base Machines Are
Coming!" *Computer*, no. 3 (1979):7–9.

Pottruck, David S. "Banking on Integration." *Datamation*, no. 11 (1979):
119–26.

Tsichritzis, D. C., and Lochovsky, F. H. "Designing the Data Base." *Datamation*, no. 8 (1978):147–51.

Test Yourself

1. A company in your area has just installed a data base management system (DBMS). What is a DBMS? Begin your explanation
   with a definition of the term *data base*. What does a DBMS consist
   of?
2. To be optimally useful to a firm, a DBMS must possess certain capabilities. Name seven such capabilities, and explain why each is
   important to the whole system.
3. What is an application data base? What factors determine a good
   application data base?
4. Identify the three general components of a data base management
   system. How do these three components relate to one another and
   function together as a whole?
5. The concepts of *schema* and *subschema* are important to an understanding of a data base. Define these two concepts. How does
   each relate to an application data base?
6. The design of data base management systems and the process by
   which data bases are generated are growing in importance. Why
   is this the case?
7. Identify four steps in the design of a flexible and practical data
   base. What is the importance of each step to the design of the data
   base as a whole?

10 Systems Analysis

As proposed by the project sponsor

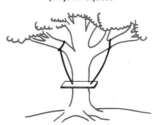

As specified in the project request

As designed by the senior analyst

As produced by the programmers

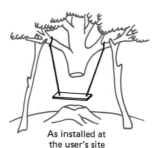

As installed at the user's site

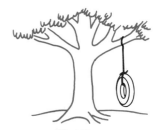

What the user wanted

APPLICATION

Computers in the Courts

The enormous backlog of court cases has long been a detriment to our justice system. An offshoot of this problem is the even more enormous amount of paperwork created by such a caseload. Solution of this problem calls for the large storage capacity and the capability of repetitive actions of a computer-based information system. How would a systems analyst approach the task of developing such an information system? This is how Milwaukee County approached it.

First, the problem was defined. In this typical urban county, more than 35,000 cases develop each year. Case data such as time, place, and type of offense, time and place of arrest, arraignment, assignment of prosecutor, trial data, and sentencing information must be entered in the court record for each case. Data about the accused and about other participants in or witnesses to an incident must also be entered. Thus the first part of the problem concerns entry of large quantities of data.

The second part of the analysis considered the difficulty of reclaiming these data quickly from the massive manual files that were used before computerization. In the current system, several offices of the justice system are concerned with the same information, and as a result, voluminous files of duplicate information are kept. The new system must avoid redundancy and allow easy access to shared storage.

After consideration of several alternative plans, a design was selected. Input would be by means of display terminals in the district attorney's and court clerk's offices. A screen format would be used so that corrections and deletions could be quickly seen and changes made if necessary. The information would then be transmitted from the terminals directly to an "intelligent" distributive processor, a processing unit that can handle online data entry and retrieval as well as online establishment of case records and criminal complaint sheets. Data would remain online while each case was pending and for at least 90 days after final disposition, so that they would be available to the court clerk and district attorney through inquiry on the display terminals. Output in the form of formal complaint sheets was to be available from a printer adjacent to the CPU.

The use of display terminals would provide a backup in case of mechanical difficulty, since the terminal could take over some of the tasks of the CPU. Also, the terminals could establish a basic case record and store it for final corrections, after which the edited version would be transmitted to the CPU.

Implementation of the system was planned in three phases. Phase I included the entry of all misdemeanor, traffic, and felony cases into the computer files so that current cases could be tracked through the computer. Phase II extended the system to the sheriff's department, public defender's office, and correctional facilities, as well as to the municipal police agencies. This would provide online inquiry capability to these agencies. Some statistical reports would also be implemented in this phase.

Phase III computerized the civil courts, including alimony, paternity, and divorce cases, making further use of the display terminals.

THE USE of a computer to solve any problem requires a complete and accurate statement of the problem to be solved and the circumstances under which the solution is required. These requirements may not seem complex, and indeed they are not if the problem has only two or three variables. But the value of a computer lies in its superb ability to handle a multiplicity of variables. Presentation of complex situations for computer action is the task of the systems analyst.

General Systems Theory

Systems analysis, as a tool, is by no means a recent development. The earliest human beings, coping with what must have seemed a hostile and chaotic world, developed simple systems that allowed them to analyze their surroundings and devise methods of survival. Most of us, too, use simple techniques of analysis for meeting our day-to-day problems. By abstracting general concepts from the observable facts (empirical data) and determining the relationships between them or their order, we are able to survive in our world. We are constantly, often without being aware of it, processing data to produce information. This system of analysis may be as complex as the development of the science of mathematics, or as simple as a child's learning to distinguish the color red.

Historical evidence of human systematic thinking dates back to the earliest Greek philosophers, who were attempting to find an intelligible order, or *kosmos*, in the universe. The basic statement of systems analysis, still valid today, was in fact defined by Aristotle in the proposition "The whole is more than the sum of its parts." This simple statement emphasizes the importance of a system's organization or order and is a keystone of what we now call *systems theory*.

As philosophy developed into the early sciences, mathematics was increasingly used as a tool. Where the order of a system was not readily apparent, scientists used mathematical descriptions to understand how the universe was ordered. This analytical approach involved the breakdown of how the universe was ordered.

An organized approach to systems as a special tool of scientific investigation did not develop until the 1930s, when Ludwig von Bertalanffy began to describe the discipline he called the general system theory. He devised "a logico-mathematical field whose task is the formulation and derivation of those general principles that are applicable to 'systems' in general."*

* Ludwig von Bertalanffy, *General System Theory: Foundations, Development, Applications* (New York: Braziller, 1968), pp. 32, 253.

275

General system theory provided a unified way of viewing phenomena and a common vocabulary for different fields. Its usefulness became apparent as it was quickly adopted after the Second World War as a tool for everything from biology to electronics, astronomy to business organization.

What Is a System?

"System" is a frequently used and rather simple word, but it can mean many things to different people. For this reason, and in order to understand the basics of general system theory and systems analysis, a precise definition is important. People who work with computers and those in business management, mathematics, and science use the word *system* to mean *a set of elements* that are interrelated and interact toward one or more common goals or objectives.

In the simplest terms, the relationships between elements in a system can be diagrammed as:

Input ⟶ Process ⟶ Output

Feedback, that is, information exchanged between elements in a system, may be added. This leads to more complex relationships between the elements of the system but also (at best) to greater efficiency:

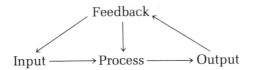

Systems may be *abstract* or *concrete*. Abstract systems contain elements that are concepts, such as languages, number systems, and philosophies. Abstract systems are created by (a) defining the component elements and (b) expressing the relationships between these elements. Statements of such relationships are usually expressed as axioms and postulates. A common error when dealing with abstract systems is to confuse the concept with the physical symbol representing it. For instance, a numeral is a physical symbol, but the number it represents is a concept. It is the number that is an element of the system, not the arbitrary numerical symbol.

A concrete system is one in which at least two of the elements are actual, physical objects. It is possible to determine the properties of these elements and their relationships through observation and empirical research. This type of system is the one we are most often concerned with in business.

Systems may also be classified as *static* or *dynamic*. When there are no changes in the condition of the system or its environment over a certain period of time, the system is said to be static during that period. A dynamic system is one in which changes take place over a specified period of time.

It is often useful to classify systems according to the type of relations between their elements. These relations may be *spatial,* as in a static system in which physical objects remain in fixed positions. Spatial relations are also found in dynamic systems when the positions of physical objects change with respect to their environment but maintain their relationship to each other. Our solar system is a good example of this.

A system's elements may also be related by their sequence in time, either absolutely by clock time or relatively by terms like earlier, later, and so on. Time relations are present in all dynamic systems.

Nearly all dynamic systems also display cause-and-effect relationships. This law of cause and effect most readily applies to irreversible processes that happen in a given period of time. The cause happens at a certain point in time, and the effect appears at a later time. In complex dynamic systems, however, in which several processes may be going on at the same time, the cause-and-effect relationships cannot always be clearly seen. It may be difficult to determine the precise beginning and end of every process. If it is necessary to clarify causal relationships in such a system, input/output relations can be substituted for cause and effect. In this way, concern then shifts to initial and final results; it is not necessary to be concerned with the processes in between.

Logical relations, usually found in systems dealing with concepts, operate on the elements of a system by comparing them according to the rules of logic. A computer program is a good example of logical relationships between conceptual elements in a system. The steps of the program constitute the elements of the system; these steps are interrelated through such logical operations as "if A then B," "either A or B," or "A and B."

Mathematics is a special form of logical relations. It is a system whose elements are the variables or numbers we deal with every day. The rules of this system are the processes—addition, subtraction, multiplication, division—or relationships, such as inverse proportions, that may exist between the elements. These rules can be used to depict or describe a situation that exists in the real world. For example, addition (the additive mathematical relation) accurately represents the total cost of an item as the sum of the costs of each individual element in that item's production.

The Hierarchy of Systems

When a system is defined as either static or dynamic over a period of time, that definition implies that the system's boundaries remain the same during that period. The concept "boundary" expresses the separation of a system from its environment. If the boundaries of a system are changed, a static system may become dynamic, and vice versa. If a 50-story skyscraper is viewed as a system whose boundaries include only the building, then the system is static, for certainly there is no change or movement in such a large structure. However, if the boundaries are redefined to include only the top story, then the system is dynamic. This is because structural engineering requires that such a tall building be designed to sway slightly in high winds, causing the top stories to move a measurable amount.

The above example illustrates the nesting phenomenon, or hierarchy, of systems. Another example is the human body, composed of several basic systems: the skeletal system, digestive system, circulatory system, and so forth. Any of these systems may be further divided into subsystems; for instance, the digestive system contains such organs as the stomach, small and large intestines, esophagus, and so on, each of which is, in turn, a subsystem composed of living tissue.

Figure 10-1   A hierarchy of systems

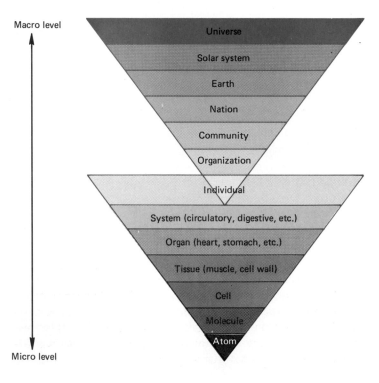

278

Now consider the human body as an element of a larger system—the species *Homo sapiens*. The original system has now become part of a supersystem. This nesting process may be continued ad infinitum in either direction, down to the micro level (in this case, the various substructures within a cell), or up to the macro level (the world of universes). Thus, all of reality becomes a hierarchical system of systems. Depending on the phenomena we wish to observe, we may consider every system in itself or as part of another, larger system. (See figure 10-1.)

Systems in Data Processing

A system, then, is a set of interrelated elements that interact toward one or more common goals. In data processing, the term is applied to two different concepts. There are computer, or hardware, systems, and there are information systems. In an information processing system, hardware and software, along with human, financial, time, data, and information resources, constitute the interrelated and interacting elements.

Management Information Systems

In business, the system we are most concerned with is the organization. Unlike an abstract or a purely mechanical system, the organization is made up of entities sharing one or more common goals. Furthermore, these entities must be willing and able to perform actions related to the pursuit of their goals. A group of people who would all like to see a fence built around the town dump do not constitute an organization. But when the same group cooperates to get the lumber and nails and to build the fence, it has become an organization.

Subsystems and Divisions of Labor

Although each person in the group must help to erect the fence, it is not necessary for each one to do exactly the same job. As a matter of fact, it is much more efficient to divide the work. All organizations have a functional division of labor in pursuit of their common purposes, with each division or subsystem of two or more entities pursuing its own course of action. Organizations may be divided according to function (production, marketing, finance, personnel), space (sales territory or regional division), and time (advance promotion for a new product).

At least one division or subsystem in any organization must be responsible for system control. This subsystem determines the desired goals for the system and its component subsystems. Then it compares the achieved outcome with the desired outcome, and determines what adjustments in the organization's behavior might make the outcome more nearly approach its goals. A small organization (such as our fencebuilders) may have the entire group as its system control division. However, the individuals or groups in an organization that determine the goals are not necessarily the ones who carry them out.

Communication: Systems for Information

In order for the members of an organization to know what needs to be done to achieve their goals, an exchange of information is critical. Information is the result of the perception and interpretation of processed data. Information is always new; that is, it is previously unknown or unrealized. The value of information depends on its usefulness within an immediate context.

In an organization, information consists of processed data. Members of the organization need specific information in order to do their jobs. Without information, the goals of the organization cannot be accomplished. Of course, in any organization, every member does not need to have all the information available at any time; communication in an organization means not only the spread of information but also getting the information to the people who need it. For instance, information that an assembly-line worker at an automobile plant has called in sick is not vital to the vice president in charge of production at company headquarters. On the other hand, the information would be absolutely necessary to the assembly-line supervisor, whose job it is to assign a temporary replacement.

A typical business organization. Business organizations generally consist of three subsystems: operations, management, and information. The *operations subsystem* includes all the people, materials, and activities involved in the function of the organization. In a shoe manufacturing organization, for example, the operations subsystem comprises all the employees, equipment, buildings, leather, and manufacturing processes involved in making and distributing shoes.

The *management subsystem* encompasses all the people and activities involved in the planning, controlling, and decision-making aspects of the operations subsystem. Management in the shoe factory decides such matters as how many and what kinds of shoes will be produced, the size of the inventory, and the amount of future production.

The *information subsystem* acts as a pipeline between all the other subsystems of the organization. It comprises all the people, ideas, machines, and activities involved with satisfying the organization's information requirements. The information subsystem processes data gathered from the operations subsystem into inventory records, performance reports, and so on. From these come all the necessary information for management, segments of the operations subsystem, and external users, such as customers and government. Data input from the interface of the information subsystem and external users (customer orders, government reports, and so on) is made available to management and operations. Finally, through the information subsystem, management provides operations and external users with data in the form of budgets, requisitions, forecasts, schedules, and so forth.

The role of the computer in information management. As a machine that collects, stores, transmits, calculates, and displays data, the computer can be an invaluable tool in the information subsystem. Although commonly used for traditional data processing, it is capable of doing much more than billing and accounting. A computer-based *management information system* (MIS) can generate information that is a direct aid in the decision-making process.

To supply all the necessary and appropriate decision-oriented information, an MIS must include: decision-oriented reports, a hierarchical structure, and decision support systems. Decision-oriented reports present information in a format related to the method by which the information is to be used. The hierarchical structure is aimed at providing general information to upper management while supplying middle and lower management with more detailed information. Finally, decision support systems allow the computer to take over several of the actual decision-making steps.

Organizing the MIS

There are basically six methods of organizing information in an MIS, one or more of which may be used for any business organization. Each concentrates on a particular aspect of the decision-making process.

Filtering is the process of screening unwanted elements from some data as they are communicated from one point to another. The data are summarized and classified to provide persons at different management levels with more or less detailed information as needed. The management subsystem usually consists of strategic, tactical, and technical levels of decision making. Strategic decisions are the broadest levels, while technical decisions are very specific levels. Thus, strategic decision makers need generalized reports, while technical decision makers need reports on specific elements of the operations subsystem.

The *key variable method,* unlike filtering, focuses on certain factors or parameters that have an impact on the total performance of the organization. These include such factors as sales, share of the market, new and cancelled orders, and lost customers. Reports of key variables allow management to see current trends immediately and, if necessary, to concentrate on certain target areas.

Monitoring reduces the amount of irrelevant data by automatically isolating certain information to be provided to the decision makers. Monitoring can be accomplished by *variance reporting, programmed decision making, or automatic notification.*

Variance reporting, also called expectance reporting, requires that data representing actual events be monitored and compared with data representing expectations. The difference between actuality and expectation is variance. This is then compared to a control value to see whether variance is significant enough to be reported. In this way, the computer reports only important deviations from normal events to the decision makers. To take proper advantage of this tool, a systems analyst must establish a reasonable norm, decide on an acceptable variance, and establish a procedure to collect performance data and compare it with the norm.

Programmed decision making relegates to the computer all routine repetitive decisions, leaving the human decision makers more time to spend on less routine decisions. An example of programmed decision making could be purchasing. Periodically, all outstanding purchase orders must be reviewed to compare the scheduled delivery date with the dates on which the items are needed. This can be tedious and time-consuming in an organization that has hundreds of purchase orders outstanding at any given time. By programming a computer to decide which orders need to be expedited, the purchasing agent is freed for more creative decision making.

Automatic notification makes use of the computer's huge memory to keep track of large and sometimes confusing amounts of information. The computer is programmed to produce needed data at periodic intervals. In a large hospital, automatic notification might be used to help sort out constantly changing doctors' instructions for the nursing care of several patients. Unlike programmed decision making, an automatic notification system only scans the large data file, leaving decisions on action to be taken to the individual decision makers—in this case, the nurses.

The *modeling method* of designing information output relies on constructing as accurate a logical or mathematical model as possible. This requires that a real-world problem be defined or described in terms of its essential variables. These variables are then arranged in sequence and assigned values if necessary. Some data are then run through the modeled system to test the output obtained. The major advantages of a model are its structured description of a complex situation and its ability to allow several courses of action to be tested before implementation. However, the model represents only

(Bill Longcore)

This systems analyst's office, containing a variety of systems and office procedure literature and documentation for existing programs, is typical of the environment in which systems are developed.

an abstraction of reality. Poorly designed models will not be applicable to real-world situations. Care must be taken to use the modeling method with judgment.

INTERROGATIVE METHOD REQUIRES USER INTERACTIVITY

All of the methods mentioned so far have one thing in common: once implemented, they require no special action on the users' part. But in the *interrogative method*, the user must request the necessary information from the system. Since it is difficult to anticipate all information requirements when a system is first implemented, the ability to interrogate the system for specific information is very useful. For this reason, the interrogative method is often programmed into the system as a support to the filtering, monitoring, or modeling methods. However, it requires an extensive data base that is organized so that a variety of users can access needed elements, and this can be expensive.

The final method to be discussed here is that of the *strategic decision center*. Strategic decision makers are concerned with choices that affect the growth and development of the organization as a whole, and are affected by factors outside of the organization itself, including social, political, and economic variables. For this reason, most data bases cannot provide sufficient information.

The role of the strategic decision center is to supply data about relevant external factors. This can be done by: (1) Collating and indexing publications and documents from outside sources for quick retrieval; (2) gathering and summarizing documents from government and other organizations; (3) interfacing with the organization's data base to gather key variables useful at the strategic level; and (4) gathering external data for storage in the data base. Several types of equipment and media can be made available for presentation of the information in its most convenient form, including television, cathode ray tube displays, movie projectors, and so on.

Structured Systems Analysis

Once an information system has been developed according to one or a combination of several of the above methods, then the job of the systems analyst is done, right? Wrong! A business organization is a dynamic system. Its environment is changing all the time. New products are developed, prices change, means of production wear out and are replaced, government regulations or their interpretations shift, new labor contracts go into effect, and so on. An information system is similar to a large physical resource such as a factory, which must be maintained and modernized to keep up with continuously changing conditions. Maintenance can help keep a system responsive for a while; however, there comes a point in time when a major overhaul or modernization is the most efficient way to adjust the system to reality.

The Life and Death of a System

The development stages of a system have been likened to a life cycle. Every system has a beginning, and eventually reaches a terminal stage that requires renovation before it can function once again. The very first stage in system development is conception. During this stage, the system is defined and analyzed, alternative plans are developed, and a trial system is designed. The system is born when the developmental plans are implemented. During adolescence the system is tried and evaluated, and new approaches are tested. Maturity is reached when the system provides the most benefit to its users. Finally, the system begins to age; now, substantial maintenance is required for the system to meet the needs of the organization. When this is no longer feasible the system dies, to be replaced by a new system. In a good organization, this new system will be conceived before the old one dies. (See figure 10-2.)

Systems analysis today is often referred to as "structured"; that is, it follows a logical sequence of separate stages, with emphasis on the definition of the problem. This approach to system development involves users from the earliest stage in the process. The success or failure of any system ultimately rests with the individuals who will use it. If the system meets user needs, it will be effective. If not, all the time, effort, and money spent to devise it will have been wasted.

Structured systems analysis is also said to be "top-down": The problem is first conceived from an overall perspective, and then subdivided into logical units that can be separately analyzed. As each phase of system design is completed, it is reviewed by other systems

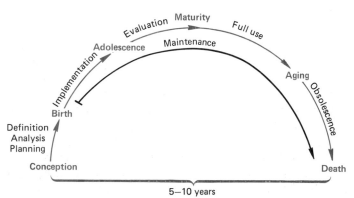

Figure 10-2 The life cycle of a system

analysts. This review process is known as a "structured walk-through."

Generally, structured systems analysis involves seven stages; definition, analysis, planning, design, implementation, evaluation, and maintenance. At every stage, written documentation is produced.

Definition. Even before analysis begins, it is necessary to *define* a system's objective or goal. A system may require analysis for several reasons. Perhaps there is a problem either with an existing system or in a particular department of the organization. Perhaps a new requirement has been imposed on the organization in the form of a new law, a new service or product, a change in the competition, or some new management procedure. An organization's adoption of a new idea or technology may require a change in the MIS; this might be true, for example, if an optical card reader were added to existing computer equipment. Or, systems analysis might be initiated simply to find a better way of doing what is already being done.

The purpose of every system is to provide information in an output format that meets the needs of the users. Therefore the output component of the system must be designed at an early stage in the process. Too often, systems design starts by collecting data—but this may be based on assumptions that are not valid and often leads to a dead end.

No matter why a systems analysis is undertaken, the first phase must be to have a clear, concise definition of the goals and performance requirements of the proposed system.

Analysis. The next phase in the development of a new system is *analysis* of the existing system. To accomplish the objective that has been defined, it is necessary to see whether the existing system is in need of some minor repair or a major overhaul. Study of the existing system also indicates the resources available for the new system. Finally, knowledge of the existing system will be needed when it is time to phase out the old and begin operating the new.

To analyze an existing system, analysts review the direction in which the work flows within the organization and the decision-making processes involved. They must also review the information flow needed to support these decision processes. Once this is done, the deficiencies in the existing system can be isolated.

An existing system may be deficient in inclusion or structure. Inclusion deficiencies refer to information, technology, and personnel that are lacking in the system. Structure deficiencies pertain to how information, technology, and personnel are organized throughout the system. Both kinds of deficiencies must be dealt with if the new system is to be both effective—producing the desired information—and efficient.

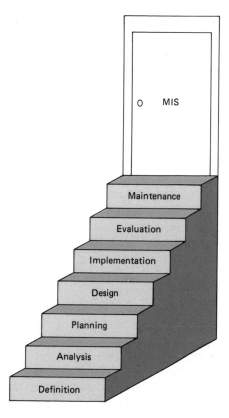

Figure 10-3 Steps in constructing a management information system

Planning. The next phase is *planning.* During this phase, alternative solutions to the problem as it was defined in the first phase are considered. Each plan must be evaluated logically and in terms of economy, accuracy, feasibility, and efficiency. A flowchart (see chapter 11) is usually made for each plan and checked for any potential problems or missing links. It is much easier to correct problems at this stage than when a system is being implemented. Some of the plans may be translated into mathematical models and simulated by a computer manipulation of synthetic data to see if they produce the desired results. Finally, after considering such factors as staff and hardware requirements, the timetable for system completion, and costs, a working plan is selected from which the system will be designed.

Design. The *design* phase of a system's development is the engineering phase; it is at this point that the actual programs are engineered or created. The way in which the task is approached depends on the particular system being developed. The system analyst and programmers will consider how many and what types of human/ma-

287

chine interfaces are needed, which components of the system should be batch and which online, what type of data storage is to be used, and so on. Some or all of these decisions may have to be tailored to existing computer equipment, or may have been decided earlier, during the planning stage.

System design may begin on the function and subfunction level. Each data processing function may be designed separately by programmers. Then each must be checked and tested to ensure that all necessary information is provided and that each subfunction is compatible with the others and with the system as a whole.

Even after the computer programs have been developed and tested, there is more to be done before the design is complete. Detailed flowcharts and/or decision tables are made to guide maintenance and any later modifications in the design. Specific operating procedures must also be documented; these include general rules and policy, forms and transcripts, operating instructions for data collection devices and other equipment, and error correction and other emergency procedures. All of the information is usually published in a procedures manual.

Procedures manuals are also needed for the computer operators. These manuals must be equipment-oriented and cover whatever is necessary for normal operations, operating schedules, data handling procedures, and any emergency procedures. Finally, training programs are required for both the people who will operate the system and the management personnel who will use the data in their decision processes. Written material, classroom hours, and audiovisual aids needed for training must also be designed. Some of this documentation may be updated to reflect specific changes made during the implementation stage.

Good business practice requires that a company be audited periodically. Part of the job of the auditors is to safeguard the assets of the company. Today, to a large extent, records of company assets exist on magnetic media. Traditionally, however, they existed on paper, in books and files. In a traditional manual system, auditors understood the steps involved in processing data, and had developed controls for auditing such systems. Now, auditors must become familiar with the computer-based systems widely used today. It is being suggested that auditors be included in the design phase of a system, to provide usable controls that until now have generally not been included in system design.

Implementation. After a system has been designed, the analyst and programmers begin the most difficult part of their task—*implementation.* Converting from the existing system to a new one may involve changes in equipment. This may require extensive rewriting or recompiling of existing programs to make their coding compatible with the new equipment. Many new computers and peripherals, however, have been designed to be "plug-compatible" with other equipment; extensive rewriting may not be necessary if such equipment is used.

System conversion often changes from one data processing method to another. This may only involve replacing one group of activities with another. Usually, though, extensive procedural changes must accompany the new system, especially when changes in equipment and data processing are involved.

Procedural conversions can refer to both the changes in the activities performed by the computer and the sequence in which it performs them. Procedural changes are almost inevitable when a major subsystem is being implemented.

There are four basic approaches toward implementing a new system: direct, parallel, modular, and phase-in.

Direct implementation is the immediate startup of the new system that is coincident with the discontinuation of the old. This approach may be called "cold turkey." Although inexpensive, it involves a high risk of failure at the time of changeover, since there is no backup to the new system. Direct implementation may be feasible for a very small or a simple new system, or when the old one is judged completely worthless. Occasionally, the design of a new system is so radically different from an old one that any comparisons between the two are impossible, and the direct method of implemention must be used. Because there will be no backup capability, problems must be anticipated and reduced to the bare minimum. The number of "bugs" normally expected to show up in a new system must be worked out by careful preimplementation testing when direct conversion is attempted. There is no opportunity for "on-the-job training" of a new system.

Parallel implementation allows both the old and new systems to operate simultaneously for a time. In this way, outputs from the two systems can be compared and differences reconciled. After a reasonable adjustment period during which reviews of the new system's performance are made by the systems analyst, operating personnel, and users, the old system can be discontinued.

The main drawback to this approach is the cost of maintaining duplicate facilities and personnel to run the dual system. Given the high degree of protection against failure, however, the additional expense may well be justified.

Modular implementation, sometimes called the "pilot approach," refers to the implementation of a new system piece by piece. The system's users within the organization are grouped into modules, and each user module enters the new system separately. Thus, inventory reports for one product group or the products from one location may be processed by the new system before the total system is implemented for all products. The advantages are that the risk of failure is localized, and errors can be corrected on a small scale before further implementation is attempted. Modular implementation also allows personnel to train in a "live" situation, so when the new system is implemented in their area, they will have had "hands-on" experience. Modular procedure is, however, somewhat time-consuming and not feasible for every system.

Phase-in implementation is similar to modular conversion, except that the system, instead of the organization, is separated into modules. For instance, the data collection activities for the new system may be implemented first, then the new data base access, storage, and retrieval, then another segment, and so on until the whole system has been phased in. Each time a module is phased in, an interface with the old system must be developed to allow them to work together. The advantage of this approach is that it allows a gradual switchover to the new system. The disadvantages are that it may not be applicable in many systems or subsystems, and additional costs may be incurred in developing temporary interfaces.

A very important part of any new system's implementation is the creation and conversion of data files. The old system's files may have to be modified in format, content, and/or type of storage medium. A systems conversion may involve changing all these aspects simultaneously. Almost always, existing files must be converted to a new format to fit the needs of the new programs. To convert a file to a new format, a one-time program must be written. The only function of this special startup software is to read in the data in the old format and produce the data in the new format for use by the new system.

Special startup software is also needed when creating a new file to set up a special physical or logical storage location. This location is referred to as a "dummy" file. Once this dummy file is created, the new system can begin to store data.

It is often necessary to set up elaborate control procedures to ensure the integrity of files during conversion. Backup files are usually created to ensure against the loss of information in the event of a processing error or a disaster in the data center. Unless the new system uses a different storage medium, backup files are created by the same procedures as for the original files.

Evaluation. The sixth phase in the system life cycle is *evaluation.* After a system has been implemented, it must be tested to see that it is doing efficiently and effectively what it was meant to do. Testing is done throughout the development of the system; for example, logic modules are tested by the programmer early in the design phase to ensure that all input transactions are accounted for, that all files are closed at the end of a transaction, and so forth. The next level is *program testing*, which assures that all logical modules are compatible and that all outputs are produced accurately. *Sequential testing* makes sure that two or more interfacing modules work properly together.

When all tests are accomplished, the systems analyst is ready to test the computer system. This requires testing all the programs to be implemented as part of the system and making sure that all inputs produce the desired outputs. To a great extent, the users provide on-going evaluation. But thorough evaluation by analysts is always necessary.

Finally, after the new system has been implemented, *systems testing* can be done. This is the most comprehensive stage of evaluation, involving not only the total computer system but all the supporting clerical procedures. In systems testing, an event is followed from its occurrence through its processing to its reporting, which is used as a decision-making tool. At this point, the people who are to use these tools, the decision makers themselves, can be polled to get their views on the effectiveness of the system and how it might be improved.

In addition to evaluating the system design, the analysts must evaluate the systems analysis methodology they themselves used. What problems did they encounter? How did they attempt to solve them? What could they have done better? Such self-analysis will provide them with feedback, improving their ability to design systems in the future. Any errors or flaws are traced back through all the processing steps until they are defined and resolved.

Maintenance. Once the new system has been implemented, evaluated, and modified, the job of the systems analyst is still not over. The informational needs of an organization are constantly changing, and the system must change to meet these needs. In fact, as much as 90 percent of the staff time devoted to a system during its life cycle may be spent in maintaining it. This time will be divided between two phases: the learning curve and routine maintenance.

The *learning curve* starts immediately after implementation. Since the system operators and users are learning the system, excessive errors are to be expected. To keep these errors within design limits, close monitoring and possibly some retraining may be necessary. During this early life of the system, equipment and programs fail most frequently; provisions must be made to find the problems and to correct them as soon as possible. It is also during this time that discrepancies in the system logic begin to show up; these also require prompt action.

APPLICATION

How a System Goes Wrong

Having examined the steps in a structured systems analysis, we can appreciate what happens when a "nonstructured" analysis—that is, one that does not follow a logical sequence of separate steps—is attempted.

A perfect example is the Unified Management Information System, a system being developed for the U.S. Department of Agriculture's Farmers Home Administration. After six years and $17 million, this project is five years behind schedule and will have used up an estimated $42 million when and if it is ever completed. What went wrong?

The system was intended to keep track of Farmers Home Administration's financial assistance programs, involving more than $30 billion and more than 1.25 million farmers; but the requirements analysis was never completed. In other words, the problem was never adequately defined. What is more, during the six years spent on the system so far, no attempt has been made to monitor and analyze changing users' needs. It is not possible to design an efficient and effective information system without a working knowledge of what it is to accomplish.

Next, there was no comprehensive system development plan—but equipment was ordered anyway. And when it came to the design phase, the information system's developers were not provided with detailed data on the capabilities and limitations of the computer hardware that had been contracted for until four months after the machinery had been selected. Problems like these, along with other serious technical drawbacks, plagued the design phase of the Unified Management Information System's analysis. Structured system analysis would have made the difference.

During their life cycle, all systems require some *routine maintenance*. There may be random problems or failures that require immediate attention to prevent degeneration of the system. Or there may be changes in the system's environment that require modifications in system operation. Sometimes, due to human error such as negligence or misinformation, the system will not be in compliance with its design, requiring action to correct the error. This last type of problem should be constantly monitored to prevent such errors from getting out of control.

Summary

The use of the computer as a business tool requires the techniques of systems analysis to reduce "real-world" problems to computer-synthesized systems. Systems analysis is analogous to human thought processes: concepts are abstracted from observations, and a sequence or a set of relationships is defined.

By definition, a system is a set of elements that are interrelated and interact toward one or more common goals. Systems may be abstract or concrete; it is the concrete system, in which at least two of the elements are physical objects, that business is most concerned with. Systems also exhibit a "nesting" phenomenon; any given system is composed of several subsystems and is itself an element of a larger supersystem in the hierarchy.

In business, the type of system we are most concerned with is the organization. This is a system whose elements are entities willing and able to perform activities related to the pursuit of a common goal.

Organizations are divided into subsystems that perform specific functions. The subsystem responsible for control of the organization is called the *management subsystem*. The *operations subsystem* includes all the employees, materials, and activities involved in pursuing the goals of the organization. The *information subsystem* provides the management subsystem with data for decision making and relays the decisions made to the operations subsystem.

A computer-based *management information system* (MIS) can be an invaluable tool for all three organizational subsystems if it is properly organized. There are six basic methods of MIS organization: filtering, key variable, monitoring, modeling, interrogative, and the strategic decision center.

To develop an efficient and effective MIS using one of these methods, a structured systems analysis must be conducted. This analysis consists of seven steps: definition, analysis, planning, design, implementation, evaluation, and maintenance.

Definition pinpoints the objective or goal that the MIS being developed is to accomplish. When this has been done, any existing system can then be *analyzed* to see where its deficiencies are. Next, several possible systems are *planned* to take care of these deficiencies. Of these several systems, the one that seems to be able to do the job most efficiently is selected for *design*. The design stage is the point at which the actual programs that will make up the MIS are engineered.

When the programs have been prepared and preliminary testing done, the MIS is ready for *implementation*, putting into operation the new MIS. There are four basic approaches to implementation: direct, parallel, modular, and phase-in. When the new system has been implemented according to one of these methods, it is then time to *evaluate* the system to see if it is successful; that is, does it provide the required output from the given input in an efficient and effective manner? If not, what changes must be made to obtain useful output?

The final stage of the system's life cycle continues until its death: *maintenance*. Since the organization and its environment are constantly changing, a viable MIS must also change to meet every need.

Key Terms and Phrases

analysis
definition
design
direct implementation
evaluation
filtering
implementation
information subsystem
interrogative method
key variable method
learning curve
maintenance

management
 information
 system (MIS)
management
 subsystem
modeling method
modular
 implementation
monitoring
operations subsystem
parallel
 implementation

phase-in
 implementation
planning
program testing
routine
 maintenance
sequential testing
strategic decision
 center
systems testing
systems theory

Sources of Additional Information

Alexander, M. J. *Information Systems Analysis, Theory and Applications.* Chicago: Science Research Associates, 1974.

Burch, John G., Jr., Strater, Felix R., and Grudnitski, Gary. *Information Systems: Theory and Practice.* 2d ed. New York: Wiley, 1979.

Couger, J. Daniel, and Knapp, Robert W., eds. *Systems Analysis Technique.* New York: Wiley, 1979.

Davis, Gordon, and Everest, Gordon, eds. *Readings in Management Information Systems.* New York: McGraw-Hill, 1976.

Ryan, Hugh W. "Structured Methods: An Analysis of Current Practices," *Computerworld,* no. 49 (1979):9–24.

Yourdon, Edward. "Introducing the Structured Life Cycle." *Computerworld,* no. 49 (1979):1–8.

Test Yourself

1. What is meant by the phrase "hierarchy of systems"?
2. The field of data processing is concerned with two kinds of systems. What are they, and how do they differ?
3. What is the role of feedback in an operational system?
4. Why are information processing systems developed?
5. Briefly describe the three subsystems in a business organization.
6. What is a management information system? How does it function?
7. Describe the six methods that may be used, separately or together, to organize information within an MIS.
8. What is structured systems analysis? Why can we speak of the "life cycle" of a system?
9. Describe the steps in developing a system; relate these steps to the phases of the life cycle of a system.
10. What are some factors that should be evaluated during the planning phase of systems analysis?
11. What four basic approaches may be used to implement a new system? What are some advantages and disadvantages of each?
12. Why should a new system be evaluated *after* it has been implemented?

11 Flowcharts

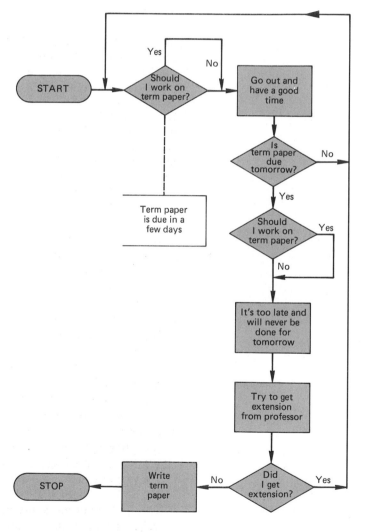

APPLICATION
Penn Mutual Flowcharts Progress

When the Penn Mutual Life Insurance Company of Philadelphia adopted structured programming several years ago, the system analysts and designers faced a problem: how to communicate their system and program decisions to the staff members who were to use the system. Previously, computer systems had been described in a narrative fashion to users within the company. But users of one component of the system were unable to understand how their function related to the system as a whole, and users in one department had little notion of what happened in another department.

With the move to structured programming, analysts decided to use graphic tools to show all users within the company how their system worked and where each department and individual fit into the overall system. A simple diagram was the first step. Rectangles were used to show data input and output. Circles indicated processes, and in some cases subprocesses, that affected data between input and output. Arrows linked rectangles and circles to show the data flow between input, processes, and output, while small labels—data flow, data store—described what was going on. Larger labels provided the additional detail that was needed. Taking up less than one page, this diagram made clear to every user at Penn Mutual exactly how the overall system was organized.

But this diagram did not distinguish between the different kinds of processes, procedures, or storage that took place at different points within the system. To show this, another level of diagram was used, and each step or process in the system was broken down into its component parts and described. Each type of storage, each interim or partial output—all were diagrammed and described by means of brief labels. Thus, for a single department, all of the steps of each function were diagrammed and clarified.

These flow diagrams helped users to "get their bearings" rapidly in the new system. After orientation with the flow diagrams, users were ready to turn to the more detailed pages of the project system report that included detailed data element descriptions and a project glossary, in which every step was described in user-oriented terms.

Among the benefits noted by Penn Mutual: All users on staff understood more clearly both the old and the new systems, and learned quickly how the new system interfaced with ongoing processes. Conflicts and other problems in coordinating data flow or processes were clearly seen and could be resolved early in the planning stages, instead of showing up later on. The time required for users to review the system during development, including the time required for users to become familiar with the new system during implementation, was reduced. And programmers could program more efficiently because the graphic model accurately reflected the structured design of the program.

There was, however, some resistance. Staff members working on projects that had started with other systems were reluctant to see their months of work discarded. And other workers needed time to adjust to the new intraorganizational lines of communication. But the clarity and efficiency of the new approach was convincing.

DEVELOPING an information processing system that will meet the requirements of the user effectively and efficiently is no simple task. The task is often made more difficult by the very specifications that define the proposed system. For example, systems specifications tend to emphasize individual procedures, such as payroll processing. This emphasis on separate processes tends to conceal the actual flow of data within the system as a whole. Also, specifications often define a system in terms of separate files and programs. As a result, the logic underlying a system is not always apparent; and systems designers may find it difficult to identify and analyze alternative solutions to a particular processing problem.

As computer use expanded, the need for a way to represent complex data processing systems clearly became apparent. More people were involved in information processing at different stages. A way had to be found for those who planned and designed a system to talk with those who would operate it and use its output.

It was easy to see what was needed: a language or other device that would facilitate communication between workers who had different backgrounds and different kinds of interactions with the business and its computer systems. Ideally, such a language or device would have to be simple to use and easy to learn. It should be "readable" so that important features and patterns of the system can be highlighted. It should be unambiguous and not introduce any uncertainty about what data and operations are essential and/or desirable. And it should be independent of any individual computer or computer language so that communication about a computer system can be generally applicable to different equipment and thus provide flexibility to the users.

Various languages and techniques have been developed to deal with the problem of describing computer functions: mathematical formulas, written descriptions, and programming languages. These have obvious drawbacks. Mathematical formulas, for example, are not easy to read. Written descriptions tend to be wordy and may be ambiguous. Program languages require special knowledge and are designed to describe processing, not general data operations.

The solution was the graphic device known as a *flowchart*. It uses standardized symbols to depict a system—logical data flow, processes, and operations of computer systems and programs. The flowchart is a tool that can be used by systems analysts, designers, and programmers, but it is also accessible to nonspecialist users of computer systems.

The use of flowcharts is not restricted to computer-based systems or operations. Rather they can function as a tool for representing any logical flow of information through any kind of system or organization. Indeed, flowcharts have come to be used in most phases of system development and functioning, including problem definition, systems analysis, systems design, programming, debugging, conversion, documentation, operation, and maintenance.

In this chapter, however, our concern is primarily with the use of flowcharts in the computer environment. The historical development of this technique—often called *flowcharting*—will be reviewed before we focus on specific flowchart symbols and their use in systems flowcharts. (Program flowcharts will be discussed in greater detail in chapter 12.) We will also examine decision tables, which can be alternatives or supplements to flowcharts.

Development of the Flowchart

John von Neumann and his associates at the Institute for Advanced Study in Princeton were the first to make systematic use of graphic techniques to represent computer functioning. They were also the first—as early as 1947—to write about the use of flowcharting. The basic principles and approach that they established then are still valid today, though the technique of flowcharting has changed in many details since von Neumann's time.

During the 1950s, the conventions and standards used in flowcharting developed more or less haphazardly. Computer users, either individually or in collaboration, decided when and where to use what symbols or conventions. Usually users chose those symbols employed by the manufacturer of whatever equipment was in place. Manufacturers frequently supplied plastic templates for drawing their chosen flowchart symbols to purchasers of their computers and peripherals. At the same time, though, some large users developed their own conventions and standards.

By the early 1960s, the need for a standardized set of conventions and symbols was becoming apparent. A committee working through the Business Equipment Manufacturers Association (BEMA) and the American Standards Association (ASA) published the first set of flowchart standards in 1963. Known as American Standard X3.5, this set of standards was subsequently revised a number of times. A major revision in 1970 was intended to make X3.5 conform more closely to the standards previously set by the International Organization for Standardization (ISO). In 1969, ASA changed its name to American National Standards Institute, or ANSI (pronounced "ann-see"). Consequently, the American Standard is now known as the ANSI X3.5 Standard and is the most widely accepted set of flowchart conventions in use today.

Thus, the development of flowcharts ran parallel to the development of computers. As the complexity of these computer systems increased, the need for clearer representations of computer systems grew. The earliest computer systems were quite simple, often performing only a few kinds of calculations. It was easy for users to understand how such a simple computer system replaced a step or two in the manual system that continued to be used. But today's highly sophisticated online real-time systems are complex, accessing integrated data bases from locations all over the world and interfacing with other systems. Flowcharts are a valuable and effective aid in the development of today's complex computer systems. The ANSI X3.5 Standard clarifies the use of flowchart symbols and techniques, and provides a basic type of description understandable (or easily learned) by any individual. It makes possible the efficient exchange of information not only between individuals working on a system now, but also between those who in the future will have to operate, maintain, and revise that system. In this way the ANSI X3.5 Standard contributes to continuity.

Flowchart Symbols

Three kinds or groups of symbols are used in constructing flowcharts: basic, additional, and specialized. A clear and useful flowchart can be constructed using only basic and some additional symbols. The use of specialized symbols is optional.

The ANSI X3.5 Standard specifies the shape of all symbols but not their size. Size is usually a matter of convenience and space. The same symbol may appear in more than one size on the same flowchart. All lines used in drawing all symbols or linking them, however, should be of the same width or thickness.

Basic Symbols

The four basic flowchart symbols represent input/output, processing, flowlines, and annotation. All four types are illustrated in figure 11-1.

The *input/output symbol* is a rhomboid, or equilateral parallelogram. It can represent input or output or the operations of input or output. Thus, in figure 11-2, this symbol is used for both input and output. The symbol can be used no matter what kind of media, format, or equipment is being referred to.

The *processing symbol*, a rectangle, represents transformation of

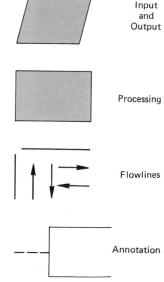

Input and Output

Processing

Flowlines

Annotation

Figure 11-1   The four basic flowchart symbols

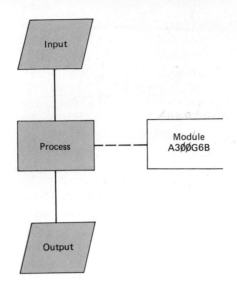

Figure 11-2 A simple flowchart using only the four basic flowchart symbols

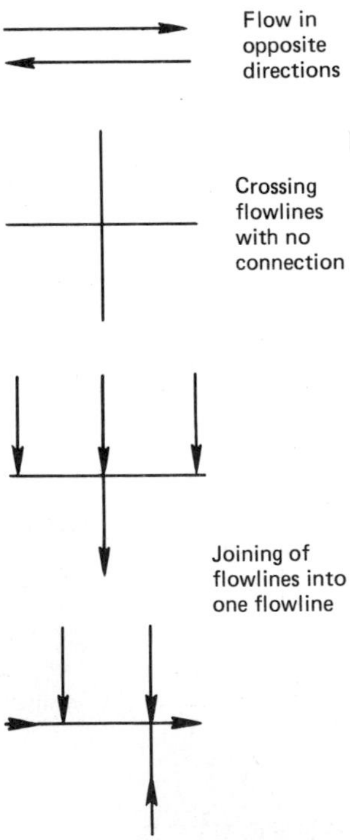

Flow in opposite directions

Crossing flowlines with no connection

Joining of flowlines into one flowline

Figure 11-3 Conventions in the use of flowlines

data, logical operations on data, or movement of data. It is also used as a general-purpose symbol when no specific symbol is specified in ANSI X3.5 for a particular purpose.

A *flowline symbol* commonly appears as an arrow of variable length between two other symbols. Flowlines indicate the sequence of operations on data or the transmission of data (data flow). Flowlines usually alternate with other symbols and thus indicate the sequence in which those symbols are to be read. Flow in opposite directions is preferably represented by two parallel flowlines pointing in opposite directions, rather than by a single flowline with an arrowhead at each end.

The general direction of flow in flowcharts is consistent with the normal direction of English prose, from top to bottom and from left to right. When the data flow follows this basic pattern, the flowlines may appear without arrowheads, and a left-to-right, top-to-bottom direction is assumed. But if the data flow contains any significant deviations from this overall pattern, arrowheads must be used to identify the direction. This is true also for flowlines that may be ambiguous.

As a rule, flowlines should not cross one another. If this is necessary, however, any arrowheads that would lead into the point of crossover should be removed. An arrowhead on a flowline that crosses another indicates a *conjunction* of flowlines. Compare the examples of crossing and joining illustrated in figure 11-3, which illustrates conventions for using flowlines. Note that when two or more flowlines join together to form a single flowline, arrowheads are used at every junction to eliminate any ambiguity.

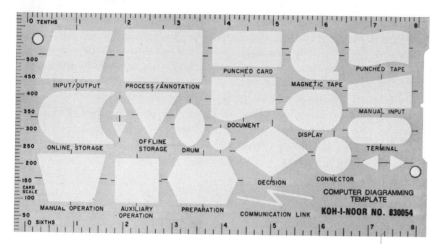

Flowcharting is facilitated by the use of a plastic template such as this one.

An *annotation symbol* is used to identify comments, explanations, and descriptive material that appear directly on the flowchart. It appears as a large, elongated bracket or open rectangle, connected with a dashed line to the symbol to which the annotation refers.

Additional Symbols

The main purpose of additional symbols is to make a flowchart easier to read and more convenient to use. With the basic symbols alone, virtually every operation could be diagrammed in its essential details by a flowchart. But a flowchart of a complex system using only the basic symbols would be much more difficult to follow than a flowchart using some specialized symbols. The three important additional symbols are the connector, the terminal, and the parallel mode. (See figure 11-4.)

The *connector symbol* is a circle, representing a flow sequence usually shown in detail elsewhere. An *entrance connector* (inconnector) *symbol* has one flowline leaving it, but no flowlines entering; the *exit connector* (outconnector) *symbol* is just the reverse, with one flowline entering and none leaving. Every outconnector must be associated with one inconnector. However, a single inconnector may have any number of associated outconnectors, or even none.

Connectors are used to break up a long flow diagram into smaller parts than can be shown on a given page. This connector symbol can also be used to join converging lines of logic flow and to identify diverging lines of logic flow.

The *terminal symbol* can represent the beginning or end of an operation or process, or it can represent a break in the flow diagram.

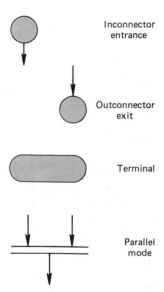

Figure 11-4 The additional flowchart symbols

301

Use of the terminal symbols is not restricted to the beginning or end of the complete flowchart. It can also be used to replace a connector symbol at the beginning or end of a major data flow sequence within the entire system. As a symbol for a break in the normal sequence, the terminal symbol can be used to represent a variety of events, including starts, stops, interrupts, and so on.

The *parallel mode symbol* consists of a pair of parallel horizontal lines, one or more entry flowlines, and one or more exit flowlines. It is used to indicate the beginning or end of processes that take place at the same time.

Specialized Symbols

The three major groups of specialized symbols are used for specifying *media, peripheral equipment,* and *processing operations.*

The *document symbol* is the most used of the four media symbols, and is shown as a stylized representation of a piece of paper. It stands for hard-copy input or output of all kinds. The other media symbols are stylized representations of *magnetic tape, punched tape,* and *punched cards.* The punched-tape symbol is used to represent tape of any material. The punched-card symbol can represent any kind of punched card (except a time card, which is represented by a document symbol). (See figure 11-5.)

Of the eight equipment symbols, two refer to types of data, one to data communication, and five to types of storage. (See figure 11-6.)

The *display output symbol,* a stylized cathode ray tube, stands for any kind of soft-copy data, such as might appear on a CRT display screen. It may also be used to represent intermediate output that controls ongoing processing, such as data/information that appear on CRTs in real-time situations and that will be utilized immediately for further processing. The *manual input symbol* stands for data obtained from manually operated equipment such as keyboards, transaction records, light pens, and so on.

The *communication link symbol,* a zigzagging flowline, indicates data flow between one electronic medium or type of equipment and another. Arrowheads are added as necessary to show the direction of flow.

Each of the five storage symbols represents a different stage or medium of storage. The *disk storage symbol* can represent disk storage devices of any kind but usually refers to magnetic disks. The *drum storage symbol* commonly refers to magnetic drums, but it can represent data stored on any type of drum device. The *core storage symbol* represents data stored in magnetic cores or similar high-speed secondary storage. The crossed lines in the symbol represent the two

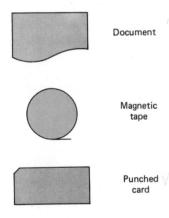

Document

Magnetic tape

Punched card

Punched tape

Figure 11-5 Specialized flowchart symbols I: the four media symbols

302

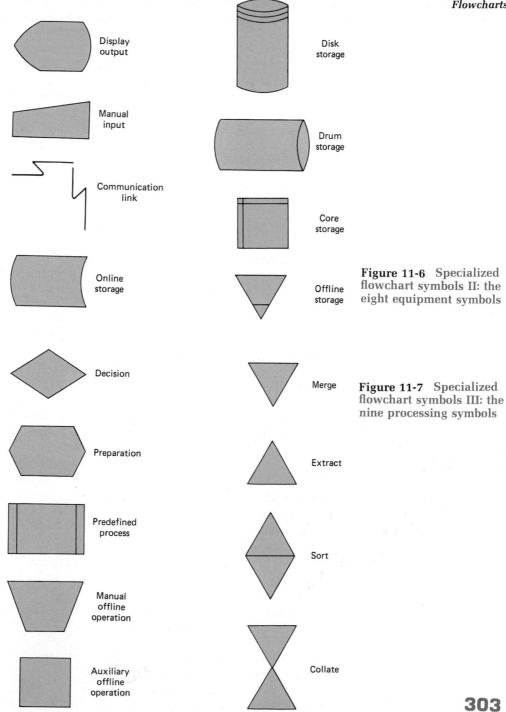

Display output

Manual input

Communication link

Online storage

Decision

Preparation

Predefined process

Manual offline operation

Auxiliary offline operation

Disk storage

Drum storage

Core storage

Offline storage

Merge

Extract

Sort

Collate

Figure 11-6 Specialized flowchart symbols II: the eight equipment symbols

Figure 11-7 Specialized flowchart symbols III: the nine processing symbols

303

lines of electric current in a magnetic core element. The *online storage symbol* stands for data stored in any kind of online storage device, whether intermediate or external, and might include magnetic drums, tapes, cards, or cores. The *offline storage symbol* stands for any data stored offline, regardless of the medium or equipment used, and is usually used to represent manual files.

Of the nine *processing operation symbols* (see figure 11-7), the most frequently used is the diamond-shaped *decision symbol*. This symbol can represent decisions, testing, comparisons, or switching operations—any stage in processing, in fact, where one of two or more possible sequences is to be followed. At least two flowlines always leave a decision symbol.

The *preparation symbol*, a hexagon, stands for operations that are not directly involved in the production of output. Operations on the program itself, such as control, for example, would be represented by a hexagon.

The *predefined process symbol* indicates one or more operations that have been specified in greater detail elsewhere, and is used to refer to a subroutine.

The *manual operation symbol* refers to any offline operation in which speed is determined by a human operator, such as in offline keyboard data entry. Conversely, the *auxiliary operation symbol* represents any offline operation in which speed is not determined by a human operator.

The remaining four symbols—*merge*, *extract*, *sort*, and *collate* —all stand for basic operations on data files. The definition of collate in flowcharting, however, differs from the common meaning of this word, and the collate symbol stands for a combination of merge and extract.

Multiples can be shown in flowcharting in a variety of ways. Usually several of the same symbols are drawn to overlap. (See figure 11-8.)

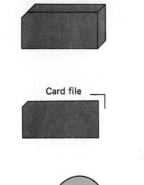

Deck of cards

Card file

Three magnetic tapes
treated as a group

Figure 11-8 A few flow-chart conventions for showing multiples

System and Program Flowcharts

Flowcharts are used to diagram both systems and programs. System flowcharts provide a macrolevel description or overview of information flow, summarizing the input and output processed and produced by all the sequences of operations, procedures, and programs involved. A system flowchart indicates the general flow of information through an organization, or the various interactions of many files and processes. Program flowcharts, on the other hand, use a microlevel focus to diagram detailed data transformations in a segment of the system.

A program flowchart shows *how* input becomes output. It usually represents a detailed breakdown in outline form of the process indicated by a single symbol in a system flowchart. System flowcharts generally tend to be less complex than program flowcharts, even though they may use a greater variety of symbols.

There is not necessarily a distinct dividing line between program and system flowcharts. Given a reason—and a large enough sheet of paper—any system can be diagrammed in great detail. But for practical purposes, it is customary to distinguish between the detailed description provided by the program flowchart and the overview shown on the system flowchart.

System Flowcharts

A *system flowchart* provides a macroscopic view by charting the general flow of information through an organization and/or the general processing interactions and relationships of the many files in a complex computer-based system. Certain conventions have been established concerning format, symbols, and annotation appropriate to system flowcharts.

Basic format. The component elements in a flowchart of an organization or system must be arranged in a way that makes the flow clear to the reader. By convention, system flowcharts achieve clarity by following a basic format, often referred to as the "sandwich rule." That is, every process symbol (the "filling") has an input symbol (the "bread") above it and an output symbol (more "bread") below it. Since the output of one process often represents the input for the following process, the format may become a multilayered "sandwich" consisting of alternating layers of data symbols and process symbols (sometimes referred to as a "Dagwood sandwich"). But no matter how many layers the sandwich has, it must begin with an input "slice" and end with an output "slice."

Identification. A flowchart with the format just described will be informative only to someone who already knows *what* input, processes, and output are involved. To anyone else, however, it will be the barest of outlines. The convention used to make the outline clear to any user is to identify each input, process, and output. This is usually done by writing an identifying label within each symbol outline. Coded terms may be used for these components, but identifications may also be written in "plain English" for readers unfamiliar with the code or terminology. Identifying labels do not refer to the

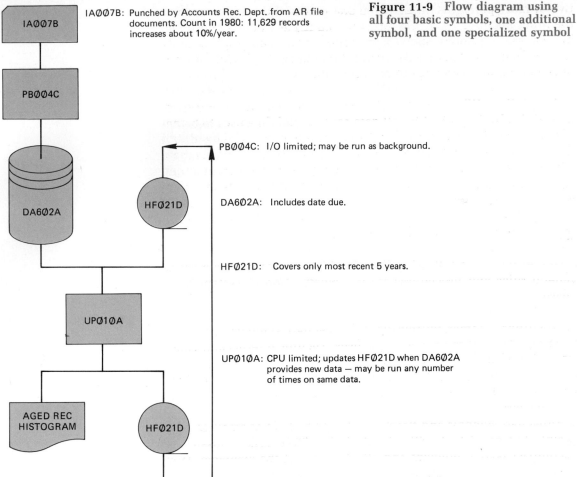

IAØØ7B: Punched by Accounts Rec. Dept. from AR file documents. Count in 1980: 11,629 records increases about 10%/year.

PBØØ4C: I/O limited; may be run as background.

DA6Ø2A: Includes date due.

HFØ21D: Covers only most recent 5 years.

UPØ1ØA: CPU limited; updates HFØ21D when DA6Ø2A provides new data — may be run any number of times on same data.

Histogram is on printer.

type of data medium or the equipment to be used. Figure 11-9 shows the identification used to clarify a single system flowchart.

Specialized symbols. The use of specialized symbols can improve the clarity of a system flowchart even further. For example, a flowchart could indicate hard-copy output by using a document symbol.

Connectors and cross-references. The availability of connector symbols to divide a flowchart into distinct parts is especially useful when a system flowchart is too large to fit on a single page. For maximum clarity, all input and output of each part of the system must be identified by cross-referencing. When a flowchart is broken into two or more parts, the output from one part of the system becomes the input to another part. Both output and input can be represented by the same symbol and identification and then appropriately cross-referenced. This use of connectors makes it possible for the flowchart on any one page to be self-contained.

Annotation. When a system flowchart is broken into two or more parts, it is also important for all data sources and data uses to be defined. Annotation can supplement cross-referencing and data identification. Where annotation symbols and copy threaten to become a jumble, the annotation can be set in a column in the margin at one side of the chart. (See figure 11-9.) Annotation columns are commonly used for information that cannot be otherwise conveniently displayed in the flowchart, such as the volume of input and output, control procedures, and equipment required.

Guidelines. The following list of guidelines constitutes a set of general rules and procedures for the construction of system flowcharts.

1. Identifying names written within flowchart symbols should be chosen to meet the needs of the user. Technical terms and codes can be understood by few people.
2. Identification should be brief and consistent. The same item should be identified by the same name wherever it appears in the flowchart.
3. Flowchart symbols and flowlines should be kept as small as possible but consistent with visual clarity. This makes possible a compact layout, efficient and effective use of the available page space, and easier reading.
4. Sufficient space should be left around major flows (unless they are converging). When unrelated flows are shown close together, it is difficult to tell what is happening.
5. Flowlines should be combined wherever possible to minimize the number of lines that must be shown entering or leaving a process symbol.
6. Flowline crossings should be avoided wherever possible; connectors and cross-references are clearer.
7. Specialized symbols should be used wherever possible to increase the information contained on the flowchart and thus make it more useful to the reader.
8. Annotation and cross-referencing should be used wherever they will help the reader understand the flowchart more easily. But these techniques should not be overused or allowed to clutter up a chart.

9. All operations performed on data *before* they enter the system as input should be specified. Omission of such information from system flowcharts, a very common failure, reduces their usefulness.

Preparation. As a general rule, preparation of a system flowchart should begin with the parts that are most familiar to the preparer. Then the flowchart can be extended in both directions—forward toward final output and backward to initial input. The notations and conventions specified in ANSI X3.5 should be followed.

Program Flowcharts

Program flowcharts focus on the sequence of processing operations by which input is transformed into output, and detail the different types of data involved. A program flowchart usually requires more symbols and presents a more detailed view than a system flowchart.

Also, because of their detail, program flowcharts are commonly divided into two or more parts. Consequently, connectors and cross-references become all the more important.

The conventions governing program flowcharts are similar to those established for system flowcharts, with some important exceptions. Because of their detail and complexity, program flowcharts cannot follow a simple format principle such as the sandwich rule. Rather, the overall format of a program flowchart tends to follow a sequence in which several process symbols are linked by flowlines. One or more input/output symbols will usually appear near the beginning of this sequence and again near the end.

Basic format. Program flowcharts can be constructed using the standard basic and additional symbols. Program flowcharts begin and end with terminal symbols. They usually include one or more program *loops*. A loop is essentially a process or subroutine that should be repeated as many times as the processing of the data requires (see figure 11-10).

Identification. Written identifications of data are important in program flowcharts. Although English terms can be used, they may be too long to fit within the outlines of the flowchart symbols. (Since program flowcharts tend to require more symbols than the system variety, the size of the symbols tends to be smaller as well.) Symbols used in one or another programming language may be too specific to

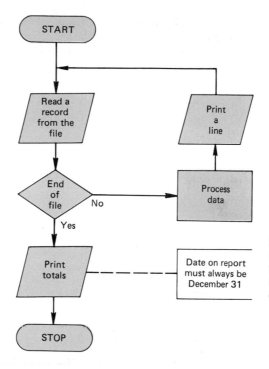

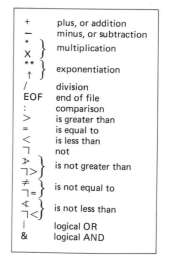

Figure 11-10 Flowchart showing special coding within the symbols and an annotation column to explain the coding

describe operations and manipulations of data that must be shown in a flowchart. They also may be unfamiliar to many users.

To meet the need for comprehensive flowchart descriptions, notational schemes have been proposed. Figure 11-11 shows a list of the generally accepted symbols.

Specialized symbols. The specialized symbols that appear most often in program flowcharts are those for decision, preparation, predefined process, merge, extract, sort, and collate. Because program flowcharts usually map the processing performed in the computer itself, they normally do not include any symbols for manual or auxiliary operations. Since the focus of the program flowchart is on processing, input/output and storage media are usually not significant; therefore the basic, rather than the specialized, symbols for such features are most often used.

Connectors and cross-references. A complete flowchart is almost always too big to fit on a single page. A program must almost always be broken down into segments and shown on separate pages. The detail shown may include one or more alternative paths of information flow and a number of converging and diverging flowlines. It is easy to produce a flowchart in which symbols are bunched together

Figure 11-11 Notation symbols for flowcharts

309

or where lines look like a tangle. By using connectors and cross-referencing, a clear, straight-line flow pattern can be achieved.

Note that when a flowchart is broken down into several parts, each part requires a connector symbol to indicate the break—an outconnector on one for exit and an inconnector on the next for entry. Cross-references help the reader to find the entry connector for a given exit connector.

Annotation. The annotation symbol is particularly useful in program flowcharts. It is more frequently used to indicate values, such as the number of times a loop is to be executed, and to explain specific features.

Guidelines. Guidelines for constructing a program flowchart are similar to those for system flowcharts but with some important differences.

1. As with systems flowcharts, names and symbols should be chosen to meet the needs of the user.
2. The names should be brief and consistent.
3. The level of detail should be consistent throughout the flowchart. In other words, the amount of detail used in one part of the chart to represent an operation should be essentially the same as the amount of detail used in other parts of the chart to represent other operations.
4. The flowchart should be simple and clear, with sufficient space around symbols.
5. Data processing operations should be clearly distinguished from operations in the program itself. The latter should be identified by a preparation symbol.
6. The general flow should be from top to bottom and from left to right. Entrances should appear at upper left, exits at lower right.
7. The use of successive connector symbols should be avoided. Also, entry and exit connectors should be consistently positioned with respect to the symbols to which they are attached.
8. Connectors and cross-references should be used to minimize the crossing of flowlines.
9. There should be only one entrance flowline to a symbol and, with some exceptions, only one exit flowline from a symbol. One important exception is the decision symbol, which must have more than one exit flowline.

Preparation. Constructing a program flowchart is always, to some extent, a trial-and-error process. Two general approaches help to reduce the number of trials and amount of errors.

One approach is to <u>follow the general sequence involved in the ac</u>tual <u>processing of a program</u>: prepare to read input, read input, process input data, produce output, and end processing. In fact, each stage of a program can usually be considered as involving all five steps.

HIPO and Pseudocode

HIERARCHY INPUT
PROCESSING OUTPUT

Another <u>approach to flowcharting is to draw a hierarchical series</u> of <u>flowcharts, each showing more detail than the preceding</u> one, <u>until the desired level of detail is achieved.</u>

A variation contains elements of both these approaches. It is known as <u>H</u>ierarchy plus <u>I</u>nput-<u>P</u>rocessing-<u>O</u>utput, or <u>HIPO, and in</u>cludes <u>the input and output of each program module, where</u> the usual flowcharts describe <u>only structures and functions</u>. HIPO is the visual counterpart of top-down structuring in system and program design (which we will examine in chapter 12). HIPO exists as a set of

Preparation
of a HIPO program
diagram

(Bill Longcore)

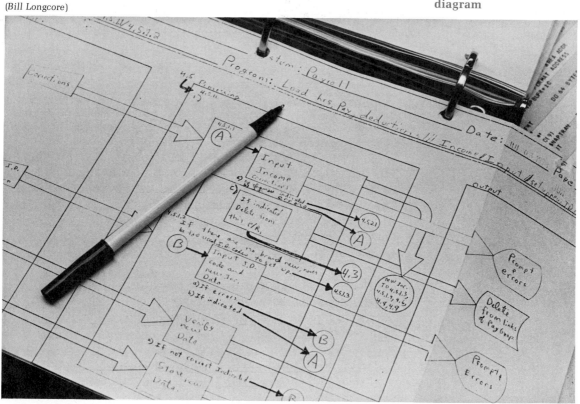

HIPO

charts that move from the most general or broadly descriptive level to the most specific or detailed level. The extent of detail shown at each level is determined by the needs of programmers and users.

HIPO was intended by its designers to provide more documentation throughout the programming process than was possible in a flowchart. In this way, a HIPO representation could lead to better communication between programmers, systems designers, auditors, and users. The varying degrees of detail shown in a set of HIPO charts make them particularly useful for the different individuals who must work with the system or program at various stages of its development and implementation.

Pseudocode is an alternative technique for developing flows of logic. Essentially, pseudocode uses brief English language statements to represent the logical steps required to solve a programming problem. For example:

```
DOWHILE more records in file
      move name address social security number to output area
   ENDDO
```

can replace an entire flowchart sequence. This technique has been used informally for many years by knowledgeable programmers.

Decision Tables :

Complex
  APPLICATIONS

There is another alternative to the flowchart, the *decision table*. A decision table provides a clear visual representation of the "actions" to be taken under specified conditions in a computer program. For a complex application, a decision table may provide a more straightforward and useful way to examine processes than a flowchart, and it is likely to be easier to prepare.

Features of a Decision Table

A decision table represents one or more of three fundamental features—conditions, actions, and rules. A *condition* is a factor or criterion that must be considered before a "decision to act" can be taken. An *action* is the step or set of steps to be followed when a specified condition or set of conditions is met. A *rule* is a combination of specified conditions and associated actions. Figure 11-12 shows the relationship between these three components in a simple decision table.

Heading				(Rule Identifiers)		
			R1	R2	R3 . . .	
Con- dition Identi- fiers	C1 ---- C2	Condition statements		Condition entries		
Action Identi- fiers	A1 ---- A2	Action statements		Action entries		
	Notes:					

Figure 11-12 Components of a decision table

Double or heavy lines divide a table horizontally and vertically into four major parts: condition statements, condition entries, action statements, and action entries. Each condition and action appears in the table as both a statement and an entry.

Other features of decision tables include an identifying title or code for the table itself; rule, condition, and action identifiers (R1, C1, and A1, respectively); and notes or comments expanding, if necessary, on any items in the table.

Types of decision tables. In a *limited entry decision table,* the condition and action statements are complete in themselves, and therefore the condition and action entries simply show whether the stated condition exists or the specified action has been taken. (Condition entries are indicated by N for "not existing," Y for "yes, it exists," and—or a blank if the condition does not apply. Action entries are indicated simply as X if the action is to be taken or executed, and—or a blank if no action is to be taken.) The name of

ITEM REORDER PROCEDURE		R1	R2	R3
C1	REACHED EOQ	Y	N	N
C2	SALES TREND FAV	—	Y	N
A1	ORDER ITEM	X	X	—
A2	RETURN FOR APPROVAL	—	—	X
Note: Be certain that the latest EOQ information is used.				

Figure 11-13 Example of a limited entry decision table

Note: EOQ = economic order quantity, the inventory level of an item that has been predetermined as the level at which reorders are necessary if sales volume is to be continued.

313

ITEM REORDER PROCEDURE		R1	R2	R3
C1	EOQ	REACHED	NOT REACHED	NOT REACHED
C2	SALES TREND	–	FAVORABLE	UNFAVORABLE
A1	ORDER ITEM	APPROVE	APPROVE	DON'T APPROVE
A2	RETURN FOR APPROVAL	–	–	RETURN TO SALES

Figure 11-14 Example of an extended entry decision table

ITEM REORDER PROCEDURE		R1	R2	R3
C1	REACHED EOQ	Y	N	N
C2	SALES TREND	–	FAVORABLE	UNFAVORABLE
A1	ORDER ITEM	APPROVE	APPROVE	DON'T APPROVE
A2	RETURN FOR APPROVAL	–	–	X

Figure 11-15 Example of a mixed entry decision table

this type of table is derived from the limited function or information provided by each entry, hence its name. (See figure 11-13.)

In an extended entry decision table, on the other hand, the condition and action statements are not complete in themselves, but require the information in the entry boxes, such as "approve" or "consider." Since the condition and action entries indicate more than a single N, Y, X, or —, their function is considered to be "extended" beyond that of the limited entry. (See figure 11-14.)

A mixed entry decision table combines the characteristics of both limited and extended entry tables. (See figure 11-15.)

Decision tables can be either vertical or horizontal in arrangement. The logic of both types is identical.

Decision Tables vs. Flowcharts

Decision tables with a few neatly labeled boxes may seem clearer and simpler than flowcharts with a variety of symbol outlines and clusters of flowlines. But the choice of one in preference to the other depends on how they are to be used.

Flowcharts are particularly useful for mapping programs that are straightforward and contain a minimal amount of branching. They are especially well suited for showing sequences of operations and the flow of information from one component of a system or program to another. They can also depict different kinds of processing operations, and make other distinctions graphically clear as well.

But flowcharts can be difficult and tedious to prepare. They tend to become cluttered as the programs that they map become more complex. In addition, flowcharts are difficult to revise. It can even be difficult to determine whether a flowchart adequately describes a given program or could be improved. For this reason, a flow or gap may not show up until the program is actually in operation.

In contrast, all decision tables share a standard tabular format that is very easy to draw. The conditions and actions are also very easy to read and to follow. With some exceptions, the clarity of a decision table—unlike that of flowcharts—increases as the program becomes more complex. Moreover, decision tables are easier to check for completeness, and they are easier to revise and update. Finally, a decision table makes possible communication between personnel that is as good as, or even better than, that of a flowchart. One important consequence of better communication is that the application or problem in question tends to be more clearly defined.

Originally, the use of decision tables required translation into a programming language, but software packages now make it possible to bypass this step. The use of these decision table translators, available for several computer languages, has improved programming efficiency.

Among the disadvantages of decision tables is the reluctance of personnel trained in flowcharting to shift to a new and different device. A serious disadvantage is that the conventions governing decision tables prevent branching. In decision table terms, branching is an action entry that requires reference to another table. For a program with several branching operations, decision tables would be cumbersome.

But decision tables can be used at most levels of an organization and are a practical solution for a variety of functions. For example, they can be employed for applications in accounting, personnel, manufacturing, and engineering, as well as for program writing and related applications. Also, they can serve as effective communications links between the various personnel involved in the analysis, design, programming, and use of computer systems. While not a perfect solution for all the problems of developing computer systems and programs, they make a valuable contribution to solving some of those problems.

Summary

The *flowchart* is a technique or method for graphically depicting the logical data flow, processes, and operations of systems and programs. The term *flowcharting* refers to the creation and use of flowcharts. Although they are particularly useful for the analysis and design of computer-based systems and operations, flowcharts can also be used to depict other types of information flow and organizations.

A technique for representing information flow and processing should be easy to use, simple, easily readable, unambiguous, and independent of specific information media or processing equipment. Flowcharts satisfy these criteria more successfully than any other method developed to date. In particular, they are easier for the nonspecialists to learn and use.

The standards governing the symbols and conventions used in flowcharting are those contained in the ANSI X3.5, which also specifies the shape but not the size of the symbols.

Flowchart symbols fall into three main classes: (1) *basic*, (2) *additional*, and (3) *specialized*. A complete and informative flowchart can be developed using only the first two types. The use of specialized symbols is optional.

The four basic symbols are: (1) *input/output*, (2) *processing*, (3) *flowline*, and (4) *annotation*. The normal direction of flow is from top to bottom and from left to right.

The three additional symbols are: (1) *connector*, (2) *terminal*, and (3) *parallel mode*. The specialized symbols consist of three groups for specifying (1) *media*, (2) *peripheral equipment*, and (3) *processing operations*.

System flowcharts provide a macrolevel view of the overall pattern of information flow. *Program flowcharts* provide a much more detailed microlevel view of data transformation. The basic format of system flowcharts follows the *sandwich rule*: input/process/output. Program flowcharts usually consist of a series of operations symbols that are linked by flowlines.

Guidelines for constructing flowcharts emphasize ways to clarify information and meet the needs of all users. Identifications for symbols should be brief and used consistently. Crossing of flowlines should be minimized.

Decision tables are an alternative method of representing information flow and processing. A decision table shows three elements: *conditions*, *actions*, and *rules*. When compared with flowcharts, decision tables have a simpler format and are easier to revise. *Pseudocode*, another way of expressing program logic, uses brief English language statements.

Key Terms and Phrases

action	communication link	conjunction
annotation symbol	symbol	connector symbol
collate	condition	decision symbol

decision table
display output
  symbol
document symbol
entrance connector
  symbol
exit connector
  symbol
extract
flowchart

flowcharting
flowline symbol
input/output symbol
manual input
  symbol
merge
parallel mode
  symbol
peripheral equip-
  ment symbols

processing opera-
  tion symbols
processing symbol
program flowcharts
rule
sort
system flowcharts
terminal symbol

Sources of Additional Information

Chapin, Ned. "Flowcharting with the ANSI Standard: A Tutorial." *Computing Surveys*, no. 2 (1970):119–43. Reprinted in *System Analysis Techniques*, edited by J. Daniel Couger and Robert W. Knapp, pp. 128–61. New York: Wiley, 1974.

———. *Flowcharts*. New York: Auerbach Publishers, 1971.

Couger, J. Daniel, and Knapp, Robert W., eds. *System Analysis Techniques*. New York: Wiley, 1974.

Fergus, Raymond M. "Decision Tables—What, Why and How." *Proceedings, College and University Machine Records Conference*, pp. 1–20. University of Michigan, 1969. Reprinted in *System Analysis Techniques*, edited by J. Daniel Couger and Robert W. Knapp, pp. 162–79. New York: Wiley, 1974.

Gane, Chris, and Kain, Jim. "Structured Analysis Tools Please Users—Cut Efforts." *Infosystems*, no. 6 (1978):100–104.

Weinger, Gerald R. "You Say Your Design's Inexact? Try a Wiggle." *Datamation*, no. 9 (1979):146–49.

Test Yourself

1. What is a flowchart, and why is it used?
2. Which characteristics should be included in any medium or method used to describe information flow and sequence of operations?
3. What is ANSI X3.5?
4. Name three kinds or groups of flowchart symbols.
5. Name and draw or describe the four basic flowchart symbols.
6. There are some customs, or conventions, that are generally agreed upon and followed in constructing flowcharts. Why are such conventions important? Describe three of them.
7. What is the function of a flowline symbol? What is the convention for showing the normal flow of direction in a flowchart?

317

8. How could you clarify or provide additional information about a step or operation shown on a flowchart?

9. Which processing operation symbol may appear most frequently on a program flowchart, and why?

10. What do the specialized flowchart symbols represent? Why are they likely to appear more often than basic symbols in a system flowchart?

11. Name three alternatives or supplements to flowcharting.

12. What are the three fundamental features of a decision table? Describe the relationships between them.

13. Decision tables and flowcharts can be used to describe the process in a system. Which of these would be a better communications tool for describing a problem or process to the personnel who will use the system? Explain your answer.

12 Program Preparation

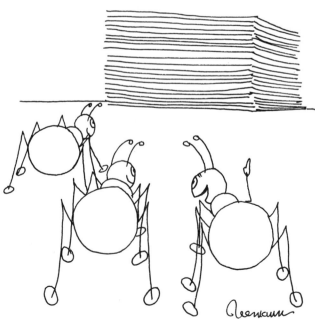

By permission of Tom Niemann

"Looks like a good program. Climb in, everybody."

APPLICATION

A Program for Any Date

Problem: To develop a program—an algorithm—to find the day of the week for any date from the year 1582 to 20,000. Source of information: the Gregorian calendar.

In the Gregorian system, a year has 365.25 days, and every fourth year is a leap year of 366 days. Thus, any year between 1582 and 20,000 whose number can be divided by four is a leap year. Centennial years (1600, 1700, 1800, and so on) are leap years only if they can be divided by 400. The millennial years (2000, 3000, and so on) are *not* leap years if they are divisible by 4,000.

A 365-day year has a total of 52 weeks and one extra day; a leap year therefore has 52 weeks and two extra days. Thus, if January 1 falls on a Monday one year, it will fall on a Tuesday the next year if that year is not a leap year.

Now we can begin to see what we need to develop this algorithm. We must know: (1) The day of the week for a reference date; (2) the number of years between the reference date and the date in question; (3) how many of these years are leap years. From this information, we can calculate how many extra days must be added to the reference table to find the day of the week of the date in question. (In this algorithm, we will represent Monday as 1, Tuesday as 2, and so on.)

First, we need to calculate whether a year is a leap year and how many leap years occur in a given period. There are four basic tests to see if any year, say 1900, is a leap year. If it can be divided by the integer 4 with no remainder, it is a leap year unless it is a millennial year, or, as in this case, a centennial year. If it can be divided by 100 with no remainder, it is a centennial year. As was mentioned above, 400 and 4,000 are also key numbers. If the year can be divided evenly by 400 and not by 4,000, then it is a leap year.

Following these four tests, we take our year 1900 and divide it by 4, 100, 400, and 4,000. But what we are interested in is whether 1900 is evenly divisible by each of these dividends, or whether there is a remainder. The remainders are, respectively, 0, 0, 300, 1900. Reviewing, we can see that 1900 is a centennial year but *not* a leap year because it can be divided evenly by 4 and 100 but not by 400. If a zero remainder is represented by a binary 1 (on) and a nonzero remainder by a binary 0 (off), the computer will be able to store the results and logically test to see whether the conditions for a leap year are met.

To determine how many leap years there are in a given period, let us use January 1 of the year 0 as our reference date. The year 0 is not a leap year. To find the number of leap years between January 1 in the year 0 and January 1, 1900, find the integer quotient of $(1900 - 1) \div 4$, or 474. The number of centennial years between 1900 and 0 is $(1900 - 1) \div 100$, or 18. The number of years that pass the test of divisibility by 400 is $(1900 - 1) \div 400$, or 4. So far, we have 474 years, 18 of which are centurial, but only four of which are divisible by 400. This gives us $474 - 18 + 4$, or 460 leap years. But what about the millennial years? The only millennial year between 0 and 1900 is the year 1000. Since it is not divisible by 4,000, it is a leap year. This brings our total up to 461.

Now, to find the day of the week of January 1, 1900, we take the number of years between 0 and 1900 and add an extra day for each. We then take the number of leap years, 461, and include an additional extra day for each. This gives us $1900 + 461$, or 2,361 extra days.

Because the same day of the week comes around every seventh day, we divide 2,361 by 7, to get 337 weeks and 2 days. The reference date of January 1 in the year 0 was a Saturday (we calculated backward to discover this), so January 1, 1900, was a Monday.

Once the day of the week of the first day of any year is known, the same principles can be applied to calculate the day for any date in that year. Just add up the number of days between the date in question and January 1, divide by 7, and take the integer remainder. This is the number of extra days.

If we combine all our information into a general algorithm, we end up with five steps. If we represent the date that we are interested in finding the day of the week for as M/D/Y, we can proceed as follows: (1) Find out whether Y is a leap year. (2) Store a list containing the number of days in each month, that is, 31, 29, 31 . . . if Y is a leap year. (3) Find the number of extra days between January 1, 0, and M/D/Y by adding Y to the number of leap years between January 1, 0, and January 1, Y. (4) Use the results of Step 2 to add up the number of days in Y, up to and including the day D of the month M. (5) Add the results of Steps 3 and 4 and call it X. The number corresponding to the day of the week for M/D/Y is then equal to one plus the integer remainder of $(X - 1) \div 7$.

Source: Bhairav Joshi, "Day-of-Week Algorithm Works to 20,000 A.D.," *Computerworld*, January 14, 1980, pp. 36–42.

 PROGRAM is a written set of specific instructions that causes the computer hardware to perform required tasks in the appropriate sequence. A computer can only do what it is programmed to do. If there is an error in the program, there will be a corresponding flaw in the computer's functioning. Indeed, it is a truism that computers do not make mistakes, but people do; computers will correctly execute the flawed programs.

Every program should be viewed as a component of (or a module within) a given system. (A system that is very small may consist of only a single program.)

Preparing a program is not just writing instructions. Before a programmer can code even a single statement, a considerable amount of planning must be done and numerous decisions made.

In complex programs, the framework or structure of the program is crucial. Teams of programmers are often needed to complete a large program on schedule; only a standardized structure can integrate the contributions of team members into a coherent whole. Testing and debugging are necessary to ensure accuracy; only a logical sequence will prevent specified procedures from becoming a programmer's nightmare.

These and other considerations have led to the development of several programming approaches: top-down design, GOTO-less programming, and modularization, among others. In this chapter we will discuss these approaches and the relationship between them. We will also examine their roles in planning, structuring, and writing a computer program.

Planning the Program

The essential steps in program preparation are: planning the program, structuring the program, and writing the program. Final considerations in program preparation relate to the needs of the user for documentation and maintenance. (See figure 12-1.)

Defining the Problem

If formal systems analysis precedes programming, then to a great extent the problem will have already been defined. In that case, the programmer would, of course, refer to any flowcharts or other documentation produced during that analysis. But in some organizations, analysis is the responsibility of the programmer, who must begin at the beginning and solve the problem from both a systems and a program perspective.

The first step in planning a program is to define the problem to be solved. This seems obvious; after all, how can a programmer begin to

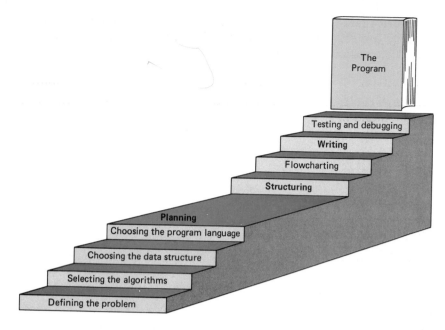

Figure 12-1 Steps in program preparation

work toward a solution without first understanding the problem? Yet all too often this is exactly what happens. The initiative for a new system may come from a bank, consulting engineers, or company executives who have a good grasp of overall objectives but may not be aware of the difficulties the system presents to the programmer. This lack of communication at the outset results in the need for extensive debugging and program patching later on.

In chapter 10, problem definition was discussed from the point of view of the system—a "macrolevel" perspective. Once the problem has been defined on the system-oriented level, though, programmers must begin to deal with the particular steps that might be taken to solve it. The overall problem or objectives must be broken down or redefined into a series of related problems that are more limited in scope. The combined solutions of these "microlevel" problems, which will eventually lead to solution of the larger or system-oriented problem, constitute the program or programs.

Ideally, the planning process should start with a personal conference between the system originator and the programmer. This allows the programmer to learn the originator's needs before a single step is coded. Based on this conference, a formal or informal specification should be written. This "spec" should define the program problem and yet be flexible enough to allow for additional information or modifications in program design.

323

Selecting an Algorithm

Once the problem has been identified, the next step is to select the best method for solving it. If the problem is a familiar one, standardized algorithms may be available from program libraries. An *algorithm* is a series of logical steps that must be followed to solve a particular problem. But if standard algorithms are not suitable, a new algorithm must be written. New algorithms are then added to the program library.

When all the necessary algorithms are listed, the programmer should check program libraries, exchange organizations, and other computing installations to see if programs have been written for these algorithms. Frequently, a large portion of the most detailed work will have already been done. Even in this case, though, the programmer may have to make some modifications or adapt the program to a different programming language. If the precise programs specified by the list of algorithms are not available, there may be some that will accomplish the same task through a different but acceptable alternative algorithm.

Choosing the Data Structure

Next, the data file organization—sequential, direct access, and so on—is selected, based on the requirements of the algorithms being used and the computer hardware available. Additional hardware may be needed to handle new files. Whenever possible, the programmer should opt for data structures that reduce the program's complexity. This effort will usually be most appreciated at the debugging stage.

Choosing a Programming Language

Selecting the appropriate programming language is the final step of program planning. Several factors are usually involved in this decision. The language may be predetermined by the data processing department (or "shop") or by the availability of personnel who know a certain language. The computer for which the program is being written may influence the decision, since smaller computers may have only one compiler.

The application and special requirements of a program are the most important factors in choosing a language. Depending on the problem, several levels of programming may be required. Low-level programming languages are very close to machine language or binary. It is tedious to write programs in *low-level languages* and also difficult to detect and correct errors in such programs. But these languages have advantages for special purposes. *High-level languages* are closer to the language used by humans, and are therefore easier to write programs in and to correct. However, their use requires a compiler to translate their terminology into machine language for the computer to follow.

Low-level languages. In some computer installations, equipment has been adapted for the use of microlanguage. This is the most basic level of programming available. In microprogramming, the microprogram directly controls every register in the CPU. In this case, even the simple loading of a single storage location might take several lines of microinformation. In microprogramming, therefore, the programmer must specify every step in minute detail. In most systems using microprogramming, the microinstructions are stored in read-only memories, inaccessible to the programmer. Where the microinstructions are accessible, however, the ability to redefine the computer's functions by using microlanguage can be a tremendous tool.

The one language that can be used directly by the computer is *machine language*. It is written in binary by the programmer, and therefore no translation within the computer is necessary. Although it is precisely what the computer requires to perform the requested data processing tasks, machine language is very difficult for humans to use.

In an attempt to make programming more manageable for humans, *assembly language* was developed. Instructions in assembly language consist of a symbolic code, usually a letter or combinations of letters, as opposed to the binary code of machine language:

Machine language operation code for "add": 011100
Assembly language symbol for "add": A

Assembly language instructions are translated within the computer into binary code on a one-to-one basis; that is, every assembly language symbol translates into a binary coded instruction. (See table 12-1.)

Assembly language is, however, more than just a glossary of instructions in symbolic coding. It also includes *macroinstructions*. A macroinstruction consists of a predefined series of assembly language statements that are often used as a group in a specific sequence to perform a particular task.

Programmers sometimes choose to work with assembly language in order to make full use of a particular computer's capabilities. In

Table 12-1 A Sample of Assembly Language

Instruction	Symbolic code
Add	A
Add Halfword	AH
Branch and Link	BAL
Branch on Condition	BC
Compare	C
Compare Halfword	CH
Convert to Binary	CVB
Decimal	P
Divide	D
Divide Decimal	DP
Halt I/O	HIO
Load	L
Load Address	LA
Move Numerics	MVN
Multiply	M
Multiply Decimal	MP
Set Clock	SCK
Set Storage Key	SSK
Start I/O	SIO
Store	ST
Store Character	STC
Store Halfword	STH
Subtract	S
Subtract Halfword	SH
Test and Set	TS
Translate	TR
Translate and Test	TRT
Write Direct	WRD
Zero and Add Decimal	ZAP

certain cases, assembly language may make possible a problem solution that would not be feasible in a higher-level language.

There are a number of different machine languages and assembly languages, each associated with the hardware of a different manufacturer. Different vendors offer different machine languages. All are binary, but the specific coding differs. Programmers who choose to work in machine or assembly language must learn the specific binary or symbolic coding characteristic of the hardware available to them.

High-level languages. Beyond the machine languages are several high-level problem-oriented languages designed for specific areas of concern. These include: COBOL, or COmmon Business-Oriented Language; FORTRAN, or FORmula TRANslator, a scientific and

(Joseph L. Sardinas, Jr.)

A program consultant uses a number of reference manuals while preparing an application program.

(Joseph L. Sardinas, Jr.)

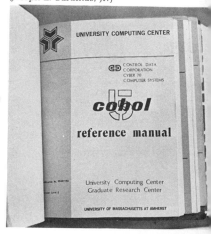

technical language; list processing languages like LISP; multipurpose languages like PL/I; and BASIC, an interactive mathematical language. (See chapter 13.) Despite the large assortment, however, a programmer will often find that no one high-level language is ideal for all aspects of a particular project. In this case, the most suitable language is selected and extended as necessary. Extension is accomplished by writing subroutines in other languages to perform specified tasks. The programmer must then rewrite the program's instructions as a series of calls on subroutines.

A solution to the tedium of high-level language extension is the use of a precompiler. A precompiler is designed to accept statements tailored to a particular program and automatically generate the calls on various subroutines. Precompilers are often used for simplifying a particular language so that beginning students can start programming sooner. A precompiler can be designed for doing interval arithmetic, where the answers are expressed as real number intervals that are guaranteed to contain the theoretical results. More versatile precompilers (AUGMENT, for FORTRAN, is one example) can accept programs with normally unacceptable data types, generate the appropriate subroutine calls, and prepare a program acceptable to the standard compiler for a given language. By combining several precompilers with AUGMENT, standard FORTRAN can be extended to deal with virtually any type of nonstandard data.

Structuring the Program

Once the program strategy is planned, the programmer can begin to build the structure and develop the related logic. The simplest way to structure a program is in a direct sequence, with one step executed right after the other. Most programs, however, do not lend themselves to this simplicity. Before we can examine the techniques for developing logic and structuring programs, however, it is necessary to describe the construction of a program in general.

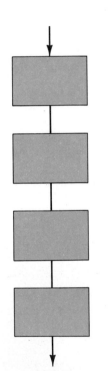

Figure 12-2   Skeleton flowchart diagram of simple sequence

Basic Programming Operations

All programs, even the most complex, consist of one or more of three basic operations: sequence, conditional, and loop. These operations can relate to each other in a variety of ways in order to detail virtually any programming problem that comes along.

Sequential operation.   In a sequential operation, statements are executed in the order in which they occur, one right after another. (See figure 12-2.) It is often necessary to interrupt the sequential order of execution and direct the computer to continue executing at some other place in the program. This is referred to as *branching*. A GOTO statement in the program directs the computer to the appropriate place; a second GOTO statement is needed to send the computer back into the sequence after the branch steps have been executed. A really complex program may become a mass of GOTO statements, making the program flow hard to follow and increasing the chance for both human and computer errors.

Conditional operation.   The conditional operation allows the program to follow one of two branches in a forward direction, if certain conditions have been met. If a certain condition or test is met, the computer is directed to execute one sequence of steps; if it is not

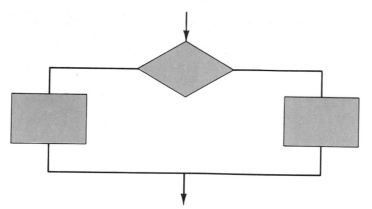

Figure 12-3 Skeleton flowchart showing IFTHENELSE condition

met, the computer is told to execute another sequence. The paths of these two sequences will eventually meet, so that the sequence of the entire program continues, regardless of which path is taken. (See figure 12-3.)

A conditional statement may be used to test whether the values resulting from previous steps in the program are equal to a figure that has been predetermined. In computing a payroll, for example, the program may instruct "If days worked equal 10, then GOTO subroutine XYZ. If not, then continue along branch EFG." This is called an IFTHENELSE statement, because the computer is in effect told, "If a certain condition exists, then do such and such, but if not, then do a specific something else."

Depending on the needs of that point in the program, there are three possible outcomes of an IFTHENELSE condition: transfer control to another point in the program, using a GOTO statement; transfer control to a subroutine; and assign values to specific variables and continue executing.

Loop. The *loop* of DOWHILE operation allows some steps in the program to be repeated. (See figure 12-4.) Before the computer can begin executing the steps in a loop, there is a decision statement similar to the conditional IFTHENELSE. This decision statement is a logical expression that must be evaluated. Usually the decision statement must evaluate a variable quantity, which is expressed as a numeral. The decision statement refers to the value of this control variable: "N is less than 10." While this statement is true, the computer is directed to execute a sequence of steps called the process and then to reevaluate the decision statement. This continues until the statement becomes false; then the computer resumes execution of the rest of the program.

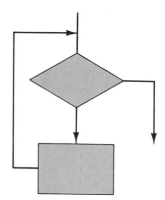

Figure 12-4 Skeleton flowchart showing loop

329

The control operation variable that is tested by the decision statement must be changed by one of the processing steps in the loop. Otherwise, the computer will execute loop after loop, endlessly. Because the control variable is usually a numeral that counts, a step in the process increases it by one each time the loop is executed. When the desired number, say 10, is reached, the decision statement "N is less than 10" will be false and the loop will end.

Structured Programming Techniques

From experience, programmers have developed several techniques or approaches to the logical grouping of these operations. It has long been the case that the design of the system or application was from the top down, moving from the general to the more specific, while the programming was designed from the bottom up. In *bottom-up programming*, the more detailed or lower-level routines are coded first. These are tested and completed before the higher-level routines are coded. The routines are combined at each successive level, with each higher level acting as a test of the assumptions made at the lower levels.

When the lower levels are coded first in this manner, driver routines are usually needed for testing. A driver routine sends data to a routine and receives output, thus simulating the operation of the finished program. The driver may also print out intermediate results for the programmer's inspection. Driver routines are inserted in a program; these sections are known as the throwaway code because they are usually designed to be removed from the program after it has been thoroughly tested and is finished.

The bottom-up approach produces a few problems. It is not unusual for each routine to work correctly with its driver but then fail when the routines in the whole program are executed together. This may be due to changes in specifications since the earliest routines were coded, or it may be due to poor communication between the programmers who worked on separate routines. In order to correct the design, parts of the existing code may have to be patched, the whole problem recoded, or the design modified to fit the most recent or thorough code. This loop of redesign, recode, retest, and branch back to redesign may go on until time has run out and the program must be put into production—bugs and all.

Top-down programming. The alternative to the sometimes haphazard bottom-up approach is to use *top-down programming.* This technique begins with the most general statement of the program and divides it successively into more specific routines. (See figure

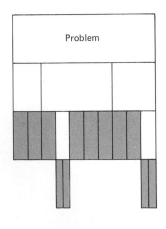

Problem

Subcomponents that will be designed as distinct modules

Figure 12-5 Top-down design

330

12-5.) At each level, program stubs are substituted for routines that are to be coded at lower levels. These program stubs consist of the most minimal amount of coding needed to execute the program. Any detailed coding is deferred until the very last stage of program development.

With top-down structuring, the design, coding, and testing of the entire program are done concurrently, as opposed to bottom-up structuring, which allows testing of the entire program only after all the coding has been finished. Top-down structuring is therefore not plagued by the frantic batching and redesign needed by bottom-up structures.

Modularization: Programming's atomic theory. Closely related to the technique of top-down structuring is that of *modularization*. Modularization, in fact, takes the top-down concept a step further by subdividing each subroutine into modules that are totally self-contained. A module is a compilation of statements that perform a single function: to transform input to output when the module is executed. These statements are collectively referred to by the module name, a one-sentence description of its function.

A module may be called up by the operating system or by another module; however, it always returns control to its caller. To the caller, or invoking module, the invoked module is a "black box." All that is needed to describe the module is its name and its output. All instructions necessary for executing that module are contained within it.

This concept of modularization offers several advantages, especially for large programs being written by several programmers simultaneously. The program design is simplified and easier to modify if necessary. Modularization also allows for more complete testing, since any part of the program can be tested by simply feeding dummy input to the appropriate modules. Furthermore, the creation of "black box" modules to perform certain functions makes it possible to store commonly used modules in program libraries.

There are of course some disadvantages with modularization. It may require increased storage size and greater compile, execution, and load times. The lack of intermodule communication is another problem in some cases. These disadvantages are largely offset, however, by the reduced development and maintenance costs of a modular program.

GOTO-less programming. As we have seen, the three basic operations of sequence, IFTHENELSE, and looping can be combined in any arrangement to solve any programming problem. However, as programs became more complex, it became apparent that extensive

331

branching led to increasing numbers of errors. It seemed as though the more GOTO statements a program contained, the more likely it was that errors would occur. Then it seemed logical that the removal of GOTO statements would produce a program relatively free of bugs from this cause. The controversy over this theory still rages. It is probably not possible or advisable to program completely without GOTOs. But it is clear that *limiting* the number of GOTO statements makes a program considerably easier to handle.

The main objective of GOTO-less programming is to keep the program flow in a forward direction and as close as possible to simple sequencing. Some steps in the sequence may have to be skipped when an IFTHENELSE statement is read or repeated in a DOWHILE routine, but in GOTO-less programming the exit from these operations is always forward to the next step in the sequence.

Program Flowcharting

As we saw in the previous chapter, a flowchart is a graphic "map" that uses standard symbols to represent logic. Program flowcharts use the same symbols as systems flowcharts but are usually more detailed. Instead of depicting the sequence of activities in an organization, program flowcharts depict the steps to be executed in a specific computer program. Figures 12-2, 12-3, and 12-4 are skeleton flowcharts showing sequential operation, conditional operation, and looping, respectively.

Although the flowchart is intended to simplify communication, it can itself become a communication problem if not prepared correctly. Ideally, it should be neither too detailed nor too general. The labels for each symbol should contain enough detail so they are understandable and informative. Cryptic messages that only the programmer understands are no help, especially when even the programmer cannot read them six months later. Neatness counts, especially in flowcharting.

Structuring the Individual Module

In a modularized program, each of a number of modules will consist of the program for a logical subcomponent of the total program's problem. A structured program consists of its component modules joined together with other logically structured modules and submodules. A module exists as an entity, a complete "package" of a distinct segment of a program: It fits into a given compartment or niche within the structure of the overall program. Each module must be executed in its entirety before the next logical module can be called upon.

Debugging: Toward Painless Extermination

Modularization and top-down design have been developed because, by their very nature, they make *debugging* easier. Yet, this does not mean that programmers can forget about debugging. Errors in both syntax and logic are still found in the best modular designs. The compiler can detect errors in syntax (such as TOO instead of TO), but errors in logic can be identified only by the programmer's

(Joseph L. Sardinas, Jr.)

Debugging is often a team effort. Here, three programmers review a computer-generated program listing to locate a bug.

333

use of debugging statements. These are intentional additions to the program. Provisions must therefore be made for debugging so that programmers are able to detect and correct program bugs efficiently.

Several steps can be taken within the program modules themselves to lead to better debugging. It is not difficult, for instance, to insert special debugging output statements in a module while it is being designed. The resulting printouts can then be used to verify that the module received the expected input, performed the operations correctly, and output the correct results to the calling program. These debugging statements must be made independent of the module, however, so that their removal does not interrupt normal operation. Also, since all the debugging statements are not needed in every test run, there should be some provision for activating and deactivating each of them separately.

Another debugging technique is to insert special counters at key points in the program. In the event of a catastrophe—loss of power, perhaps—the counters will indicate how far operations had progressed before the program terminated. Counters can also be used to flag the most frequently used routines and help the programmer determine what is critical in terms of efficiency.

Advance planning is important for efficient debugging. If debugging statements are simply inserted in the program as the need arises, even more debugging will be necessary—to debug the debugging statements themselves. One prime example of the need for organized debugging is the case of business applications program auditing. For many years, individuals in data processing have designed systems and developed programs without regard to the auditor's job. While external auditors from public accounting firms may be primarily concerned with the fairness of their client's financial statements, the internal auditor must be concerned with financial, compliance, efficiency, and effectiveness audits as well. The computer cannot be isolated from these considerations of sound management and business practices. For this reason, auditors should participate in systems development and design from the earliest stages. Often an auditor may not become aware of a system's inadequacies until it is running, and at that point it is difficult and costly to improve auditing interfaces.

Adapting the program design to permit concurrent auditing of the program can make the auditor's job much easier and more effective. By writing tagging and tracing routines right into the program logic, output of test transactions can be obtained as they flow through the system. This locates problems, which can then be resolved immediately; by the time periodic auditing locates a problem, many processing weeks or even months of errors may have accumulated.

Concurrent auditing can be done by an integrated test facility, which uses the actual system to provide information on the transactions, controls, and logic of the system. In a parallel test facility, which serves the same purpose, test transactions do not flow through the live system. Instead, they are run through a copy of the logic and partial data base. Both of these methods require the consideration of auditing practices from the beginning of program design and structuring.

Writing the Program

The final phase of program development is the actual writing. This means coding the program as designed into a language that the computer can understand. Since this language has already been selected during the planning stage, the programmer must work within its particular guidelines.

Coding the Program

One of the first steps in program coding is to label the program blocks. The term *block* is used to denote a group of related program statements. If the chosen language permits, it is usually helpful to give each block a name related to the function that it performs. These names are limited to a certain number of characters by the particular program language's restrictions. Any individual statements within the blocks that may be called during program execution must also be labeled. They are usually given names that reflect both the relative position of the statement in the block and the block name.

The next part of coding is to choose names for variables, those entities whose values will change during processing or over a period of time. For the sake of clarity, variable names should be as precise as possible, indicating the quantity of the variable represented. Using the same variable names as were used in the algorithms and flowcharts is the most practical method.

After all the variables are named, the programmer can concentrate on coding the body of the program. The debugging statements to be included in the program should be coded along with the rest of the statements, with some means of telling them apart from regular programming statements so that they can be removed once testing has been done. Declarations and other statements that provide information for the utility routines can be grouped together, since they do not affect the readability of the program. Any nonstandard compiler features that modify the program language should also be grouped together into one module. This prevents confusion and makes it possible to remove them as a group.

In most cases, input and output data formats are determined by program specifications. However, the programmer may have some leeway and should use it to design the input and output for maximum user convenience. Inputs should, if possible, be in a sequence or order that is natural from the user's point of view. If any reordering or reorganization is necessary, it can be coded into the program. Output should be clearly identified so that the user does not end up with a list of numbers that cannot be deciphered.

The actual coding depends on the program language being used, but the programmer's approach to coding is related to the program structure. In bottom-up programming, the more detailed lower-level routines are coded first. In a top-down structure, however, the main program routines will be coded first. The simplest method of top-down coding is to complete the design before any coding is done. Coding begins with the main program and continues for each successively lower level; coding for each level is completed before coding for the next level is begun.

In its most thorough form, however, top-down design and coding proceed together level by level; that is, the main program is both designed *and* coded before successive levels are designed. There are some striking advantages to this total top-down approach. By coding as close as possible to the design stage, the program can be communicated in concise code, instead of by flowcharts, diagrams, and wordy descriptions. Because programming is often a team effort, improved communication between the members of the team will improve understanding and efficiency. Also, putting down programming ideas in code often makes clear the difficulties that might not otherwise be seen. These difficulties can then be avoided when coding the lower levels of program logic. Finally, total top-down coding greatly facilitates top-down testing.

Testing and Debugging

After the program has been coded, it must be tested to make sure that it accomplishes what it is supposed to (and does not do what it is not supposed to do). It is usually a good idea for a programmer other than the one who developed the program to do the final testing. This is because of the natural human tendency to focus on the familiar. Thus, programmers are most likely to test those features that they have developed, and will probably overlook features that perhaps should have been inserted. The programmers who developed the program might detect errors within their logic, but they are not likely to notice basic errors in the program design itself.

A series of more or less standardized steps has been found most effective for program testing:

Review. The first step is to go back and review the problem definition, algorithms, data structures, and flowcharts. It is here that documentation shows its value. This review ensures that the problem has been properly understood and that the intended program design will indeed solve it.

Code verification. In the next step, the code is compared with the flowcharts to be sure that the logic implemented in the code matches the logical steps drawn in the charts. This checking step may be done either before or after the code has been entered into the system.

Proofreading the program. After the code has been transcribed into the system, a printout or some sort of visual output of the program must be proofread. The proofreader checks for typographical errors, misspellings, or irrelevant comments that may have been inserted. At the same time, program statements can be checked to be sure that they are stated correctly. One misspelling can cause the computer to come to a halt when a program is running, and a misplaced comma or incorrectly arranged words can wreak havoc when a program is executing.

Desk checking. Before the program is run, some desk checking will help catch glaring logic errors. The program statements are executed by hand, using a few simple cases.

Compilation. If no errors are detected, the program is ready for compilation. A diagnostic compiler can pinpoint errors in program language, such as misspelled variable names, undefined variables, and so on.

Actual testing. Once the program is compiled, it is ready for on-the-computer testing. There are two major approaches to testing that parallel the two structuring approaches. Bottom-up testing, still the most commonly used method, starts by testing individual modules separately, using driver routines. This stage is called "module" or "unit" testing. At the next stage, the modules are joined into subsystems, each of which is tested as a whole. Finally, the subsystems are integrated into larger and larger test groups until the entire program has been tested.

337

Top-down testing, like top-down structuring and coding, starts by testing the main program and adds the modules one by one as each subsequent level of the program is tested. The testing begins with a sort of skeleton of the main program. The first few top levels of the program are implemented; any lower-level modules called by them are replaced by dummy program stubs. As the testing progresses, more and more lower-level modules are added until the whole program has been tested.

Top-down testing, although applicable to any program structure, is most effective with top-down structuring and coding. In a total top-down environment, the main program would be designed, coded, and tested before the modules on the next level are designed, coded, and tested, and so on. Even less thorough top-down testing, however, has its advantages, one of which is easier debugging. Because top-down testing starts with a known skeleton or framework and adds a new module for each test, it is easy to detect "bugs" as they enter the system. If the old version worked but the new version doesn't, then it is reasonable to assume that the "bug" is in the last module added to the program. The programmer can focus on that module to find the bug. And since the major interfaces of the program are tested first, the major bugs are usually detected first, instead of being carried along through the whole test.

Another advantage to top-down testing is that it avoids the inverted-pyramid effect of the bottom-up approach. Programmers using bottom-up testing often correct all the trivial errors early in the testing stage, only to discover a major error right before their programming deadline.

Program verification. After all of the testing runs have been made and the bugs located and dealt with, the next step is *verification* of the program. Although all logical errors may have been corrected, it is still necessary to see that the program's output is accurate and makes sense. Verification for accuracy is similar in concept to checking an arithmetic problem. It may be done by performing independent calculations, either by hand or on another computer. Verification may also be done by reverse calculation, working backward from the results to the initial data (in principle, this is the same as verifying the results of a subtraction problem by addition). But if this is done by computer, it may require a program as large in scope as the problem being checked!

Sometimes an independent programmer will be asked to perform tests to verify the results obtained by another programmer. In any case, if the program passes muster during verification, it is cleaned up, and any unneeded debugging or counting statements are removed. Then the program is ready to go.

Once the program has been finished, it is important to assemble adequate documentation. If the program has been planned and written systematically, much of the documentation will have already been prepared. An accurate record of the program eases operation for the user and permits future modifications. For these reasons, documentation is essential both to the programmer and the user.

Documentation

There are two types of documentation: programmer's or technical documentation, and operational or user documentation. The technical documentation package should include: (1) A complete statement of the problem; (2) a description of the algorithms and data structures used; (3) a description of the program logic and copies of all the flowcharts; (4) a sequenced listing of all the program steps; (5) a description of the testing and verification procedures and results; and (6) operating instructions, including program structures, data structures, input formats, output formats, error messages, and any abnormal conditions that might occur.

User documentation is similar to technical documentation, but because users do not need a great deal of technical detail, documentation for their purposes should be very condensed. The problem statement, algorithms, and data structures should be given in only enough detail to explain what the program does and why. Flowcharts and program listings are usually omitted, as are testing results. The operating instructions, on the other hand, are essential to the user and should be included in their entirety. After all, the program is no good if the user does not know how to make it operate.

Maintenance: An Ongoing Affair

Inevitably, a program that was thought to be finished will produce a few bugs once it is operating. Indeed, it is impossible to anticipate every set of circumstances that might occur during execution and to debug the program accordingly in advance. It is during the life of the program that good documentation is needed to make program maintenance possible, if not always easy.

Maintenance is somewhat more complicated than ordinary debugging, because the errors being corrected are in a program that was believed to be in its final form.

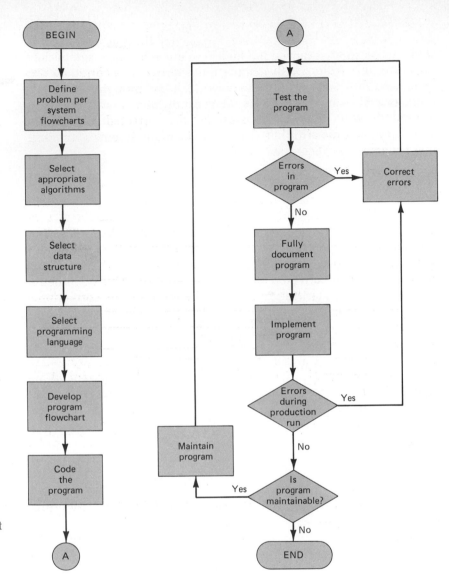

Figure 12-6 Flowchart summarizing steps in solving a problem by computer

First, the error should be documented by stating the symptoms and the conditions under which it occurred. In this way, any recurrence of the same error will not be a mystery to future users. Next, the decision as to how to correct the error has to be made. Since major program changes are difficult at this stage, the correction should not drastically affect other portions of the program if at all possible. Isolating a correction will be easier if the program has been modularized properly.

340

The correction must then be tested. The program with the necessary changes should be run with a duplicate of the master file data. It is unwise to test the correction by running it with the original data, because other errors might destroy the original. The corrected program should be tested under the conditions that brought the error to light, as well as under the original test conditions in which the error did not show up. This will ensure that the corrected program not only eliminates the error but also meets the requirements of the original program specifications.

When the program correction has been tested successfully, a history listing should be made of any instructions removed from the program or new instructions inserted. Only then should the main program file be changed. Any necessary changes should also be made in the algorithms, program structure, and flowcharts. The final documentation will then include a description of the error, its effects and conditions, and also the program statement, algorithms, and so on in both corrected and uncorrected form. This documentation will serve to alert future users to the error and its correction.

Maintenance is also required to update programs as the information requirements of the organization change. Programs may have to be modified to provide new types of output, to accommodate additional categories of input, to incorporate additional processing stages as new needs arise, and so on. As long as organizations change internally in response to various needs, program maintenance is required to be certain that data processing is directed to the goals of the organization.

Summary

There are three main steps in program development: planning, structuring, and writing.

The planning stage of a program's development begins by defining the problem. This definition requires communication between both programmer and user. Once the problem has been specified, algorithms to solve it can be selected. An algorithm is a series of logical steps, much like a recipe, that must be followed to solve a particular problem. Program libraries, exchange organizations, and other data processing groups are good sources of preexisting algorithms for frequently recurring problems. Naturally, good programmers do not want to reinvent the wheel. Of course, new algorithms must be devised for many situations.

Data file organization and program language selection are the next steps in program planning. These factors are determined by the computer hardware to be used, as well as by program requirements. The language itself may be a low-level assembly language or one of the many high-level problem-oriented languages for business, scientific, or technical applications.

The second stage of program development is structuring. There are three basic types of statements that can be combined to structure a program: sequential, conditional, and loop. In a sequential program, all statements are executed one right after the other in the order in which they occur. This method is uncomplicated but not often applicable to a complex program. The GOTO statement is used when necessary to break the sequence and send the computer to execute a statement somewhere else in the program. A second GOTO statement might then be used to bring the computer back to its place in the sequence.

The conditional or IFTHENELSE statement consists of a test condition and two different paths. If the test is true, the computer executes one set of steps; if it is false, the other set of steps is executed. These two paths merge at some point so that the rest of the program sequence continues, regardless of which path is taken.

The loop or DOWHILE statement directs the computer to repeat execution of a set of steps until a certain condition is met. A counting variable is usually used to keep track of how many times the loop has executed. Within the loop, there must be a step that modifies this counting variable; otherwise, the loop will execute indefinitely.

These three basic operations can be combined in various ways to accomplish what needs to be done in a program. One method of program design is the bottom-up approach, which involves designing the lowest levels of the program first. These pieces of the program are then combined into higher and higher levels until the entire program is designed.

Top-down structuring, on the other hand, begins by designing the overall program. The main program is then divided into successively smaller routines, with the details of the lowest-level routines added last. Closely related to this technique is the concept of modularization, which subdivides each routine into self-contained modules identified only by their function name, input, and output.

GOTO-less programming is another approach to programming that attempts to eliminate some confusion by keeping the program flow in a forward direction. The theory is that the number of errors in a program increases with the number of branches or GOTO statements; therefore, limiting the use of the GOTO statement should lead to a decrease in errors. This theory is still the subject of controversy, as many programmers think the GOTO statement has a legitimate place in programming.

The final stage of program preparation is the actual writing or coding. Each statement is expressed in the chosen program language.

Blocks of statements must be labeled, variable names chosen, and input and output formats finalized.

After coding is completed, the program must be tested, debugged, verified for accuracy and usefulness, and documented. These last steps provide information for the program's future operation and maintenance.

Program Preparation

Key Terms and Phrases

algorithm
assembly language
block
bottom-up programming
bottom-up testing
branching
conditional operation
debugging
high-level language

loop
low-level language
machine language
macroinstructions
modularization
sequential operation
top-down programming
top-down testing
verification

Sources of Additional Information

Hughes, Joan K., and Michtom, Jay I. *A Structured Approach to Programming.* Englewood Cliffs, N.J.: Prentice-Hall, 1977.
Mitchel, Joe. "Expanding the Small Business System." *Datamation,* no. 12 (1979):126–30.
Yohe, J. M. "An Overview of Programming Practices." *Computing Surveys,* no. 4 (1974):221–45.

Test Yourself

1. What is a computer program?
2. List the three essential steps in program preparation.
3. List the steps usually followed in planning a program.
4. Describe the three basic operations common to all programming.
5. Explain the difference between bottom-up and top-down programming.
6. List some advantages of modularization.
7. List some disadvantages of modularization.
8. What is the goal of GOTO-less programming, and how attainable is it?
9. What is the purpose of a program flowchart?
10. List some ways to plan ahead for the debugging step in program development.
11. List the steps used in testing a program.
12. List the essential part of technical documentation.

343

13. Explain the difference between technical and user documentation.
14. Explain why program maintenance is important and what it involves.
15. List some of the factors involved in choosing a programming language for a particular application.

13 Programming Languages

John Glueckstein

"From your résumé here, it's obvious you're fluent in COBOL, PL/I, and FORTRAN, but your English stinks."

APPLICATION
Ada to the Defense

Unlike human languages, which evolve haphazardly as the result of interaction between users, computer languages are typically created for a purpose. A group of users design a logically consistent language to articulate particular problems.

Careful planning has not prevented the great proliferation of specialized computer languages and variants of these languages. The situation has even been referred to by some as the "new tower of Babel." The three military services alone were using five specialized languages (some not officially standardized) as well as FORTRAN and COBOL. As a result, the Department of Defense (DOD) decided to take action. At least once, DOD had stepped into the muddle of computer languages to assist at the birth of the business-oriented language COBOL. Now, DOD has decreed that a common language be invented to enhance communication between programmers.

In a typically thorough manner, DOD polled various computer applications areas regarding the language features they required. It was found that identical requirements for a wide range of program applications would make it possible to define one language to serve almost all areas.

A committee was created to specify the characteristics of the new language. Twenty-three existing languages, including several used for similar purposes in other nations, were analyzed to see if any met the specifications fully enough to serve as a common language; none did. Committee members did decide, though, that a few existing languages might provide a foundation for the new language, and ultimately Pascal became the base language.

A "first-cut" version of the language, appropriately entitled "Strawman," was set up to initiate comment and criticism. Strawman was circulated to military departments, other government agencies, the academic community, and a number of foreign technical computer experts. Their suggestions were incorporated into a revised set of specifications titled "Woodenman." Additional review stages were named "Tinman" and "Ironman." The final set of requirements, growing ever stronger, was embodied in "Steelman." These requirements were the basis of a four-way competition between subcontractors. Four years after the idea for a new language began to gleam in DOD's eye, a winning design was selected.

The new language is named Ada, to honor Ada Augusta, Countess of Lovelace, who assisted Babbage and is now acknowledged as the world's first programmer. The selection and approval process included contacting the descendants of Lady Lovelace in England for permission to use her name.

Ada's development continues and the Army is expected to be the first of the armed services to implement it. The Navy and the Air Force are more reluctant to abandon their present programming languages. But DOD expects Ada to fulfill their expectations, not only in military but also in a wide range of other high-pressure, real-time applications.

Source: Robert L. Glass, "From Pascal to Pebbleman . . . and Beyond," *Datamation*, no. 8 (1979):146–49.

A S WE HAVE SEEN, computers accomplish their tasks as instructed by programs. Computers understand instructions expressed in machine language, which consists of "binary" instructions specifying that this element be "0," the next a "1," the next a "1," and so forth. The actual coding for these instructions varies from machine to machine, depending on the particular way in which the internal circuitry of the machine is arranged. Coding helps humans translate instructions into machine language.

The following set of instructions might be a machine language coding that directs the computer to add two numbers together. The first group of three digits of each line represents an instruction; the second grouping of three digits refers to the storage location address in main memory:

```
001 200
002 201
003 202
```

The operations necessary to perform the "addition" function must be explicitly detailed in the numbered codes that the machine understands. Instruction 001 directs the computer to place the contents of address 200 into the accumulator. Instruction 002 indicates that the contents of address 201 are to be added to the accumulator contents. Finally, instruction 003 directs that the contents of the accumulator be stored in location 202.

Machine language is not particularly useful for programming. One step removed are "assembly" or low-level languages. The instructions are coded in symbols that are somewhat easier for programmers to use than machine language. Assembly language coding is translated by an assembler, or translation program, into machine language within the computer.

Assembly language is not too different from machine language: one instruction in assembly language generally translates directly into one instruction in machine language. The addition of two numbers could be coded in assembly language in this way:

```
LDA  A    (Put the contents of A into the accumulator.)
ADD  B    (Add the contents of B to A in the accumulator.)
STA  C    (Store the results in C.)
```

Location 200 is now symbolically called "A," 201 is "B," and 202 is "C." The instructions themselves are given in "shorthand" symbols: LDA for "load accumulator," ADD for "add," and STA for "store the contents of the accumulator." Assembly language programming, which still requires a detailed knowledge of how computers work, is used to direct the most efficient operation of computer hardware.

Compiler or high-level languages are designed for humans. These various languages are written to be useful for the solutions of particular kinds of problems, and their vocabularies may be specifically tailored to those problems. A single instruction in a high-level language corresponds to a whole sequence of machine language instructions. For this reason, translation to machine code is fairly complex. The translation or compiler programs have been previously written by professional programmers and are contained within the computer's permanent library of programs.

Instructions in a high-level language are usually "Englishlike" and use common mathematical expressions, and the syntax of the language is easily understood. Therefore, coding in a compiler language is much easier than in assembly or machine language. The addition of two variables might now simply be stated:

$$C = A + B$$

The computer has been programmed to understand the concept of "addition" and knows what detailed operations must be executed. Correspondingly, that information is lost or hidden from the user, and there may be a reduction in the efficiency (speed) with which a program is run. However, these are not usually limitations for the general computer user.

Compiler Languages

Various computer languages have been developed to satisfy specific purposes. Programming languages are sometimes classified as "interactive" or "noninteractive." (See table 13-1.) *Interactive languages* allow programmers and users to interact directly with the computer while the program is being generated or executed. Interactions, such as inputting new data or changing program instructions, usually take place via a data terminal.

Table 13-1 Classification of Programming Languages

Interactive Languages	Noninteractive Languages
BASIC	COBOL
APL	FORTRAN
Pascal	PL/I
Ada	ALGOL

(Marc Anderson)

BASIC, Pascal, and APL are interactive programming languages.

The immediate feedback provided by interactive languages makes them ideal for the novice user who can systematically learn to build up complicated programs from simple functions. Beginners profit from the prompt detailed error messages. The disadvantage is that program execution times are tremendously increased. Examples of interactive languages are BASIC, APL, and Pascal.

(Marc Anderson)

COBOL and FORTRAN are among the most frequently used noninteractive languages.

Noninteractive languages are used for programs designed to be executed by the computer, generally without interruption by the programmer. Programs in noninteractive languages tend to be more complex, and longer computation times may be required. Noninteractive languages are preferred when only the final answer and/or report is desired; these languages include COBOL, FORTRAN, PL/I, RPG, and ALGOL.

Interactive Languages

BASIC

BASIC is an acronym for *B*eginners' *A*ll-purpose *S*ymbolic *I*nstruction *C*ode. It was developed at Dartmouth College by Professors J. G. Kemeny and T. E. Kurtz under a grant from the National Science Foundation and extended by General Electric. BASIC was designed as an interactive, general-purpose language with special concern for the needs of the novice user.

BASIC uses simple English words in its instructions and, wherever possible, familiar math symbols, such as + and − for addition and subtraction. It is therefore a language that is easy to learn and remember. Beginners can start programming very quickly in BASIC to solve simple problems.

The sample programs shown below have certain features in common that are characteristic of the earlier established programming languages. Each instruction is preceded by an identifying number; the sequence of increasing numbers usually corresponds to the sequence in which instructions are to be executed. An END statement is required to indicate that the set of program instructions is complete. (In some more recently developed languages or variants of the existing languages, instruction identifying numbers are not required; the translation program will itself be responsible for maintaining the instruction order.)

BASIC can be used in a simple desk calculator mode:

```
100 PRINT 5 + 4 + 3 − 2
110 END
```

If the above instructions were typed into the terminal, BASIC would return the number "10."

A slightly more sophisticated BASIC program, to compute the sum of two numbers, A and B, looks like this:

```
100 INPUT A,B          (Read A and B from the termi-
                        nal.)
110 PRINT "A + B = ", A + B (Compute A + B and print its
                        value.)
120 END
```

This program would request two numbers, A and B, to be typed into the terminal and would then print "A + B = __" (the dash indicates the actual numerical value of A + B).

A BASIC program to add a series of three sets of two numbers might look like this:

```
 90 FOR I = 1 TO 3
100 INPUT A,B
110 PRINT "A + B = ", A + B
115 NEXT I
120 END
```

The program will go through its sequence of steps three times (for I = 1, 2, and 3), each time requesting different values of A and B.

BASIC programs can very rapidly become more complicated. Although designed to be an interactive language, it can also be operated noninteractively. Extended BASIC has capabilities that make it a powerful general programming language.

APL

APL is an acronym for *A Programming Language*, designed by K. E. Iverson while at Harvard University in the early 1960s. APL was intended to be a language that could describe procedures in information processing. The language structure encourages efficient organization of program instructions into "procedures" or "functions." Like BASIC, APL may also be used in the desk calculator mode: typing "13.5 + 3.2" into the terminal will yield the answer "16.7."

While APL can be utilized quite rapidly by the beginner to solve simple problems, its real power lies in its emphasis on arrays of numbers and array manipulation. An *array* is a grouping together of numbers that have been assigned a common variable name. For instance, the array A could include the numbers (3, 4, 6). The individual numbers would be designated A(1), A(2), and A(3).

APL is more symbolic than BASIC, and a sequence of commands in an APL program is more often composed of mathematical symbols rather than English word commands. However, the symbols it uses are not all commonly used symbols, and the coding is not, as it is in

BASIC, a simple variant of English language commands. For example, the instruction "t/A" means "total the elements in array A." The special symbols required by APL do not appear on the standard terminal keyboard. An expanded keyboard including both standard and special APL symbols, usually available as an option, is required when programming in this language.

Most other languages perform the addition of two arrays of numbers, A = (3, 4, 6) and B = (2, 1, 3), by a sequence of instructions like the following:

DO 6 I = 1,3
6 C(I) = A(I) + B(I)
to form the array C = (5, 5, 9)

The APL instruction would simply be:

A + B

and the program would return the answer:

5 5 9

APL "knows" that the addition operation (+) means to add the first number in array A to the first in array B, the second in A to the second in B, and so on.

A *matrix* is a two-dimensional array of numbers ordered in horizontal rows and vertical columns:

$$M = \begin{pmatrix} 1 & 2 & 3 & 4 \\ 5 & 6 & 7 & 8 \\ 2 & 4 & 6 & 8 \end{pmatrix}$$

Many of the fundamental operations in APL are complex matrix operations that require several program steps in other languages. For example, "taking the transpose" of a matrix means interchanging the rows and the columns:

$$\text{the transpose of } \begin{pmatrix} 1 & 2 & 3 & 4 \\ 5 & 6 & 7 & 8 \\ 2 & 4 & 6 & 8 \end{pmatrix} \text{ is } \begin{pmatrix} 1 & 5 & 2 \\ 2 & 6 & 4 \\ 3 & 7 & 6 \\ 4 & 8 & 8 \end{pmatrix}$$

In APL this fairly complicated procedure can be instructed by a single symbol: M. This and other similarly efficient symbol instructions are the reasons why APL is such a compact and powerful language.

Pascal was designed in 1968 by Niklaus Wirth of the Federal Institute of Technology (ETH) in Zurich, Switzerland, and it has been used increasingly ever since. Its name honors the French mathematician and philosopher Blaise Pascal, who at the age of 19 invented the first of the many "arithmetic machines" (see chapter 2). The language was designed to be reliably and efficiently implemented on the available computers and to be suitable for teaching computer programming and for writing systems software.

The proper use of Pascal reinforces structured programming; it requires, for example, the clear definition of all variables and constants at the beginning of the program. Efficient program design is, in a sense, built into the writing of a Pascal program. The result is programs that are easier to code, debug, and maintain.

Like BASIC, Pascal uses familiar mathematical symbols and English-like commands, and can be easily learned and implemented. Let us consider again the problem of adding two integers, A and B. The Pascal program would appear as:

```
VAR A,B :INTEGER    (A statement that the variables A and B are
                     integer numbers.)
READ(A,B)           (Read the values of A and B.)
C = A + B           (Set C equal to the sum of A and B.)
WRITELN (C)         (Write the value of C.)
```

In Pascal, as in BASIC and APL, the format of the output does not have to be specified. (In noninteractive languages, or for more complex programs, it is necessary to specify output formats.) However, using Pascal, the variables A and B did have to be designated as integers before the program could be executed. (Other options for the variables A and B are REAL and COMPLEX.) This kind of specification may seem unnecessary and inefficient for a short and simple program like the one above. However, in more complex programs, it is more efficient for the programmer to be forced to organize program commands and variables before entering the maze of a complex sequence of calculations.

As a last example of Pascal programming, let us consider the problem of adding three sets of two integers:

```
VAR A,B :INTEGER
LABEL 1
1:READ(A,B)
C = A + B
WRITELN(C)
FOR 1:=1 TO 3 DO 1
```

The sequence of reading in the two variables, A and B, totaling them to form C, and printing out the value of C, is performed three times. Even in this simple program, we can see how Pascal prevents errors. Having to make a LABEL identification beforehand of all numbered instructions lessens the possibility that, as the program grows larger and more complex, two separate instructions might be tagged with the same identifying number. With only a few additions in program coding, the capabilities of a simple program have been greatly increased. Even a single program can be organized and included as part of a more complex program without substantial recoding.

Noninteractive Languages

COBOL

COBOL stands for *CO*mmon *B*usiness-*O*riented *L*anguage. Until the advent of COBOL, no programming language existed that specifically addressed the requirements of business data processing and could be used on a variety of different computers. The federal government, understandably one of the largest users of data processing equipment, pressed for the creation of a standardized, business-oriented programming language. In 1959, at the insistence of the Department of Defense, a committee was formed for the express purpose of creating such a language. The committee was composed of computer users in both government and industry.

The initial specifications were presented in 1960 by the *CO*nfer-

(Joseph L. Sardinas, Jr.)

Partial listing of a COBOL program. This particular program is featured in the Appendix to this book. Display of the program on the CRT enables the programmer to make changes directly as needed, without having to generate paper output.

```
LHH
      FILE SECTION.
      FD PRINT-FILE
            LABEL RECORDS ARE OMITTED
            DATA RECORD IS PRINT-LINE.
      01 PRINT-LINE.
            02 FILLER            PIC X.
            02 DATA-LINE         PIC X(132).
      WORKING-STORAGE SECTION.
      77 PRESENT-YEAR            PIC 9999, VALUE 1981.
      77 PRINCIPAL               PIC S9(13)V99,  VALUE 24.00.
      77 YEARLY-INTEREST         PIC S9(11)V99.
      77 STARTING-YEAR           PIC S9(4),  VALUE 1627.
      01 ANSWER-LINE.
            02 FILLER            PIC X(25).
            02 FILLER            PIC X(23),
                                 VALUE "BALANCE TO DATE EQUALS".
            02 EDITED-PRINCIPAL  PIC $,$$$,$$$,$$$,$$9.99.
            02 FILLER            PIC X, VALUE ".".


      PROCEDURE DIVISION.
      A0010-BEGIN.
            -
```

ence on *DA*ta *SY*stems Language (CODASYL). Three requirements had to be met: (1) Provide a standardized input format that was usable by all computers; (2) provide a source program that was easily understood; and (3) include terminology for commercial applications. COBOL was to be a machine-independent language that used a syntax closely resembling that of English and avoided the use of special symbols as much as possible. The language was to be tailored to the demands of commercial data processing.

Commercial data processing involves large volumes of data. The amount of actual computations performed on each data element is relatively limited, but the amount of information generated, and subsequently the output, is quite large. For example, COBOL might be used in assembling statistical information about the employees of a particular company. The "data file" would be a list of all the employees of that company. Each file entry or data element would include the employee's name, address, age, profession, length of employment with the company, and salary. The computer could be programmed to deliver tables of employee distribution according to age, sex, and profession. Furthermore, correlations may be made between various factors such as age, length of employment, and rate of pay. While the volume of information gained from the program is quite large, no detailed mathematical computations have been made on the data itself. Programs that perform this type of data processing and also catalogue inventory, personnel, or clients are expected to enjoy repeated use over a long period of time. It is important that these programs be well documented so that they may be easily understood by each new generation of users.

The structure of a COBOL program requires that extensive documentation be incorporated into the text of the program itself. Every COBOL program must specify program identification, the particular peripheral hardware to be used, and the names of all files of data used in the program.

Adding two variables together in COBOL might be coded as:

COMPUTE C = A + B.   (The period [.] is necessary.)

It is not unusual to use more descriptive names for the variables in a COBOL program:

COMPUTE GROSS-PAY = BASE-PAY + OVER-TIME-PAY.

Such descriptive names make COBOL especially accessible to users in a business environment. Most of the shortcomings of COBOL occur in use by personnel who do not adequately understand the language.

FORTRAN

FORTRAN, the shortened form for *FOR*mula *TRAN*slation, was originally developed in 1957 by IBM for the 704 computer. The development of FORTRAN represented an experiment in the more efficient compilation of algebraic formulas. Today, it is the most widely used programming language for scientific and mathematical computations. The introduction of FORTRAN is said to have increased tenfold the number of scientists and engineers using digital computers. The current version of FORTRAN is FORTRAN IV.

The syntax of FORTRAN is Englishlike and easily understood. For simple computations, the program structure is very much like that of BASIC or Pascal. The following program will add two variables, A and B.

```
     READ 14, A, B          (Read in the values of A and B,
  14 FORMAT (F6.3,F6.3)      according to the format specified.)
     C = A + B               (Add A and B to obtain variable C.)
     PRINT 16, C             (Print out the value of C,
  16 FORMAT (F6.3)           according to the format specified.)
     END
```

Any input or output instruction in FORTRAN must be formatted. The format above specified as F6.3 reserves a field for the number that has six digits including the decimal point, with three digits after the decimal point.

Until COBOL was developed, FORTRAN was used for many business data applications. COBOL was designed to perform simple computations on a given body of extensive data. FORTRAN can perform complex calculations, such as those required to calculate the orbit of a satellite. A large number of factors are involved, such as the satellite shape and mass, its initial orbital velocity, and the frictional resistance it will encounter. These factors must be incorporated into a number of complex calculations, but the data output is meager compared with the amount of computation required. These computations usually employ standard mathematical formulas that are already coded and exist as part of an extensive FORTRAN scientific library.

PL/I

PL/I stands for Programming Language (I). (Note that the Roman numeral I is always used.) PL/I was developed in the mid-1960s jointly by IBM and the representatives of two customer groups, SHARE, a scientific users' organization, and GUIDE, its commercial counterpart. The objective of the committee was to synthesize into one language the best features of the many existing languages, incorporating the most recent advances in theoretical language design.

The preceding discussion has distinguished between the needs of business and scientific programming. However, the increasing accessibility of computers has led to an increased sophistication in computer usage, and has made apparent the large region of overlap between scientific and business applications. Familiarity with computer processing techniques and mathematical manipulations has encouraged the use of more sophisticated accounting procedures in industry and business. Increased computer use in the biological and social sciences has demonstrated the need for some business data processing features, especially the ability to perform relatively simple calculations on large bodies of data with well-documented print-outs. The convergence of scientific and business requirements has been encouraged by technological developments in computer hardware. By using more versatile logic circuitry to handle a wider variety of data, a single machine may provide a wider variety of data processing capabilities with equal efficiency.

PL/I was developed to meet the common needs of the business and scientific programming communities. It is a modular language: the user can successfully write programs knowing only a portion, or "module," of the total language. This means as well that the programmer who is interested in only one aspect of the language (for instance, the nonnumeric data handling capability that can be called the "businesslike" aspect of the language) may operate as if other features of the language did not exist.

The computational features of the language encourage structured programming in much the same way as Pascal does. The feature of PL/I that makes it a powerful language for commercial applications programming is its use of "structures," or categories, of data. For example, if a stockroom contains erasers, pencils, nuts, and bolts, the stock can be classified by arranging it in a hierarchy. A number is assigned to each level of the hierarchy:

```
1 SUPPLIES
  2 OFFICE
    3 ERASERS
    3 PENCILS
  2 HARDWARE
    3 NUTS
    3 BOLTS
```

There are two categories of supplies, office and hardware. There are two categories of office supplies, erasers and pencils. Nuts and bolts compose the hardware. Each grouping is a structure.

The advantage of using structures is that entire groups of input and output data can be referred to by one structure name, SUPPLIES, rather than reading in ERASERS, PENCILS, NUTS, and BOLTS separately. In FORTRAN, these items would have to be read in individually. Programming and executing efficiency are enhanced by the use of structures. As a result, PL/I is compatible with structured programming, modularization, and top-down design.

ALGOL

ALGOL is the acronym for *ALGO*rithmic Language. It is an elegant, highly logical language, similar in concept to APL. ALGOL was devised by an international committee as a language that would easily express algorithms. The first version was published in 1958; the current version is referred to as ALGOL 60. The language has a strong appeal for mathematicians, who can describe the steps of a computation in a reasonable, readable way that is suitable for instructing a computer.

Two versions of ALGOL have been defined. "Reference ALGOL" is the defining language. Some of the basic characters of Reference ALGOL are not available on certain keypunches or other input devices. This situation generates "Hardware ALGOL," a condensed version of Reference ALGOL, adapted to the number of characters available on input equipment.

The following illustrates the way ALGOL might be used to program the addition of two variables, A and B:

```
begin
real A,B,C
A: = read; B: = read;
C: = A + B;
output (C);
end
```

The "begin" and "end" statements must appear at the start and finish of each program, respectively. The term *real* sets aside space in the computer for the variables A, B, and C (if A, B, and C were integers, we would use the statement "integer A,B,C"). The program reads the first data value and assigns it to variable A, reads the second data value and assigns it to variable B. The sum of A and B is assigned to variable C, which is finally printed out. Each executed statement ends in a semicolon (;). The coding is not quite as simple to read as FORTRAN or other more Englishlike languages. The advantage of ALGOL is its ability to express many program steps compactly. A single program line instructs the computer to perform the same calculation as the six program lines above:

begin *output* (*read* + *read*);
end

"Talking" to Computers

In the languages of human beings, the same idea may be expressed in a multitude of ways. As we have just seen, the same is true of programming languages. The ultimate task performed by the computer may be the same, but the instructions directing it to do that task are phrased differently.

Consider the simple operation of adding the value of variable A to the value of variable B and designating the result as variable C. The descriptive FORTRAN statement would appear as:

C = A + B

while in PL/I, the same statement would be expressed as:

C = A + B;

The only noticeable difference between the two statements is the presence of the semicolon (;) after the B in the PL/I statement. The same instruction in COBOL, however, looks very different:

ADD A,B GIVING C.

Given these instructions, computers with compilers for FORTRAN, PL/I, and COBOL, respectively, would perform the same operations and, using the same data, come up with the same results.

The Need for Standardization

The different high-level languages may direct the same operations (adding together two variables, for example) and yet express those ideas quite differently. One dialect of a human language may be unintelligible to the speaker of another dialect; the analogous situation exists for computer languages. Problems of communication exist even between different versions or dialects of the same programming language.

The different ways of expressing the same idea in a high-level language are usually developed by the hardware/software vendors. A COBOL program written for a computer manufactured by company ABC might not run on a computer manufactured by company XYZ. One user may need a detailed vocabulary to describe a certain set of frequently used operations, while another user has no need of those operations and requires a totally different processing sequence. One user may need to see the output displayed on a screen and must therefore have the relevant instructions incorporated into the programming language, while others need reams of paper output that also must be appropriately programmed.

ANSI. To prevent the breakdown of communication between users of a common programming language, the American National Standards Institute (ANSI) has attempted to standardize certain computer languages. ANSI is the coordinating body for a federation consisting of some 900 companies and 200 trade, technical, professional, labor, and consumer organizations, all of which require standards of various kinds. (ANSI is concerned with standards affecting construction materials, electronic components, photographic and medical equipment, and much more, in addition to programming languages and other computer-related factors.)

ANSI does not itself develop standards, but encourages competent organizations to do so. It helps identify which standards are required and establishes timetables for their completion. It further ensures that the standards will achieve general recognition and acceptance for use. Finally, it provides for the effective representation of U.S. interests in international standardization.

How Programmers Choose a Language

To a great extent, the decision regarding the primary programming language to be used in a computer environment is made when the computer is purchased. Ideally, this is the time when the types of problem solving that will be used should be evaluated. The user and the computer vendor together determine the hardware and software capabilities that will be required for the user's predicted applications.

A market research organization might need machines and programs able to perform long, large, complex mathematical computations. FORTRAN might be chosen as the primary language, and limited hardware would be supplemented with an extensive library of FORTRAN programs. A bank, which requires input and output of quantities of data, would be likely to purchase a great deal of hardware to perform those functions and choose COBOL as its preferred programming language.

Programmers are thus subject to the environment in which they operate, and are influenced by the nature of the problems to be solved. In some situations, programmers may prefer an interactive language, which allows program instructions to be changed more easily.

Programmers may not always want or be able to use the higher-level symbolic languages. Or they may not be able to use the same languages for all parts of a program. If a particular function or operation does not exist in the vocabulary of the language chosen, it will have to be written in. Sometimes this can be done only by using the basic vocabulary understood by the machine itself.

There probably will never be a truly universal programming language. Realistically, though, it should be possible to design a language specific enough to deal effectively with a limited range of problems, yet general enough to be understood by a group of programmers having widely differing interests. One solution may be the development of Ada as a general-purpose language that will meet the needs of a large range of applications.

Programmers have strong personal preferences for working with particular languages, and may be unwilling to abandon those languages. An international human language, Esperanto, has been developed but is not widely used. However, English has evolved naturally as the most commonly used language in many types of international interchanges, particularly in scientific research. Non-English-speaking scientists are encouraged to become bilingual in English and their native language, or at least to have some knowledge of written, technical English. Perhaps a similar situation will evolve for computer languages, with one preferred language emerging. Certainly, as the use of computers becomes more widespread, the "general" computer user will become more sophisticated and perhaps more comfortable working with several languages.

Summary

Computers understand machine language, which expresses operations in binary (on-off) form. Programming languages were devised to enable humans to communicate with computers.

There are two main categories of programming languages: (1) assembly or low-level languages, which are one step removed from machine language, and (2) compiler or high-level languages, which are closer to the vernacular. High-level languages are generally used in writing computer programs.

Some programming languages are *interactive*, allowing the user to get immediate and ongoing responses from the computer. Interactive languages are most likely to be used in a real-time environment and with terminals. BASIC, APL, and Pascal are important interactive languages.

Noninteractive programming languages are suitable for programs that are to be executed by the computer in their entirety, without intervention by a human operator. COBOL, FORTRAN, PL/I, and ALGOL are major noninteractive languages.

BASIC (*B*eginners *A*ll-purpose *S*ymbolic *I*nstruction *C*ode) is particularly suited to the needs of the novice user. It is a general-purpose language, easy to learn and use, with few syntax rules. BASIC uses familiar English terms and arithmetic symbols, and is interactive and powerful.

APL (*A P*rogramming *L*anguage) is tailored to the needs of information processing. It is concise, consistent, and powerful, and can be learned easily. APL lends itself to use in units or modules.

Pascal is named for the French philosopher/mathematician Blaise Pascal. It is particularly suited to structured program design, executes rapidly, and is being used increasingly with mini- and microcomputers.

COBOL (*CO*mmon *B*usiness-*O*riented *L*anguage) was designed especially for business applications. It is particularly well suited for processing large files with a minimum of calculations and for generating substantial amounts of paper output. It can be compiled on many different kinds of computers, and is said to be *machine independent* for this reason.

FORTRAN (*FOR*mula *TRAN*slator) was developed for scientific and mathematical applications in which a great deal of calculation must be done on relatively little data. However, before COBOL was available, the mathematical precision of FORTRAN lent itself to business applications as well.

PL/I (Programming Language/I) is a powerful composite language, combining aspects of a number of other programming languages and adding new capabilities of its own. Its strong points include the capability of being modularized and therefore its use in top-down programming.

ALGOL (*ALGO*rithmic *L*anguage) is particularly useful to mathematicians who must deal with complicated steps in calculations.

There are many more languages than those mentioned here. To bring some measure of standardization to this field, the American National Standards Institute (ANSI) promotes communication between groups in the computer and related industries and coordinates the development of new languages and procedures.

The language chosen for a program is often determined when the computer hardware is acquired. Programmers tend to choose the languages with which they are most familiar. Ideally, the language most suited to an organization's needs or a particular type of application should be chosen.

Key Terms and Phrases

ALGOL
American National Standards
 Institute (ANSI)
APL
array
BASIC
COBOL

FORTRAN
interactive languages
matrix
noninteractive languages
Pascal
PL/I

Sources of Additional Information

Anderson, Decima M. *Computer Programming: Fortran IV*. New York: Appleton-Century-Crofts, 1966.
Ehrman, John R. "The New Tower of Babel." *Datamation*, no. 3(1980):156–60.
Fletcher, Dennis; Glass, Robert L.; Shillington, Keith; and Conrad, Marvin. "Pascal Power." *Datamation*, no. 8 (1979):142–56.
Sanderson, Peter C. *Computer Languages: A Practical Guide to the Chief Programming Languages*. London: Newnes-Butterworth, 1970.

Test Yourself

1. Explain the difference(s) between a high-level language and an assembly language.
2. How is an assembly language instruction converted into machine language coding? Why is this necessary?
3. What happens when a single coded instruction in a high-level language is converted by a compiler?
4. How do interactive and noninteractive languages differ?
5. What is the key difference between instructions in APL and BASIC? How does this reflect the purpose of each language?
6. Why is Pascal considered to be the "language of the '80s"?
7. What is the impact of a FORMAT statement in the FORTRAN language?
8. Why was PL/I developed? Why was COBOL developed?
9. What is the primary advantage of ALGOL?
10. What is the purpose of the American National Standards Institute (ANSI) with respect to programming languages?
11. Name some limitations that a programmer might face in choosing a computer language to solve a given problem.

Unit IV
Data Processing Management

14 Managing the Data Processing Department

Nick Hobart, Datamation

". . . and if any of you have a problem, please remember that my input keyboard is always open."

APPLICATION

Information—The Path to the Top

In the business community, information is power. It is the key to productivity and thus to the accomplishment of the goals of the business organization. This puts information managers in a strategic position, since they are responsible for gathering, analyzing, organizing, and communicating data—the facts necessary for the conduct of business.

In May 1980, these points were emphasized in the keynote address heard at the National Information Conference and Exposition in Washington, D.C. "I see information becoming management's prime source for productivity," pronounced James J. Crenner, chairman of Dun & Bradstreet. Urging information managers to become more involved in the overall management of their companies, he continued: "The main thing is simply to get aboard, get involved. Be more valuable to your chief executive than your job description would indicate you should be.

"It behooves every person who looks at or touches information to get on the general management team," Crenner stated, ". . . to suggest to all levels of general management those things which could open doors to new products and services, those things which could streamline and speed the way to increased productivity."

The openings will be there, because general management usually does not understand computerization thoroughly enough to get along without information managers. Of course, information managers must be alert to the implications of their product—processed data—for the company as a whole. They will have ample opportunity to demonstrate that their expertise in handling the organization and communication of information is indispensable.

The rewards for information managers who take a broader view should come in a very short time, the Dun & Bradstreet executive forecast, as top management realizes that "information is indeed the key to productivity and bottom-line progress within business. . . ." The contribution made by data managers will become increasingly visible. No longer will production, marketing, and finance positions be the only tracks to top-level promotions. Information management, "an area of business which is undergoing a nuclear explosion," is going to be the jumping-off point for chief executives in the business organization of tomorrow.

Source: Jake Kirchner, "Managers Urged to Aim for Top," *Computerworld*, June 2, 1980, pp. 1, 6.

THE SCOPE of information handling has changed rapidly in the last two decades. New problems of increasing complexity have brought forth new technologies to solve them. All this progress has in turn affected the way in which the data processing department of an organization functions; today's trend toward more organized and better structured management is an answer to these needs.

In the past, isolated data items were gathered and used by computer operating personnel, passed on to various levels of management, and finally ended up in the accounting and financial departments. It was here that data processing became somewhat specialized, although it was still only a branch of the accounting department. As the use of electronic equipment expanded the data processing function, it became an activity in its own right, serving all levels and departments of the business organization. But usually the responsibility for data processing remained with the accounting or other operating departments. And these departments, because of their own focus, were unable to take a broad view of the place the information system had within the organization. Under these circumstances, information management was somewhat haphazard.

As the trend toward specialization and centralization increases, several tendencies are changing the structure of the data processing department. These include the consolidation of files into larger and larger data bases and the development of management information systems to handle them.

Managers of data processing departments must keep their departments up to date with new technical developments and newly emerging standards. They must also assign responsibilities to staff members in such a way as to foster creativity as well as technical skills. And they must manage effectively and efficiently on a day-to-day basis, coordinating data activities with the needs and goals of the organization.

Managers supervise both the work of their departments, in this case the data processing activities, and the people in their depart-

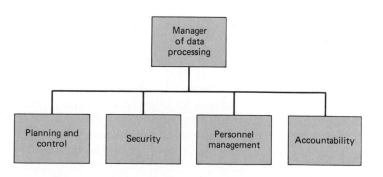

Figure 14-1 Responsibilities of the data processing manager

369

ments. There are four major aspects of data department management: (1) organization, (2) management planning and control, (3) accountability, and (4) security. (See figure 14-1.) With modern data bases that may contain confidential information, and with the increased reliance on the data center and its equipment, security has become quite important; this aspect will be discussed in chapter 15. Our discussion in this chapter will concentrate on the other functions.

Managing Personnel: Organization

The organization of a data processing department is concerned with the allocation of human resources. Human resources are people— people who serve as computer operators, programmers, systems analysts, and technicians. Organization of the department depends on three elements: (1) mission statement, (2) department structure, and (3) personnel management.

The Mission Statement: Goals

The *mission statement* defines both the goals of the data processing department as a whole and the role it plays as part of a larger business organization. Just as in any group endeavor, the data processing activities require goal congruence; that is, everyone in the department should be working toward the same end. A clearly defined and documented mission statement, approved by higher management, lets both the data processing personnel and the users in other departments know what is expected of them. Of course, no one mission statement is final. Because an organization and its goals are constantly changing as needs and situations change, the mission statement must be revised. It should be reviewed and updated periodically to reflect any changes in the data processing department's responsibilities.

Department Structure and Location

The department structure is the chain of command. Usually it is documented in the form of an organization chart. The organization chart diagrams the limits of authority, outlines responsibilities, and indicates reporting relationships within the department. The structure of the data processing department can be regarded from two different aspects. There is, first, its location within the structure of the larger organization. Second, there is the internal structure within the department itself. Because the services provided by the data processing department are vital to all levels of most organizations, both aspects are equally important.

Location within the organization. A data processing department can be positioned in one of three ways within the organization it serves. First, it can be linked to the larger organizational unit that contains its primary user. For example, if accounting is the most important customer, then data processing personnel would report to the Finance Department, of which accounting is a part. This alternative, sometimes known as *operational location,* gives each major group its own independent data processing activities; other groups with only minimal data processing requirements may purchase services from one of these independent data processing departments or from outside as needed. This allows computer time to be "dedicated" or reserved for certain priority activities. (See figure 14-2.)

Figure 14-2 Organization chart of operational location—data processing departments located next to the organizational units they serve

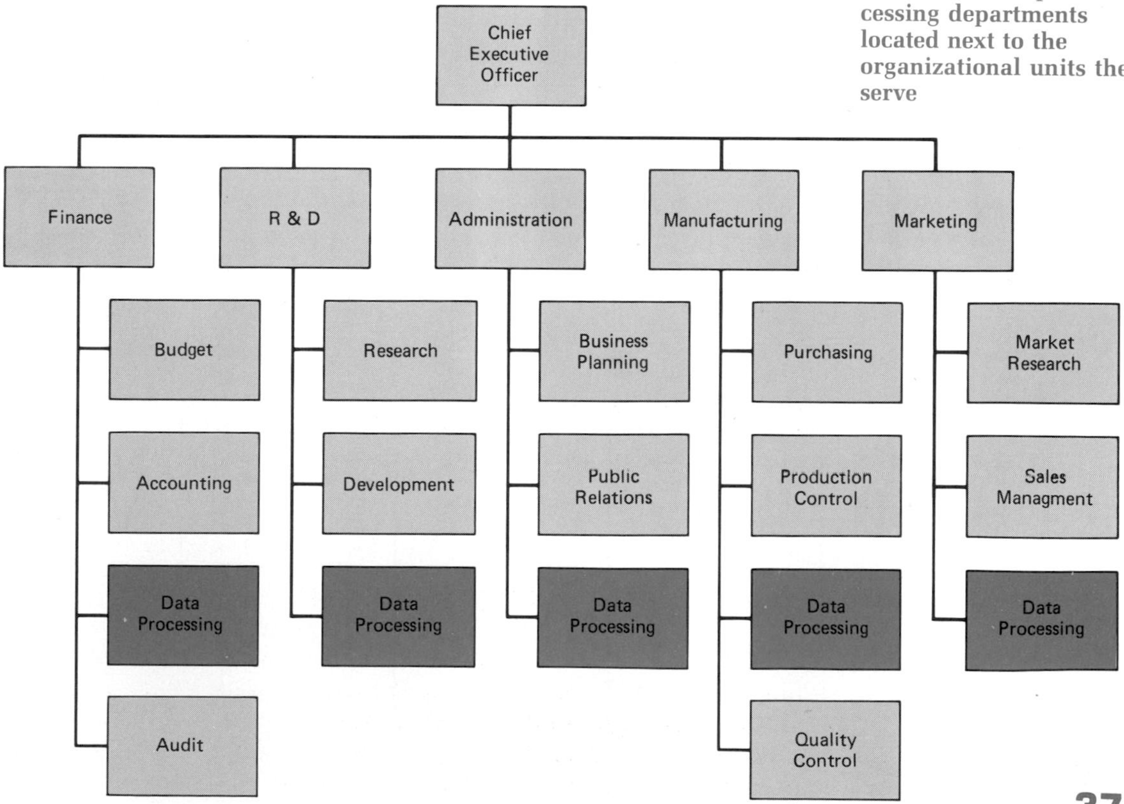

371

This decentralized approach is now best suited to larger organizations, where there is little sharing of data bases. Where it exists, it is difficult to integrate data processing functions or to standardize corporate policies relating to data processing. Another disadvantage is that corporate control of data processing applications is hindered, since the data processing department is within a particular operational unit. In the future, however, as distributed data processing using distributed data bases becomes more widespread, decentralization will be more practical, and more companies of every size will be organized in that way.

A second possible structure locates data processing activities within an existing service group that is separate from the operational units it serves. In this case, data processing might be a part of Administration, equal to such other departments as Planning or Public Relations. (See figure 14-3.) Control of the data processing operations and equipment belongs totally to this central department, and user departments are billed for costs on a per-job basis or by division of annual costs according to usage.

This centralized approach is best suited to small or medium-sized organizations, or to a large organization where there is a great amount of data-base sharing between departments. It allows better information system planning and integration, and also promotes full

Figure 14-3 Organization chart of centralized location—the data processing department as part of a central service group

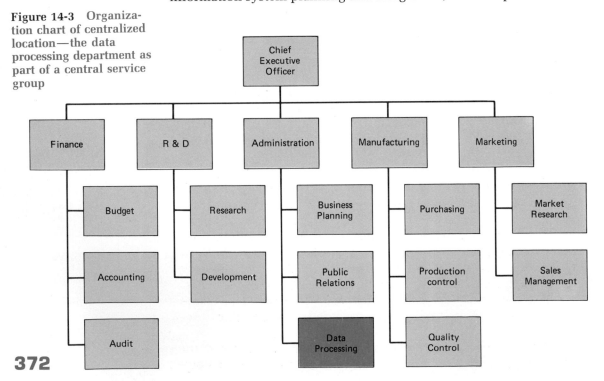

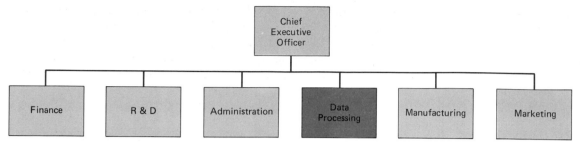

Chief Executive Officer

Finance | R & D | Administration | Data Processing | Manufacturing | Marketing

Figure 14-4 Organization chart of independent location—the data processing department as a self-contained unit reporting at the same level as other operating units

utilization of the central computer system. To be successful, however, the centralized data processing staff must be aware of the needs of its users. This is more difficult in large organizations. Also, priorities must be carefully established among users to allow optimum use of computer time. Increasing the amount of data processing equipment and the size of the staff to handle peak demand is an expensive solution to priority problems.

One solution to centralization difficulties is to divide the data processing responsibilities between a central headquarters and several regional offices. Data processing operations are standardized, but with leeway for the solution of problems unique to a particular location. Although each regional office has some autonomy, all report directly to the central data processing headquarters; control is not returned to the operating departments.

The final alternative for organizational location is an independent data processing department that reports directly to the head of the whole organization. This department reports at the same level and has the same importance as the principal operating and staff functions. (See figure 14-4.) Such an approach is desirable when data processing is an integral part of accomplishing the organization's objectives; examples include commercial banks, insurance companies, and airlines.

Internal structure of the data processing department. Once the location of the data processing department in the larger organization is established, the internal structure of the department itself must be decided on. Several structural models are available; the choice between them depends on the type of organization and its objectives. The most basic structural pattern divides responsibility among three line groups (technical support, applications systems development, and operations) and one staff group (management). These four groups report directly to the manager of data processing. (See figure 14-5.)

Technical support: The division of responsibilities within the technical support group can vary greatly, depending on the data pro-

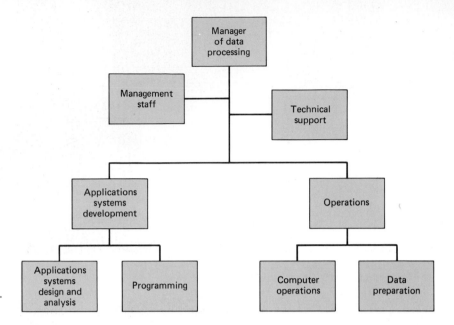

Figure 14-5 Internal
structure of the data processing department

cessing environment. One typical three-way division for a fairly large department provides system programming, standards and methods, and system evaluation functions. System programming includes creation and maintenance of the operating system software, administration of the data base and its related software, and user training. Standards and methods tasks include the development, publication, and updating of all standards and the maintenance of a technical library for all applications and software systems. Finally, the system evaluation tasks are to evaluate system performance, adjust the hardware configuration, and request software adjustments from the system programming personnel. System evaluation is also responsible for suggesting long-range hardware and software improvements.

Applications systems development: The applications systems development group may assign responsibilities to its personnel in one of two ways: by skills required to do a task or by type of applications system. Grouping by skills means dividing the work to be done into: (1) applications systems analysis and design and (2) programming. The work is assigned by project; usually one of the systems analysts who worked on a particular project from its inception will be appointed project manager. The analysts and designers work on the project, passing it on to the programmers when they are finished; all the work is under the project manager's supervision. Often some programmers are made responsible for what is called maintenance

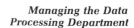
(Bill Longcore)

The data processing manager at this college computer center has a view of the computer room from her office. In these two rooms, all essential activities take place.

(Bill Longcore)

The computer room itself, although small, contains a variety of equipment. Counter-clockwise from right can be seen four direct-access disk drives, a console display (partially concealed), the CPU (at rear right), two different printers, magnetic tape drives (partially concealed at left), a card reader, magnetic tapes stored on shelves, and a card punch. The flooring is raised and perforated (see chapter 15) for air circulation and protection from water damage.

375

programming, that is, handling minor modifications to existing programs or quick requests for outputs from existing files.

The second method of organization—by type of applications system—divides the data processing workload into groups such as management information systems, marketing, finance, manufacturing, and so on. Each of these applications systems has its own group of analysts, designers, and programmers. Whereas grouping by skills allows a designer to work on any type of applications system, grouping by type means a designer will always work on the same kind of applications system, such as marketing. This way of organizing projects by type is appropriate for data processing departments serving several important users with complex systems, each requiring specialized and detailed knowledge. Organization of workload by type is also useful in cases where the users have little or no systems expertise. In these cases, the data processing specialists must act in place of the users to make certain decisions. This specialization can lead to less efficient utilization of data processing personnel, however, and also to the emphasis of applications over technical skills.

Operations: The operations group serves two major functions—production support and operation of equipment. Production support includes scheduling and coordination, job control, and other services such as program libraries. Equipment operations include all actual equipment functions, including computer and offline operations and data preparation.

This is not the only way in which the operations group may be organized. Smaller data processing departments may have much simpler arrangements, less production control, and data preparation, library, and equipment operations groups reporting directly to the manager of operations.

Personnel Management

The administration of the people involved in data processing is a key part of the department's organization. The data processing manager, like any other manager, interacts with staff through five functions: (1) recruitment, (2) career development, (3) performance evaluation, (4) administration, and (5) position definition.

Recruitment. In most business organizations, the selection of new employees is usually supervised by the personnel department, but the various department managers generally provide a list of qualifications for the job and interview candidates. The data processing manager has these responsibilities for the technical staff. The foremost requirement for an applicant is technical ability, but personal qualities such as emotional stability are important also. Heavy responsibilities accompany the handling of large amounts of financial, personal, and other data, and for this reason reliability and honesty are important. Past job performance is a good indicator of what can be expected from an applicant. A background check should include personal references and an investigation into a prospective employee's qualifications for bonding.

Training and career development. New employees must be given orientation and training in order to perform well in their new jobs. Existing staff members must receive training to keep up to date with the latest technical developments. Training for career development must allow qualified employees to advance along prescribed career paths.

Training may come from several sources: on-the-job training, professional seminars and conferences, trade schools, colleges, and in-house training programs. In-house training programs are especially useful for data processing personnel; they provide special training as the need arises, and help to attract new employees eager to learn more about the field.

Performance evaluation. All managers must be aware of their employees' potential and their strengths and weaknesses. At the same time, employees must be made aware of how well they have performed and what their shortcomings are. Regular, formal performance evaluations serve both these purposes. They also provide a basis for equating pay with performance (it has been said that a paycheck is a report card for grownups) and an opportunity for the manager to help improve performance. Finally, periodic performance reviews establish documentation on the department's performance history. Quarterly reviews are usually recommended for managers and supervisors, while analysts and programmers might do well with monthly reviews, since their assignments tend to last about a month.

Administration. The person supervising the data processing department is responsible for seeing that the goals and objectives of the department and of the organization as a whole are achieved. Effective supervisors must be sure department employees know their duties and meet their responsibilities. Not every person is able to assume a managerial role. It is not unusual for an individual with technical ability to be promoted to an administrative position for which he or she is not prepared.

Security is a critical concern to most data processing departments. Decisions and actions to prevent possible fraud or misuse of infor-

377

mation are an administrative responsibility. Security procedures—identification, searching, restriction of materials to authorized personnel only—must be instituted. Since many computer frauds involve collusion, separation of the various duties that must be performed in the data processing department may deter some illegal or unethical activities. Supervisors should separate such staff functions as authorizing a transaction, processing the data, processing the input and output, and management of the data files.

Rotation of personnel is another useful administrative tool. Rotation can prevent one employee from dominating a particular area. Mandatory vacations for all key personnel are likewise helpful, since errors or fraud are often discovered while the perpetrator is not around to cover up. (A "workaholic" employee who passes up a vacation should arouse suspicions.)

The termination of employment in the data processing department is a matter that administration must handle very carefully. Many stories are told of irate employees who were given two weeks' notice, and then erased tape files or destroyed valuable equipment. For this reason, an employee should be required to leave the premises immediately after being dismissed or given notice; two weeks' or one month's severance pay is a good investment when weighed against the possibility of sabotage.

Position definition. The preparation of *job descriptions* and titles for all personnel in the data processing department is a major administrative task and tool. Specific job descriptions and titles will vary from one organization to another, depending on the objectives of the data processing department and its environment, including size, type of work done, workload, and other factors. For instance, a small department of five to 10 employees may have a difficult time matching job titles with the actual duties performed in a large 200-employee department. The kind of system being developed also affects job titles and responsibilities. An environment in which large integrated data bases are handled will require specialized data base design and maintenance jobs. A department dealing with a large number of users will have specialized systems design and analysis jobs.

Positions in Data Processing

The data processing department's workload determines to some extent how duties will be assigned. If the workload in systems development is limited, the systems analysis, design, and programming functions might be combined into one job title. If the production

Figure 14-6 Job families
in data processing

Supervisory Positions	Administrative Job Family
Manager of data processing	Job setup clerk
Manager of systems development	Control clerk
Manager of operations	Operations librarian
Project controller	Technical librarian
Production support manager	Supply clerk
Planning specialist	Aides
Systems Job Family	**Operations Job Family**
Systems analyst	Console operator
Systems designer	Peripheral equipment operator
Systems consultant	Chief terminal operator
Methods and procedures analyst	Production coordinator
Management information	Scheduler
systems analyst	Keypunch operator
Operations research analyst	
	Technical Support Job Family
Programming Job Family	System programmer
Programmer	Data administrator
Maintenance programmer	Communications analyst
	Standards controller
	Configuration manager

workload is low, library maintenance, production support, and related functions might be combined under one title. Generally, there
are six broad groups, or job families, of data processing positions:
systems, programming, operations, technical support, administration, and management. (See figure 14-6.)

The systems job family. The *systems job family* is involved with
establishing the system's requirements. The most common job title
in this family is systems analyst. The systems analyst is responsible
for gathering and analyzing data and its relationship to organization
objectives and for developing an economical and effective system. In
some large organizations, the systems analyst's job function is subdivided into several specialized jobs including: systems designer,
management information systems analyst, operations research analyst, systems consultant, and methods and procedures analyst.

The programming job family. The *programming job family* comprises those positions responsible for preparing working computer
programs. The most common job title is programmer. Programmers
often specialize in either applications programs or program maintenance. Applications programmers prepare data processing systems

379

Operations, technical support, administrative, and supervisory personnel work in close proximity to their equipment in this computer facility.

for the user's applications; maintenance programmers modify and update existing programs.

The operations job family. The *operations job family* includes all the positions involved with the actual operation or control of the operation of computer hardware. Some typical job titles in this family are: console operator, chief terminal operator, peripheral equipment operator, keypunch operator, scheduler, and production coordinator.

The technical support job family. The *technical support job family* covers the jobs that require knowledge of the entire data processing activity. One title, system programmer, refers to the person who generates, modifies, and maintains the operating system and related software. Other titles are: data administrator, communications analyst, configuration manager, and standards controller. Some of the positions in the technical support family, notably data administrator and communications analyst, involve many system development functions as well as technical support functions. They are placed in this family because they perform their system development functions for the entire data processing group.

380

Job Title Systems Analyst	**Grade**
Reports To Manager of Systems Analysis and Design	**Date**
Job Titles Supervised Directly	**Approximate No. of Positions**

None

Narrative Description

Gathers and analyzes information for developing and modifying data processing systems. Designs and specifies systems and methods for installing them and supervises or guides their installation. Evaluates operational systems and recommends improvements. Works closely with personnel in problem areas to gather information and define systems objectives. Documents fact-finding and study results. Makes formal presentations of findings, recommendations, and specifications in formal reports and in oral presentations.

Responsibilities

1. Defining requirements for improving or replacing systems.
2. Ensuring cost effectiveness of recommendations.
3. Guiding systems development and implementation activities, sometimes acting as a project manager.

Duties

1. Define requirements for analytical studies.
2. Document current systems operations.
3. Perform interviews and other data gathering.
4. Apply current technology to solution of problems.
5. Prepare specifications for system improvements.
6. Define systems security and control procedures.
7. Develop systems testing and conversion plans.
8. Fulfill administrative reporting requirements.
9. Supervise other project personnel as required.

External Job Contacts

1. Managers and personnel in user departments.
2. Operations management and scheduling personnel.
3. Programming personnel.

Qualifying Experience

1. Bachelor's degree (preferably including courses in statistics, mathematics, accounting, computer sciences) or equivalent.
2. Training in systems analysis with special emphasis in project management, user relations, data gathering techniques, written and oral communications, and management information systems. Knowledge in the subject matter area(s) is desirable.
3. Minimum of six years work experience, four of which must have been in data processing. (Two or more of the four years must have been in programming or systems positions.) Graduate education and experience may be interchanged on a year-for-year basis.
4. Thoroughly familiar with problem analysis and oral and written communications.

Achievement Criteria

(Courtesy of IBM)

Figure 14-7   A data processing job description

The administrative job family. The *administrative job family* includes all the nontechnical support positions for the entire data processing activity. While the persons holding these positions may have extensive data processing skills, their general administrative and support skills are of primary importance. These personnel support the operations, systems development, and management functions by filling positions as: control clerk, job setup clerk, operations librarian, supply clerk, and computer aide. Administrative job titles primarily involved with support of the system development function are: technical librarian and programming aide. The administrative job family also includes training coordinators and budget and costing specialists.

Supervisory positions. Management personnel must have supervisory skills as well as data processing expertise. Some supervisory job titles are: manager of data processing, manager of systems development, manager of operations, and production support manager. There are, in addition, management jobs that oversee technical planning and administration needs. The titles of these jobs might be project controller and planning specialist.

Regardless of how job titles and duties are finally assigned, there should be a written job description for each position. A good job description includes a job title, a brief description of the work assignment, a grade or salary level, and a classification that identifies the position within the organization. The job description should also contain the job title to which the position in question reports and the job titles that it supervises directly. A paragraph should list the duties and responsibilities of the position, and another should outline the qualifying experience and desired education or training. A sample job description is shown in figure 14-7 that appears on page 381.

Managing Department Work

Planning, control, and accountability are three management functions that relate directly to data processing activities. On a short-term basis, it may be satisfactory to conduct data processing activities without the benefit of an overall plan. However, to fulfill the organization's goals, a long-range implementation plan is needed. This overall plan gives the data processing department a framework within which to develop and implement applications systems. It also provides direction and a sense of purpose for data processing personnel.

Planning

There are six steps in the development of a master plan:

1. Establish objectives.
2. Identify what activities must be performed to achieve these objectives.
3. Determine the necessary resources.
4. Define the time available for each activity.
5. Determine in what sequence the activities are to be performed.
6. Establish controls to see that the activities are carried out to achieve the desired objectives.

It is customary to set up a steering committee or other management group to complete these tasks. While final control over the integrated plan rests with the top levels of management, the manager of data processing and the technical staff should be consulted. When decision making is too far removed from those who will have to implement the decisions, costly and inefficient procedures are likely to result.

A long-range plan for a data processing department consists of three elements: the strategic plan, the specific projects plan, and the resources plan.

The strategic plan. The *strategic plan* is a broad outline of developments and achievements that may be expected over a period of three, five, or even 10 years. It may include such long-term management objectives as development of a data base management system, distribution of data base activities to users, installation of an advanced data communications system, and implementation of system standards. The strategic plan may have to be changed in response to new situations and even new technology, but the goals should be broad enough to remain fairly stable even in the event of change.

The specific projects plan. Specific projects are those that the users and the data processing department management can foresee over a period of one to three or, perhaps, five years. Some of the projects in the *specific projects plan* may already be approved and scheduled. Other projects may still be in planning stages and tentatively scheduled. Intended projects are those without even preliminary scheduling commitments. Specific projects plans tend to be somewhat less stable than strategic plans. Users can readily make changes and deletions in any planned or intended projects.

The resources plan. The *resources plan* lists the personnel, hardware, software, and data base requirements needed to support the strategic and specific projects plans. It outlines the projected allocation of these resources and estimates their cost. This plan is reviewed and updated at least once a year, and frequently more often.

Management Control

Management control examines how the data processing resources are being used and measures their performance against the strategic plan. It also has a diagnostic aspect: If targeted projections are not being met, why not? What can be done about it? The control function operates at two levels: project control and operational control.

Project control. Project control starts in the planning stage by seeing that projects are properly selected. This control is concerned that projects are developed according to a standard systems development methodology. Project selection should include evaluation of the relative value of proposed projects to their users and a cost/benefit analysis.

Once a project has been selected, it must proceed through a standard development process. This allows the major effort to be concentrated on the project itself and not on the methods used to develop it. A project is best developed in phases. For each phase, responsibilities should be spelled out and review points established. Costs and schedules can be recalculated as each major phase is completed. This provides a check on the progress of the project.

Operational control. Management of the production of the data processing department—the hardware and software—is the goal of operational control. Sets of standard instructions facilitate this management task. Standard instructions should include *run books* that tell the operator how to run a job, what input and output are expected, and what to do if the job aborts. Daily and weekly schedules are also a standard operational tool. Schedules note the relationships between different jobs, as well as the days and times at which each job should be run.

Operational control must also analyze schedules in comparison with capacity. Will scheduled jobs be completed on time? It may be necessary for management to make schedule adjustments or to increase capacity before a job reaches the critical stage. A forecast of load versus capacity is also helpful. An analysis of machine downtime is still another scheduling tool; it shows hardware replacement and repair needs, indicates maintenance policies that may need to be revised, and outlines the productivity of data processing operations in general.

Accountability

Data processing managers are responsible for the formal accounting of their departments. Running a data processing department requires the expenditure of substantial sums of money to pay for equipment, maintenance, staff, overhead, supplies, and more. The control of expenditures is implied in the term *accountability*, and is managed through a budget. Accountability includes two basic components: identification of expenditures by source and allocation of expenditures.

The *chargeout system* is a means of both identifying and allocating expenditures. In a chargeout system, all resources consumed — disk space, data entry cards, programmer time, and so on — are listed, and costs are allocated to each on some rational basis. (A rational basis for allocating costs might involve cost of supplies, hourly rate of employee time, a percentage for overhead, and so on.)

A chargeout system, once established, can be changed to meet different objectives. For instance, if new systems development is to be encouraged, the chargeout system can be adjusted to increase allocation of funds for that purpose. Increased funding can be provided in several ways: New systems development may be subsidized wholly or in part, or on a fixed-cost basis, instead of being charged for resources consumed.

In addition to allocating costs to resources, the chargeout system must satisfy user requirements and adequately provide for new hardware. User satisfaction may be measured in terms of how a user rates service against cost, production time, and quality. Are the user's deadlines being met in the most efficient way? Are operations procedures and capacities being monitored to keep costs down and avoid excessive staff or machine resources?

Project backlog is another indication of how well a data processing department is meeting user requirements. If there is a large backlog, perhaps human resources are being used inefficiently, or hardware maintenance requirements may have been underestimated.

The rapid changes in information handling over the past 20 years have led to the development of the data processing department as a unique part of business organizations. Management of data processing activities has become more than a secondary duty of another department; it is important in its own right to provide efficient and effective operation of an increasingly important department.

Summary

Data processing management consists of four major functions: (1) organization, (2) management planning and control, (3) accountability, and (4) security.

The organization of a data processing department deals with the allocation of human resources: operators, programmers, systems analysts, and so on. It consists of three basic elements: mission statement, department structure, and personnel management.

The mission statement defines both the goals of the data processing department as a whole and its role in the larger organization. This ensures goal congruence; that is, everyone should be working toward the same end. The department structure is the chain of command; it outlines each employee's authority, responsibilities, and reporting relationships. The structure can be regarded from two aspects: (1) its location within the larger organization and (2) the internal structure of the data processing department itself.

Within the data processing department itself, there are four basic groups: (1) technical support, (2) applications systems development, (3) operations, and (4) management. All four groups report directly to the manager of data processing.

The technical support group may divide responsibilities in a variety of ways, depending on the data processing environment. One three-way division provides system programming, standards and methods, and system evaluation functions.

The applications systems development group may assign its personnel according to skills required to do a task, or according to type of system. Grouping by skills divides the work to be done into (1) applications systems analysis and design and (2) programming. Personnel in each division work on all types of applications programs.

Grouping by type of system divides the workload and the personnel into areas of specialization, such as management information, manufacturing, marketing, or finance. Systems analysts and programmers will work on only one type of applications program from one of these categories. This specialization is useful for developing complex systems requiring special expertise.

The operations group serves two major functions—production support and equipment operations. Production support includes scheduling and coordination functions, job control, and such services as program libraries. Equipment operations cover all the actual equipment functions, including computer and offline operations and data preparation.

Personnel management in the data processing department has five principal components: (1) Recruitment is the selection and hiring of new employees for the department. This, of course, must be done in a manner to assure the availability of good technical skills. (2) Career development provides a path for employee improvement, besides a way of increasing technical skills. (3) Performance evaluation is necessary to see that an employee's responsibilities are lived up to and that the employee is aware of the quality of his or her performance. (4) Administration oversees the attainment of the goals and objectives of the data processing department. (5) Position definition provides job titles and descriptions for all personnel in the department.

Management planning and control are concerned with the actual activities of the data processing department. Long-range planning consists of the strategic plan, the specific projects plan, and the resources plan. Management control, both project and operational, examines how data processing resources are being used and measures their performance. It also diagnoses and corrects any problems in program development.

Accountability is the function of management responsible for the large expenditure of funds involved with running the data processing department. Accountability includes two basic elements: the identification of expenditures by source and the allocation of expenditures.

Key Terms and Phrases

accountability
administrative job family
chargeout system
job description
mission statement
operational location
operations job family

programming job family
resources plan
run books
specific projects plan
strategic plan
systems job family
technical support job family

Sources of Additional Information

Awad, Elias M., ed. *Issues in Business Data Processing.* Englewood Cliffs, N.J.: Prentice-Hall, 1975.

Burch, John G., Jr., and Sardinas, Joseph L., Jr. *Computer Control and Audit.* New York: Wiley, 1978.

Whitmarsh, John. "Consultant Decries Patchwork DP Planning." *Computerworld*, October 29, 1979, p. 18.

Test Yourself

1. In what three ways can data processing departments be located within an organization?
2. What are the three line groups that make up the internal structure of the data processing department? State some functions of each.
3. In what ways does a data processing manager interact with staff?

4. What are the six families or categories of data processing positions? Name two job titles in each.
5. What is a job description? What information should it include?
6. What are the steps involved in developing a master plan?
7. What is a strategic plan? A specific projects plan? A resources plan?
8. What is the function of management control? At what two levels does the control function operate?
9. What is meant by the term "accountability"?

15 Computer Security

Brooke Stauffer

"The increase in computer crime is frightening."

APPLICATION
The Vulnerable Computer

In March 1973, a former employee of the Equity Funding Corporation of America
—a California-based insurance company—reported to the New York State Insurance Department that the company was involved in a large-scale conspiracy to defraud its customers. The same employee also revealed the details of the fraud to a Wall Street insurance analyst. In just days, the value of Equity Funding shares on the New York Stock Exchange plummeted, and before the month was out, various state and government agencies began investigating the matter. After three years of investigation, several officers of Equity Funding, including its board chairman, were indicted on charges of fraud, tried and convicted, and sent to prison.

To many professional observers and to the public, one of the most fascinating aspects of the Equity Funding scandal was the part played by computers in perpetrating the crime. Part of the complex fraud involved creating about 64,000 insurance policies for nonexistent clients. These fraudulent policies existed only within the company's computers.

The "fake" policies, as well as genuine ones, were then sold to reinsurers, insurance companies that buy insurance policies from other companies. (Reinsurance is a standard means by which insurance companies spread their liabilities.) A reinsurer would pay off on an insurance policy when Equity Funding notified it of a claim.

In less than 10 years, Equity Funding had created an estimated $2 billion in computerized but fictitious insurance policies (as well as more than $1 billion in genuine policies), and had received from reinsurers over $1 million in payments on false claims. Most of the "take" went into the company's own accounts as "current earnings." However, unknown even to the managers of the conspiracy, a few of their colleagues in the crime found a way to move $144,000 into their personal bank accounts. (There's no honor among computer thieves, either.)

In part, the fraud succeeded for as long as it did because the company officers assigned a special computer code to their false policies. Thus, when auditors came to check the company's books, the conspirators could exclude the records of those policies for as long as necessary.

The money lost by the reinsurers was only a fraction of the total, however. The real victims of the fraud were the company's customers, who had in good faith invested many millions of dollars in premiums and shares. The total—some $100 million—represents the largest sum of money lost to date through a single computer crime.

THE EQUITY FUNDING scandal, in addition to being a spectacular fraud, was also unusual in that it was a conspiracy. Usually, computer criminals work alone, aided only by a computer terminal (and sometimes not even that), and walk away with an estimated average of several hundred thousand dollars.

It is widely believed that the reported instances of criminal computer misuse represent the tip of the iceberg. And criminal misuse of computers is only part of a much greater and more serious problem —*computer security*. It has become increasingly clear that computers are vulnerable to a wide range of abuses, intentional and unintentional. In addition to unauthorized access and fraudulent misuse, computers have been burned, sunk, bombed, and even shot. They have been the victims of unintentional error, power failures, natural disasters, and sabotage.

Computers are at the mercy of their power supply—no electrical input means no computer output. In an age of brownouts, blackouts, and energy crises, an uninterrupted power supply has become an increasingly important aspect of computer security. One of the most serious physical threats to computers is fire, in part because of the difficulty in putting out a fire without damaging the computer or creating a worse hazard. In addition, computers are vulnerable to sabotage and a variety of natural and unnatural hazards.

Given all these potential risks, it is hardly surprising that computer professionals and users are devoting considerable thought and effort to the problems of protecting the security and integrity of computers. What constitutes adequate security controls for one computer installation may differ from those for another. Good security begins with a thorough analysis of the risks a given computer installation is vulnerable to.

And finally, just as computers can be abused and damaged by human beings, they can be used to abuse and damage human beings. The potential for invasion of privacy by computers is in many ways the most important problem of computer security.

A Hierarchy of Hazards

To many data processing managers, the term "computer security" means primarily the physical security of the computer and of data files, records, and programs. In recent years, however, the meaning of the term has been broadened to include access to and interaction with a computer and its data files, records, and programs.

In general, there are two main types of potential danger to computers: the danger of physical damage and the danger of misuse or theft by humans. But these categories often overlap. Humans can do —and have done—physical damage to computers. Our hierarchy of hazards generally proceeds from the most likely to the least likely. (See figure 15-1.) Regardless of their relative importance, however, the following discussion of potential dangers underscores the need for a thorough analysis of risks by those responsible for a computer's security.

Unintentional Error

According to some security experts, unintentional errors account for more losses than all other hazards combined. Unintentional errors are those errors or malfunctions accidentally caused by a human agent, software, or hardware. Humans are the major source of such errors, either through acts of omission, neglect, incompetence, or plain absentmindedness. To err may be human, but computers are not forgiving and often transform a trivial mistake into an unexpected disaster.

A classic example of how a relatively minor oversight can lead to disaster via the computer involved a company with a large inventory of an obsolete item. The company decided to reduce this undesirable inventory by selling the item well below cost. As the inventory was sold off, sales were entered into the computer, which noted that the item was selling very well in the sales reports it generated. The computerized reorder system automatically issued a reorder for more of the same item—at a much higher price than the company was selling it for. The inventory continued to sell fast, so the computer ordered still more. A third reorder was completed before the mistake was detected. It was a mistake that cost the company tens of millions of dollars—a very painful way to learn a lesson. Indeed, it was ulti-

Figure 15-1 Hierarchy of hazards

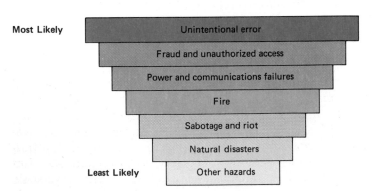

mately discovered that the item was so out of date, and the national inventory so small, that the company was buying its "new stock" from the same suppliers that had just bought the company's old stock! It was literally buying its own stock from itself and paying heavily for the privilege.

It is often said in such cases that the computer "made a mistake." That, of course, is not true. It is people who make mistakes. The computer just does what it is told to do. In this case, the mistake was not omitting inventory sold below cost from the automatic reorder program. More often than not, the mistake occurs when recording data or instructions in a computer program. A recent example occurred when a programmer gave the wrong field specifications in a program for calculating tax refunds for the Internal Revenue Service. As a result, the computer either calculated the wrong amount or gave no refund where one was due.

However, not all unintentional errors involve information processing. In one well-known case, a computer operator at the *Los Angeles Times* put a container of coffee on top of an IBM 370/158. The operator apparently was quite tall. A shorter colleague, not seeing the coffee, got too close, accidentally bumped the machine, and knocked the container over. Coffee—and, worse, milk and sugar—spilled into the computer. The total cost to the *Times*—downtime, resetting, and repair—was about $39,000. A very expensive cup of coffee!

Fraud and Unauthorized Access

The hazards of fraud and unauthorized access are second only to unintentional error in financial importance. However, they may represent a greater potential threat. While accidents do not actively look for an opportunity to happen, they are, in a sense, invited by an appropriate set of conditions. Fraud and unauthorized access, on the other hand, are definitely unwelcome and usually uninvited.

Time magazine has called computer fraud a growth industry. Some experts think it may be a boom industry. And a leading authority on the subject—Donn B. Parker of SRI International—expects organized crime to move into this industry, as it has into so many others, during the next decade. According to Parker, the actual number of computer crimes during the 1980s can be expected to fall, but the amount involved will be much more than the present national average of $450,000 per occurrence. Computer security systems will become increasingly effective, but so will computer criminals. Computer crime will be a career for professionals. But computer security will be aimed at protecting against large-scale losses, so there will still be room for the small-time hobbyist, who currently accounts for most computer crime.*

Fraud refers to intentional deceit used for personal gain. Frauds are perpetrated by a variety of means: infiltration, tapping of communications lines, or electronic eavesdropping (with a computer and its peripherals acting as transmitters); unauthorized reading of data records through an online terminal; physical removal of files and other sensitive documents; masquerading as an authorized user; and installation of a "Trojan horse"—that is, the input of innocent-looking data that, in fact, contain secret instructions to the computer.

Unauthorized access occurs when an individual who does not have the authority to do so is able to obtain information or actually alter data within the computer. Unauthorized access includes physical access to the computer facility, which may be simply a matter of walking in, thus exposing the computer to physical damage, as we shall see below in the discussion of sabotage. Depending on the circumstances, unauthorized access may or may not involve a fraudulent act.

Why does an individual commit computer fraud? The main reason is the same as for most crimes of theft and financial gain—greed. A study of employees who committed computer fraud found that many were living beyond their means. Other motives include financial problems, ego gratification (an employee may see the potential for fraud as a challenge), and revenge, or just "getting even" (with a supervisor, for example) for a real or imagined grievance.

Curiously enough, computer frauds are often committed by individuals who are considered "model" employees. According to a profile developed by Donn Parker, the perpetrator is usually young (under 30), a manager or skilled technical professional, and regarded by the supervisor as bright, motivated, reliable, and trustworthy. Such employees are not criminals by nature and do not have arrest records. The opportunity was there, and they gave in to temptation.

It is especially difficult to detect a computer crime or identify the perpetrator. In one instance, a bank customer noticed that his bank balance was always short a few cents at the end of each month, although the amount never exceeded $.25. Upon being notified of the discrepancies, the bank simply credited the missing amounts to the customer's account, since in each case the "error" was less than $2.00. The customer was not satisfied, however, and insisted that the discrepancies were the result of a computer crime. The bank called in the FBI. Investigation revealed that a bank employee was siphon-

* Tom Henkel, "DP Crime Seen Hitting New Heights in 1980s," *Computerworld*, November 5, 1979, p. 17.

ing off very small amounts of money from randomly selected accounts in the computer system and transferring them to his or her own account in the same system. There was no way to identify the criminal, since the account receiving the stolen amounts was indistinguishable from the accounts being robbed. And no money was being taken out of the system—it was simply being transferred from various legal accounts into the employee's legal account. This kind of computer crime has become known as a "salami" technique because it removes one thin "slice" at a time.

The problem of detecting computer crimes and criminals is compounded because of the number of people who may have access to terminals. In the days of manual data processing, very few individuals could affect the actual bookkeeping. When fraud or embezzlement was detected, it was usually possible to trace it back through the paperwork. Also, each individual's handwriting was identifiable. But digital blips on magnetic tapes tell no tales and can be entered or altered by anyone with access to a terminal.

According to an FBI estimate, only one in every hundred computer crimes is detected; of these, only one in eight is reported to the appropriate authorities. Often, the most frequent reason is that the resulting publicity would weaken public confidence and thereby damage the firm's reputation and financial position.

When the criminal is caught, tried, and convicted, the sentence is often surprisingly lenient. There are several reasons for this. First, computer criminals are not violent, have done no physical injury to another human being. They are often members in good standing in their communities. Second, the public does not get emotionally involved when the target of a crime is an impersonal entity such as a bank. And third, the law is not clear about what constitutes a computer crime. An irreplaceable data file may be worth a great deal of money to the company that owns it. (Computer tapes have actually been "kidnapped" and held for ransom.) But legally, the theft of a file is usually considered as only petty larceny.

This situation has gradually begun to change in the past few years. Sentences for computer crime are getting more severe, and Congress is beginning to consider the need for clear legislation in the area of computer crime.

Power and Communications Failures

A large CPU may consume as much as $30,000 to $40,000 worth of electricity in one year. Not only do computers demand a lot of electricity, but they want it in a particular form—400-plus cycles per second—in order to protect against power-line noise. (Standard

395

household alternating current has a frequency of 60 cycles per second.) Variations and interruptions in the power supply can cause massive disruptions to data processing activity, and can even result in the loss of electronically stored data. Areas of rapid population growth, heavy manufacturing areas, rural areas, and areas subject to frequent lightning storms are subject to power interruptions.

Online systems are the most sensitive to power fluctuations, but all CPUs and peripherals can be affected. The majority of electrical problems involve power reductions (brownouts) or failures (blackouts). Curiously enough, a blackout does not represent a serious threat to computer functioning. Blackouts are relatively rare and most of them are quite short. According to one study, 85 percent of all power failures last less than 11 minutes, and half less than 6 seconds. But *power surges* that occur when large computers and their peripherals are turned on can create serious problems as well. For example, the electric current needed to keep an IBM 370 executing is

(*Sola Electronic*)

The control panel of an uninterrupted power supply (UPS).

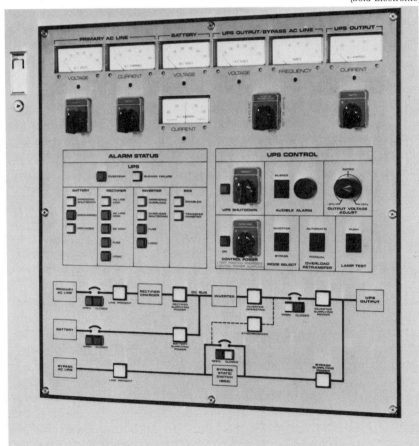

128 amps, but as much as 1,000 amps may be needed for the brief moment when the computer starts up. This amount of current, delivered suddenly, may actually damage delicate components of the computer circuitry.

But far more common than blackouts are a variety of small disturbances that can easily damage computers and the data they contain, not to mention the reputation of the people operating them. The most frequent small power reductions are the fluctuations known as transients, or glitches. They last only a few milliseconds but cause considerable trouble by producing sudden increases and decreases in voltage. Brownouts often occur because the power supplier reduces the voltage by as much as 10 percent during periods of great demand. The effective voltage drop in the computer itself may be more than twice as great. Lightning sometimes produces power surges in a computer's circuitry, but more often it causes voltage dips of up to several seconds.

Various devices have been developed to provide noise-free, uninterrupted power. The best known of these is the *uninterrupted power supply* (UPS), a battery-powered, solid-state device that maintains the required current if the commercial power fails. A UPS is an expensive form of protection, and the expense is not always justified. For instance, a computer manager could decide to spend $250,000 or more on a UPS to ensure that the computer stays "on the air." But staying on the air is pointless if the terminals that access the computer also lose their power. With the rapid growth of distributed data processing, the entire network and its lines of communication must be protected.

Fires

Fires pose a serious threat to computer facilities. Computer rooms are often filled with combustible materials such as printout paper and punch cards. The electrical cables required by a computer system may be wrapped in combustible plastic. If the cables overheat, this wrapping may catch fire. Much of the computer equipment itself may consist of plastics vulnerable to fire. Thus, although the incidence of fire may be low, the damage that could be caused is greater than might result from almost any other hazard. Equipment may have to be replaced, and stored data may be irretrievably lost. Even a relatively minor fire can result in significant downtime. When a major activity is dependent on a computer, any interruption can have a great effect. A fire in a telephone switching center in New York City in 1975 was put out promptly. But there was so much damage to the computer installation that it took a week to restore tel-

Ionization detectors set into the ceiling of a computer installation can detect invisible products of combustion even before there is smoke, noticeable fire, or appreciable heat.

ephone service to one large section of the city. The ultimate cost of the damage ran into millions of dollars.

Fires in computer installations are fought with water, carbon dioxide, and an anticombustion gas called Halon. Each method has its drawbacks.

It is dangerous to use water in an electricity-laden environment. Water may put out the fire but electrocute an employee. Sprinkler systems are often installed in computer centers, but they are designed to protect records and combustible materials around the computer rather than the computer itself. By the time a fire is hot enough to trigger the sprinklers, the computer equipment is often badly damaged.

The use of carbon dioxide to fight fires also involves serious risks. This heavy gas will effectively smother a fire. It will also smother anyone in the area. Consequently, carbon dioxide cannot be used until all personnel have been cleared from the affected area. By the time the gas can be sprayed on the fire, considerable damage may have been done.

Halon, a chemically inert gas, is nontoxic and effective against fires in concentrations of 5 percent Halon to 95 percent air. At this concentration, the gas is considered relatively harmless, even though it can cause drowsiness and disorientation. Moreover, direct exposure to the gas during the first 30 seconds after its release may produce frostbite. In addition, Halon systems are extremely expensive.

At this time, no one fire prevention system is best for every installation. An important recent advance, however, is the development of ionization detectors. These respond to combustion products even before smoke forms and give early warning. Until a reliable and effective fire prevention system is developed, the extent of potential damage can be minimized by careful management. DP managers should follow two important rules: (1) Store records or duplicate records in a building separate from the computer installation, and (2) keep to a minimum the amount of combustible material in the computer installation itself.

Sabotage and Riot

The records of computer crime include a number of cases in which computers have been the victims of physical assault. These attacks have been committed by computer personnel, irate customers, and politically motivated groups and individuals. During the Vietnam War, for example, antiwar groups and radicals bombed and sabotaged a number of computer installations, particularly those on the campuses of universities believed to be doing research for the Department of Defense. In Italy, terrorist groups bombed more than two dozen computer centers in the late 1970s. A particular target of these groups are the headquarters of multinational corporations. Efforts to track down the terrorists in Italy have been hampered by the fact that one of the first installations bombed contained the records of drivers' licenses.

With the exception of the antiwar protests, attacks on computers in the United States have usually been the work of individuals. The motive is often a desire to strike back at what is seen as the impersonality and insensitivity of "the machine." Computers have even been shot with a gun! The targets included an insurance computer in Charlotte, North Carolina, an IBM 1401 in Olympia, Washington, as well as computers in Australia and South Africa.

As computer use increases, the damage caused by such attacks will have an increasing impact on the institutions using the computers. The only prevention is strictly controlled physical access to the computer installation.

Natural Disasters

In comparison with the other causes of damage to computers, natural disasters are rare. Accordingly, many users underestimate the risk involved and concentrate on preventing accidents, thefts, and sabotage. But natural disasters do occur and can be devastating. This type of event, legally termed as an act of God, includes fire, floods, earthquakes, and lightning.

Acts of God cannot be prevented, but adequate planning can reduce their impact. The best protection is to locate the computer facility in a "safe" place. Like nuclear power plants, computer centers should not be in locations that are exposed to predictable catastrophic damage, such as earthquake faults. One company, for example, put its computer facility in a suburban shopping and office mall, only to learn too late that the site was below the level of the flood plain. Neither the ground floor nor the top floor (of a multi-storied building) are choice locations.

Other Hazards

There are any number of random hazards that are difficult to define and anticipate. Computers are sensitive to temperature and humidity levels and require air conditioning. Lack of temperature control in the computer facility may cause temperature fluctuations in the computer. Excessive heat can affect the circuitry of LSI chips and may even produce changes in their shape. High humidity can cause deterioration of magnetic tape surfaces, card jamming, and corrosion of electrical contacts. Low humidity, on the other hand, increases static electricity, which can disrupt operations involving magnetic media. In one such case, a disruption resulted from the static electricity that was produced by simply moving a metal chair across an uncarpeted floor. The downtime was considerable.

Air conditioning is important in the control of other environmental features besides temperature and humidity. There must be a steady flow of air from floor to ceiling so that detectors in the ceiling will sense smoke or fire. Inadequately filtered air can interfere with the operation of magnetic tapes and disks.

It is impossible, of course, to think of everything, but two examples will illustrate the need for planning and vigilance. In late 1979, just before the 1980 census was to begin, the computer center of the U.S. Census Bureau—containing $40 million worth of hardware—was accidentally flooded by its sprinkler system. This might have been a minor problem if a different kind of sprinkler head had been installed. As it was, the system poured out 500 gallons of water, completely destroying two Univac 1108s and damaging two other computers. The cost of this accident was more than $7 million dollars as well as months of lost time.

Much less expensive—though potentially more dangerous—was the experience of an executive who went to his office on a Sunday morning. Parked just outside the company's computer center was a fully loaded gasoline truck—with its brakes on fire. Unfortunately, the computer center was located on a truck route. A better choice of site would have averted such a hazard entirely.

Security Controls

No two computer installations are exactly alike or have precisely the same security requirements. Consequently, the implementation of security controls at any facility requires a careful analysis of the security requirements of that particular installation. It is probably not possible to achieve perfect security. In each situation, someone must define the risks and decide what controls will ensure the desired degree of security. A *risk analysis* should determine which security measures would be most useful in a given case. It should also include a cost/benefit analysis of proposed measures. Are the proposed measures worth the cost? In any security analysis, there are a number of factors that must be considered. The most important are discussed in the following section.

Goals of Security Control

A security system should consist of several levels of control. If the control at one level fails, another control will reduce the impact. These control levels can be thought of as goals, defining the kinds and extent of security the system is intended to provide. An ideal security system would probably consist of the following five levels of control. (Also see figure 15-2.)

1. Deterrence: The goal is prevention of any loss or damage.
2. Detection: Since absolute deterrence is impossible, methods are set up to note hazards as early as possible and to report on them promptly.
3. Minimizing loss or disaster: Procedures and facilities are set up to reduce the effect of loss or damage. Duplicate files, for instance, will mitigate the effect of losing the master files.

401

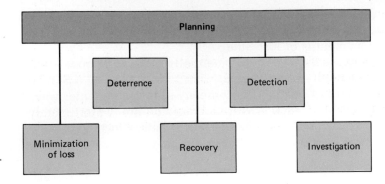

Planning

Deterrence

Detection

Minimization
of loss

Recovery

Investigation

Figure 15-2 Goals of security control

4. Investigation: In the event of loss or damage, the causes should be determined as quickly as possible. This information can aid in security planning for the future.
5. Recovery: Every computer security system should include a plan for reestablishing normal operations as quickly as possible following a loss or disaster.

As a matter of practical fact, recovery is the most neglected aspect of computer security. More than a few security experts have publicly lamented the widespread absence of contingency plans. It is difficult to overemphasize the importance of such plans. Today, a financial institution eats and breathes data processing. The loss of its data processing operation for one or two weeks might mean bankruptcy. Yet many organizations have no contingency plans whatsoever. For small computer installations in which replacing equipment would represent a major expense, no plan at all may be the best solution. But for larger facilities, this would be extremely risky. Sometimes a timely warning makes no difference: In 1979 a data processing firm in New Jersey began "looking for a plan" after a mild earthquake. The company, located on the Ramapo fault (by no means as active as the famous San Andreas fault in California), recognized the possibility of a major quake striking the area. But the development of a contingency plan should not require a warning, because more often than not there is no warning.

Contingency planning. A proper contingency plan consists of a set of procedures for personnel to follow in the event of serious accident or disaster. The contingency plan should be carefully prepared, printed, given to all employees who will be involved in the recovery operation, and rehearsed. The plan should have the following general features:

1. A list of personnel (and their alternates) who will implement the plans and the responsibilities of each person.

402

2. A description of recovery operations and procedures.

3. A priority list of materials to be saved in different kinds of disasters.

4. Contingency contracts and arrangements for use of backup equipment (for example, mutual assistance agreements with other companies).

5. The acquisition of important backup equipment not covered by contingency contracts and the storage of this equipment in another location.

Physical Location

The location of a computer facility provides the first line of defense. The following guidelines to location selection can greatly reduce a computer's exposure to hazard.

1. Remote site: Ideally, a computer facility should be located at a safe distance from airports, radar installations, heavy traffic, steam boilers, and so on. The greater the distance, the better.

2. Separate building: Control of physical access is always enhanced if the facility occupies a building of its own. Location in a building shared by other tenants means exposure to hazards created by them. On the other hand, a separate building makes the installation more vulnerable to damage from its own power, water, and air supplies and breakdowns of its communications lines. All of these should be protected or placed underground.

The computer itself should not be on the top or ground floor or in

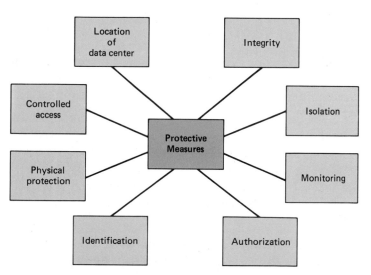

Figure 15-3 Factors in risk analysis

the basement. The computer is best placed in the center of the building, and the supporting floor should be reinforced.

3. Identification: The site should have no signs to identify it to strangers.

4. Location of backup facilities: These should be far enough from the main facility to be protected from the same hazards, but close enough to make a quick return to normal operations.

Control of Physical Access

The control of physical access is the second line of defense. If unauthorized personnel cannot get to the computer, the risk of damage by human agents is greatly reduced. Access to computer facilities is most commonly controlled by a number of measures. Preferably, several of the following should be used in combination.

1. Guards and escorts: All entrances to the computer facility should be guarded. Any unguarded entrances should be locked. No visitors should be allowed to tour the facility unescorted.

2. Sign-in/sign-out registers: At the very least, all personnel should sign in and out and indicate the time in a register or logbook. This provides a record of those who have been in the computer facility at any time. Registers that incorporate a computerized signature analysis device are particularly effective. Duplication of the pressure and the time taken to write a signature is even more difficult to achieve than a successfully disguised handwriting.

3. Cards and badges: Optically or magnetically coded cards are probably the most popular form of access control. Authorization can be reduced or extended by simple modification of the card. In addition, the card authorization can specify the place and times of entry permitted. Badges should be used for identifying authorized personnel and visitors. They are most effective if they are color-coded and carry a picture of the wearer.

4. Closed-circuit monitors: Television monitors, cameras, and intercom systems are more effective in controlling a large area than individual entrances and exits.

5. Double-door entries and one-way emergency doors: The use of a *double-door entry* means that an individual passing through the first door enters an area sealed off from the computer. It is necessary to open the second door to get to the computer from the "trap" area, which may be observed by a guard or through a closed-circuit television monitor. One-way doors open to the outside only, giving personnel a means of exiting without allowing unauthorized entry.

6. Paper shredders: Access by cleaning and building maintenance personnel may be unavoidable. A paper shredder makes waste paper useless as a source of information, especially if it produces microconfetti, which absolutely cannot be reconstructed.

An adequate security plan will probably include one or more of the following protective devices.

1. Drains and pumps: These devices will help to reduce the destructive potential of water from burst pipes, floods, or fire hoses.

2. Emergency power: The most important power protection is that provided by a backup system such as the UPS, discussed on page 397.

3. Coverings: Plastic covers for equipment not in use can reduce water damage.

4. Fire control: Protection against fire is very important. The three main types of fire protection systems have been discussed on page 398. In addition, the materials of the walls and ceilings should have a fire-resistance time of at least 1 hour, and all air ducts should be equipped with fire dampers.

Integrity

The *integrity* of a system refers to its reliability, or the assurance that it is complete and functioning properly. In the context of a computer security system, integrity means that the system carefully and correctly controls such aspects as access. For example, if someone is authorized to retrieve item A from a file, the system will provide item A and nothing else. Similarly, the system will erase processing information when a job is completed, thereby preventing unauthorized reading by anyone else.

Isolation

Perhaps the most basic concept of information security is that of the "need to know." *Isolation,* also known as compartmentalization, minimizes the number of people who know the details of an entire operation. The tighter the security, the less access any one individual has to information that does not directly concern him or her. Isolation can be achieved by several methods.

1. Disconnection and separation: This type of isolation involves the logical or geographical separation of the elements of a system. For example, no one individual is given access to programs *and* the operation of the computer *and* the design of the system. Personnel who input transactions are not given access to programs.

2. Least-privilege access: Any information security system will allow different degrees of access to different staff members, according to the needs of the job.

3. Obfuscation: The term *obfuscation* means hiding or obscuring. In computer security this form of isolation most often takes the form

of encoding information (encryption). The method has several drawbacks, however. It increases overhead. Also, many codes can be broken with relative ease. Finally, all codes require a key—and if one person has a key, someone else may be able to gain access to it.

Identification

A security system that uses isolation techniques must be able to identify users who have been authorized for access to the computer itself. How does the computer know that the person contacting it is, in fact, authorized to do so? Depending on the degree of security involved, the user may be identified by name, terminal, file, or program, or by some combination of these. There are four major identification methods:

(*Margarete Lyons/Stellar Systems*)

The Identimat hand-reader system can be programmed to recognize the unique handprints of any individual. Entry into the system is gained either through insertion of a card or keying in of a special number.

1. Identification items: These may be codes, keys, badges, coded cards, phone numbers, ID numbers, or encryption keys, which are items in the possession of the user. They have the disadvantage that others may gain possession of them.

2. Items of knowledge: Such items, known to the user but not physically accessible, may be passwords or prearranged sequences of questions and answers. The effectiveness of this method is a function of how often the item is changed. The more frequent the change of a password, say, the less likely it is that it will be stolen.

3. User characteristics: There are two important types of identifying characteristics. Dynamic characteristics involve an action or behavior of the user, such as the individual's handwriting or way of walking; genetic or physical characteristics are fingerprints, voice patterns, and eye color. The technology for the identification of all such characteristics by a computer is not commercially available, although experimental efforts are continuing.

4. Terminal location: Terminals can be assigned different degrees of privileged access to information according to their location. For example, if many people have access to a terminal, that terminal would provide only the most limited access capabilities. If terminals must be moved, their access privileges must also be changed.

Authorization

Authorized users must be further identified according to the specific level of authority. An effective security system must have procedures for determining who has access to particular parts of the data base, who has the authority to add and delete data, and so forth.

Users must be classified according to the categories of activity and

User of File A	Authorized to				
	Read only	Write only	Read and write	Delete	Add
1	x				
2		x		x	
3		x			x
.					
.					
.					
N			x		

Table 15-1 Table of Authorization

information for which they are authorized. The result might be an authorization table (see table 15-1).

Identification codes can be assigned to users and to categories of access. A user must enter his or her identification code and the code for the access category into the computer before being able to do the necessary computer work.

A security program is written for the computer. This program enables the computer to recognize user identifications and to match them with levels of authorization. A user authorized to read only will not be able to delete or add, because the security program will not permit it. Security programs must also provide for changing identification, authorization, and security requirements. They should also include a routine for automatically reporting any attempted violations of authorization restrictions.

Monitoring

A monitoring system is a program that guards the security system. It provides a continuing check on the functioning of the security system. Implicit in the concept of monitoring a computer system is the recognition that a violation of security can and probably will occur. Sooner or later, accidentally or intentionally, a security control (or perhaps several) will be neutralized or broken.

An effective monitoring system will be able to:

1. Detect security violations, such as a mismatch of user and terminal identification codes or unauthorized requests for files.

2. Lock up the computer system to prevent further use under specified circumstances. A "lockup" might be triggered, for example, by repeated attempts to use an incorrect identification card.

3. Report exceptions and trends. Any exceptional conditions should be reported and reviewed. The complete absence of such re-

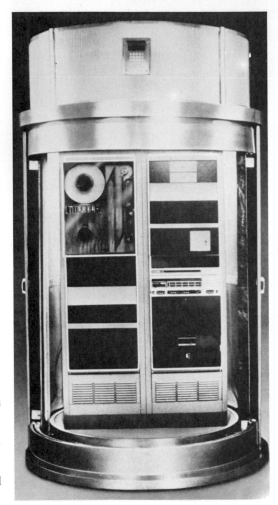

A "portable" computer enclosure is prefabricated and therefore easy to install virtually anywhere. Security is combined with environmental control through these features: heating, ventilation, and air conditioning; both internal and external fire detectors; an automatic Halon fire-suppression system; independent power packs; both audible and visible alarm units; dust shield and protection from water and explosion damage. A rotating turntable provides total access to all components contained within.

(Transaction Security, Inc.)

ports may be a sign that users are subverting the security system. The monitoring system should also collect data about user access for later review. This information would identify each user, terminal, type of processing, date, and time of day.

Invasion of Privacy

The problem is not new. As long ago as 1890, an article in the *Harvard Law Review* warned of the need to protect the individual's "right to be left alone" against invasions by "recent innovations and business methods." One of the authors was Louis Brandeis, later associate justice of the Supreme Court and one of the Court's greatest defenders of the right to privacy. Congress did not begin to deal with the problem until the 1950s. With the advent of computers, public concern for the right to be left alone has steadily increased. A Louis Harris poll taken several years ago showed that more than 70 percent of the American public felt that they began to lose their privacy the day they opened their first charge account, applied for a loan or a credit card, or bought something on the installment plan.

This concern has made itself felt in state legislatures as well as in Congress. These state legislatures have passed more than 150 privacy statutes, and Congress itself has passed more than half a dozen major laws to deal with different aspects of privacy. These include the Freedom of Information Act (1966), the Fair Credit Reporting Act (1970), the Privacy Act (1974), and the Right to Financial Privacy Act (1978). Because of the number of bills introduced and the resulting activity, the 95th Congress (1977–1979) was sometimes referred to as the "Privacy Congress."

Reasons for Concern

The concern for privacy has been increasing because of the explosive growth of information in computer files. The concern is well founded: Computer systems today do not protect personal and sensitive information.

There are three major reasons for this lack of protection. First, most of the computer systems now in use were designed before privacy became an issue of computer security. Second, there is still no comprehensive set of security criteria for designers of computer systems to follow. And although public concern over lack of privacy is growing, business managers generally do not share this concern; it is therefore of low priority in the average data processing department.

Although the public sees the computer as a potential "Big Brother," it is not the real culprit in violations of privacy. Computers can only do what they are told to do. It is, for example, well known that insurance companies ask applicants for much more information than is actually needed—including hospital records and psychiatric reports. Once this information is collected, it is often passed along to other companies in the industry through a central clearinghouse that stores information about policyholders. In fact, clients cannot find out directly from their insurance companies what *medical* information is in their files. The companies will send such information only to a physician, who then may decide whether or not to transmit it to the client.

Government agencies also accumulate enormous amounts of in-

409

formation about people. The potential for abuse is equally great. The line between the use of computers for administrative efficiency and their potential use for electronic oppression is easily blurred.

What should information collectors—private business or government agencies—be allowed to do with the personal information they collect? Should they be able to buy or sell such information without restriction? (Even state agencies have been known to sell lists of addresses to private companies. Such lists can be extremely valuable sources of potential customers.) And how much does a business or government agency have the right to know about individuals?

Recommendations

A very important step in the direction of resolving these and related problems was taken with the formation of the Privacy Protection Study Commission in 1974. The report produced by this commission in 1977 made three major policy recommendations:

1. Minimize intrusiveness in individual record keeping. Information-collecting organizations should inform customers and clients of their policies and practices in using the information they receive. Also, personal information should not be obtained by means of misrepresentation.
2. Maximize fairness in treatment of individuals. The record-keeping organization must recognize that individuals have an "assertable interest" in not having personal information distributed to other organizations without their consent.
3. Create enforceable rights of confidentiality. Individuals should have the right to take legal action against any record-keeping organization that violates their privacy.

A number of the commission's recommendations were incorporated in the Right to Financial Privacy Act of 1978.

There will, of course, be additional costs resulting from the implementation of privacy regulations. At present, it is not clear how great the costs may be or who will bear them. Costs and most issues affecting privacy in the age of electronic information must still be resolved. It is already clear, though, that data processing managers must become as concerned as the general public about the rights of individuals to privacy.

Summary

The problems associated with computer security and privacy are increasing, a trend that is expected to continue through the 1980s. DP managers must be aware of the variety of hazards that computers are subject to and take appropriate measures. In order of decreasing likelihood, the main sources of damage to or misuse of computers are: (1)

Unintentional error, probably responsible for more losses than all other hazards combined. (2) *Fraud* (intentional deceit for personal gain) and *unauthorized access* (illicit access to information or modification of data, as well as physical access to a facility). (3) *Power and communications failures*—CPUs are particularly sensitive to fluctuations in their power supply; an important protective device is the UPS, or uninterrupted power supply. (4) *Fires* pose a very serious threat since the materials in a computer room, including the equipment, are often combustible; damage from water or other fire-suppressing substances is also a hazard. (5) *Sabotage*—computers have been physically attacked by individuals and by politically motivated groups. (6) *Natural disasters* include fire, flood, lightning, and earthquakes. (7) *Other hazards* include temperature changes and extremes of humidity, to which computers are quite sensitive.

The goals of a security system should be deterrence, detection, minimization of loss, investigation, and recovery to normal operational status.

Factors to be considered in planning a security system include: (1) *Control of physical access* by various means (guards, logbooks, cards and badges, monitors, restricted entrances and exits, and paper shredders). (2) *Physical location,* ideally away from major hazards and in a separate building from other organizational activities. (3) *Physical protection of equipment* (by drains and pumps, backup power sources, coverings, and fire controls). (4) *Integrity* (assurance that the system security functions as intended). (5) *Isolation,* also known as compartmentalization (access to information only on a need-to-know basis). (6) *Identification* by various means to ensure that a computer user is authorized to gain access to the machine (keys, badges, codes, user characteristics, and terminal locations). (7) *Authorization* (who has authorization to do what), controlled by a computer program written for that purpose. The aim is to minimize the number of people who know all the details of the entire operation. (8) *Monitoring* of the security system to see that it functions properly.

Invasions of privacy make possible the misuse and abuse of personal information. DP professionals need to increase their awareness of the rights of individuals to privacy.

		Key Terms and Phrases
authorization	obfuscation	
closed-circuit monitors	power surges	
double-door entry	risk analysis	
identification codes	unauthorized access	
integrity	uninterrupted power supply (UPS)	
isolation		
least-privilege access		

411

Sources of Additional Information

Block, Victor. "Privacy Impacts DP World." *Infosystems*, no. 6 (1979): 94–96.

Burch, John G., Jr., and Sardinas, Joseph L., Jr. *Computer Control and Audit.* New York: Wiley, 1979.

Krauss, Leonard I., and MacGahan, Aileen. *Computer Fraud and Countermeasures.* Englewood Cliffs, N.J.: Prentice-Hall, 1979.

Lettleri, Larry. "Disaster Recovery: Picking Up the Pieces." *Computer Decisions*, no. 3 (1979):16–27.

Murphy, John. "Support Systems and Sources." *Modern Data*, no. 7 (1974):46–52.

Parker, Donn B. *Crime by Computer.* New York: Scribner, 1978.

Smith, August. "Data Processing Security: A Common Sense Approach." *Data Management*, no. 5 (1977): 7–13.

Sykes, D. J. "Positive Personal Identification." *Datamation*, no. 11 (1978):179–86.

Whieldon, David. "Clean, Steady Power Prevents Problems for Mainframes." *Computer Decisions*, no. 5 (1979):46–60.

Whiteside, Thomas. "Annals of Crime: Dead Souls in the Computer: I and II." *The New Yorker*, August 22, 1977, pp. 1–14, and August 29, 1977, pp. 1–16.

Test Yourself

1. What is meant by the term "computer security"?
2. What are some of the hazards that might endanger a computer facility?
3. Computers are often blamed for making a mistake when a customer receives an inaccurate bill. Should computers be blamed? Defend your answer.
4. What is a UPS?
5. How can data processing managers minimize potential fire damage?
6. What is the purpose of risk analysis?
7. Name the five levels of control in a security system.
8. What is the purpose of a contingency plan? What features should it include?
9. Your company's computer facility contains a CPU, two terminals, four desks, and a bookcase of reference manuals in one large room, with supplies and magnetic tapes stored in an alcove. How would you control physical access to this facility?
10. Why are many people concerned about invasion of privacy in relation to computer systems?

16 Trends in Computer Applications

(By permission of Tom Niemann)

"Ms. Robinson, you've got real class."

APPLICATION

Computers and Medicine

There are seven million severely handicapped people in the United States—those for whom the loss of sight or hearing, impaired walking ability, or the inability to use their hands prevents self-sufficiency and lessens the quality and enjoyment of life. In the new field of rehabilitation engineering, supplemental appliances are being designed to bring new mobility and sensory perception to the handicapped. New prosthetic devices containing microprocessors can be operated by breath, voice, or muscle contractions. Among the most promising developments:

- A voice-activated controller that can move a wheelchair and instruct a robotic self-care arm, designed for use by quadriplegics.
- An artificial arm that responds to muscle contractions in the upper arm and can be moved at will. Electrodes implanted in the stump of the amputated arm are translated by a microprocessor in the prosthesis, making possible such typical arm movements as grasping objects and bending at the wrist and elbow.
- An artificial hand that can sense both touch and slippage, can duplicate the wrist rotation and grasping motions of a human hand.
- A hearing device that consists of a series of electrodes implanted in the cochlea of the inner ear. The electrodes are connected to a miniaturized microphone and computer worn by the deaf individual. Sounds picked up by the microphone are translated by the computer into electronic signals and sent via the electrodes to stimulate a specific location in the cochlea, where they are perceived as speech.
- A visual prosthesis in which 64 electrodes are implanted in the cortex, the visual response area of the brain (located at the back of the head). A miniaturized television camera and microprocessor set in "eyeglasses" receive light emitted by a source and transmit the image electronically to the cortex for perception.

Computers are also used during appliance development to simulate a range of conditions and for testing. In the hearing device, for example, computers tested the responses of electrodes to varying sound frequencies that simulated the patterns of human speech. Computers are also used to design the weight of artificial limbs within acceptable humanlike limits.

Computer data processing is a component of regular health care services. Computers can ask the questions necessary to obtain a medical history, and can actually assist in the diagnosis itself. At a clinic in Edinburgh, Scotland, for example, all new patients must "talk" to a computer terminal. The computer asks a number of questions that are to be answered by pressing the "Yes" or "No" button. A "?" button asks the computer to restate a question that is not clear to the patient.

The same technology makes remote-site diagnosis possible. At Logan Airport in Boston, a medical "studio" is linked via computer and television to Massachusetts General Hospital. With the aid of a nurse in the studio, a physician at the hospital can get the results of various tests (cardiograms, urine analyses, and blood counts), make a diagnosis, and even sign a prescription for a patient at the airport.

We are not yet living in a bionic community—and it is not likely that we ever will be. But the computer technology barely out of the laboratory, or just over the horizon, will increasingly be an aid to human life and health in the years to come.

T
HE OUTLINES of computer development in the future can be seen in the trends that are with us today. One key trend in computer technology is miniaturization. Another is the growth of the telecommunications industry and the spread of computer networks, which are making distributed data processing possible. And related to all these developments is the increasing variety of applications pertinent to business, industry, and government. (Some of these applications—electronic mail, robotics— still sound to us like things in a science fiction novel, and yet prototypes exist today.)

In this chapter we will review the trends in computer use and development, with emphasis on their implications for the business community. We will look also at some problems of social policy posed by this new technology, and raise questions about human and governmental priorities in research and development as well as questions about personal privacy and national security in the telecommunications era.

Trends in Computer Use and Development

The big story in the computer industry has always been *growth*. At the end of the 1970s, the decade that marked the greatest expansion of the field to date, increases continued dramatically. The worldwide value of the installed base of mainframe computers from U.S. manufacturers went from $89 billion in 1978 to $97.9 billion in 1979, a 10 percent increase. Of this total, about $45.3 billion represented the value of the 49,696 mainframe computers installed abroad, while $52.6 billion represented the value of the 53,243 units in the United States. IBM led the way, accounting for some 62.6 percent of all units installed worldwide. In 1979, personal computing was up 60 percent, peripherals up 40 percent, and minicomputers up 25 to 30 percent over the preceding year. (See figure 16-1.) One analysis of the computer industry predicted revolutionary developments in computer hardware by the end of the decade.*

Trends in Hardware

Computer categories are rapidly becoming blurred. At one extreme, superminis are competing with the smaller general-purpose mainframes, while new desktop units are competing for the micro-

* Standard & Poor's industry survey, "Office Equipment Systems and Services, Basic Analysis," Section 2, May 15, 1980.

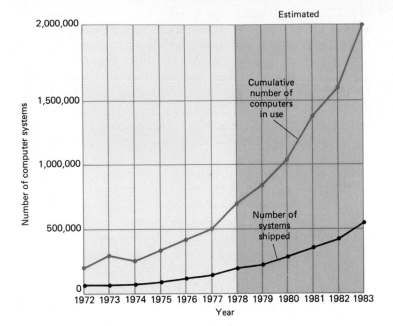

Figure 16-1 Computer activity of U.S. manufacturers
Source: Adapted from Standard & Poor's industry survey, "Office Equipment Systems and Services, Basic Analysis," Section 2, May 15, 1980, p. 017. Based on data supplied by International Data Corp.

mini market at the other end. The minis and micros of the last five years are making possible computer applications in small businesses, schools, and homes, applications that were unheard of only a short while ago. Much of this new equipment permits greater interaction between computer and user. Consequently, we can expect a steady increase in the use of computers for education, for entertainment, and for a variety of "personal" computing uses.

The trend toward miniaturization affects "big" machines as well. Improvements in microelectronic technology are bringing lower-cost and smaller hardware within reach of individuals and small businesses, and are providing greater storage capacity and main memory, as well as faster speeds of operation and information retrieval, in smaller housing and at lower cost. Increased production of smaller equipment is lowering costs and bringing greater data processing capacity to more users of large-scale equipment.

At the same time, nontechnological developments in the nation and the world that are enhancing computer usage and development include the energy crisis, international political competition and pressure, new government regulations that require management of massive amounts of data and disbursement of large sums of money, and greater public acceptance of the desirability of change.

Minicomputers. Sales of computers costing between $2,000 and $25,000 increased more than 30 percent in 1979, and are expected to continue at that level or higher each year. The main memory of these

A minicomputer, the HP-85, is teamed with an equally compact printer and graphic plotter to bring calculating power directly into the research laboratory.

(Hewlett-Packard Co.)

machines ranges from 10K- to 128K-bytes, their size from tabletop modules to that of a three- or four-drawer file cabinet. Thus the prefix "mini" refers to relative size, not to computer power. Today's minicomputer is used primarily for processing either a single large application or several smaller programs. In recent years this segment of the industry has been growing at an average rate of more than 20 percent per year. The availability of these machines has created a new market of "small" users, as minicomputers have enabled small installations such as a company department or branch office to assume responsibility for its own data processing. Among the advantages that minicomputers bring to small businesses are access to all file records, total interaction (compared to the batch processing of a large centralized system), and cost savings similar to those of corporations using large central computers. Traditional minis have been supplemented by superminis and microminis, each reaching into a different segment of the market. The anticipated growth is greatest for the superminis, which are already replacing large and standard computers of the previous generation. As minicomputers of every size find an ever-larger niche, the auxiliary hardware they require is experiencing complementary growth as well, and so are software and services geared to this market.

417

Desktop computers. Increasingly, the term "desktop" is being used to describe a wide range of microprocessor-based systems that include home and school computers as well as small business systems. Perhaps the most explosive of all computer growth areas, microcomputers first made their appearance in the late 1970s, and annual increases of around 30 percent per year were being predicted for the 1980s. (See figure 16-2.) Microtechnology advances that give greater storage capacity to these units, and also provide plug-in accessories at low cost, will further increase the audience for these systems; so will the development of software that enables the noncomputer-trained individual to use them effectively.

Microcomputers are classified by the number of bits that can be handled at one time by their microprocessor CPUs. The long-popular eight-bit processors began to be succeeded by 16-bit devices in 1978, and are expected to be replaced in turn by 32-bit processors before the 1980s are over. The microcomputers of 1990 will have CPU storage capacity equal to or greater than that of today's large computers.

At present, business microcomputers are typically single-terminal, transaction-oriented devices of limited capacity. They require tape or disk storage of both programs and data. Increasingly, though, these devices are being linked with networks that make up for their relatively small main memory.

In the meantime, single-chip microcomputers are available for a variety of specialized applications. They are used to control fuel consumption in cars and provide useful information to the driver; to keep track of rodeo riders' ratings and schedules on the rodeo circuit; to design toys; to provide a variety of services in drugstores (for example, keeping customer prescription profiles and recording multidrug interactions so that customers are not given dangerous combinations of medications)—and much more.

Figure 16-2 The microcomputer market in 1979 and 1984 according to end-user category

Source: Adapted from Standard & Poor's industry survey, "Office Equipment Systems and Services, Basic Analysis," Section 2, May 15, 1980, p. 017. Based on data supplied by International Data Corp.

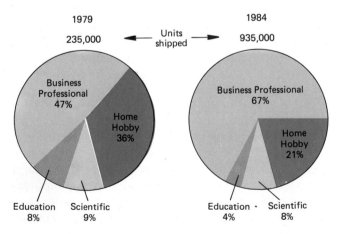

Speed. The standard cycle time of today's fast computers is 30 to 50 nanoseconds. But computer scientists expect to produce a Josephson junction computer with a 3-nanosecond cycle time within the next decade. Josephson junctions are superconductors and the fastest electronic switch known (see also chapter 2). A complete computer based on the superconducting technology will be contained in a 2-inch cube, and will be as much as 50 times faster than the fastest computers now available. Superfast computers of this kind would be of particular value in such special applications as computerized weather forecasting (see chapter 5). But even where speed is not crucial, such fast cycle times would mean the ability to process 50 times as much data in the same amount of time. And it may also mean correspondingly lower costs.

Communications. In a 1980 ruling, the Federal Communications Commission (FCC) deregulated the *equipment production* segment of the telephone industry. (The FCC, however, still has jurisdiction over telephone *service*.) This ruling served notice that the traditional distinction between data processing (manipulation of data) and telecommunications (transmission of voices and visual images) is fast disappearing. An immediate effect of the ruling was to give the American Telephone and Telegraph Company (AT&T), a leading common carrier, permission to develop customer-oriented telecommunications products and to enter the field of data processing. No longer are AT&T, General Telephone and Electronics, and similar companies able to provide only the channels by which computers communicate; now they can, through subsidiaries, produce equipment for use with their communications facilities as well.

Among the first results are "smart" telephones; these will automatically redial a number that had been busy, store and record messages, locate a customer at other numbers, screen out undesirable calls, set up conference calls between more than two parties—and more. Devices that would connect coast-to-coast telephone calls in 2 seconds, a fifth of the time required at present, and high-speed data transmission networks that could process, store, retrieve, and distribute information between numerous users are also expected to be among the early consequences.

Software and Services

At present, a major deterrent to even greater growth in the use of mini- and microcomputers is the relative scarcity of software for these machines. But the direction of change can already be seen as companies specializing in software production enter the market.

APPLICATION
DDP at TI

Distributed data processing involves a network of remote-site, intelligent terminals, each capable of communicating with all the others, and perhaps with a centrally located CPU, and each having access to the files and programs of the others. Texas Instruments is a corporation with 48 plants in 18 different countries. The company began installing a minicomputer DDP network in 1971. It now has a distributed system linking together more than 5,000 terminals and 200 remote job entry stations, handling a workload of 6,000 batch jobs and 320,000 separate transactions daily, and is supported by a communications network that includes satellite channels. TI expects to expand this system to 25,000 terminals and 10,000 minicomputers by the mid-1980s.

Two of TI's most important applications illustrate why DDP is necessary: a real-time customer service system and an in-factory production control system. The customer service system maintains computer file records of the service history of all equipment sold, constantly updated inventory records of parts and equipment, and real-time status reports on every request for service. A subsystem schedules every customer request for service and accesses all data pertinent to every service job.

The in-factory system manages work in progress by controlling production queues and flow rates. Known as DAPS (for Distributed Application Processing System), it keeps track of some 20,000 lots in 550 stations in 20 shops. DAPS, together with a Factory Order and Control System (FOCS), links 170 terminals at 10 sites in four cities. These two systems operate around the clock, with time out only for system maintenance and related procedures. The advantages of DDP for Texas Instruments seem obvious and essential as a high-technology manufacturer moves into the future. Yet middle-level management personnel did not readily accept the capabilities of the system when it was first introduced, and continued to rely on informal word-of-mouth communication to update information.

Source: Ron Person, "How TI Distributes Its Processing," *Datamation,* no. 4 (1979):98–103.

This activity can be expected to increase as the potential audience for these products expands. Indeed, computer programmers are "moonlighting" as the "authors" of commercial software programs. Already, business and personal computer users are finding it less costly to buy software programs, which are becoming available for a wide range of applications, than to invest the time, money, and personnel required to develop applications programs themselves.

Software development is lagging far behind that of computer hardware, and industry sources doubt whether the soaring demand for software can be met in the years ahead. A major reason for this phenomenon is the lack of trained personnel—a shortage that is expected to continue well into the future. It is predicted that software-related occupations, such as systems analyst and programmer, will have the highest growth rate of any profession in the next decade.

As the computer industry expands into the consumer market, the software and services needed to attract that market are being developed. Among the services already available to make the purchase of personal units more practical are subscription information networks. A typical network provides international news, stock market quotations, restaurant information, games, and even a home real-estate service, as well as a message interchange for subscribers. There is a one-time installation fee and per-hour usage charges priced differentially for peak or business (daytime) usage and off-peak or consumer (evening) usage. The New York Times Information Bank provides an archive of information as well as up-to-the-minute news for subscribers; another network specializes in programs and information aimed at the computer hobbyist.

Applications Today and Tomorrow

The online real-time society is coming. Already computers are in our schools, in our places of work, in our homes—all around us, perhaps *on* us, and, in some instances, *inside* us. But few people are aware how widespread the influence of computers is today.

The dollar volume of the data processing industry has doubled at five-year intervals since 1970. By 1990, user spending on data processing in the United States is expected to increase from its present value of slightly over 2 percent of the gross national product (GNP) to about 13 percent. By that time, too, at least 20 percent of U.S. workers will need some knowledge of data processing to carry on their jobs, and the jobs of 60 percent will *depend* on data processing to one degree or another.

In Unit I, we examined the roles that computers play in our lives today, and looked at the astonishing pace of developments in technology over the short life span of these machines. Now we will survey predictions for the computer world of the future, and examine some of the issues that will face us as we move inevitably into the computer society.

The vice-president of a bank can, by depressing a few keys on the keyboard of her computer terminal, view staff memos on the terminal's screen. She can answer each one immediately. Her responses are delivered instantly to associates at branches of her bank in her own state, elsewhere in the nation, and at affiliated banks overseas. It is not necessary for any of these associates to be at their desks when our vice-president is sending her messages to them; their own computer terminals are storing the communications, holding them until the addressees have time to view them and respond. Meanwhile, the vice-president is depressing a few more keys to view financial data stored in a CPU at another bank location. She can also view the overtime records of the branch's staff.

The Office of Tomorrow

In the office next door, another bank vice-president has the same equipment on his desk. But he does not use it—he hates to type and sees himself as a "talker." He prefers to dictate into a machine and have his messages transcribed for transmission through normal postal channels. In a few years, though, he will be able to utilize computer power without having to confront a keyboard. Voice-recognition devices will solve his problem. Voice data entry and voice-response technology are still in the early stages of product development, but when they achieve the ability to recognize wide vocabularies and continuous speech and are marketable at competitive cost, the users and applications will be waiting.

Two other technological developments whose impact will increase in the next decade are optic electronic mail and optical recognition devices. Both are already in use for limited applications, but have enormous potential for changing the way we work and do business over the next decade.

Electronic mail. The first significant application of electronic mail was the introduction of Mailgram by Western Union in conjunction with the U.S. Postal Service in 1971. The success of this service has contributed, at least in part, to the installation of electronic "mailboxes" by some corporations. For Cook Industries, which deals in the buying and selling of commodities, electronic mail solved the problem of delayed communications. Messages from around the world were reaching Cook's centralized communications department in Memphis almost instantaneously, but were then delayed several hours or more for copying, before being sent on to their ultimate destination. A system of some 90 CRT terminals, each in contact (via a computer center in Chicago) with the major commodities exchanges in Chicago and New York, provided mailboxes. A printer in each of 21 departments could provide hard-copy output for all terminals serving that department. To read the mail received at an electronic mailbox, the user enters both an identification code and a password. Individual codes appear on the CRT screen when mail is received to alert a particular addressee or those staff members concerned with the mailed information.

Citibank of New York is another company that has already made electronic mail a part of its 16 management work stations. Each work station—which includes a minicomputer, several disk drives, a printer, a communications line and modem, and a CRT-keyboard terminal—is run by one manager and a secretary.

With further developments in telecommunications, we can expect to see offices with Picturephones that connect individuals who are thousands of miles apart. Business personnel around the world will be able to hold "face-to-face" conferences without leaving their own offices, and they will be able to exchange printed information almost instantaneously, even while a conference is in progress—all with the aid of voice-recognition technology.

Micrographics. Originally used as a backup system to store information from original documents as protection against loss or damage, micrographics has emerged as a viable adjunct to office management. It offers a solution to a number of common office problems: increasing costs of paper, increased computer output volume, increased amount of space required for information storage, increased time consumed in information retrieval from paper-storage file systems, and lack of cross-referencing in paper file storage systems. Micrographics includes microfilm, microfiche, computer output microfilm (COM), film processors, and media such as reels, cassettes, and cartridges. Digital signals from magnetic tape or direct from a computer are accepted by a COM recorder, which converts the digital input to analog signals, displays them on a screen or other output medium, and can expose the resulting microfilm for accessing. Microfilm/fiche readers enlarge film or fiche images and project them onto a screen for viewing as needed. Reader-printers can project film or fiche onto screens as well as print paper-output copies.

As the advantages of this technology become apparent, the use of COM units is likely to grow by 20 percent every year in the 1980s. Microfilm output costs are lower than paper copying; microfilm storage costs are about $1/45$ those of paper, and take up only 2 percent of the space that paper would require. COM is likely to replace magnetic tape storage in many applications as well, because it costs about a fourth as much and requires only 1 percent of the storage space.

An even greater advantage, though, is likely to be the ability of COM and other micrographics products to interface with other data and communications technologies. For example, electronic mail will automatically convert to COM for storage and retrieval. The implications for organizations with sizable data processing requirements—government agencies, stock exchanges, news services—are enormous.

423

Manufacturing

The first computer-controlled manufacturing plant went into operation in 1959. There are at present more than 200 different computer-aided manufacturing (CAM) systems available on some 40 to 50 different computers. The following predictions have been made for the end of this decade:

1. Eighty percent of in-process and finishing technology in manufacturing will be automated and computer-controlled.
2. Computers will generate processing plans and control 30 percent of all manufacturing.
3. Fifty percent of the labor involved in small-component assembly will be replaced by automation.
4. Fifty percent of the work force on the plant floor will be skilled engineers and technicians.
5. Computer-aided design (CAD) will be used by 20 percent of the total number of manufacturers.
6. Fifteen percent of assembly systems will use robotic technology.

General Motors, which has been using CAD for over a decade, expects that by 1990 approximately 90 percent of all the new machines in its manufacturing and assembly plants will be computer-controlled. The value of computer process control became dramatically apparent to the company as the market for smaller, fuel-efficient cars expanded rapidly. Following the oil embargo of 1973, GM had to redesign, assemble, and test a new generation of automobiles. Their Vehicle Structural Analysis Program (VSAP) uses CRT consoles to evaluate the structural characteristics of designs. The program makes it possible to "assemble" mathematical models of the various components of a new car and then run it through a computer-simulated road test—all long before the actual test model is built.

Robotics. Robots have been imagined—and in some cases feared—for decades. At this very moment, more than 3,000 robots are at work in American industry in such companies as General Electric, Westinghouse, and Ford. Yet, American industry is lagging well behind the Japanese, who employ about 7,000 robots and are currently working to develop the first completely robotic factory.

Robots are already in use as mail carriers, picking up and delivering materials between work stations in large offices and factories. These machines are self-starting, self-stopping, and self-charging.

At present, the most sophisticated robot available in this country is the PUMA 500. This Programmable Universal Machine for Assembly is a small robot weighing 120 pounds, with a maximum arm reach of 3 feet. Looking very unlike the standard robot of science fiction, PUMA consists essentially of an arm mounted on a cylinder that is hooked up to 75 pounds of electronic brain. PUMA can lift a maximum load of 5 pounds and can position it with an accuracy of four-thousandths of an inch. Since 95 percent of automobile parts weigh 3 pounds or less, PUMA is finding wide use in the automobile industry. General Motors, for example, already has about 15 robots on its assembly lines. Because PUMA occupies about as much space as a human worker, it can be installed within existing production systems. PUMA is also quiet and will not disturb human workers as it goes about its business.

Such robots can be used for a variety of tasks—welding, paint spraying, loading, riveting, and so on. Moreover, a single robot can be easily modified to perform any and all of these jobs by attaching a different tool to the end of its arm and reprogramming it. Reprogramming may be as easy as leading the robot "by the hand" through the series of movements it will have to perform in a particular process. PUMA's "brain" records the movements, and the robot is "ready to go."

Robots are not going to take over in the world of the future. They will, however, be given more specialized assignments, and will be created with additional capabilities. The manufacturer of PUMA is

This "mailmobile" is programmed to go through the corridors of an office, stopping at every work station so that mail can be deposited and picked up.

(Courtesy of Sears, Roebuck & Co.)

working on a robot that will be able to shear Australian sheep. Robot-icists are also working on a seeing model called Consight, which will have a relatively simple "eye" and brain. This second-generation robot will be able to take over a large number of simple assembly-line tasks that are too dull or too dangerous for efficient or safe production by humans.

Government and Military Applications

Government uses of computer technology range from the mundane to the global. At one pole, for instance, are the computerized space suits that NASA is developing for the astronauts who will be using the space shuttle. These suits feature a microprocessor-based display and control unit located on the chest of the suit. The astronaut wearing the suit will be able to read a small display screen simply by looking down. Among other things, the screen will provide instructions for dealing with malfunctions of the suit. If there are two or more malfunctions, the screen will list them in order of importance.

National security and defense. The communications system serving the U.S. armed forces is a network of 35 large computers in 27 different locations worldwide. Wimex (for WWMCCS, or World Wide Military Command and Control System) is presently being replaced by a more up-to-date system. Wimex has had some unfortunate failures, at least one of them extremely dangerous: In November 1979 it falsely declared a missile attack. Determining that Wimex had made a mistake cost its managers 6 minutes of severe anxiety.

The U.S. military's communications network AUTOVON (*Automatic Voice Network*) is the largest private telephone network in existence. AUTOVON transmits both data and voice over the same lines, encoding calls for security when necessary, of course. The push-button AUTOVON telephones have four priority keys in addition to the usual 12. The "P" (priority) key allows the caller to preempt ordinary calls, while the three other priority keys are able to preempt successively higher levels of priority calls. A special tone informs the speaking parties that they are being interrupted by a higher-precedence call. If a given telephone is not "authorized" for a particular priority level, a caller pressing the unauthorized key is told by a recording that the call cannot be made from that phone.

AUTOVON also includes "hot lines," telephone links that provide an almost instantaneous connection between predetermined locations. AUTOVON can automatically set up a conference call when a user dials a number keyed to a predetermined list of conferees.

Law enforcement. The prosecutor's office in Suffolk County, New York, has installed a computer-based case management system that records key information about a defendant, the status of the charge(s) brought against him or her, the time, place, location, and result of "events" (such as arraignment) in the history of a particular case, and information needed for notifying all interested parties of an upcoming event in a case. Data entered by voice appear on a screen to be edited and validated immediately. Once stored, data can be accessed by docket number, case number, or name of defendant.

The Millburn, New Jersey, Police Department installed a system known as COPS (Computerized Optimal Police System) a few years ago. By sharing it with the police departments of five nearby towns, the cost to each town is reduced to the equivalent of one police officer's annual salary. This system can search records for an individual's criminal history or an outstanding warrant, if any, while the officer requesting the information waits in a patrol car. The confidentiality of the system's records is also protected.

Education, Entertainment, and Personal Computing

According to one estimate, the amount of information that will be available in computer software formats will increase fourfold by the time that a child born today graduates from college. By the time that graduate is 50 years old, the amount of information will have increased 32 times. Skilled workers will probably have to retrain several times during their working careers just to keep up with important developments. The increased availability of personal computing will put all of this information literally at everyone's fingertips. Instruction at every level will be increasingly interactive and individualized. Education will tend to become lifelong, as computer software brings up-to-date continuing education to a mass audience. Specialists and professionals in all fields will rely less on memorizing large amounts of factual details as they turn to a computer for reference and updating.

Education. It has been predicted that by the year 2000 most college students will own an inexpensive, briefcase-sized computer much more powerful than the mainframes found on today's campuses and costing about one-thousandth as much. This portable computer will produce words, pictures, and sounds. Programs for teaching different subjects will also be available in software formats so that students can use their computers as ready-reference notebooks.

Some computer authorities have begun to express concern about a new form of learning handicap—computer illiteracy. By computer illiteracy is meant the inability to use computers to perform various tasks. Changes in school curricula are being made so that children can become familiar with, and use, computers at an early age. Already, the newest status symbol a school can show off to parents is a computer room, but it will not be long before this prestige facility becomes widespread and commonplace.

Entertainment. The chief area of growth for computer-based entertainment is the home, or personal, computer. TV games, chess, and hobby programs are so far the leading entertainment applications. On a professional level, cartridge devices are now available that can substitute for a radio disk jockey. With random access to as many as 78 cartridges, such a device serves as part of a microcomputer-based system that can operate a radio station—unassisted—for an entire week. Similar technology can program complex audiovisual presentations and create special effects in film and video studios.

Personal computers get serious. In 1980, Texas Instruments offered a personal computer with easily replaceable software modules. These modules include: various teaching programs for children (with color, sound, and motion); a variety of financial programs (from home budget management to securities analysis); and, of course, entertainment programs (among them, a three-level chess player). TI plans a constantly expanding library of such programs. Already available to users is a telephone link that provides access to wire-service news reports, weather information, and stock quotations. And the model incorporates a voice synthesizer—it can actually talk! Only a few months later, the Tandy Corporation announced a hand-held computer that cost less than $300 and two other models with innovative abilities priced well under $1,000.

Toward a Computer Morality

All great technological advances bring risks as well as benefits. The technology of the industrial revolution created new wealth and a higher standard of living for many in the nineteenth century. But for the men, women, and children who worked in its factories, that revolution often meant dangerous working conditions, unhealthy living conditions, debilitating disease, and early death. The second industrial revolution—as the computer revolution is sometimes called—has its own benefits and risks. It is, certainly, creating new wealth and a higher standard of living for many people. And while it does not bring unhealthy working conditions (quite the contrary!), it does pose other kinds of problems for our society.

Throughout history, knowledge—especially technical knowledge—has brought power to those who possessed it. In this age of computers, it is especially true that information is power. In the opinion of many, it is the ability of computers to store vast amounts of information that makes them a real threat to individual freedom. The nature of the problem becomes clear when we begin to consider the variety of data banks that are currently used to hold personal information. Table 16-1 shows a *partial* list of the types of data banks and a few uses of each.

Invasions of Privacy

Of course, a great deal of computer-stored data are collected with the consent of the individuals in question, but much is not. (In the early 1970s, it was revealed that the Department of Defense had files on 25 *million* Americans and on thousands of organizations—including the American Civil Liberties Union and the National Association for the Advancement of Colored People.) Moreover, much of these data are anything but confidential. Government departments exchange information about individuals. It is frequently sold for marketing purposes—which explains why your name is on the mailing lists of organizations you never heard of.

Table 16-1 Types of Data Banks

Data Bank	Used For/In	Data Bank	Used For/In
Financial	Credit status Banking information	Organizational	Armed forces Membership lists Personnel files
Governmental	Business information Economic data Property owners	Job Qualifications	Educational records Professional group membership IQ test results Aptitude test results
Health, Education, and Welfare	Educational Job opportunities Unemployment Medical	Service	Insurance Libraries
Marketing	Mailing lists	Social	Computerized dating
Medical	Hospital Medical Psychiatric	Travel	Reservations Rentals

A free society thrives on the free flow of information—but the unregulated exchange of data can become an invasion of privacy. The world has seen many examples of how data collection can be abused. Some dictatorships use computers to record the activities of dissidents, and collect names for secret police roundups. Indeed, our own Secret Service uses this procedure to identify individuals who might pose a physical threat to our own or visiting government leaders. Many states keep computer files on criminals and suspected criminals. There is considerable justification for maintaining files on known and even suspected criminals and also on suspected spies. But what about people who may associate with known criminals, or work with suspected undercover agents? What about employees of a government unit, a public agency, or a company engaged in secret or sensitive work for the government? What about ordinary citizens—teachers, factory workers, accountants? Where should record keeping stop? What kinds of records should be kept?

The full impact of this issue remains to be faced. Legislative action, both federal and state, will be required. Controls will also be needed within the computer industry itself. Many suggestions have been offered: expanded use of more intricate electronic safeguards in computer systems to prevent unauthorized use; legislation to prevent abuse of computer information by private or government agencies; ready access for individuals to the information filed about them, with ready recourse in case of error or damage.

But before corrective action can be taken, some kind of consensus about the problem will have to be reached. This will not be easy because many people believe that a government's right to know takes precedence over the individual's right to privacy. Others take just the opposite view. Whether we control computers or whether computers are used to control us may well depend on where and how we draw the line between these two extremes.

Other Social Problems

The displacement of workers by machines that can do their jobs more efficiently is known as technological unemployment. To what extent are computers replacing human workers? In what industries?

It is clear that the computer society is creating many new jobs and many new kinds of jobs. According to one estimate, 50,000 more computer programmers are needed *right now*.* But the computer industry requires personnel who are highly trained. Meanwhile, the individuals who formerly performed their tasks manually and were

---

* "Missing Computer Software," *Business Week,* September 1, 1980, p. 51.

perhaps less technically skilled—clerks, typists, bookkeepers—will have more difficulty finding jobs, and will receive comparatively lower salaries for their work.

How can we provide the technical training for the jobs of the future? And can we ease the transition for those who will have to "re-tool" for new careers? These challenges must be met from several different directions.

The business community must provide transitional jobs and on-the-job training. It must assume responsibility for the human implications of technological progress. This will not, in an age of inflation and high interest rates, be easy or inexpensive. It will take a fore-sighted management to follow up an investment in up-to-the-minute hardware with an investment in the future careers of presently un-derskilled employees. Flexible scheduling of work assignments may make it possible to keep highly trained men and women in the work force and allow them to raise children at the same time. Government assistance will be needed to encourage the upgrading of both equip-ment and human resources. Tax incentives and outright grants of money could variously be used to attain different goals. Federal, state, and local government will also have to encourage new educa-tional options. The creation of new bureaucracies to deal with such problems should be avoided—but is probably inevitable.

The education community will have to show the imagination nec-essary to reach out to a new market and expand the offerings avail-able in continuing education programs. Flexibility could bring credit courses to where the students are—in industrial neighbor-hoods, in the workplace itself, and even in such innovative locations as shopping malls.

Clearly, the solutions pose still other problems. A shorter work week might provide employment for more people. It will also pro-vide time for continuing education and other leisure pursuits. As people receive more technological training, will they be able to pur-sue leisure activities of a cultural nature, or will they have lost the knack of reading for pleasure? Will they be passively glued to their CRTs in their leisure time, perhaps playing computer games, or will they seek out a variety of creative activities? Time, as well as human nature, holds the answers.

Setting Priorities

Late in the summer of 1980, the National Science Foundation, which is the U.S. government's primary arm for financing basic re-search, agreed to withhold funding of a research project in computer encoding. The reason was that the National Security Agency, which

431

collects intelligence by electronic monitoring of worldwide ground and satellite communications, became interested in the project. The academic and scientific communities were alarmed: If independent research in encoding is not supported and the results made public (as is the case with research in other scientific areas), how will we develop the cryptographic techniques to protect against the invasion of individuals' privacy? If scientists are funded by the National Security Agency, some of their results may be classified as secret; but what uses will be made of their work?*

This episode illustrated other problems as well. Government sponsorship of basic research has ultimately made possible many developments of benefit to industry and to consumers. Clearly, the withdrawal of government funding—or different regulations for funding different kinds of research—will hamper innovation and scientific creativity, and interferes with the free flow of ideas between laboratory and marketplace.

Who is to decide? And who will decide whether research with potential military applications should be better rewarded financially than research into medical problems? Will financial incentives be given to industry to develop computer-aided prosthetic devices, while computer applications for education go unfunded?

What, as a nation, are our priorities? What *should* they be? These questions are often put to the electorate in debates over defense budgets or social programs, but the computer components of those budgets are seldom isolated. When politicians talk about a $2 billion price tag on a jobs-for-youth program, how can we find out the amount of money that will be needed to keep computer records and develop a program to match skills and interests with available jobs?

We simply do not know how our national computer research and development funds are being spent. Is it any of our business? How can we decide? At least, let us begin to ask the right questions.

The future of computers is already discernible and promises to be exciting. But it will require further adaptation on the part of an informed citizenry—a citizenry that has already begun to feel both awe and trepidation for the capabilities of these powerful machines.

Summary

The developments in computer technology and data processing over the next decade are hinted at by today's trends. The major technological developments are expected to come with miniaturization, with

* John Noble Wilford, "Science Agency Blocks Funds to Aid Research on Computer Coding," *The New York Times*, August 27, 1980, p. A1.

smaller, faster, and more sophisticated computers that have greater storage capacity and computing power than those available today. The single-chip microcomputer may become the basic component of tomorrow's computer system. Josephson junctions and bubble memories will provide the faster electronics in smaller-than-ever formats that will make it all possible.

The major developments in computer usage will come with the expansion of distributed data processing (DDP) and the growth of the telecommunications service industry. Interactive language use will surpass the use of more limited, technological languages, especially as small systems and personal computing expand.

The trends to both DDP and personal computing will reinforce the increased demand for software. A greater variety of applications for business, education, and personal uses will be demanded—and today's experts do not expect the software market to be saturated even by 1990.

In industry, 50 percent of small-component assembly will be automated by 1990. Computer-aided manufacturing (CAM) and design (CAD) will become increasingly important in many production processes. The office of the future will be largely computerized, with electronic mailboxes and minicomputer systems that will enable a manager and a secretary to run a small department. Another important area of development will be robotics, with "seeing" and "brainy" robots coming into use within the decade.

Over the next 10 to 20 years, the development of computer technology and usage will raise many serious issues of ethics and social policy. Chief among these will be the threat to privacy and individual freedom represented by computer data banks. Whether these issues are resolved to our benefit or to our harm depends not so much on the potential of computers as on our attitude toward computers and our use of them.

"The Challenge of Distributed Systems." *EDP Analyzer*, no. 8 (1978):1–13.

Evans, Christopher. *The Micro Millennium*. New York: Viking, 1980.

Feidelman, Lawrence. "Microcomputers Mean Business." *Infosystems*, no. 6 (1979):104–106.

Kelley, Neil. "Developing a Network." *Infosystems*, no. 10 (1977):99–102.

Martin, James. *The Wired Society*. Englewood Cliffs, N.J.: Prentice-Hall, 1978.

Matisoo, Juri. "The Superconducting Computer." *Scientific American*, May 1980, pp. 50–65.

McCorduck, Pamela. *Machines Who Think*. New York: Freeman, 1979.

"Missing Computer Software." *Business Week*, September 1, 1980, pp. 46–56.

Sources of Additional Information

433

Test Yourself

1. Describe in general terms the advances being made in computer software relative to those being made in hardware.
2. List some nontechnological developments that have affected the development and use of computers.
3. Explain the difference between the terms "mini," "supermini," and "micromini."
4. What are some applications of microcomputers?
5. How does superconducting technology promise to affect the capabilities of future computers?
6. What effect will the 1980 FCC deregulation of equipment production have in the area of data processing?
7. Briefly explain the concept of "electronic mail."
8. What are some advantages of micrographics?
9. What is robotics, and how does it affect manufacturing?
10. List a few government applications of computers.
11. What is technological unemployment?
12. How does increased computer usage threaten individual privacy?
13. What new problems will increased automation of factories create for management?
14. Describe how OCR machines are contributing toward solving the data-entry bottleneck.
15. In terms of gross national product, what is the outlook for user spending on data processing?

Appendix

- **An Introduction to Programming Languages**
  BASIC
  COBOL
  Pascal
- **Acronyms Used in Computer Data Processing**
- **Electronic Data Processing Periodicals**

MANHATTAN PROGRAM

```
10   REM THIS PROGRAM CALCULATES THE BALANCE
15   REM THAT WOULD HAVE ACCUMULATED TO DATE
20   REM HAD THE INDIANS INVESTED AT 6.5%
25   REM THE $24.00 THEY RECEIVED IN PAYMENT
30   REM FOR MANHATTAN
35   REM Y1 IS THE STARTING YEAR, 1627
40   REM Y2 IS THE PRESENT YEAR, 1981
45   REM P IS THE STARTING PRINCIPAL, $24.00
50   READ Y1,Y2
55   READ P
60   REM MULTIPLY PRINCIPAL BY INTEREST RATE
65   REM GIVING YEARLY INTEREST, P1
70   LET P1 = .065*P
75   REM ADD YEARLY INTEREST TO PRINCIPAL
80   REM GIVING UPDATED BALANCE
85   LET P = P1 + P
90   REM INCREMENT YEARLY COUNTER BY 1
95   LET Y1 = Y1 + 1
100 REM IF PRESENT YEAR REACHED, PRINT RESULTS
105 REM IF NOT, REPEAT LOOP
110 IF {Y2 - Y1}> = 0 THEN 220
115 PRINT "BALANCE TO DATE IS";P
120 DATA 1627
125 DATA 1981
130 DATA 24.00
190 END
```

THIS APPENDIX is designed to give the reader a brief introduction to the principles of programming in BASIC, COBOL, and Pascal. For each language, a program has been written that will compute the amount of return on $24.00, invested at an annual interest rate of 6.5 percent. The program is titled MANHATTAN since $24.00 was paid to the Indians for the island of Manhattan in 1626, so interest payments theoretically would have begun the following year. Wherever possible, relevant examples from the program will be used to illustrate the discussion of the programming procedure. Certain topics have general applicability to all three languages, such as hierarchy of arithmetic operations, file processing, and use of computational loops. These will be treated in detail in the discussion of BASIC, and more briefly in the COBOL and Pascal discussions.

In general, the discussions of the three programming languages will parallel each other. However, the languages and their usages are sufficiently different so that this is not always possible. The discussion of COBOL, for example, requires a detailed description of the program structure, which is more rigidly defined than that of BASIC or Pascal. These discussions are not intended to be thorough treatments of the languages. They should be regarded as extended glossaries, giving enough vocabulary and syntax for a reader to understand and write a simple program in each language. These discussions also convey some sense of the different nuances of each language in expressing the same problem. The procedure of signing on and running a program will be illustrated only for the BASIC program.

BASIC

Computer programs in BASIC are generally entered into the computer by typing instructions into a terminal. We describe below one particular way of accessing the computer to write, edit, or run programs in BASIC. Accessing procedures vary with the particular machine used at a particular installation. More detailed information can be provided by the computer center used.

Sign-On Procedure

Assuming the data terminal is "online," waiting to transmit instructions to the computer, the user types in:

```
LOGIN
```

and presses the RETURN key to signify that the input is complete. The system then requests the user to enter her or his password or user number, and something similar to the following is displayed:

```
ON AT 17:30 FRIDAY FEBRUARY 13, 1981
       USER NUMBER, PASSWORD
```

The use of a password protects the programmer's files from use by others. The user enters his or her password and again presses the RETURN key. The terminal immediately types over the password to protect it from disclosure. After receiving a valid password, the computer responds with:

```
READY
```

The user then specifies the particular computer language to be used by typing:

```
ENTER BASIC
```

The computer again responds with:

```
READY
```

At this point, the user may begin to type in BASIC instructions.

The BASIC Character Set: Creation of Variables and Constants

Three types of characters are used to form the symbolic words of the BASIC vocabulary:

1. Alphabetic characters: `ABCDE . . . . . Z`
2. Numeric characters: `0123456789`
3. Special characters: `. , " + * - / = {}<>$` and blank or space

The BASIC vocabulary consists of "verbs," which are the computer operations, and "nouns," which are the elements that are operated on. There are two kinds of nouns, *constants* and *variables*. Nouns are composed by the programmer. The BASIC vocabulary is used to construct the instructions that constitute the program.

Constants. As the name suggests, constants are numerical quantities whose values do not change during the course of the computer calculation. In the `MANHATTAN PROGRAM`, for example, the interest rate, .065, is a constant. Valid characters for a BASIC constant are numeric characters, + (plus) or − (minus) signs, and a decimal point. If no + or − sign precedes the numerical value of the constant, a + sign is assumed (that is, it is assumed that the number is positive). The following are examples of valid (will be accepted by the machine) and invalid (will not be accepted) constants:

Valid constants	Invalid constants	Reason invalid
3.156	A42	Alphabetic character not allowed.
+.0214	42,156	Comma not allowed.
−.356	X	Alphabetic character not allowed.
11	4Y	Alphabetic character not allowed.

Variables. Variables represent quantities whose values may be changed during the course of a computation. A "variable name" is assigned to a particular storage location in the computer. Variable names represent quantity concepts such as hours worked or total sale, and may designate data stored either in numeric or character form. The numerical value of a particular quantity is placed in that location. The variable may be used by the computer several times during a computation. Although the actual numerical value of the variable may change during the course of the program, the variable location name represents only one numerical quantity at a time. In the MANHATTAN PROGRAM, the yearly balance, P1, changes as the interest accrues. Y1 (starting year) is designated a variable because it is used as a "counter" (see below). Its value changes during the course of the program. Y2, present year, is also made a variable since the programmer might want the flexibility of updating or changing the value of the final year.

BASIC provides for both numeric and string variable names. A *numeric variable name* may be either a single alphabetic character, or a single alphabetic character followed by one numeric digit:

Valid numeric variable name	Invalid numeric variable name	Reason invalid
A	A,	Comma not allowed.
Y	YZ	Two alphabetic characters not allowed.
K3	3K	Alphabetic character must appear first.

A *string* is a sequence of letters, digits, and/or special characters stored under a single variable name. A *string variable name* consists of a single alphabetic character followed by a dollar sign ($):

Valid string variable name	Invalid string variable name	Reason invalid
N$	N6$	Only one character can precede $.
A$	3$	Numeric character not allowed.

String variable names may represent character strings such as:

```
"THE ANSWER IN INCHES IS"
"SEPT. 25, 1981"
```

Program Syntax

In every language (human as well as computer), there are certain conventions for arranging words meaningfully. In an English language sentence, for example, adjectives precede nouns, the subject of the sentence usually precedes the predicate, and clauses are separated by commas. These conventions constitute the syntax of the language. Before treating specific BASIC program statements, we will discuss a few rules of general program syntax that must be followed in writing programs in the BASIC language.

Line numbers. Each statement of the program must be assigned a "line number" so that the computer knows the order in which statements are to be executed. The line numbers may take positive integer values only, ranging from 0 to 99999; each statement must have a different line number. The statements are then performed sequentially according to their line number, from low number to high number. When composing a program, it is wise to leave unused numbers between instructions in case there is a need to add intermediary instructions later on. See the printout of the MANHATTAN PROGRAM on page 436.

The REMARK statement. The general form of the REMARK statement is:

line #   REM comment

The REMARK statement aids the programmer by providing documentation of the program steps. In the MANHATTAN PROGRAM, lines 10 through 30 are REMARK statements that identify the program and outline its purpose. Other REMARK statements are lines 60 and 65, which elucidate the symbolic calculations being performed, and lines 35 and 40, which identify the meaning of the symbols used.

The END statement. An END statement must conclude every BASIC program. That statement must be assigned the highest number in the program. The general format of an END statement is:

line #   END

The mathematical operations are indicated by *arithmetic operation symbols*. Note that some BASIC symbols differ from the common symbols of pencil-and-paper arithmetic.

BASIC arithmetic operation symbol	Operation	BASIC arithmetic expression
+	addition	A+B
−	subtraction	A−B
*	multiplication	A*B
/	division	A/B
** or ↑	exponentiation	A**B

An arithmetic expression is a relation in which BASIC nouns (constants or variables) are linked by arithmetic operation symbols.

When several operations are to be performed, the computer follows a hierarchy or sequence in performing those operations. Consider evaluating the expression:

(4*(3*A)**2+6)/B

   (ii)   (i)

If more than one set of parentheses appears in an expression, the operations called for within the innermost set of parentheses (indicated by *i* in our example above) are performed first. Then the operations indicated within the next innermost set of parentheses (*ii*) are performed, and so on.

There is an established order of priority that determines the sequence of BASIC operations to be performed within any set of parentheses:

Priority	Operation
first	exponentiation
second	multiplication or division
third	addition or subtraction

In the example above, the expression 3*A is within the innermost (*i*) set of parentheses, so it is evaluated first. Within the outer set of parentheses (*ii*), exponentiation takes precedence over other operations, so 3*A is next raised to the power 2. Since multiplication takes precedence over addition, the expression so far is next multiplied by 4; 6 is added to the result, and then the entire expression is divided by B. (Therefore, if A = 1 and B = 2, the numerical value of the expression would be 21.)

The LET Statement

The computing process *involves the assignment of values to variables.* This involves:

1. Computation of an expression, using various operations that act upon variables and constants.
2. Assignment of that expression to a variable.

In BASIC, assignment of an expression to a variable is accomplished with the LET statement, which has the following format:

line #   LET variable = expression

The expression may be a constant, variable, or a combination of constants, variables, and arithmetic operations. The computer will evaluate the expression on the right side of the equal sign and assign that value to the indicated variable on the left side of the equal sign. The following are examples of use of the LET statement:

Valid use of LET statement	Invalid use of LET statement	Reason invalid
LET B = 2	LET 2 = B	Variable on right side of = sign.
LET Y = A∗B/C	LET A∗B/C = Y	Expression on left side of = sign.
LET N$ = "NUMBER"	LET N3 = "NUMBER"	N3 invalid character string variable.

In the MANHATTAN PROGRAM, lines 85 and 95 are further examples of use of the LET statement.

Input/Output Statements

The computer must be provided not only with specified operations or procedures, but also with the data to be operated upon. In a BASIC program, data are provided to the computer by DATA and READ statements.

The DATA statement. The general format of the DATA statement is:

line #   DATA constant-list

The *constant list* consists of numeric or character string constants separated by commas or semicolons. Several DATA statements may be made in a program, and they may be located anywhere in the program before the END statement. In the program example, the following DATA statements appear:

```
120 DATA 1627
125 DATA 1981
130 DATA 24.00
```

These data could also be declared in a single statement:

```
122 DATA 1627,1981,24.00
```

The computer reads in all constants from all **DATA** statements, forming a single list headed by the first constant designated in the first **DATA** statement and completed by the last constant in the last **DATA** statement.

In the program example, the computer would form this internal **DATA** list:

```
1627
1981
24.00
```

The READ statement. **READ** statements instruct the computer to process data. The **READ** statement(s) will process the list above, for example, in sequence, beginning at the top. The general format of the **READ** statement is:

line #   **READ** variable-list

The constants in the data list are read in sequentially and assigned the corresponding variable names. The instructions:

```
50 READ Y1,Y2
55 READ P
```

result in the following assignment of data values to variable names:

```
Y1 1627
Y2 1981
P  24.00
```

The INPUT statement. The **INPUT** statement allows data to be provided to the program in an interactive way. When the program encounters an **INPUT** instruction, it will suspend operation until the programmer has typed in the data, followed by a carriage return. The computer will signify to the user its readiness to accept data by printing a question mark (*?*). The program will continue after the data have been entered and a carriage return has been keyed in to signify end of data input. The general format of the **INPUT** statement is:

line #   **INPUT** variable-list

The **INPUT** statement is like a **READ** statement in function: It is used to assign values to variable names, but those values are now pro-

443

vided directly by the programmer rather than by using a DATA statement. Since the program uses only a question mark to indicate the need for data, it is a good practice to precede each INPUT statement in the program with a PRINT statement that causes the computer to type out the identification or description of the data to be entered. This procedure is especially important if there are several INPUT statements in the program.

The PRINT statement. The PRINT statement directs the computer to provide printed output. Specific kinds of output may be called for in a PRINT statement. The general format of the PRINT statement is:

line #   PRINT { variable
                   literal
                   arithmetic expression
                   combination of the above }

The instruction "PRINT variable-name" will result in print output of the value of the variable, be it numeric or character string. For example, the sequence:

```
10 LET N$ = "A IS"
20 LET A = 3
30 PRINT N$,A
40 END
```

results in the output "A IS 3".

A *literal* expression, unlike a variable name, represents only one value, its "face value." A literal expression may consist of alphabetic, numeric, or special characters in any combination. A *character string literal* must be enclosed in quotation marks. The instruction:

```
200 PRINT "BALANCE TO DATE EQUALS"
```

will result in the literal "BALANCE TO DATE" being printed.

Numeric literals do not have to be enclosed in quotation marks. The instruction:

```
201 PRINT 100
```

results in the numeric literal 100 being printed.

The computer can also print the values of arithmetic expressions. The following set of instructions:

```
44 LET A = 40
45 LET B = 60
46 PRINT A + B, A + 6, B/2
```

results in the printed output:

```
100 46 30
```

The instructions described so far direct the computer to perform its operations in a sequential manner. Instructions will be performed in the order of their instruction number. But this is not always the most efficient way of writing or executing a program. Very often, the same few sets of operations are repeatedly performed on a large set of data. It is more efficient to direct the computer to repeat, or loop over, those same sets of operations for all the data.

Unconditional GOTO. Suppose we wished to multiply each one of a list of numbers by a factor of 2, and print them out. A sequential way of programming this would be:

```
10 READ A
15 LET C = 2*A
20 PRINT "A = ";A;"C = ";C
25 READ A
30 LET C = 2*A
35 PRINT "A = ";A;"C = ";C
40 READ A
 . . .
80 DATA 1,3,5,8,6
85 END
```

The program repeats the group of operations:

```
READ A
LET C = 2*A
PRINT "A = ";A;"C = ";C
```

for each new data value, A. Recognizing this, a more efficient way of writing the program is to direct the computer to simply "loop over" or repeat that group of instructions, 10, 15, and 20. This is accomplished with the *unconditional transfer* GOTO *statement*, illustrated in the following example:

```
10 READ A
15 LET C = 2*A
20 PRINT "A = ";A;"C = ";C
25 GOTO 10
30 DATA 1,3,5,8,6
80 END
```

The general format of the GOTO statement is:

line #   GOTO transfer-line

The transfer statement (transfer from line 25 to line 10, rather than to line 30) is *unconditional*. Each time the program encounters the instruction on line 25, it will transfer control to line 10. (When no further data can be read, the program will print `LINE10:END OF DATA`, and program execution will be halted. We will see how to avoid this problem later.)

Conditional transfer statements. BASIC programs become far more powerful once decision making is incorporated directly into program operations. The decision making is performed by *conditional transfer statements.* Examples of conditional transfer statements are `IF...THEN` and the `FOR` and `NEXT` statements.

The general format of an `IF...THEN` statement is:

line #   `IF` test-condition `THEN` line #

("`GOTO`" is implied in the `THEN` part of this statement.)

The test condition is usually a relation between data items. If the test condition is met, the program is transferred to the specified line. If the test condition is not met, the program proceeds normally to the next sequentially higher line number.

The condition or relation to be tested may involve either numeric or character string data. Relational symbols are usually used to express the relationships between data items or to define test conditions. The standard relational symbols are:

BASIC relational symbol	Meaning	Numeric example
$<$	less than	$A < B$
$<=$	less than or equal to	$C <\, = 10$
$>$	greater than	$X + Y > Z$
$>=$	greater than or equal to	$B3/F >\, = 15$
$<>$	not equal to	$A <> B$
$=$	equal to	$D + E = F$

In the `MANHATTAN PROGRAM`, line `110` contains the instruction:

`IF (Y2 - Y1)> = 0 THEN 70`

This can be translated as, "If we have not calculated the principal up to the present date, we must perform the computations another time (`GOTO 70`). If we have completed the computation, we are ready to print the answer (instruction `115`)."

A method of counting the number of loops performed is needed. (This avoids receiving an "error message" due to insufficient data; see above.) This can be accomplished in two ways, using the `IF...THEN` statement.

First, a *trailer value* could be included with the data. In this example, a trailer value, `0`, is specified in lines `12` and `35`:

```
10 READ A
12 IF A = 0 THEN 80
15 LET C = 2*A
20 PRINT "A = ";A;"C = ";C
25 GOTO 10
30 DATA 1,3,5,8,6
35 DATA 0
80 END
```

The trailer value cannot be an actual data value. When the program encounters the value 0 in the data input, it recognizes that no further data are to be read in.

Second, a *counter* or *index variable* could be set up to limit the number of loops the program will perform. If there are only five separate entries, a counter variable, K, would be incremented each time a loop was completed. Execution would be halted when K = 5.

```
2 LET K = 0
5 IF K = 5 GOTO 80
10 READ A
15 LET C = 2*A
20 PRINT "A = ";A;"C = ";C
22 LET K = K + 1
25 GOTO 5
30 DATA 1,3,5,8,6
80 END
```

The FOR and NEXT statements. Because looping is so important in programming and used so often, BASIC provides ways for us to express this concept more concisely than through the use of either counters or trailer values. These are the FOR and NEXT statements. The general format of the FOR statement is:

line #   FOR variable-initial-value TO final-value STEP step-value

Using the FOR and NEXT statements, the above program sequence can be rewritten to use seven instead of nine separate steps:

```
5 FOR K = 1 TO 5 STEP 1
10 READ A
15 LET C = 2*A
20 PRINT "A = ";A;"C = ";C
25 NEXT K
30 DATA 1,3,5,8,6
80 END
```

In conjunction with the NEXT statement (see below), the FOR statement begins the loop sequence and continues it for as long as speci-

447

fied. In the example above, the FOR statement performs all of the following:

1. The counter variable (K) is set equal to its initial value (1).
2. The variable is tested to see if it has exceeded the final value (5).
3. If the final value has not been exceeded, the subsequent program steps are performed.
4. If the final value has been exceeded, program control is transferred to the instruction immediately following the NEXT instruction, in this case line 30, and thus prevents the loop from being repeated again.

The NEXT statement, ending the loop sequence, does the following:

1. It adds the step value (that is, the amount by which the variable is increased by each loop sequence) to the current value of the control variable.
2. It returns control to the FOR statement.

File Manipulation

In the examples discussed so far, the data were supplied to the program either by DATA statements or INPUT statements. Very often, large quantities of data must be read in, processed, and updated, such as the payroll information for employees of a company or the inventory of a particular store. Such data are usually stored permanently on magnetic disks or tapes; these data are referred to as a *file*, and the manipulation of the data is called *file processing*.

The first step in file processing is naming the file, so that space will be allocated to it and it may be subsequently referenced by the program. The general form of the command used in the IBM system to name a file is:

FILE "file-name"

This might be entered, for example, as:

FILE PAYROLL

Once the file has been given a name, it must be *opened*, or unlocked, before any processing can be performed. This is done via an OPEN statement:

OPEN file-number, "file-name", file-type

The file-number is a reference number for the file that is chosen by the programmer. The "file-name" is the previously chosen name (here PAYROLL). The "file-type" is either INPUT or OUTPUT. An INPUT file is one from which data will be read; an OUTPUT file is one on which data will be written. The two are distinct: you cannot write on an INPUT file, nor can you read from an OUTPUT file.

The file processing analogous to the READ and PRINT statements are:

GET file-number:variable-list

to read from a file, and:

PUT file-number:variable-list

to write data onto a file.

After the data have been written onto a file, the file must be closed to ensure that the program does not inadvertently access and perhaps change its contents. This is done with the statement:

CLOSE file-number

The RUN Statement

After all program instructions have been entered, the program is ready to be translated into machine language and then executed. This is accomplished by typing in the instruction:

RUN

If errors have been made in programming, the computer will respond with an error message indicating which line is in error:

LINE 40: SYNTAX ERROR IN EXPRESSION

If no errors have been made in programming, the program will then be executed and the answers given.

COBOL

Three types of characters are used in COBOL:

1. Alphabetic characters: ABCDE . . . . . . Z
2. Numeric characters: 0123456789
3. Hyphen: -

In addition, a variety of special characters are used for specific purposes.

449

COBOL VERSION

MANHATTAN PROGRAM

```
 1        IDENTIFICATION DIVISION.
 2        PROGRAM-ID.          MANHATTAN-PROGRAM.
 3        AUTHOR.              PUT-YOUR-NAME-HERE.
 4           DATE.             SEPT-25-1981.
 5           REMARKS.          THIS PROGRAM CALCULATES THE BALANCE
 6                             THAT WOULD HAVE ACCUMULATED TO DATE
 7                             HAD THE INDIANS INVESTED AT 6.5%
 8                             THE $24.00 THEY RECEIVED IN PAYMENT
 9                             FOR MANHATTAN.
10
11
12
13        ENVIRONMENT DIVISION.
14        CONFIGURATION SECTION.
15        SOURCE-COMPUTER.     CDC-CYBER-74.
16        OBJECT-COMPUTER.     CDC-CYBER-74.
17        SPECIAL-NAMES.       "1" IS PAGE-TOP.
18        INPUT-OUTPUT SECTION.
19        FILE CONTROL.
20        SELECT PRINT-FILE ASSIGN TO OUTPUT.
21
22
23        DATA DIVISION.
24        FILE SECTION.
25        FD PRINT-FILE
26            LABEL RECORDS ARE OMITTED
27            DATA RECORD IS PRINT-LINE.
28        01 PRINT-LINE.
29            02 FILLER         PIC X.
30            02 DATA-LINE      PIC X(132).
31        WORKING-STORAGE SECTION.
32        77 PRESENT-YEAR      PIC 9999, VALUE 1981.
33        77 PRINCIPAL         PIC S9(13)V99, VALUE 24.00.
```

```
34        77 YEARLY-INTEREST      PIC S9{11}V99.
35        77 STARTING-YEAR        PIC S9{4}, VALUE 1627.
36        01 ANSWER-LINE.
37           02 FILLER            PIC X{25}
38           02 FILLER            PIC X{23},
39                                  VALUE "BALANCE TO DATE EQUALS".
40        02 EDITED-PRINCIPAL  PIC $,$$$,$$$,$$$,$$9.99.
41        02 FILLER            PIC X, VALUE ".".
42
43

44        PROCEDURE DIVISION.
45        A0010-BEGIN.
46            OPEN OUTPUT PRINT-FILE.
47        A0020-INTEREST-CALCULATION.
48            MULTIPLY PRINCIPAL BY .065 GIVING YEARLY-INTEREST ROUNDED
49               ON SIZE ERROR GO TO A0040-PROGRAM-ERROR-1.
50            ADD YEARLY-INTEREST TO PRINCIPAL
51               ON SIZE ERROR GO TO A0050-PROGRAM-ERROR-2.
52            ADD 1 TO STARTING-YEAR.
53            IF STARTING-YEAR IS EQUAL TO PRESENT-YEAR
54               GO TO A0030-PRINT-ANSWER.
55            GO TO A0020-INTEREST-CALCULATION.
56        A0030-PRINT-ANSWER.
57            MOVE PRINCIPAL TO EDITED-PRINCIPAL.
58            MOVE ANSWER-LINE TO DATA-LINE.
59            WRITE PRINT-LINE AFTER ADVANCING PAGE-TOP.
60            CLOSE PRINT-FILE.
61            STOP RUN.
62        A0040-PROGRAM-ERROR-1.
63            DISPLAY "YEARLY-INTEREST FIELD TOO SMALL--JOB ENDED.".
64            CLOSE PRINT-FILE.
65            STOP RUN.
66        A0050-PROGRAM-ERROR-2.
67            DISPLAY "PRINCIPAL FIELD IS TOO SMALL--JOB ENDED.".
68            CLOSE PRINT-FILE.
69            STOP RUN.
```

Variables and Constants

In COBOL, variables are referred to by *identifiers,* or data names. An identifier can be from one to 30 characters in length, must begin with an alphabetic character, and cannot begin with a hyphen. No blanks or characters other than those specified above can be used. As is true for any language, certain combinations of characters cannot be used as identifiers. These are "keywords," such as `MOVE`, `SE-LECT`, and `GOTO`, and they are reserved for specific purposes in the standard COBOL vocabulary. Some examples of valid and invalid identifiers are:

Valid identifier	*Invalid identifier*	*Reason invalid*
`PRESENT-YEAR`	`24-342`	Must have alphabetic character.
`YEARLY-INTEREST`	`A.B.C.`	No special characters (.) allowed.
`YEAR-2`	`YEAR - 2`	No blanks allowed.

There are three kinds of data values or constants in COBOL. *Numeric literals* are numerical constants. These literals may contain from one to 18 digits, a + or − sign preceding the number, and a decimal point. The decimal point must not appear on the right end of the number because it may be confused with a period (`.`), the COBOL punctuation mark.

Valid numeric literal	*Invalid numeric literal*	*Reason invalid*
`1200`	`1,200`	Comma not allowed.
`151`	`151.`	Decimal point on right end not allowed.
`-14.2`	`14.2-`	Hyphen should not follow number.

Nonnumeric literals are also called *character strings.* These literals are always enclosed within quotation marks, and can be composed of any permitted character except quotation marks. Blanks are treated as separate characters. If numbers are enclosed within the quotes, they are treated as alphanumeric characters and cannot be used in arithmetic statements. Nonnumeric literals may be from one to 120 characters long. Examples of nonnumeric literals are:

```
"BALANCE TO DATE EQUALS"
"HELLO"
"14.6"
```

A *figurative constant* is a constant to which a specific data name has already been assigned; these are among the special reserved words in the COBOL vocabulary. ZERO (ZEROS, ZEROES) always represents the value 0. SPACE (SPACES) always represents one or more blanks.

Program Structure

The structure of a COBOL program is strictly defined. Every program is organized in four divisions, which must appear in a fixed sequence. These divisions and their functions are:

1. IDENTIFICATION: Identifies the program.
2. ENVIRONMENT: Describes the computer and peripheral devices used.
3. DATA: Describes files, record layouts, and storage.
4. PROCEDURE: The program logic.

The COBOL coding form. A special coding sheet is generally used for writing COBOL programs. The coding sheet contains 80 numbered columns, separated by vertical rules into five fields:

Columns 1–6 are used for instruction sequence numbers. Columns 73–80 are reserved for program identification; use of this field is optional but may be helpful to the programmer. Columns 8 and 12 are both important markers. The names of divisions, sections, and paragraphs, as well as descriptions of files and records, must begin at column 8, which is known as Margin A. Most other entries start at column 12, which is known as Margin B.

Division titles, paragraph names, and sentences must be followed by a period and a blank. Nothing else can be written on the same line as a division title. In the MANHATTAN PROGRAM, lines 44 and 45 are the names of a division (PROCEDURE DIVISION) and a paragraph (A0010-BEGIN), respectively, and so begin at Margin A.

Identification Division

The first division of the COBOL program must include a program name (or PROGRAM-ID). The program name must begin with an

453

alphabetic character and be composed of alphabetic and numeric characters. The entries that follow are optional, but if they are used, they must appear in a specific order:

1. `AUTHOR.`
2. `INSTALLATION.` (that is, name of computer installation)
3. `DATE-WRITTEN.`
4. `DATE-COMPILED.`

The name of the program on page 450 is `MANHATTAN-PROGRAM.` Space for the author is allotted (`PUT-YOUR-NAME-HERE`), and the date that the program was written is included (`SEPT-25-1981`). Also included are some `REMARKS`, beginning at Margin B, explaining the purpose of the program.

Environment Division

The hardware used in the running of a given COBOL program must be described in the `ENVIRONMENT DIVISION`. This division may include a `CONFIGURATION SECTION` that lists the source computer on which the program was compiled and the object computer on which it is to be run. In the program example, the `ENVIRONMENT DIVISION` starts on line `13`, and both the source and object computers have been identified as `CDC-CYBER-74`.

The second section in the `ENVIRONMENT DIVISION` is the `INPUT-OUTPUT SECTION`, which must be specified whenever there is to be input or output for a program. In COBOL, the data that form the input and output have usually been assembled into files. This section identifies the files to be used in the program, and assigns them to specific input/output devices (card reader, line printer) under a `FILE-CONTROL` paragraph. The assignment is made using a `SELECT` statement. There must be as many `SELECT` and `ASSIGN TO` statements as there are files in the system:

`SELECT` file-name `ASSIGN TO` equipment-name.

In the program example, no data are read in from an input file, so there is only one `SELECT` statement, assigning the file `PRINT-FILE` to `OUTPUT` (line `20`).

Data Division

The `DATA DIVISION` contains a description of all data to be handled by the program. Both input data and output data (for example, printed results) are included here. The DATA DIVISION contains two subdivisions:

1. The FILE SECTION is used to describe all input and output files.
2. The WORKING-STORAGE SECTION is used to store all information created by the program, such as intermediate results or tables of constants used as references by the program.

A file is a collection of related *records*. A record is a collection of related *fields*, and a field is an item of information. For example, a file, PAYROLL, could be composed of the payroll records of each company employee. Each record contains several fields, or items of information: name, company number, regular and overtime hours worked. In a COBOL program, files and records are described by means of FD statements, record levels, and "PICTURES."

The FD statement. Each file used in a COBOL program is associated in the FILE SECTION with an FD or File Description statement. The general format of an FD statement is:

```
FD file-name
   LABEL RECORDS ARE  (OMITTED )
                      (STANDARD) .
```

Tape and disk files are usually labeled and therefore STANDARD. Record labels are omitted on card files and print files. In the program example, LABEL RECORDS ARE OMITTED, since the output file is a print file (line 26).

Record levels. Record description entries follow the FD entry. To organize information more clearly, records are grouped by *levels*. All items on the same level will have the same level number. *Level 01* is the most inclusive level and is used to identify the record name. The 01 level number always begins at Margin A. All higher numbered levels (02-49) begin at Margin B. For example, if the file PAYROLL contains one record, EMPLY-RECORD, the program might be structured this way:

```
01 EMPLY-RECORD
      02 NAME
      02 NUMBER
      02 HOURS
            03 REGULAR-HOURS
            03 OVERTIME
```

455

The PICTURE statement. Even with all this, the description of the record is not yet complete. The type and size of every field of the record must be explicitly described. This is done with a PICTURE statement, which has the form:

$$\left\{ \begin{array}{l} \text{PIC} \\ \text{PICTURE} \end{array} \right\} \text{field-indicator (field-size)}$$

where the types of field indicators are:

X alphanumeric field (any computer character)
9 numeric field (digits and + and − signs)
A alphabetic or blank field (only letters and blanks)

A numeric field having three spaces (for the number 134) may be written either PIC 9(3) or PIC 999. If we wish to set aside a field for a number having a decimal point, we use V to indicate the position of the decimal point. PIC 9V99 indicates a three-place (not four) numeric field with a decimal point between the second and third digit.

Value as entered	Picture	Number stored
0012	99V99	00.12
3157	9V999	3.157
125	99V9	12.5
125	V999	.125

The V is not required when the decimal point is on the right: PIC 999V should be expressed as PIC 999.

An S preceding the picture field indicates that there may be a sign (negative) associated with the number. The total number of field sizes must add up to the record size. To accomplish this, a FILLER can be used to designate a field that will not be occupied by data, but is there merely used to fill out the record size.

The dollar sign ($) used in the PIC description (line 40) is referred to as a floating dollar sign. A separate position in the output field is reserved for the $ in the printed output. Moreover, the $ is placed or "floats" next to the leftmost nonzero digit of the answer.

Value	Picture	Printed output result
1023	$$$$.99	$10.23
0005	$$$.99	$.05

The picture specification for the record EDITED-PRINCIPAL is:

PIC $,$$$,$$$,$$$,$$99.99

and results in the printed answer for the current balance:

$108,298,442,544.15

In the MANHATTAN PROGRAM, lines 25 through 30 in the DATA DIVISION indicate that the file, PRINT-FILE, contains a single record, PRINT-LINE, which has two fields, a FILLER and DATA-LINE.

```
01 PRINT-LINE.
      02 FILLER        PIC X.
      02 DATA-LINE     PIC X(132).
```

Working storage. The WORKING STORAGE SECTION indicates information that will be created by the program, such as intermediate results of program computations, or other information not associated with files, such as counters for program looping procedures or tables of constants to be used in the calculations. Some items stored here may be unrelated to any other data items and therefore need not be included as part of a data structure: isolated constants are an example of this. These data items are assigned a level number 77. All level 77 items must be declared at the beginning of the WORKING STORAGE SECTION, before any records are declared. In the MANHATTAN PROGRAM, the constant values, PRESENT-YEAR, PRINCIPAL, YEARLY-INTEREST, and STARTING-YEAR, are level 77 and are declared before the record ANSWER-LINE. VALUE statements are used to assign particular values to constants. For example:

```
77       PRESENT-YEAR    PIC 9999, VALUE 1981.
```

Procedure Division

The actual problem solving is performed in the PROCEDURE DIVISION. The PROCEDURE DIVISION is organized into paragraphs. Each paragraph is identified by a name, beginning in Margin A. Paragraph names are used in looping and branching procedures. Each paragraph is composed of a group of related sentences specifying a procedure to be performed. In the MANHATTAN PROGRAM, the paragraph A0020-INTEREST-CALCULATION contains the actual computational instructions, while A0030-PRINT-ANSWER includes the instructions to produce the printed solution.

Each COBOL program must be terminated by a STOP RUN statement, which is the last statement executed by the program.

Arithmetic Operations

The arithmetic operations of COBOL are like those of BASIC. There are five arithmetic operation symbols:

COBOL arithmetic operation symbol	Operation	COBOL arithmetic expression
+	addition	A + B
−	subtraction	A − B
*	multiplication	A * B
/	division	A / B
**	exponentiation	A ** B

These symbols must be separated from each side of the variables they are operating upon by a blank space. Otherwise the mathematical operation will be confused with the variable name:

A−B   is a variable name.
A − B is the operation of subtracting B from A.

Mathematical operations on COBOL variables and constants may be performed using the verb COMPUTE. The general format of the COMPUTE instruction is:

$$\text{COMPUTE data-name-1} = \begin{cases} \text{arithmetic expression} \\ \text{data-name-2} \\ \text{numeric literal} \end{cases}$$

For example:

    COMPUTE A = B + C.   arithmetic expression
    COMPUTE A = B1.   data-name-2
    COMPUTE A = 3.14.   numeric literal

Like the LET statement in BASIC, the expression to the right of the equal sign is evaluated and then assigned to the variable on the left of the equal sign. The hierarchy of operations performed is the same as for BASIC:

1. Where parentheses exist, the expression within the innermost set of parentheses is evaluated first, then the expression within the next innermost set, and so on.
2. For a given expression, disregarding parentheses, exponentiation takes priority over multiplication and division, which take priority over addition and subtraction.

COBOL also uses the verbs ADD, SUBTRACT, MULTIPLY, and DIVIDE to perform arithmetic operations. The general format of these instructions is:

$$\begin{matrix} \text{ADD} \\ \text{SUBTRACT} \\ \text{MULTIPLY} \\ \text{DIVIDE} \end{matrix} \begin{cases} \text{data-name-1} \\ \text{numeric literal} \end{cases} \begin{matrix} \text{TO} \\ \text{FROM} \\ \text{BY} \\ \text{BY} \end{matrix} \begin{cases} \text{data-name-2} \\ \text{numeric literal} \end{cases}$$

Unlike the COMPUTE statement, only a single operation can be performed per statement; however, several variables or numeric literals can be operated on at one time: Thus the instruction:

```
ADD 2,3,A TO C.
```

forms the sum 2+3+A+C and stores the result in C. The value of A is unchanged. If we wish the contents of variable C to remain unchanged as well, we may use the statement:

```
ADD 2,3,A,C GIVING D.
```

The sum 2+3+A+C is stored in D, while the contents of A and C remain unchanged. Similar statements exist for SUBTRACT, MULTIPLY, and DIVIDE.

Finally, if the number of decimal places in a computed number exceeds the number allocated for its field by the PIC statement, the excess digits will simply be dropped, unless a ROUNDED statement is used to round off the number. For example if PIC 99V9 is allocated for C=A+B, and C=82.36, the program will produce the value:

```
C=82.3
```

Using the ROUNDED statement:

```
ADD A,B GIVING C ROUNDED.
```

gives the value:

```
C=82.4
```

The ROUNDED statement can be similarly used for subtraction, division, and multiplication. It is used in the MANHATTAN PROGRAM:

```
48        MULTIPLY PRINCIPAL BY .065 GIVING
             YEARLY-INTEREST ROUNDED
```

The COMPUTE statement, similar to the LET statement in BASIC, is used for expressions that involve arithmetic expressions. For other assignments (of variable to variable or variable to constant), the analogous statement in COBOL is the MOVE statement, which has the general format:

$$\text{MOVE} \begin{Bmatrix} \text{identifier-1} \\ \text{literal} \end{Bmatrix} \text{TO identifier-2 (identifier-3, etc.)}$$

The MOVE operation transmits a literal constant, or the data stored in identifier-1, into the location specified by identifier-2 (-3, etc.).

```
MOVE X TO Y           (Copies the contents of X into Y.)
MOVE SPACES TO Z,T    (Places zeroes into Z and T.)
```

459

Transfer Statements and Loops: Sequence Control Verbs

As we have seen with BASIC programs, the incorporation of decision making into the program instructions makes those programs far more sophisticated and efficient. COBOL, too, has a vocabulary for conditional and "looping" instructions.

On size error. The general format of this conditional instruction is:

$$\left\{ \begin{array}{l} \text{ADD} \\ \text{SUB} \\ \text{MULT} \\ \text{DIVIDE} \\ \text{COMPUTE} \end{array} \right\} \text{ON SIZE ERROR imperative statement}$$

If the result of a computation requires more spaces than allowed for it in a field, a `SIZE ERROR` is produced. Programmers anticipate this problem by means of an `ON SIZE ERROR` statement. This statement transfers program control unconditionally to another instruction, which has been designed to deal with the problem. In our `MANHATTAN PROGRAM`, for example, there is:

```
50 ADD YEARLY-INTEREST TO PRINCIPAL
51  ON SIZE ERROR GO TO A0050-PROGRAM-ERROR-2.
```

If `YEARLY-INTEREST` added to `PRINCIPAL` gives a result that overflows the field `PIC S9{11}V99`, then the computer will go to paragraph `A0050-PROGRAM-ERROR-2`, which instructs it to print `"PRINCIPAL FIELD IS TOO SMALL--JOB ENDED."`

Without an `ON SIZE ERROR` statement, the computer would not notify the programmer that the result of a computation was too large for the allotted field. Consequently, only part of the number would be stored, and the program would continue using the partial, and incorrect, amount.

IF statement. The general format of an `IF` statement is:

`IF` condition statement-1

Most commonly, the condition is a relation condition, similar to those used in BASIC. Statement-1 may be any COBOL statement, such as `COMPUTE Y=X+Z`, `MOVE A TO B`, `GO TO` (paragraph name). The general format of the relation expression is:

$$\left\{ \begin{array}{l} \text{identifier-1} \\ \text{literal-1} \\ \text{arithmetic-} \\ \quad \text{expression-1} \end{array} \right\} \quad \text{relational operator} \quad \left\{ \begin{array}{l} \text{identifier-2} \\ \text{literal-2} \\ \text{arithmetic-} \\ \quad \text{expression-2} \end{array} \right\}$$

The relational operators are:

```
IS GREATER THAN or IS >
IS NOT GREATER THAN or IS NOT >
IS LESS THAN or IS <
IS NOT LESS THAN or IS NOT <
IS EQUAL TO or IS=
IS NOT EQUAL TO or IS NOT=
```

The example given in the program is:

```
53        IF STARTING-YEAR IS EQUAL TO PRESENT-YEAR
54            GO TO A0030-PRINT-ANSWER.
55        GO TO A0020-INTEREST-CALCULATION.
```

If the starting year counter is equal to the present year, the program transfers control to paragraph `A0030-PRINT-ANSWER`, and the final answer is printed out. If the counter is not equal to the present year, the program returns to its interest calculation.

The same set of instructions can be written more compactly:

```
IF STARTING-YEAR IS EQUAL TO PRESENT-YEAR
    GO TO A0030-PRINT-ANSWER
        ELSE GO TO A0020-INTEREST-CALCULATION.
```

Two separate instructions have been combined into a single instruction. The general format of the `IF...ELSE` statement is:

```
IF condition statement-1
    ELSE statement-2
```

File Processing: Input-Ouput Verbs

The instructions associated with file processing are:

```
OPEN (INPUT ) file-name-1  (file-name-2, file-name-3, etc.)
     (OUTPUT)
```

and similarly:

```
CLOSE file-name-1  (file-name-2, etc.)
```

(`INPUT` or `OUTPUT` does not have to be specified for the `CLOSE` statement.)

Each file must first be opened before any reading or writing can be performed. Every file must be closed before termination of program execution to ensure that its contents will be protected from inadvertent reading or writing.

Reading data from files is done via the instruction:

> **READ** file-name (**INTO** record-name)
> **AT END** imperative statement

The computer will read only an opened **INPUT** file. The data record that is read in will automatically be moved to the area record-name in the **WORKING STORAGE SECTION**. The imperative statement is an unconditional transfer statement, telling the program where to go or what to do after all records have been read in.

Writing data onto a file is done by the following instruction:

> **WRITE** record-name-1 (**FROM** record-name-2)
> (**AFTER ADVANCING** n **LINES**)

where n is an integer. In the **MANHATTAN PROGRAM**,

> 59   **WRITE PRINT-LINE AFTER ADVANCING PAGE-TOP.**

In line **17**, **PAGE-TOP** was originally designated as **"1."** The **WRITE** instruction on line **59** tells the computer to write the record **PRINT-LINE**, after advancing the printer to the top of the next page.

PASCAL VERSION

```
                    MANHATTAN PROGRAM


{*COMPUTE THE AMOUNT OF RETURN
$24.00 INVESTED AT 6.5%*}
PROGRAM MANHATTAN {INPUT,OUTPUT};
CONST RATE=0.065;
VAR STARTINGYEAR,PRESENTYEAR :INTEGER;
    PRINCIPAL,YEARLYINTEREST :REAL;
BEGIN {*MANHATTAN*}
    PRINCIPAL:=24.0;
    STARTINGYEAR:=1627;
    PRESENTYEAR:=1981;
    WHILE PRESENTYEAR >= STARTINGYEAR DO
    BEGIN {*CALCULATION*}
       YEARLYINTEREST:=RATE*PRINCIPAL;
       PRINCIPAL:=PRINCIPAL+YEARLYINTEREST;
       STARTINGYEAR:=STARTINGYEAR+1
    END; {*CALCULATION*}
    WRITELN {'BALANCE TO DATE EQUALS', PRINCIPAL}
END. {*MANHATTAN*}
```

A glance at the Pascal version of our `MANHATTAN PROGRAM` will show that this is by far the most compact of the three languages described in this Appendix. Much of its brevity is achieved by elimination of the "housekeeping" information contained in the `ENVIRONMENT` and `DATA` divisions of a COBOL program. You will note also that a Pascal program lacks the line numbers that are in BASIC and COBOL. This is a symbol-oriented and very efficient programming language.

The Pascal Character Set: Identifiers and Constants

As with the other languages described, the character set for Pascal includes both alphabetic and numeric characters as well as special symbols. Words may consist of both alphabetic and numeric characters formed according to syntax rules. Like COBOL, Pascal has a limited vocabulary of reserved words that may not be chosen as identifiers by the programmer. We will examine some syntax rules and reserved words in the discussion below.

Identifiers. Pascal *identifiers* or *variable names* must begin with an alphabetic character, which may be followed by any combination of letters and numbers. A name should contain no spaces. It may be any length, but only the first eight characters of any identifier can be distinguished by the computer. Additional characters are used only to clarify meanings for programmers and users. Thus, `THANKYOU1` and `THANKYOU2` will be read as the same variable. Both upper- and lower-case letters may be used.

Valid identifier	Invalid identifier	Reason invalid
`MAXTEMP`	`MAX TEMP`	Space between characters not allowed.
`AB`	`A-B`	Includes character that is not alphabetic or numeric.
`A1B1`	`1A1B`	Starts with numeric instead of alphabetic character.

Each Pascal identifier must be further described according to its *attribute* or type. Two frequently used numerical attributes are `INTEGER` and `REAL`, denoting whole numbers (integers) and decimal or fractional (real) numbers, respectively. Every variable used in a

Pascal program must have its attributes designated in a *declaration* appearing at the beginning of the program. The declaration has the form:

```
VAR variable-name-1, variable-name-2, . . . , {:INTEGER;
                                               {:REAL;
```

In simple programs, the keyword `VAR` should appear only once, but can refer to more than one variable declaration:

```
VAR STARTINGYEAR,PRESENTYEAR :INTEGER;
    PRINCIPAL,YEARLYINTEREST :REAL;
```

is valid, but:

```
VAR STARTINGYEAR,PRESENTYEAR :INTEGER;
VAR PRINCIPAL,YEARLYINTEREST :REAL;
```

is not valid.

Constants. Numerical *constants* may be used directly in computations. In the BASIC and COBOL versions of the `MANHATTAN PROGRAM`, for example, the yearly interest is compiled by direct multiplication of the current principal by .065 (6.5 percent). To make the program more readable, we could use the constant term `RATE`, denoting the interest rate. This makes it clear that the numerical factor, .065, multiplying the principal value, is the interest rate. The definition of a constant is accomplished by:

```
CONST  name-1 = value-1;
       name-2 = value-2;
              etc.
```

In the `MANHATTAN PROGRAM` example, the statement is:

```
CONST RATE=0.065;
```

Unlike variable quantities, constants by definition cannot be changed during the course of a program. Constants should always appear before variables in a program.

Assignment of values. In Pascal, values are assigned to variables by means of the following statement:

```
variable-name:=expression;
```

As in BASIC, the expression may be a variable, constant, or computed expression, and appears on the right side of the combination symbol ":=", which can be read as "is assigned the value of." The variable to which the expression is assigned appears on the left side of the combination symbol ":=".

Valid assignment	Invalid assignment	Reason invalid
`A:=4.3;`	`4.3:=A;`	Variable on right side
`B:={A+SUM}/2;`	`{A+SUM}/2:=B;`	of ":=".

General Program Structure

The general form of a Pascal program is:

```
*comment summarizing program function*
PROGRAM name {INPUT, OUTPUT};
    definitions and declarations
BEGIN {*name*}
    body of program
END. {*name*}
eor (end of record)
data
```

(The indentations are for visual clarity only, and are not otherwise significant to the program.) The selection of a program name is subject to the same rules as used for identifier names. `INPUT` and `OUTPUT` designate the input and output files (for example, card reader and line printer). All constants and variables used in the program must be declared before the body of the procedure is entered. `BEGIN` and `END` are keywords delimiting the procedure(s) specified by the *name*. A period (`.`) must immediately follow the `END` marker after the main procedure. The body of the program consists of a sequence of instructions or statements. Each statement must be followed by a semicolon (`;`).

Compound statements. A series of separate simple statements, each of which specifies a single operation (be it an input/output operation, arithmetic operation, or assignment) may be grouped together into a *compound statement*. The limits of the compound statement are set by marker keywords such as `BEGIN` and `END`. The compound statement is a single programming unit, and an entire procedure may be treated in Pascal in the same way that a single simple statement would be. The general format of a compound statement is:

```
BEGIN
    statement-1;
    statement-2;
        . . . .
    statement-n
END;
```

A semicolon (;) appears after each of the component statements in the compound statement, except for the last statement. The utility of the compound statement will become clear in the discussion of re-petitive procedure.

Arithmetic Expressions

The symbols used as the Pascal arithmetic operators are:

+   for addition of both integers and real numbers.
−   for subtraction of integers and real numbers.
*   for multiplication of integers and real numbers.
/   for division giving a real number result; operands may be either integers or real numbers.
DIV for division giving an integer result; operands must both be integers.
MOD for the remainder of an integer division. The result is an integer, and both operands are integers.

Examples using the last two operators are:

```
13 DIV 4 IS 3
13 MOD 4 IS 1
```

Unlike many programming languages, Pascal has no special operator for exponentiation.

The hierarchy of operations is the same as for BASIC and COBOL:

1. Where parentheses are present, the expression within the innermost set of parentheses is evaluated first, then the expression within the next innermost parentheses, and so on.
2. Within a set of parentheses, multiplication and division have priority over addition and subtraction.

READ and READLN Statements

The Pascal READ statement is an input instruction that processes data in a way similar to that of the BASIC READ statement. The format of the input statement in Pascal is:

READ (variable-names,separated by commas);

The data to be used in a Pascal program do not appear within the body of the program itself, but are grouped together in data statements usually appearing after the program statement. Each data statement may contain one or more data values. The READ statement causes the data to be read in sequentially, beginning with the first data entry in the first statement and ending with the last entry in the last statement. Each data entry is read in only once.

The `READLN` (variable-names) statement differs from the `READ` statement in one important respect: It tells the computer to skip over all data following the last data statement and go to the next line.

Suppose that the `MANHATTAN PROGRAM` read in values of the variables (rather than assigning values to them in the body of the program, as was actually done). If the data appeared as follows:

```
(data statement one) 24.00 1627
(data statement two) 1981
```

then the statements:

```
READ {PRINCIPAL};
READ {STARTINGYEAR,PRESENTYEAR};
```

would result in the following assignment of values to variables:

```
PRINCIPAL     24.00
STARTINGYEAR  1627
PRESENTYEAR   1981
```

But if we were to use the statements:

```
READLN {PRINCIPAL};
READLN {STARTINGYEAR,PRESENTYEAR};
```

an error would result, for after reading in the value `24.00` for `PRINCIPAL`, the computer would skip to statement two for its next data entry. It would expect to read in two data values and would find only one.

WRITE and WRITELN Statements

Similarly, output is obtained by a WRITE or WRITELN statement:

```
WRITE (variable-names, separated by commas);
WRITELN (variable-names, separated by commas);
```

`WRITELN` differs from `WRITE` in that the printer (or other output device) moves to the beginning of the next line after printing the variable names specified in the `WRITELN` statement. In addition to printing variable names, the `WRITE` statements will print out *literal character strings*. These are groups of characters delimited by single quotation marks (`'`), as in:

```
WRITELN {'BALANCE TO DATE EQUALS',PRINCIPAL}
```

The form of the output can be specified by means of descriptive integers following the statements of variables to be printed out. Since `PRINCIPAL` is a `REAL` variable, we might specify its format as:

```
PRINCIPAL : 10 : 2
```

The `10` specifies the *minimum* field width for `PRINCIPAL`. If the item requires more spaces, as many as are needed are used. The second integer, `2`, denotes the number of digits to be printed after the decimal point. The second integer applies only to `REAL` variables, since integers are not specified with a decimal point.

Unconditional Transfer: The GOTO Statement

An unconditional transfer of program control can be accomplished by the `GOTO` statement, which has the following form:

```
GOTO label;
   . . .
label: statement;
```

A statement *label* is an integer of not more than four digits. A labelled statement might appear as follows:

```
4321: READ {A};
```

The execution of the `GOTO` statement, `GOTO 4321`, causes the program to jump to the instruction whose label is specified, that is, `READ {A}`. Integers that are used as labels must be declared as such. The `LABEL` declaration would precede the declaration of variables in the program:

```
LABEL 4321;
```

Conditional Statements

The simple conditions or relational expressions of Pascal are similar to those of BASIC or COBOL. The relational symbols are:

Symbol	Meaning
=	is equal to
<>	is not equal to
>	is greater than
>=	is greater than or equal to
<	is less than
<=	is less than or equal to

The combination characters (such as <>) cannot have a blank space separating the characters. A condition consists of two variables, constants, or arithmetic expressions separated by a relation:

arithmetic-expression-1   relation   arithmetic-expression-2

For example:

```
2<>3
A=B
X+Y>5
```

The IF...THEN statement. The IF...THEN conditional statement has the following format:

```
IF condition THEN
    statement-1;
```

Statement-1 may be a compound statement. If the condition tested is true, the program performs the operation or series of operations specified by statement-1. If the condition is not true, statement-1 is passed over and the next statement in the program is performed.

The MANHATTAN PROGRAM contains the compound statement named CALCULATION. The sequence of statements composing CALCULATION computes the current principal value of the investment. Instead of the loop construction actually used in the program, we could employ an IF...THEN construction:

```
IF PRESENTYEAR>STARTINGYEAR THEN
  BEGIN {*CALCULATION*}
    YEARLYINTEREST:=RATE*PRINCIPAL;
    PRINCIPAL:=PRINCIPAL+YEARLYINTEREST;
    STARTINGYEAR:=STARTINGYEAR+1
  END; {*CALCULATION*}
```

The program will iterate the CALCULATION statement as long as PRESENTYEAR is greater in value than STARTINGYEAR (which serves as a counter here). When the condition is no longer satisfied, that is, when we have reached the present year, the program will go to the next statement, in this case, to the WRITELN statement.

Another form of the IF...THEN statement appears as:

```
IF condition THEN
    statement-1
ELSE statement-2;
```

Statement-1 may also be a compound statement. In our example:

```
IF PRESENTYEAR>STARTINGYEAR THEN
  BEGIN {*CALCULATION*}
    YEARLYINTEREST:=RATE*PRINCIPAL;
    PRINCIPAL:=PRINCIPAL+YEARLYINTEREST;
    STARTINGYEAR:=STARTINGYEAR+1
  END; {*CALCULATION*}
ELSE WRITELN {'BALANCE TO DATE EQUALS',PRINCIPAL};
```

Repetitive Execution

Pascal explicitly provides looping procedures that allow the repeated execution of a sequence of statements. These are the `WHILE` loop and the `REPEAT` loop.

The general form of the `WHILE` loop is:

```
WHILE condition DO
    statement;
```

The statement may be a compound statement, so the `WHILE` instruction can specify a procedure involving several operations. An example of a `WHILE` loop appears in the `MANHATTAN PROGRAM`:

```
WHILE PRESENTYEAR>STARTINGYEAR DO
  BEGIN {*CALCULATION*}
    YEARLYINTEREST:=RATE*PRINCIPAL;
    PRINCIPAL:=PRINCIPAL+YEARLYINTEREST;
    STARTINGYEAR:=STARTINGYEAR+1
  END; {*CALCULATION*}
```

The `REPEAT` loop could also be used to accomplish the same thing. This loop has the general form:

```
REPEAT
    statement;
UNTIL condition;
```

The statement, again, may be a compound statement. `REPEAT` and `UNTIL` are keywords that serve as markers for the loop procedure; thus `BEGIN` and `END` are not needed to set off the compound statement.

The above procedures can be expressed in a `REPEAT` loop as follows:

```
REPEAT {*CALCULATION*}
    YEARLYINTEREST:=RATE*PRINCIPAL;
    PRINCIPAL:=PRINCIPAL+YEARLYINTEREST;
    STARTINGYEAR:=STARTINGYEAR+1
UNTIL PRESENTYEAR=STARTINGYEAR;
```

The FOR...DO loop. Another type of loop procedure uses a counter or index variable as a loop control. The `FOR...DO` loop has this format:

```
FOR counter-variable:=initial value TO final-value DO statement;
```

Again, the statement may be a compound statement.

Letting `K` represent our counter variable, we can, for example, write the procedure for finding interest in the `MANHATTAN PROGRAM` over the first five investment years:

```
FOR K:=1 TO 5 DO
  BEGIN {*CALCULATION*}
     YEARLYINTEREST:=RATE*PRINCIPAL;
     PRINCIPAL:=PRINCIPAL+YEARLYINTEREST;
     STARTINGYEAR:=STARTINGYEAR+1
  END; {*CALCULATION*}
```

In this case, CALCULATION will be performed five times, computing the interest on the $24.00 principal for five years, from 1627.

When the programs are executed, the sum accumulated to 1981 is found to be $122,834,800,994.64.

Acronyms Used in Computer Data Processing

ALU—arithmetic logic unit

ANSI—American National Standards Institute

A/R—accounts receivable

ASCII—American Standard Code for Information Interchange

AUTOVON—Automatic Voice Network

bpi—bits per inch

BPI—bytes per inch

bps—bauds per second

CAD—computer-aided design

CCD—charge-coupled device

COM—computer output microfilm

CPS—characters per second

CPU—central processing unit

DBMS—data base management system

DDP—distributed data processing

DES—Data Encryption Standard

DML—data manipulation language

EAROM—electrically alterable read-only memory

EBCDIC—extended binary coded decimal interchange code

EDP—electronic data processing

EDSAC—Electronic Delay Storage Automatic Calculator

EDVAC—Electronic Discrete Variable Automatic Computer

EFT—electronic funds transfer

ENIAC—Electronic Numerical Integrator and Calculator

EPROM—erasable programmable read-only memory

FDM—frequency division multiplex

GIGO—garbage in–garbage out

IBG—interblock gap

IC—integrated circuit

I/O—input/output

IRG—interrecord gap

ISAM—indexed sequential-access method

LED—laser- or light-emitting diode

LPM—lines per minute

LSI—large-scale integration

MFLOPS—million floating-point operations per second

MICR—magnetic ink character recognition

MIPS—million instructions per second

MIS—management information system

modem—modulator-demodulator

MOPS—million operations per second

OCR—optical character recognition

OLRT—online real time

PDSP—Programmable Digital Signal Processor

POS—point of sale

PROM—programmable read-only memory

471

PUMA—Programmable Universal
  Machine for Assembly
RAM—random-access memory
RJE—remote job entry
ROM—read-only memory
TDM—time division multiplex

tpi—tracks per inch
UPC—Universal Product Code
VLSI—very large scale integration
VSAM—virtual storage access
  method

Periodicals Relating to Data Processing

As the following list demonstrates, the rapid growth of the field has produced publications to suit every special interest. Some publications are primarily computer-oriented, some applications-oriented, and others deal with broad areas of technology. And this list is by no means complete.

Computer Decisions
Computer Design
Computer Weekly (British)
Computers and People
Computerworld (weekly newspaper)
Data Management (official journal of the Data Processing Management Association)
Datamation
Data Processing (British monthly)
Data Processing (covers IBM applications and innovations)
EDP Analyzer (monthly in-depth analysis of a particular topic)
EDP Industry Report (biweekly newsletter)

EDP Weekly (computer news summary)
IBM Systems Journal (generally, a more technical report on experience and research)
Infosystems
Journal of Educational DP
Journal of Systems Management (official publication of the Association for Systems Management)
Management Controls (published by Peat Marwick Mitchell & Co.)
Mini-Micro Systems
Office
Telecommunications

In addition, there are two useful resource compilations:

- *Data Processing Digest* (monthly reviews of articles of interest from more than 200 periodicals; semiannual index and list of reviewed publications in June and December issues)
- *Quarterly Bibliography of Computers and Data Processing* (an annotated listing of current literature categorized into explicit subject areas; covers a wide range of publications)

Glossary

How to use this Glossary: When you read the definition of a Glossary entry, note any terms in italics and look them up in the Glossary, too. Use the Index to locate the text discussions of all Glossary terms.

abacus an ancient computing device, consisting originally of stones moved on a flat surface, but most familiar as used in the Far East, as beads on a set of wires. Calculations on the abacus are based on the decimal system; all four basic arithmetic operations can be performed on it.

access the mode or manner in which a computer obtains data from storage. See also *access time.*

access time the interval required for (1) calling up an item of data from storage, or (2) storing an item of data.

accountability the control of expenditures and responsibility for formally accounting for expenditures.

accumulator a *register* commonly used to store the results of arithmetic operations.

acoustic coupler in data transmissions, a type of *modem* used in conjunction with conventional telephone lines to convert digital and acoustic signals.

action a step or set of steps, specified in a *decision table,* to be executed when a *condition* or set of conditions has been met.

add-on memory auxiliary storage capacity connected to main memory by a communications channel.

address the location of a data item in storage.

address register a *register* that provides temporary storage locations for data addresses during processing.

administrative job family in data processing departments, one of six broad groups, or families, of jobs. Common job titles include control clerk and programming aide.

ALGOL acronym for *ALGO*rithmic Language, a noninteractive, high-level programming language designed to facilitate programming of *algorithms.*

algorithm a set of rules or steps for solving a problem.

alphanumeric an adjective used to identify a character set, a code, or data as consisting of letters and digits (and, usually, special characters).

473

American National Standards Institute (ANSI) the coordinating body of a federation of commercial and noncommercial organizations; its main functions are identification of needs for standards, support of organizations in establishing standards, and publication of established standards.

analog computer a computer that operates on data in the form of a variable and continuous physical quantity (for example, an electrical voltage). See also *digital computer.*

analysis the detailed investigation of a problem, usually for breaking it down into smaller units. See also *systems analysis.*

annotation comments and descriptions added to explain symbolic or coded material in a flowchart.

APL acronym for *A* Programming Language, an interactive programming language, based on the use of *array* and *matrix* elements.

application the purpose for which a computer is used, a problem to be solved, or an operation to be performed. See also *application program.*

application data base the *data base* needed for the execution of an *application program.*

application program a computer program designed to solve a particular type of problem or perform a specific operation, such as payroll processing.

application programmer the person who writes the step-by-step computer instructions for solving a problem or performing an operation. See also *application program; systems analyst.*

arithmetic logic unit the component of the CPU that performs the arithmetic, logic, and related operations called for by a program.

array a grouping of numbers to which a common variable name has been assigned.

ASCII acronym for *A*merican Standard Code for Information Interchange, a data communications code originally based on seven bits and later modified to an eight-bit format to be compatible with recent equipment. See also *EBCDIC.*

assembly language a computer-oriented language having a one-to-one relationship between its instruction statements and *machine-language* statements; a *low-level language.*

asynchronous transmission a mode of data transmission in which each character is preceded and followed by "start" and "stop" bits, respectively. See also *synchronous transmission.*

authorization in computer security, the degree of access to a facility or computer terminal allowed to a given individual.

ball printer an output device that uses a spherical printhead, or ball, to print characters by impact. See also *impact printers; serial printer.*

band printer an output device containing a movable band or belt embossed with characters to print by impact. See also *impact printers; line printer.*

bar code a set of parallel lines of varied thickness containing encoded information that can be optically scanned by computers; the best-known example is the Universal Product Code.

BASIC acronym for *B*eginner's *A*ll-purpose *S*ymbolic *I*nstruction *C*ode, an interactive, high-level programming language that is easy to learn.

batch processing the accumulation of data for input and processing in groups, or batches.

baud in data transmission, a unit of signaling speed through a communications channel, usually stated as the number of discrete signals transmitted per second.

binary coded decimal (BCD) a notation system designed for computer use that represents each decimal digit as a binary sequence of 1's and 0's; differs from the pure *binary number system* that depends on positional notation.

binary number system a base-2 arithmetic system, in which numbers are represented as 0's and 1's. See also *decimal number system; hexadecimal number system*.

bit the basic unit of information in any system using binary notation (the term is a contraction of "binary dig*it*"); either a 1 or a 0. See also *byte*.

bits per inch (bpi) literally, the number of binary 1's or 0's that fit on an inch of track on a storage disk; a measure of storage capacity. See also *tracks per inch*.

block a group of records stored together on a tape or disk.

blocking factor the number of records stored together in a *block*. See also *interblock gap*.

bottom-up programming an approach to programming in which low-level routines are coded first and then combined and tested before the next higher level of routines is coded, and so on. See also *modularization; top-down programming*.

bottom-up testing testing a computer program by beginning with individual *subroutines* or modules and then testing increasingly larger units of the program.

branching a point in a program in which one of two alternative logical paths is to be taken.

byte a group or sequence of bits (usually eight) that is operated on as a unit. See also *bit*.

bytes per inch (BPI) literally, the number of bytes that can be contained on an inch of magnetic tape.

card-punch output computer output in the form of punched cards.

central processing unit (CPU) the component of a computer that contains primary memory, performs arithmetic and logic operations, and generally directs the activities of the computer. See also *arithmetic logic unit; primary storage*.

chain printer a line-printing output device that employs a movable printhead consisting of a series of metal slugs embossed with individual characters. See also *impact printers; line printer*.

channel a pathway for the transmission of signals; in computers and telecommunications, usually an electrical connection.

chargeout system in accounting, a method of identifying and allocating expenditures for all resources consumed by an organization.

475

closed-circuit monitor a security device, such as a television camera or intercom system, that enables security personnel to monitor an area, exit, or entrance that they cannot see directly.

COBOL acronym for *CO*mmon *B*usiness *O*riented *L*anguage, a high-level, noninteractive programming language designed for business applications.

collator a device used in card-oriented batch processing systems. It can merge, match, and select punched cards, as well as check for correct sequence.

communication link symbol in *flowcharting*, the graphic symbol (zigzag flowline) used to represent the data flow between electronic media and/or equipment.

compiler a component of *systems software* that enables a computer to translate an application program into machine-readable language.

computer output microfilm (COM) microfilm created as computer output that contains data derived from computer-generated signals.

concentrator a high-speed, high-volume *multiplexer*.

condition a factor or criterion, specified in a *decision table*, that must be met before an *action* can be taken.

conditional operation the step or steps in a program that direct the execution of one or the other of two sequences of instructions, depending on whether a particular condition or set of conditions have been met.

conjunction in *flowcharting*, the joining of two *flowline symbols*, indicated by an arrowhead on one of the flowline symbols.

connector symbol in a *flowchart*, the graphic symbol (circle) used to represent a data flow sequence detailed elsewhere.

control register a *register* for the temporary storage of information and control instructions needed to perform specific computer operations.

control unit the component of a CPU that fetches program instructions from storage, interprets them, and initiates their execution by other components of the CPU.

core memory a type of computer storage whose electronic functioning depends on current passed at right angles through magnetic cores. Because this technology was at one time a breakthrough that made possible greater primary storage capacity, the term is sometimes still used incorrectly as a synonym for central storage.

cycle time the interval required to complete a set of computer operations on a data item, particularly operations that are regularly repeated in the same sequence.

cylinder in magnetic disk storage, the amount of data that can be accessed from a disk pack by a single positioning of the access mechanism of a magnetic *disk drive*.

cylinder printer an *impact printer* containing embossed characters on a movable cylindrical printhead; one type of *serial printer*.

daisy wheel printer an output device with a printhead consisting of character-embossed tabs attached to the "spokes" of a "wheel." It is both an *impact printer* and a *serial printer*.

data base a set of nonrepetitive data files carefully and logically organized to support a variety of applications programs; a collection of data organized to be processed as an integrated whole.

data base management system (DBMS) an organized approach to information management in which all data are stored in a *data base*; a system that treats an organization's data as an integrated whole.

data base model the kinds of logical arrangements in which data items can be stored in a *data base*. There are three such models: *hierarchical, network,* and *relational.*

data management routines in *systems software,* the groups of instructions or statements that supervise the operations associated with the input, storage, transfer, and output of data.

data manipulation language (DML) a modified *high-level language* used by programmers to describe the data in a *data base* and their interrelationships.

data transfer rate the rate at which data are transferred to or from a storage location, usually expressed in bytes per second.

debugging the identification and elimination of mistakes in a computer program.

decimal number system the base-10 arithmetic system. See also *binary number system; hexadecimal number system.*

decision symbol in *flowcharting,* the graphic symbol (a diamond shape) used to represent decision choices, testing, comparisons, or switching or branching.

decision table a graphic representation of data processing operations and programs by means of a table. See *action; condition; rule.*

definition in *systems analysis,* the definition of a system's objective or intended function; the first stage in structured systems analysis.

demand paging the operation of correcting a *page fault* by loading in the *page* required for the continued execution of a program.

design in *systems analysis,* the creation of the programs that will be required by the fully functioning system; the fourth stage in structured systems analysis.

digital computer a computer that recognizes the binary digits 0 and 1, and performs logic and arithmetic operations on data coded in binary representation. See also *analog computer.*

direct-access storage device (DASD) a computer-related storage component from which a given item of data in a file can be accessed independently of any other items in that or any other file. See also *sequential-access device.*

direct implementation *implementation* of a new management information system by removal of the existing MIS.

disk drive the device that holds and rotates a magnetic disk or disk pack during data transmission; it also includes an access mechanism and several read/write heads.

display output symbol in *flowcharting,* the graphic symbol (a stylized CRT) used to represent computer-generated soft-copy data.

distributed data processing (DDP) processing in a computer system whose terminals and CPU are separated geographically but are linked together functionally in a communications network.

document symbol in *flowcharting*, the graphic symbol (a stylized sheet of paper) used to represent hard-copy input or output.

dot matrix character a character printed as a set of selected dots by a print-head that consists of an array or matrix of needles or wires. See also *shaped character.*

double-door entry a security measure that requires an individual to pass through two doors and a monitored "trap" area before obtaining physical access to a computer.

drum printer an output device with a printhead similar to that of a *cylinder printer* but which operates as a *line printer.*

dumb terminals CRT terminals with minimum capabilities; a simple I/O device. See also *intelligent terminals; smart terminals.*

EBCDIC acronym for extended binary coded decimal interchange code, an eight-bit binary code used to represent alphabetic and special characters. See also *ASCII; binary coded decimal; hexadecimal number system.*

electrically alterable read-only memory (EAROM) a semiconductor chip memory that can be reprogrammed without removing it from the computer circuitry. See also *erasable programmable read-only memory; programmable read-only memory; read-only memory.*

electronic data processing (EDP) data processing that is performed mainly or entirely by electronic equipment, primarily in a computer system, as distinct from manual or mechanical processing.

electronic printer the general term for an output device that prints by means of an electrical charge applied to special paper.

emulation the simulation, by one computer, of the processing activity of another computer.

encryption the coding of information or data in such a way as to make them unintelligible without the "key" to the code.

end-of-file marker a marker, such as a special bit sequence, that appears at the end of a record file on a magnetic tape, signaling the tape drive to stop reading. See also *end-of-reel marker.*

end-of-reel marker a marker, such as a strip of aluminum or a special bit sequence, that appears at the end of a reel of magnetic tape, signaling the tape drive to stop. See also *end-of-file marker.*

entrance connector symbol in *flowcharting*, a *connector symbol* with one flowline leaving it and none entering.

erasable programmable read-only memory (EPROM) a semiconductor chip memory that can be erased by exposure to ultraviolet light and thus made available for reprogramming. See also *electrically alterable read-only memory; programmable read-only memory; read-only memory.*

evaluation in *systems analysis*, the final testing of the effectiveness of a system; the sixth stage in structured systems analysis. See also *program testing; sequential testing; systems testing.*

exit connector symbol in *flowcharting*, a *connector symbol* with one flowline entering it and none leaving.

external page table a computer-generated table that cross-references the *virtual address* of a *page* to its *real address.*

field an item of information in a record. In Hollerith-coded punched cards, a set of one or more columns carrying a specific type of information to be processed as a single item of data.

file a group of related data items that are stored and processed together as a unit.

file activity the amount of updating and referencing undergone by a file; the extent to which a file is used.

file volatility the frequency with which the data of a file are changed.

filtering in a *management information system,* a method of organizing data by screening out unwanted data from the information flow through different levels of management.

firmware a program, contained on a silicon chip, that combines elements of hardware (memory and logic) and software (operating instructions).

fixed-point numbers fractional numbers whose decimal points are "fixed" according to some convention used in representing them, such as a specific distance from one end of a number sequence (for example, dollars and cents). See also *floating-point numbers.*

floating-point numbers fractional numbers whose decimal points are not fixed by some convention involving the length of the number itself but are implicit in other information (such as arithmetic operations). See also *fixed-point numbers.*

floating-point register a *register* capable of storing, and therefore used in arithmetic operations on, *floating-point numbers.*

floppy disk a flexible magnetic storage disk.

flowchart a graphic diagram used to represent the functioning of a system or the sequence of steps in a program. See *flowcharting.*

flowcharting the use of specific graphic symbols and techniques to represent the logical data flows, processes, and operations of computer systems and programs.

flowline symbols in *flowcharting,* the graphic symbol (arrow or line) used to represent the transmission or movement of data.

FORTRAN acronym for *FOR*mula *TRAN*slation, a high-level, noninteractive programming language particularly suited for scientific and mathematical applications.

fragmentation in multiprocessing, the occurrence of areas in main storage that cannot be used to store application programs.

frame the segment of main storage occupied by one *page* of a program.

full duplex transmission simultaneous two-way transmission through a communications channel. See *half-duplex transmission; simplex transmission.*

general-purpose computer a computer capable of executing a variety of programs. See also *special-purpose computer.*

general register a general-purpose *register* capable of storing a variety of data and program instructions.

half-duplex transmission two-way but not simultaneous transmission of data through a communications channel. See also *full duplex transmission; simplex transmission.*

hard-copy printer a device that produces a permanent, printed copy of output, usually on paper or film. See also *soft-copy printer.*

hexadecimal number system a computer-oriented base-16 arithmetic system, used for verifying computer input and output. See also *binary number system; decimal number system.*

hierarchical data model a *data base model* in which data items are organized in "levels," each item being related to only one item in the level above it and to one or more in the level below.

high-level language a programming language that approximates human language more closely than *machine language.* See also *low-level language.*

host machine in *emulation,* the computer performing the simulation; in *distributed data processing,* the central CPU.

hybrid computer a special-purpose computer capable of both analog and digital processing and used mainly for simulation studies.

identification code in computer security, a code used to identify an individual seeking access to a computer or to the data in a computer system.

impact printers hard-copy output devices that produce printed copy by causing a character image to strike against a printing medium. See also *nonimpact printers.*

implementation in *systems analysis,* the installation of a new management information system. See also *direct implementation; modular implementation; parallel implementation; phase-in implementation.*

index in storage by the *indexed sequential-access method,* the set of key numbers that permits immediate access to a given track of a magnetic disk or drum. See also *overflow area; prime area.*

indexed sequential-access method (ISAM) a system of sequential data storage that permits rapid and direct access to individual data items, as well as sequential access.

information subsystem in an organization, the functional unit responsible for all aspects of information handling by the organization. See also *management subsystem; operations subsystem.*

ink-jet printer a nonimpact output device that produces printed characters by means of jets that spray ink on the printing medium.

input generally, the data that is entered in a computer (or into a peripheral device) to be processed. Also, the process of entering such data. See also *output.*

input/output (I/O) device a peripheral device capable of performing both input and output functions; a CRT terminal.

input/output symbol in *flowcharting,* the graphic symbol (rhomboid) used to represent an I/O device or operation.

instruction register the *register* to which instructions are initially transferred one at a time during the execution of a program.

integrated circuit (IC) an interconnected set of electronic circuit elements fused together on a semiconductor chip.

integrity the reliability of a system; its completeness and proper functioning.

intelligent terminals CRT terminals capable of being programmed to perform specific functions. See also *dumb terminals; smart terminals.*

interactive language a programming language that enables the user to interact directly with the computer while the program is being prepared. See also *noninteractive language.*

interblock gap (IBG) the blank space between *blocks* of records stored on a magnetic medium; also known as *interrecord gap* (IRG).

interpreter in card-oriented systems, a device that prints—on a punched card and in a form readable by humans—the same information encoded in the punched holes in that card.

interrecord gap (IRG) the space, if any, between individual records stored on a magnetic medium; also used interchangeably with *interblock gap.*

interrogative method in a *management information system*, a technique for organizing data, commonly used in support of other methods.

interrupt handling routine any of a group of routines that take control of the computer when processing is interrupted. (The interruption may be caused by an error or may be necessary for proper processing of the program.)

invalid bit an identifier bit that indicates whether a particular *page* is in main storage.

I/O process a component of *systems software* that controls the operations of input/output hardware.

isolation in computer security, the compartmentalization of information so that access to information is on a "need to know" basis.

job generally, a program that is to be processed. Specifically, the set of data including programs, files, and operating instructions that defines a discrete unit of work to be done by the computer.

job control language (JCL) a language that programmers use to give the *operating system* the necessary specifications and instructions for handling the job.

job description a summary of the main functions, duties, and characteristics of a position, including title, grade or salary level, and work assignment.

job management routine in *systems software*, any of a group of routines that control the schedule according to which applications programs are executed by a computer.

Josephson junction an electronic switching device based on superconductive materials.

keypunch a keyboard device that encodes data by punching holes in cards.

key-to-disk device a keyboard device that encodes data on a magnetic disk. See also *key-to-tape device.*

key-to-tape device a keyboard device that encodes data on (usually magnetic) tapes. See also *key-to-disk device.*

key variable method a reporting system that concentrates on selected parameters of particular importance to the functioning of the organization; a method of organizing information in a management information system.

large-scale integration (LSI) the integration on a semiconductor chip of a large number of electronic circuit elements in a single functional unit.

laser printer a high-speed nonimpact printer that uses laser beams to print character images on a specially treated printing plate or drum. See also *nonimpact printer; xerographic printer.*

learning curve a term that refers to the initial phase of readjustment and retraining required until personnel learn to operate a newly implemented management information system with a minimum of error.

least-privilege access in computer security, access permitted according to the requirements of an individual's job.

library a set of frequently used programs and subroutines stored in auxiliary devices, ready for loading into main storage when needed.

line printer an output device that prints an entire line of characters as a unit; may be an *impact* or *nonimpact printer.* See also *serial printer.*

linkage editor a component of *systems software* that creates a load module by linking the translated application program together with smaller programs and/or subroutines that have been independently translated by a *compiler.*

loader the component of the operating system that enters an executable load module in main storage.

logarithm a number indicating the power to which a "base" number must be raised to produce a given number. For example, in decimal arithmetic, the logarithm of 100 is 2; that is, the base 10 raised to the second power (10^2) equals 100.

loop a set of instructions that is executed as a unit repeatedly as long as a particular condition specified by the program continues to be met.

loosely coupled multiprocessing system a computer system with two or more CPUs, each controlled by its own operating system. See also *tightly coupled multiprocessing system.*

low-level language any programming language that approximates *machine language* more closely than it does human language. See also *high-level language.*

machine language a language based on binary numbers that can be used directly by a computer in executing a program; machine language does not require translation by a compiler.

macroinstruction a single instruction in a *source program* that represents a set of instructions in the object program.

magnetic bubble memory an electronic memory whose basic functional element is a microscopic volume or "bubble" of magnetic polarization.

magnetic ink character recognition (MICR) a technique for "reading" characters printed in magnetic ink and translating them into computer-readable code.

main memory see *primary storage.*

maintenance the ongoing process of maintaining a computer system in proper working order. In data processing, the updating of files or programs.

management information system (MIS) a data processing system designed to aid in management decision making.

management subsystem in an organization, the functional unit responsible for planning, control, and decision making. See also *information subsystem; operations subsystem.*

manual input symbol in *flowcharting*, the graphic symbol used to represent data entered by manually operated equipment.

mark-sense input input data in the form of well-defined pencil marks made on a special form and read by a mark-sense reader.

matrix a two-dimensional array of elements; in APL, an array of numbers arranged in horizontal rows and vertical columns.

microcomputer the smallest computers currently available, containing 1,000 to 2,000 logic circuits and up to several thousand bytes of memory, all on two or three silicon chips.

microfiche a small sheet or strip of film for recording data and documents. The image size is so small that the content must be magnified in order to read. See also *microfilm*.

microfilm a spool of film for recording data and documents in greatly reduced size. The recorded images must be magnified in order to be read. See also *microfiche*.

microinstruction an instruction wired into a ROM as part of a *microprogramming* sequence.

microprogramming the incorporation in a ROM of basic operating instructions that would otherwise be part of the stored program, and thus executed much more slowly.

microprograms hard-wired programs consisting of a set of elementary instructions, each of which directs a sequence of operations, thus replacing more elaborate software.

microsecond one millionth of a second.

minicomputer a small computer, commonly desktop size and weighing less than 50 pounds. The number of logic chips can range from as few as four to as many as 600, and the memory capacity from several thousand to several million bytes. See also *microcomputer*.

MIS see *management information system*.

mission statement a statement defining the goals and functions of an organization or department within a larger organization.

modeling in data processing, a method of designing the information output to be produced by a management information system, and therefore of organizing the data processed by the system.

modem acronym for *mo*dulator-*dem*odulator; an electronic device that converts electronic signals transmitted through a communications channel from digital to analog and from analog to digital form.

modular implementation a method of introducing a new management information system by implementing one part of the system, or module, at a time.

modularization in top-down programming, a method of sectioning subroutines into self-contained program segments or modules. See also *bottom-up programming; top-down programming*.

monitor in software, a synonym for *supervisor*.

monitoring in a management information system, the process of eliminating irrelevant data from reports to decision makers.

multiple virtual storage a system of *virtual storage* that can provide the storage needed during the execution of multiple programs.

multiplexer in data communications, a device that enables a single communications channel to carry signals from two or more terminals.

multiprocessing the use of two or more CPUs in a single computer system.

multiprogramming the execution of two or more applications programs by a single CPU, more or less simultaneously.

nanosecond one billionth of a second.

network data model a *data base model* in which a given data item may be related to a number of other data items.

nonimpact printers hard-copy output devices that produce printed characters by nonmechanical techniques such as by thermal, electrostatic, or optical methods. See also *impact printers.*

noninteractive language a programming language that does not allow the programmer to interact with the computer during the preparation of a program.

obfuscation in data security, a form of *isolation,* usually involving *encryption.*

object module an application program that has been translated by a *compiler.* See also *source program.*

online a general term that refers to a state, procedure, or device involved in direct communication with the CPU. See also *online processing.*

online processing data processing performed in its entirety under the direct control of the CPU. In contrast to *batch processing,* online processing entails the immediate processing of data from the time it enters the computer system, and is typically used in applications that require constant updating of data.

online real-time (OLRT) system a system containing a number of terminals, each of which has constant online access to the CPU and thus is able to receive prompt response from the system.

operating system a group of supervisory programs that maximize effective utilization of the hardware.

operational location the subordination of a data processing department to the organizational unit that is the department's primary user.

operations job family in data processing departments, one of six broad groups, or families, of jobs. A common job title is keypunch operator.

operations subsystem in an organization, the unit responsible for day-to-day functioning. See also *information subsystem; management subsystem.*

optical character recognition (OCR) a method of data input in which a photoelectric scanner "reads" input printed in a specialized typeface.

output data that have been processed; also, the use of processed data or the result of processing data. See also *input.*

overflow area in storage by the *indexed sequential-access method,* the part of the storage file that permits the addition of new records to the *prime area* by accepting the resulting overflow. See also *index.*

page a group of blocks of data or instructions, or both, in a storage unit.

page fault the condition that results when a program being executed references a *page* that is not in *real storage.* See also *page-in-operation.*

page-in-operation the correction of a *page fault.* Also known as *demand paging.*

parallel implementation the introduction of a new management information system in which both the existing system and its successor operate
together for a period of time.

parallel mode symbol in *flowcharting*, the graphic symbol (a pair of horizontal parallel lines with flowlines) used to represent the beginning or end
of processes occurring simultaneously.

Pascal one of the newer high-level, interactive programming languages; designed for reliability and efficiency in programs for currently available
computers.

peripheral equipment symbols in *flowcharting*, the graphic symbols used to
represent the peripheral devices in a computer system.

peripherals computer components that support the activities of, and are peripheral to, the CPU; especially input, output, and auxiliary storage devices.

phase-in implementation a method of introducing a new management information system by putting one system module or functional unit into
operation at a time.

picosecond one trillionth of a second.

plaintext any information written in a form readable by humans, as opposed
to code or encrypted information.

planning in *systems analysis*, the study and analysis of alternative solutions
to a problem; the third stage in structured systems analysis.

PL/I acronym for Programming Language I, a high-level, noninteractive programming language designed to incorporate the best features of a variety
of other programming languages.

plotters hard-copy output devices that print data in the form of graphs.

pointer a data item whose function is to direct or point the computer to another data item.

power surge in electronics, a sudden brief increase in the flow of current; a
hazard in computer systems.

primary storage the component of the CPU that stores data and instructions
as required during program execution; also known as main memory (or
storage) and internal memory.

prime area in storage by the *indexed sequential-access method*, that part of
the storage medium on which data are recorded. See also *index; overflow
area.*

process approach an approach to developing a computer application that
concentrates on the computer's processing requirements in handling a single application.

processing generally, the arithmetic and logic operations performed on data
in the course of executing a computer program.

processing operation symbol in *flowcharting*, the graphic symbols used to
represent various data processing operations.

processing symbol in *flowcharting*, the graphic symbol (rectangle) used to
represent a transformation of, operation on, or movement of data.

program flowchart a *flowchart* representing the sequence of processing operations performed in the execution of a computer program. See also *system flowchart.*

programmable read-only memory (PROM) a semiconductor chip memory
that can be programmed by the user. See also *electrically alterable read-*

only memory; *erasable programmable read-only memory; read-only memory.*

programming job family in data processing departments, one of six broad groups, or families, of jobs. The most common job title in this group is programmer.

program testing in *evaluation* of a management information system, the testing of all the logical modules of a new management information system for compatibility and accuracy.

query language a *high-level language* that allows a user to interact with a computer without having to write a program.

random-access memory (RAM) computer memory whose *access time* is independent of the location of a given data item. See also *serial-access memory*.

read (1) to access data in a storage device; (2) to acquire data from an input medium or other source.

read-only memory (ROM) computer memory, usually contained as a program on a chip, permitting data to be read but not altered. See also *electrically alterable read-only memory; erasable programmable read-only memory; programmable read-only memory*.

real address the location that a data item or instruction occupies in main storage during the execution of a program.

real storage main storage during the execution of a program.

real time a term used to describe a processing operation in which *output* is produced quickly enough to affect the processing outcome.

record a set of related characters or data items treated as a unit of storage.

redundancy in a *data base*, the storage of the same data item or groups of items in two or more files.

refreshing the process of accessing stored data items in order to prevent them from dissipating.

region in *multiprogramming*, the area of main storage allocated to a particular *application program*.

register a temporary storage device of limited capacity and intended for a specific function in processing data. See also *address register; control register; floating-point register; general register; instruction register; storage register*.

relational data model a *data base model* that organizes data in terms of two-dimensional tables according to their relationship to one another.

reproducer a punch-card device that can transfer one or more data items from a master file card to one or more other cards.

resources plan a management plan that projects the needs for, costs of, and availability of various resources that are used by a company or organization.

response time the interval between the entry of data and the production of *output*.

risk analysis in the development of a computer security system, the initial stage involving the identification of possible hazards to the computer and a cost/benefit analysis of various security measures *vis-à-vis* the likelihood of a given hazard.

rotational delay the interval of time required to rotate a magnetic disk to the correct position for accessing a given data item. See also *seek time*.

routine a subsidiary program or sequence of instructions that is required frequently during the execution of a program.

routine maintenance the ongoing process of keeping a system's program routines in working order, eliminating errors and updating instructions and data when necessary.

rule a combination of a *condition* (or conditions) and an associated *action* (or actions) specified in a *decision table*.

run book a set of instructions and specifications that tell a computer operator how to run a job through the system.

scheduler a term for any of the set of *job management routines*.

seek time in magnetic disk storage, the time required for the access mechanism to move to the *cylinder* containing the data items to be accessed. See also *rotational delay*.

semiconductor memory any computer memory constructed from semiconductor materials and, specifically, printed on silicon chips.

sequential-access device a storage component from which data are retrieved by a sequential search of data files. See also *direct-access storage device*.

sequential operation processing of data according to a predetermined order or sequence of data items.

sequential testing in *evaluation* of a *management information system*, testing to determine whether successive programs are contiguous as required for processing.

serial-access memory a type of computer memory in which data items must be read in sequence before a given data item can be accessed.

serial printer a hard-copy device that prints characters one at a time, or serially. See also *line printer*.

shaped character a print character whose image consists of solid lines. See also *dot matrix character*.

simplex transmission transmission of data through a communications channel in one direction only (the direction of transmission is fixed). See also *full duplex transmission*; *half-duplex transmission*.

smart terminals CRT I/O devices that have various editing capabilities and visualizing not found in *dumb terminals*, but lack the user-programmability of *intelligent terminals*.

soft-copy printer an output device, such as a CRT display terminal, that does not produce a permanent print copy of *output*.

sorter a punch-card system device for separating cards on the basis of one or more specified data items.

source program any application program before it has been translated by a *compiler*. See also *object module*.

special-purpose computer a computer designed to perform a single specific task (such as calculation of trajectories) and usually unable to perform any other kind of task. See also *general-purpose computer*.

specific projects plan a management plan for scheduling and completing individual projects that can be foreseen over a period of a few years.

storage retention of data in a memory device for later retrieval; also, any device for retaining data for later use.

storage register a *register* for the temporary storage of data either from main memory or about to be stored in main memory.

strategic decision center a method of organizing data in a management information system, concentrating on both the external and internal factors relevant to the making of overall, or strategic, decisions.

strategic plan a long-term management plan outlining the overall developments and achievements expected over a specified period of years.

subroutine a repeated sequence of instructions within a larger *routine* or program.

supercomputers computers characterized by their very large size and very high processing speeds. Sometimes called "number crunchers" because they perform tens of millions of operations per second.

supervisor a set of *task management routines*; also called a *monitor*.

synchronous transmission transmission of data in blocks of several thousand consecutive bits at a time. See also *asynchronous transmission*.

system flowchart a *flowchart* that gives a macroscopic view of the data flow and processing interactions of an organization or computer system. Less detailed than a *program flowchart*.

systems analysis the detailed investigation of an existing organization or system to determine how its different components should be made to interact in order to fulfill certain functions.

systems analyst an individual who defines the *input* and *output* required for a particular application and develops the logical model for a computer system that will produce the desired output from the input. See also *application program*.

systems job family in data processing departments, one of six broad groups, or families, of jobs. *Systems analyst* is the best-known job title in this family.

systems software the set of programs that directs the internal operations of a computer. See also *application program*.

systems testing in *evaluation* of a *management information system*, the comprehensive testing of the system as a functioning whole.

systems theory the view that components of an organization or other entity are interrelated in specific ways (that is, they form a system), and that these interrelationships determine what that system can do and how effectively and efficiently it can function.

tape density the amount of information stored per unit area of magnetic tape, usually measured in *bytes per inch*.

target machine in *emulation*, the computer whose activity is being simulated.

task a job that the computer has begun to process.

task management routines in *systems software*, the group of routines that supervise the allocation of system resources, such as CPU time for the processing of programs.

technical support job family in data processing departments, one of six broad groups, or families, of jobs. Job titles in this family include systems programmer and data administrator.

terminal an I/O device capable of communicating *online* with a computer. Terminals commonly have a keyboard for *input* and some kind of display for *output*. See also *dumb terminals; intelligent terminals; smart terminals.*

terminal symbol in flowcharting, the graphic symbol (a stylized CRT) used to represent the beginning or end of an operation or process, or a break in data flow.

thermal matrix printer a hard-copy device that produces dot matrix characters by the application of heat to specially treated paper.

tightly coupled multiprocessing system a single computer operating system controlling two CPUs. See also *loosely coupled multiprocessing system.*

time-sharing the use of a single computer by two or more customers at the same time, without any apparent waiting time for any customer. Time-sharing is possible only in an *online real-time system.*

top-down programming a programming method that begins with the most general statement of a program and divides it into increasingly detailed sets of routines. See also *bottom-up programming; modularization.*

top-down testing in programming, testing that begins with the most general statements of the program and proceeds to increasingly smaller or more detailed units.

tracks per inch (tpi) a measure of the storage capacity of a magnetic disk, referring to the number of data-bearing tracks per inch of disk radius.

transistor an electronic switching device based on the phenomenon of semiconductivity in materials such as silicon and germanium.

unauthorized access in computer security, access to a computer facility or terminal or to data, gained illegally or unofficially.

unblocked data stored on magnetic media without any physical separation between records. See also *blocking factor.*

uninterrupted power supply (UPS) a solid-state device that supplies current when the regular source of power fails; an aid to computer security.

uniprocessor a computer system consisting of one CPU, main storage, and an I/O device.

vacuum tube an electronic switching device used in first-generation computers.

verification in testing and debugging a program, the process of comparing the results of independent calculations against program output.

verifier a punch-card system device used to detect and correct errors in data recorded on punched cards. See also *verifying punch.*

verifying punch a punch-card system device used to detect and correct errors in data input before data are punched onto cards. See also *verifier.*

very large scale integration (VLSI) the packing together of hundreds of thousands of electronic circuit elements on a single semiconductor chip.

virtual address an *address* (location) in *virtual storage.*

virtual storage external storage devices that enable a computer to access data as readily as if they were contained in primary storage.

virtual storage access method (VSAM) a double-entry method of file organization that combines indexed and sequential files, thus permitting both sequential and direct access to data.

voice output computer *output* in the form of synthesized speech.

writable control store a control memory with a *write* capacity, used mainly in *microprogramming*.

write to enter a data item in a storage device or on a data input medium.

xerographic printer a hard-copy output device that produces printed characters by a combination of electrostatic and optical techniques.

Index